HOW TO
PROBATE & SETTLE
AN ESTATE YOURSELF,
WITHOUT THE LAWYER'S FEES

The National Probate Kit

By Benji O. Anosike, B.B.A., M.A., Ph.D.

New (Revised Edition)

Copyright © 1996, 2000 by Benji O. Anosike

Library of Congress Cataloging-in-Publication Data

Anosike, Benji O.
    How to probate & settle an estate yourself, without the lawyer's fees : the national probate kit / Benji O. Anosike.-- New rev. ed.
        p. cm.
    Includes bibliographical references and index.
    ISBN 0-932704-51-4 (pbk. : alk.paper)
    1. Probate law and practice--United States--Popular works. 2. Executors and administrators--United States--Popular works. I. Title: How to probat[e] [... settle an]
estate yourself, without the lawyer's fees. II. Title.

KF765.Z9 A56 2000
346.7305'2--dc21

Printed in the United States of America
ISBN: 0-932704-51-4

Library of Congress Catalog Number:

Published by:
Do-It-Yourself Legal Publishers
60 Park Place
Newark, NJ 07102

The Publishers Disclaimer

It remains for us, the Publishers, to assure our readers that we have diligently researched, checked, and counterchecked every bit of information contained in this manual to ensure its accuracy and up-to-dateness. Nevertheless, we humans have never been noted for our infallibility, no matter how hard the effort! Furthermore, details of laws, rules, or procedures do change from time to time. And, with specific respect to probate, estate planning or settlement, trust-making, and the like, the specific details of rules or procedures (though generally not the law or the broad basic principles themselves) ofter differ from one state to another. Nor is this relatively short manual conceivably intended to be an encyclopedia on the subject, containing the answer or solution to every issue on the subject. ***THE READER IS THERE-FORE FOREWARNED THAT THIS MANUAL IS SOLD AND DISTRIBUTED WITH THIS DIS-CLAIMER:*** the publisher (and/or the author) does not make any guarantees of any kind whatsoever, or purport to engage in rendering professional or legal service, or to substitute for a lawyer, an accountant, financial or estate planner, a tax expert, or the like. Where such professional help is legitimately called for in your specific or other cases, it should be sought accordingly.

—Do-It-Yourself Legal Publishers

Acknowledgments

Our special thanks and gratitude to the following: author Norman F. Dacey ("How To Avoid Probate!") and his publisher, the Crown Publishers, Inc.; Washington D.C.'s HALT, Inc., and their authors (on "Probate"); author Murray Bloom ("The Trouble With Lawyers") and his publisher, the Pocket Books, and many many others too numerous to mention. All have, in one way or the other, by your prior deeds, pioneerintg works and/or research in this field—and by your ever unselfish readiness to share and disseminate the fruits thereof—made the present undertaking both more purposeful and easier for the present author and publishers.

Finally, we thank you, our readers, and urge this of you: Please continue to send us all those personal comments, opinions, thoughts or suggestions you might have regarding this book; or news items, newspaper accounts or clippings of probate happenings from across the country you might come across. As always, just drop us a few lines at our address (we prefer written communications, please). For us, you, the readers, are the KING and QUEEN, as the case may be! We very much value and welcome your feedback—always!!

CREDITS:
Cover design, art direction, typesetting and illustration, by Amy R. Feigenbaum and Suzanne Feigenbaum of Rivanne Advertising Creative Desktop Publishing Services, Brooklyn, NY.

Other Books Of Law By The Author

On Estate Planning:

- How To Properly Plan Your 'Total' Estate With A Living Trust, Without The Lawyer's Fees
- How To Plan Your 'Total' Estate With A Will & Living Will, Without The Lawer's Fees

On Other Subjects:

- How To Form Your Own Profit Or Non-Profit Corporation Without A Lawyer
- How To Buy Or Sell Your Own Home Without A Lawyer Or Broker
- How To File Chapter 11 Business Bankruptcy Without A Lawyer
- How To Settle your Own Auto Accident Claims Without A Lawyer
- How To Declare Your Personal Bankruptcy Without A Lawyer

Selfhelper Law Update Service

The laws governing probate and estate settlement addressed in this manual, as well as the forms and formal procedures for doing them, can and do change every now and then. Fortunately for us, this does not happen very often. Nevertheless, this necessitates at least two things: first, that a book such as this be revised and updated as frequently as possible, and, secondly, that readers as well as publishers be vigilant, always on the look out for possible significant changes that might occur.

We'll appreciate your assistance in helping us keep track of, and with, this task. *If you should come across any "local" or other form(s) or procedure(s) that are particular to your state or county or locality, or any that are new or significantly different from the ones provided in this manual, we'll like to know about it. Simply send us a written note specifying the law or procedure and/or enclosing a blank copy of the form(s).* Such material will be of valuable help to us in any subsequent editions and future updates and revisions. However, in addition to that, the Do-It-Yourself Legal Publishers researchers will further research into the matter and send you instructions on the new law or the use of the material, where necessary or specifically requested by the reader.

- -

The Selfhelper Law Update Service Response Form

TO: The Do-It-Yourself Legal Publishers • 60 PARK PLACE ., Ste. 1013, • Newark, NJ 07102

Dear Publisher,

Here's the information you invited in your HOW TO PROBATE & SETTLE AN ESTATE YOUR-SELF, as follows (*Check applicable paragraphs & add details*):

☐ I find that the laws/procedures/forms* for my county/state* seem to have changed (to be significantly different) from the one(s) in the book in the following ways:_____
_____
_____
_____

☐ Copy of the new or different form(s) is/are hereby enclosed.

My Name is:_____Address:_____
_____Zip:_____

Phone No. (   )_____

IMPORTANT: Please do NOT rip out the page. Consider others! Just make a photocopy and send that!

_____

*Cross out the inapplicable terms or words

Table of Contents

Chapter 2
CAN YOU BE AN ESTATE EXECUTOR? HERE'S WHAT IT TAKES TO BE ONE

Chapter 3
ARE YOU GOING TO BE AN EXECUTOR FOR SOMEONE'S ESTATE? THEN BE SURE THE PERSON LEAVES YOU CERTAIN TOOLS & INFORMATION TODAY, TO HELP EASE YOUR TASK TOMORROW

Chapter 4
HOW TO PROBATE AND SETTLE AN ESTATE IN ANY PARTICULAR STATE IN THE NATION

Chapter 5
'OPENING OF THE ESTATE' PART WHEN THERE IS A WILL. FIRST, GET THE WILL 'ADMITTED TO PROBATE' BY THE COURT, AND HAVE THE EXECUTOR CONFIRMED

Chapter 6
'OPENING OF THE ESTATE' PART IN A NO-WILL SITUATION.
FIRST, GET AN 'ADMINISTRATOR' FOR THE ESTATE APPOINTED

Chapter 7-A
ASSEMBLING & EVALUATING THE ESTATE'S AFFAIRS & PROPERTY:
PHASE ONE OF THE ACTUAL ESTATE ADMINISTRATION'S FOUR-PHASE PROCESS

FOREWORD: THE PUBLISHER'S MESSAGE

To All Our Dear Readers:

You may probably have been aware of one basic fact regarding probate: that probably no other area of legal practice in America has had as many complaints levelled against it by so many people for so long as the nation's probate system—the system by which the estate left behind by a dead person is settled through the legal apparatus. Victimized Americans from all walks of life, as well as independent experts, observers, commentators and writers, have for too long complained about the system and the chief operators of the system, charging them with virtually every conceivable abuse under the sun. The system has been said to be needlessly too long and time consuming, too expensive, and too rife with extortionist legal fees, embezzlement and theft of estate assets, and a variety of abuses by lawyers, judges and others who operate it.

Fewer legal issues in America have been the subject of as much sustained newspaper and magazine articles, or seen as much public outcries and media exposes as the probate system. And fewer issues have been the object of repeated legislative "study," hearings and "reform" laws in America. But just as consistently, however, such persistent manifestations of public outrage and dissatisfaction about the processes of the probate system have changed practically nothing; such so-called "reform" measures as have been undertaken all across the nation's state legislative houses ostensibly to correct the problem have been singularly distinguished by their woeful failure in bringing about any fundamental change for generations after generations.

THE ILLS AND ABUSES IN THE AMERICAN PROBATE WORLD

This manual is, in a word, a direct response to the age-long complaints of the American public, meant to confront the abuses in and of the probate system head-on—but in a new, uniquely innovative, and, for once, effective way: primarily by removing from probate the principal culprit and mastermind most singularly responsible for the state of affairs in probate, namely, THE PROBATE LAWYER.

Just like countless other articulate critics who have raised their voices before or after him on this matter, **Harper Hamilton,** a Boulder Colorado attorney and legal author, fairly accurately sums up the tragic situation in America's probate world even to this day:

> At the most traumatic time in the life of a family—the death of one of its members—down swoops the "probate lawyers" to "make it easy" for the surviving family, to "take the burden off the widow" at a time when she is in grief. Friend, they do "take."! All these expressions are laudable sounding phrases, but to be blunt about it, it's the old "probate rip off" you have heard about. Just as bad as the "divorce" racket.
>
> Typically, if any member of a family wanted to transfer property to other members of the family—during lifetime—it can be done with the ease of signing a piece of paper, recording it, if necessary, and paying any government taxes due. Simple, easy, a few minutes of your time. No big deal...
>
> But hold it! Suppose he dies and the _same_ property is to be transferred through the "Probate process." It will take the typical "probate" matter one, two, three, five years to complete. You must bear the unnecessary probate "costs," "expenses," "attorney's fees," delays, court proceedings, and on and on and on. Why is that?...[this is] to illustrate a dramatic point—how the lawyers and legislatures have continued to pull the wool over the eyes of the citizens for so long.

A NEW SOLUTION TO SUPPLEMENT THE OLD: TAKE THE LAWYER OUT OF YOUR PROBATE!

Norman F. Dacey, America's leading professional estate planner whose pioneering book, *"How to Avoid Probate!,"* remains the authentic classic in the field, makes the observation that in view of the reality that probate work is one of the lawyers' prime sources of wealth and income, "it is likely to be a long time before there is meaningful probate reform in America." This is so, he (correctly) reasons, because the legal profession generally dominates the state legislatures and the courts which must necessarily pass on the matter. Dacey adds: "Don't be discouraged, though. You need not be the system's victim. There exists a magic key to probate exemption, a legal wonder drug which will give you permanent immunity from the [lawyer's] racket."

Dacey's "magic key" to relieving Americans from the probate racket is, of course, the use of his now famous "Dacey Trusts"—principally the revocable or inter vivos living trusts—to "avoid" having one's estate pass through the probate process at all. Primarily, this is done by means of putting one's assets in such forms as would make them transferable <u>directly</u> to one's beneficiaries upon one's death.

A brilliant, ingenious and original approach to tackling the age-long probate problem, to be sure! However, here in this manual, the approach the author chooses to adopt—and prefers—is distinctively but deliberately different.

The present author's primary aim and strategy is not so much oriented towards the "avoidance" of <u>probate</u> or the probate process per se (though it wouldn't hurt any were that to be achieved or achievable). Rather, his focus is to "avoid" the use of the <u>LAWYER</u> in probate—to take the lawyer, his all-pervasive but perverse role and influence in probate, out of probate!

To put it another way, the differential strategy of the present author is to refuse any longer to give up the probate high grounds exclusively to the probate lawyer and the technicians of the law, to, if you will, "take on" the probate lawyer, and, yes, the crooked probate judge himself, at his own game and on his own grounds—thereby rendering him (or her), and the abuses of the system he makes possible, ultimately irrelevant and of no continuing practical consequence to the consumer.

Sure, the ideal solution we would all have preferred, would be for everyone and every estate not to even have to undertake probate at all. Perhaps, some day (just some day!), we shall have come to that long-dreamed-for "land of promise" in American probate when it will become a practical possibility for the bulk of estates in America to avoid the necessity for probate altogether, or, at least, to escape the traditional abuses and shortcomings rampant in the system. Unfortunately, though, we remain all too sadly aware that, as a practical reality, most estates in the nation do not yet and frequently cannot yet "avoid" probate. Most Americans must, in the meantime at least, and probably for a long time to come, still continue to pass through the probate process—and all of its attendant dreadful abuses!

For such persons, then, there needs to be a different battle strategy, some immediate *practical* means of relief or remedy in the meantime. *How do such people whose estates must undergo probate today, escape or minimize the victimization of the system in the meantime? This is the all-important question to which this book seeks to provide the answer, the void which it specifically, boldly, and innovatively seeks to fill.* It does this primarily by handing every executor or administrator—anybody whatsoever with an interest in or a need to probate or administer an estate—a practical, viable, here-and-now alternative that enables him to do the probate work by himself, thereby avoiding having to siphon off large chunks (perhaps even all) of the estate to strangers, as has been traditionally the case.

THE "HIRING" OF THIS BOOK COULD SAVE YOU $$ THOUSANDS, RIGHT OFF THE BAT!

No exaggeration is meant here. But, quite easily, at the lawyers' going rates for probate it should be obvious how and why the mere use of this book could save you an average of several thousands of dollars—easily. Here, you need no fancy calculation to make this obvious: Let's say an average estate is worth, say, $100,000 (a figure which, you should realize, is a rather conservative estimate for an average estate value, when one realizes how suprisingly easily the amount mounts upon adding together the value of such items as your home or other real estate, motor vehicles, contents of your home, life insurance proceeds, life-long savings or savings bonds, stocks, and the like). Then, a straight 5% of that value—the lawyer's average fee for probate—comes to, not one or two thousands of dollars, but FIVE THOUSAND DOLLARS ($5,000.00)!!

And, wait a minute! What if the value of the estate in question is even higher, say, $200,000, or $500,000, or $1,000,000 or greater? The point is that, right away, you can begin to see that the sky is literally the limit as to the amount of savings in legal fees alone (not to speak of the savings in terms of possible plunder and theft of the estate assets!), which the mere act of "hiring" this book, rather than a lawyer, could save you on an estate.

---

*Norman Dacey, the nation's foremost authority on probate avoidance techniques, candidly reaches the similar conclusion that the overwhelming majority of Americans still do—and probably must for the foreseeable future continue to—undergo probate. "If the inter vivos trust can, in fact, accomplish the wonderful end of avoiding probate," asks Dacey, "why is it not used frequently?" Dacey suggests the following reasons in answer to his question: 1) lack of familiarity, on the part of many attorneys and financial advisors, with what this technique can do or even how it works; 2) the traditional fear of, and unwillingness to try the new or the unknown on the part of the general public; 3) the vested interest among lawyers and representatives of corporate and financial fiduciaries to continue reaping the "very handsome legal and executors' fees" which the probate system begets.

Lest we be misunderstood or misinterpreted, however, it should be pointed out—and emphatically stated—that no book of this kind, the present one included, is necessarily meant to serve every conceivable probate case, or to solve or answer every need of a probate case. *Most ideally, the present manual will serve best almost all the needs of the average or medium-size regular estate, especially in an uncontested situation, wherein the heirs and beneficiaries are willing to compromise and to settle the estate peacefully.* Where, on the other hand, the family members, or the beneficaries and claimants are unwilling to compromise, but merely wish to battle each other to a bitter finish (which, fortunately, happens only in less than 5% of all cases), or where there's an unusually complex, larger-than-average estate involved, it may then be necessary to supplement this manual with the services or advice of a competent—and, above all—honest and trustworthy lawyer.

This manual is one of the very first of its kind ever attempted or published. Sure, lately there has been a proliferation of publications (especially since the Dacey book began to pull well at the bookstores) that purport to demonstrate to their readers varying techniques by which to *"avoid"* probate or to minimize estate taxes associated with probate. Never, however, has there been any that daringly employs this book's novel and revolutionary approach of showing the lay public how to avoid not merely <u>probate</u>, but the probate <u>*lawyer*</u>—the chief purveyor and embodiment of the worst ills and abuses in the system!

THE NATIONAL SCOPE—AND PURPOSE—OF THE MANUAL

New York State's specific probate procedures are employed in great, specific details primarily as a means of using the state's practices to illustrate the general procedures in most states. And in regard to this, there's one comforting fact for the do-it-yourselfer: that, for the most part, *the basic principles which underlie probate and estate administration are essentially identical from state to state across America.* Hence, elements of the procedures and illustrations in this manual may—and should—easily be adapted for non-lawyer probate filings and estate settlements in any state in the nation. Additionally, to further ensure that this book will be as universally useful and applicable as possible in each of the 50 states in the union and even beyond), we have taken pains to provide, in the Appendices, the basic probate rules and information specific to each state. [See the following Appendices: Appendix A (pp. 152-177), Appendix B (pp. 178-192), Appendix C (pp. 193-197), Appendix D (pp. 198-206), and Appendix E (pp. 208-215).

A CONCLUDING WORD OF ADVICE TO YOU, THE READER

In concluding this MESSAGE, there's probably no more fitting caution to leave you, the reader, with than that which is already given by none other than the venerable granddaddy of probate, Mr. Norman Dacey, the man who probably knows more about these matters than any soul in America:

> The legal establishment, promising much, has delivered only token probate reform. It is useless to hope that the abuses of probate will be corrected in our time. ***In such circumstances, it is important that every individual American who has labored to build financial security for his family— and who prefers not to name the legal establishment as one of his heirs—take advantage of the means provided to avoid the abuses. This book provides those means...***

Thank you so much.

—Do-It-Yourself Legal Publishers

Newark, NJ

'Wanna draw straws to see who handles the estate?'

Reprinted with permission from the Montgomery County Sentinel.

Introduction

WHY THE 'TAKE THE LAWYER OUT OF PROBATE' APPROACH IS A NECESSARY CONDITION IN PROBATE

ANYONE—EVEN YOU—MAY HAVE TO ADMINISTER OR SETTLE AN ESTATE TOMORROW

You may not have ordinarily thought of it. But it's not at all far-fetched: THE LIKELIHOOD OF YOUR BEING CALLED UPON TO ACT AS AN EXECUTOR OR ADMINISTRATOR for a deceased relative or friend, or of someone you are close to being asked to act in that capacity for someone else or even for you, is quite high! A harsh reality, maybe. But the point, plainly, is that with some 250 million people alive today in the United States, and still growing, sooner or later someone or the other will have to be called upon to act as an executor or administrator of just about that many number of estates!!

Suppose—just suppose—the phone rings tomorrow, from someone, and you're told Daddy or Uncle Mike has died, and that he named you the executor in his Will? Or, suppose the caller were to say that Daddy or Uncle Mike left no will, but that being you're the most trusted and closest relative available, you've been unanimously selected to act as the administrator of the estate? Now, if you are anything like the average person, you probably wouldn't have the foggiest idea about how to probate or settle an estate! And the big question for you is: HOW DO YOU KNOW WHAT EXACTLY ARE YOUR DUTIES AND RESPONSIBILITIES IN THAT CRITICAL ROLE? AND HOW AND HOW DO YOU GO ABOUT THE TASK OF CARRYING THEM OUT?

Providing you , the average person and non-expert, such vital knowledge and information, is essentially what *How To Probate and Settle an Estate Yourself, Without The Lawyer's Fees,* is all about. It, in a word, basically "walks" you through the probate and estate settlement process and procedures, step-by-step, from start to finish.

**WHY, ULTIMATELY, NOTHING WILL WORK IN PROBATE UNLESS
YOU TAKE THE LAWYERS OUT OF PROBATE**

At the heart of the strategy prescribed by this book is one underlying simple philosophy: *if all that one does is merely to eliminate the lawyer's role in any given probate case, one would have automatically and directly eliminated—or, at least, drastically reduced—the dominant source of the probate problems in that case, namely, the source of the excessive costs of probate, the plunder and embezzlement of the estate's assets by the professional "heirs" of the judicial system, and the long delays associated with the probate process! The underlying point of the book is that, ultimately, in the long run the only viable cure for the ills and abuses in probate is a non-lawyer probate.*

THE LAWYERS' HISTORY OF FEE-BUILDING DELAYS & TACTICS IN PROBATE

True, there are other costs involved in probate—fees for the filing of papers, for document reproduction, recording, appraisers, bond, the fiduciary's compensation, etc. But everyone (i.e., everyone except the probate lawyers!) agrees, nevertheless, that it is the lawyer's fees (and the lawyer's delaying formalities!) that always make the big difference, and not these other costs. As California attorney and author, **Edward E. Colby,** so well puts it, "The main expense of probate court proceedings is not the minimum court costs and expenses of about $200, but the fees for the attorney and sometimes the executor."

And the reason it has to be the lawyer's fee that constitutes the principal problem is not hard to figure out. It is this: contrary to the manner by which the compensation structure for professionals involved in most other endeavors is determined, usually made on the basis of a measure of the amount of work done, the attorney's fees in probate are typically determined in one of two ways: 1) on a set percentage of the value of the estate, or 2) on the length of time the attorney spends (or, more typically, the length of time he claims he spends) on the probate job. One team of New York area probate lawyers give the lawyers' typical rationale for their probate fees this way: given the nature of probate work, it says, "the amount of [a lawyer's] legal activity that will necessarily be required [cannot be predicted]...The key factor here is the lawyer's time. As traditionally stated, this is his stock in trade. He...provides services based on years of formal education, training and practice. His compensation must necessarily be dependent upon the value of those services. Its determination cannot be reduced to a mathematical formula."[1]

Great reasoning! Unfortunately, though, it is exactly this kind of professional logic that has *directly* given rise to much of the abuses in probate, with the probate lawyer typically at the center of all of that. For one thing, if the lawyer's compensation in probate work is supposedly to be based on "the time" expended (or alleged to be expended) on an estate, then doesn't it follow that it will work to his financial advantage to prolong, not shorten the proceedings, at least for as long as he feels he can get away with it? What would be in it for him, in other words, that would make him want to make the probate process or his involvement in it any shorter? Furthermore, how do you accurately determine that the amount of time a lawyer says he devoted just to your estate was actually so devoted? Or, that he didn't bill you a "lawyer's rate" for a clerical work which was not done by the lawyer, but actually by his secretary or a junior clerk?[2]

"Lawyers aren't too dead set against delay in probate," said **Bill Pierce,** a University of Michigan professor of law and specialist in probate procedures who, as the President of the National Conference of Commissioners of Uniform State Laws in 1968, did a lot of work on the revised 1969 Probate Code whose aim was to have eliminated much of the abuses in probate work. "For one thing, the longer something takes the more it might seem to justify their percentage fees. The long administrations of estates often provide dangerous temptation for what the bar sometimes calls 'the weak lawyer' [namely, the lawyer who buys up at a low price the estate property which the heirs may not be aware of, using a dummy company controlled by the lawyer]."

Murray Bloom, whose famous August 1961 *Harper's Magazine article,* "Your Unknown Heirs," on how politically connected lawyers and judges were quietly milking estates around New York, was the pioneering national survey that first alerted the nation to the probate 'rip off' problem by lawyers and judges, explains further: "One of the reasons lawyers love probate work is that the problem of 'ability to pay' never figures. They find out quickly how much money there is in the estate, and their percentage cut is assured."

Lawyers, being a traditionally contentious and adversarial group—"Lawyers will, as a rule, advance quarrels rather than repress them," said Mahatma Gandhi, who himself was a lawyer—have been known to crave for, even to invent and encourage probate contests. The logic is simple: if a court contest or litigation of any sort develops, everything else in the case will have to be suspended until the dispute is settled by a ruling of the judge. And, of course, THE LONGER A MATTER DRAGS ON, THE MORE APPEARANCES THE ATTORNEY MAKES IN COURT, AND THE HIGHER HIS FEES!!

---

[1]Cited from *How to Live—and Die—With New York Probate,* Gulf Publishing Co., Texas 1975 pp. 165-6.

[2]Note that a lawyer's hourly rate in probate ranges from $90 to $250 (and over)., while a secretary's hourly rate could be as low as $3.50!

"You have a pretty good case, Mr. Pitkin. How much justice can you afford?"

Drawing by Handelsman © 1973 *The New Yorker Magazine, Inc.*

Michael Richards, who directed a comprehensive national study of the probate system for HALT, the Washington, D.C. legal reform organization, quotes one Milwaukee, Wisconsin probate registrar: "Many probate lawyers use formal procedures (with the required court appearances) even though using the available informal procedures would speed up the process and take less time." Richards added that "No explanation of this practice was given. It is obvious, however, that using the slower procedures allows attorneys to submit larger legal bills."

An often cited actual instance of deliberate lawyers' delay and feet-dragging in probate involved a case in which a probate litigation dragged on and on, back and forth among the lawyers—there were eight different lawyers in all in an estate involving several millions of dollars. Then, at one point, the judge halted the proceedings and told the lawyers: "Gentlemen, if a reasonable compromise is not effected soon, the attorney's fees will eat up the [whole] assets of this estate."

California attorney **Edward Colby** relates the story often told by oldtimers of the legal profession. It was about a probate attorney and his young son who had just become an attorney also. While the father was away vacationing in some remote resort, he received the following telegram from his "naive" son: "Dad: I'm sure you'd be happy to hear the good news. I've just completed the Jones Estate that you have been working on for twenty years." The father's reply read: "Sorry about that. Now, we will both have to go to work."

By now, you are probably beginning to get the point. **The point, simply, is this: in all we do, whatever other remedies one may conceive of, there can only be, in the final analysis, one—and only one—truly fool-proof safeguard against the plundering and ripping off of an estate by** either the probate lawyer or anybody else. **AND THAT IS: to have no lawyer at all involved in the probate process!** One more, and still another and another round of "new" or supposedly "reform" laws in probate procedures will never do. Nor will any amount of probate "study commissions, " occasional media expose of the abuses, public or legislative hearings or political outcries. Haven't we had more than our share of these, again and again and again, for so long in the past, but to what effect!? And why not? After all, are those state legislatures and their "Committees on Probate" who would rule on the prposed reforms not always dominated and controlled by lawyers themselves!!

TAKE HEART, FELLOWS, PROBATE WORK IS PROBABLY BETTER SUITED TO YOU, THE NON-LAWYER, ANYWAY: IT'S INCREDIBLY ROUTINE AND SIMPLE!

Today, one thing about probate is just about as well established as one can find: the fact that what is generally billed as "legal" work in probate procedures is often shockingly simple and uncomplicated, and that much of it is merely administrative and clerical! Contrary to the impression outwardly fostered by probate lawyers and the courts, the plain truth is that, generally, there's very little, if anything at all, in probate that is truly a "legal" task—in the sense that it is technical, complex, or needy of research or adversarial proceedings over some fine points of law.

"Nine-tenths of the work here in Surrogate's isn't law work; it's routine paperwork and bookkeeping," said one veteran aide of New York's surrogate's court interviewed by the legal affairs author Murray Bloom in 1967. "Actually, the chief clerk here can handle most of what the surrogates (the probate judges) are supposed to sign. Maybe that's why there has to be so much gravy around the court: if there wasn't, nobody in his right mind would come near it...**Except for being able to hand out juicy plums, the surrogate's job is just a glorified bookkeeper's job."**

Such assessment is one that is almost universally concurred with by independent observers and experts—except, that is, for those with a vested interest in maintaining the status quo of the traditional probate system.

Leo Kornfeld, former editor of *Trusts and Estates* magazine, the leading professional journal in the field of estate administration, asserts that most things passing for probate work are generally "cut and dried...Most of the work is done by the lawyer's secretary, problems are solved gratis by the clerks of the probate court, and very little of the lawyer's own time is consumed."

Noting the fact that lawyers who probate estates in the State of Maryland charge up to 10% of the first $20,000 of an estate and 4% of the remaining value, **Michael Richards,** who headed a probate reform study for HALT, the Washington, D.C. legal reform and activist organization, adds: "Probate is one of the simplest of legal procedures. In 90% of all cases, probate does not involve legal research and writing, adversarial proceedings, or other skills associated exclusively with attorneys. Rather it is the simple listing of an estate's assets, the payment of taxes, and the distribution of funds to creditors and beneficiaries. The whole process can be as easy as filling out an IRS form."

A Western Reserve University study team of sociologists and lawyers headed by **Dr. Marvin B. Sussman,** a research sociologist, did a 3-year study in the mid 1960s under a Russell Sage Foundation grant, the object of which was to determine the estate disposition policies in the Cuyahoga County of Cleveland, Ohio. The report of the study team, which interviewed the heirs of the estates as well as 78 of the lawyers used in the probate of those estates, gave this account: "(The lawyers) like probate work all right. They said it's pretty simple, almost always just a matter of filling in forms and filing them at the proper time, and a lot of it was so routine their secretaries did the actual form-filling."[3] (Indeed, it's probably not by mere happenstance that, at least until very recently, historically the majority of persons who served as probate judges in the courts of many states were not lawyers but non-lawyers with no prior formal legal education or training of any kind. Apparently, the legal establishment of that era instinctively recognized the relative absence of real "legal" content in most probate procedures!)

[3]Cited from *The Trouble With Lawyers,* (Pocket Books: 1970) pp. 211-212.

The point here is that, except for a relatively negligible number of cases—generally cases in which serious disputes or litigation arise among heirs or estate claimants—there's generally no real, legitimate "legal question" involved, no real need for the services (and expense!) of a lawyer in probate work. Ninety-five percent or so of most probate work is essentially high school-level clerical work. Indeed, even in such instances where an estate might involve tasks that can remotely be called "technical" or specialized (such as the preparation of the income or estate tax returns, collection of estate assets or debts, transfer of title, and the like), such duties are usually NOT personally done by the probate lawyers themselves, anyway; rather, what the lawyer would customarily do in such instances is to routinely subcontract out such tasks to others, different specialists on the tasks, who would then do the actual work and supply the end products to the lawyer to file with the court!

THE EXCESSIVE LAWYERS' FEES IN PROBATE

Combine this unbelievable simplicity of estate procedures, on one hand, with the second traditional reality to which most estate administrations are frequently subjected, on the other hand, namely, THE UNUSUALLY HIGH, FREQUENTLY CONFISCATORY AND UNCONSCIONABLE FEES THE LAWYERS CHARGE FOR THE SO-CALLED PROBATE WORK. "Most of them admitted they were handsomely paid for probate work," reported the Western Reserve University investigators, referring to the lawyers they had interviewed for the study. The report added: "But a lot of the heirs weren't as happy with probate. Most of them felt that the attorney fees had been 'way too high' but there was only one case we found where a family objected to a lawyer's fees and went to court to get it reduced. It wasn't reduced."

"[Though] nearly everything we buy is made more expensive by lawyers... there is no area from which they derive a more outrageous profit than that of probate," asserts Norman Dacey, the nation's premier authority on probate. Alluding to the fact that there has always existed a continual grumbling about the "confiscatory" level of death taxes in the United States, Dacey points out that legal fees charged in connection with estate tax returns alone filed in 1973 totalled "an incredible $1,218,450,000"—an amount which, he further pointed out, "was equal to 30 percent of the total estate tax revenue collected by the federal government in that year and three times the amount collected in state death taxes for that year. Thus we see that... [probate is] a major contributor to the prosperity of the legal profession."

Dacey's estimates of the average cost of estate administrations in probate are as follows: 20% on small estates of from $10,000 to $20,000; 10% on medium-sized estates of, say, $100,000; and a smaller percentage (let's say 5%) on larger-size estates.

HALT's probate reform expert, Michael Richards, explains the "large disparity between the nature of the lawyer's services and the price that is charged" largely in terms of "the percentage fee" basis of probate work determination among attorneys. "In practice, [such price-fixing] commissions based on a percentage of the estate's value, average 5% or more of an estate value, regardless of the time or amount of work involved," he explains. "Estate assets consisting of $100,000 worth of stock can be transferred with no more time, effort, or risk than assets of only $100 in stock. Yet a lawyer can charge as much as 1000 times more in fees for the former transaction."

"PROBATE RACKET": THE HISTORY OF PLUNDER, EMBEZZLEMENT AND STEALING OF ESTATE ASSETS BY PROBATE LAWYERS, JUDGES & OTHERS

"Probate practice is a happy hunting ground for dishonest lawyers," says Norman Dacey, the famed estate planning authority and probate author—implicitly touching on one more significant reason why, in the present author's view, the non-lawyer is, by and large, the better suited and "safer" person to be entrusted with the settlement of an estate anyway.

The evidence, much of it conclusively proven and independently verified and documented, of the widespread plunder, embezzlement and out-and-out stealing of estate assets by lawyers (as well as judges) involved in probate, is overwhelming. *Here are only a very few examples:[4]*

- In a Cincinnati case, a schoolteacher, **Ruth Crittendes,** died leaving a $38,000 estate. The local bar association's fee schedule called for a legal fee of $1,347. What the lawyer took, instead, was $8,625—more than 6 times the amount allowed under the law. Furthermore, the same lawyer appraised the woman's house at $12,000, and then turned around and sold it to a fellow lawyer for $5,000.

- **Sam Wilner** died in Chicago leaving $12,000 in a bank savings account, and one surviving relative, a niece in New York. The probate court appointed a local attorney as administrator. The first attorney hired another attorney to "advise" him on the legal technicalities of withdrawing the $12,000 from the bank and sending it to the dead man's niece in New York. The two lawyers together then petitioned the court to appoint yet another attorney (a third one in the case!) to assist them.
  Five long years passed. The New York based niece heard and got nothing from the Chicago administrator. Her countless letters to the lawyer had gone unanswered. So she consulted a New York attorney on what to do. The New York attorney, in turn, hired yet another lawyer, a Chicago attorney to represent him in the matter (a total of 5 lawyers so far in a simple and uncontested estate worth only $12,000). The niece waited another ten months and nothing happened. Finally, she telephoned Norman Dacey, the national probate authority, with the problem. Dacey cited the woman's case in a subsequent appearance he made on a Chicago TV show, and only 4 days after that, the woman received a check for $5,100—all that was left of the $12,000 (just 42% of the total), and all that after nearly 6 years of delay! But that was not all. Out of the $5,100, the woman again had to pay her New York attorney $1,400!!

- **Hyde Stewart,** an Ohio postman, died leaving $22,864. The probate court appointed an administrator whose fee, by law, should have been $874. He took $2,077—nearly two and a half times what the law allowed—and the probate court approved it. He then hired an attorney, whose fee also should have been $874 to assist. But the attorney, in turn, charged $3,500 instead—four times what the law provided—and the probate court also approved it.

- When **Arthur Vining Davis** died in Florida, his estate was put through the usual lawyers' financial "probate wringer" as follows: the First National Bank of Miami drew an amount of $2,512,500 as executor; on top of that, there were not one but two "co-executors", W.E. Dunwody, Jr., a Miami attorney, and Daniel Davis, a nephew of the dead man, both of whom drew $942,187 and $628,125 respectively; thirdly, Dunwody's law firm, Mershon, Sawyer, Johnson, Dunwody and Cole, got itself paid another $1,502,000 (i.e., on top of the $942,187 Mr. Dunwody separately took!); and fourthly, still another law firm, Milbank, Tweed, Hadley and McCloy, was paid $236,000—for a grand total of over $6 million to the "unknown heirs" of the late Mr. Davis!!

- **Walter E. Hermann** died in Reno, Nevada in 1972, leaving an estate of $3 million. His son, named as executor, hired a lawyer to probate the will. The executor's lawyer promptly had the court appoint an attorney friend who practiced in a city 500 miles away to "guard" the interests of "absent heirs"—three adult daughters of the deceased who had been bequeathed $20,000 each. (The executor's attorney was later to admit that he had reached out to pick the distant lawyer from so far away because he owed the distant lawyer a favor.) The distant lawyer, however, would not travel the 500 miles distance, so he, in turn, had the Reno probate judge appoint a third lawyer who practiced in Reno, to represent him.

---

[4]The specific cases cited herein are taken from Norman Dacey's definitive *How To Avoid Probate!,* and Murray Bloom's authoritative *The Trouble With Lawyers,* to both of whom the present author remains indebted for their pioneering research work and data on the subject matter.

When the Hermann estate finally emerged from probate in 1978—6 years after Hermann's death—the lawyers had put the estate through their usual financial "probate wringer" as follows: the executor's lawyer charged a fee of $250,000, and the probate court approved it; the two attorneys who were "guarding the interests of the daughters" asked for $210,000—almost four times what the three daughters themselves, the persons they were supposedly "guarding," were to get under the will!—but the probate judge reduced it to $70,000. (The three lawyers had, among them, asked for $460,000, or 16 percent of the estate!)

At this, Hermann's son, the executor, "blew his top." Leaving aside the probate court, he went into the civil court and filed for a relief from the lawyers' exorbitant fees. The civil court judge who heard the case acknowledged that the fees allowed the lawyers by the probate court "shock the conscience of the (civil) court," and reduced the executor's attorney's probate court- approved fee of $250,000 to $80,000, while chopping down the daughters' attorneys' probate court-approved fee of $70,000 to a mere $6,000.

Then, on the pure plunder and embezzlement of estate assets by lawyers:

- When **Louis Moritz,** who had apparently spent very little and put away every penny he ever made, died in his home in a poor section of Chicago, police found $743,965 in brown paper bags on the premises. A first cousin, the closest of fourteen heirs, applied to be named administrator but the probate judge refused, choosing instead to name an "attorney." The attorney promptly stole one-half of the estate. The probate court nevertheless accepted his final accounting. The heirs protested and filed a petition in another court, the circuit court, demanding to know what had become of the rest of the money. And it was only then that the embezzlement came publicly to light. The circuit court's response upon finding that the lawyer had actually embezzled half the estate, was to order the bonding company to pay the estate $360,000, but significantly, neither the circuit court nor the probate court nor the Illinois Attorneys Disciplinary Registration Committee, which conducted an investigation into the theft, instituted any criminal action against the lawyer thief.

- In Baltimore, Maryland, **Morris Levine,** a local attorney who was engaged to probate the estate of a local businesswoman, converted to his own use $150,000 of the $180,000 insurance and profit-sharing plan proceeds in the estate, telling the family that all he collected was $30,000. Attorney Levine was tried and convicted. The Judge's punishment to him for this theft? A SENTENCE TO THREE WEEKS IN JAIL!

- In Connecticut, **the President of a tri-city bar association** was tried and found guilty of embezzling $40,000 from an estate he was entrusted with. His lawyer, obviously a skilled master of courtroom theatrics, made an impassioned, almost tearful, plea to the court asking that the lawyer-thief not be sent to jail but be given a suspended sentence because, "for a lawyer, the disgrace is punishment enough."
  The Judge apparently found no fault with this line of reasoning, for he turned the lawyer loose, as urged. An observer reported that he saw the lawyer-thief living the high life in an expensive New York restaurant a month later—this, while other men and women not having the good fortune to belong to "the honorable profession," were serving time in jail for stealing a mere loaf of bread!!

- **In one Connecticut probate court,** a hearing took place on a request to sell a piece of property owned by an estate being administered by a local bank as the executor under a will. The hearing was called to order by the Judge and it was announced that a bid of $85,000 had been received from two local lawyers. Unexpectedly, a local automobile dealer arose and bid $125,000 for the property. Startled looks were exchanged, the hearing was hurriedly recessed, and the parties adjourned to the corridor. Five minutes later, the automobile dealer withdrew his bid and hurriedly departed. The judge reconvened the hearing and the bids were canvassed. The original two lawyers were again the only bidders and the property was sold to them for $85,000. The heirs to an estate had, once again, been robbed—of $40,000 in this instance!

• On January 4, 1967, **John C. Houlihan,** a lawyer and the then Mayor of Oakland, California, was sentenced to one to ten years in prison. (Though he could have been required to make restitution for the money stolen, and could have been tried later for a federal crime of forgery, neither move was made by the legal authorities.) It had first been discovered—and at first denied and then admitted by Houlihan—that he had been stealing from the estates entrusted to his care by the courts for more than 21 years.

Houlihan had begun stealing from estates entrusted to his care in 1945. However, none of that ever came to light because between that year and 1961, when he was elected mayor, he had always managed to put the money back. But after 1961, paying back the money he took from **Mrs. Savilla Whitlock,** the widow of a former Safeway Stores executive, became impossible.

Houlihan handled Mrs. Whitlock's late husband's estate. Then, she had to be hospitalized from injuries and went into a convalescent hospital thereafter. And Houlihan's thefts from her estate began immediately. He persuaded Mrs. Whitlock's relatives to let him become the "conservator" of her estate—that is, a guardian. Ironically, for a conservatorship application to be granted by the court, the rules required that the court only had to be persuaded that there is a likelihood that the person might be 'deceived or imposed upon by artful or designing persons'— something Houlihan had no trouble in convincing the court that it existed, though he didn't add that he himself was actually going to be the one to do it!

Houlihan's thefts (totalling over $144,000) were uncovered only after Mrs. Whitlock died in 1965. Her heirs had asked Houlihan for an accounting, and when Houlihan stalled, they filed a suit demanding an accounting. And upon subsequent investigations, Houlihan was indicted by the District Attorney. Houlihan first tried to deny his crime, but later confessed to it only when he felt the evidence of his guilt had become simply overwhelming.

• By 1993, the 11th year of its operation, the New York Lawyer's Fund for Client Security, a fund created by the lawyers to reimburse the victims of crooked lawyers, had done brisk business—it had paid out $29 million to 2,200 defrauded clients.[5] *But, even with that, only one of them has ever had the distinction to come to the fund a <u>second</u> time.* Her name was **Sarah Kiss,** a mortgage broker's representative and a divorcee, and a mother of three. She had to go to the fund a second time because her stolen and recovered money was stolen again, a second time, by another thief with a law license!

First, in 1989, the lawyer who handled Ms. Kiss' divorce, **Jack B. Solerwitz,** absconded with the $70,834 she received from the sale of her house in a divorce settlement. Ms. Kiss then hired a second lawyer, **Bertram Zweibon.** In 1990, with Mr. Zweibon's help, the fund compensated Ms. Kiss for most of her losses. But Mr. Zweibon promptly stole everything she had just recouped.

Mr. Solerwitz, the first lawyer-thief who defrauded Ms. Kiss, was characterized as 'the Babe Ruth of ripoffs', in that he was convicted of stealing more than $5 million from several victims in the 1980's. He is serving 5 to 15 years in prison for grand larceny.

Compared with Mr. Solerwitz, Mr. Zweibon, the second lawyer-thief, who is now serving one to three years, was a piker: he was convicted of stealing only $2 million, including $45,000 from the estate of his mother-in-law and $30,000 from Ms. Kiss's father!

---

[5]Account as summarized from "At the Bar: Twice Stung by Crooked Lawyers, and Twice Saved by the Client Protection Fund," *N.Y. Times,* March 19, 1993. See also this report, for a more recent account of the lawyers' continuing plunder of the estate assets: "Report is Critical of Estate System in New York City—Mismanagement is Cited," The N.Y. Times, July 24, 1992, p. I.

"Fred [Miller] said to me: 'Sarah, what are you going to do with the check? You're not going to give it to another lawyer, are you?'" Ms. Kiss recalled, referring to an official of the Lawyer's Fund for Client Security which refunded her twice for the stolen money. "I told him, 'It's not going to another lawyer's escrow account in my lifetime.'"

That says it all!

IT SHOULD BE OBVIOUS WHY THIS GUIDEBOOK IS NECESSARY: TO HELP YOU REPLACE THE LAWYERS

Against the shocking and ugly background sketched above—a background of a rotten probate system rife with excessive legal fees and other unwarranted charges by the lawyers, judges and other probate operatives for essentially routine clerical work; deliberately contrived delays of months or years for the settlement of simple estates; widespread judicial and legal dishonesty and plunder of probate assets and so on—could there really be any question about the crying need and urgency for a better way of doing probate in America!?

Now, however, with this book in hand, the average non-lawyer should be fully equipped to handle by himself or herself, the probate work of an average estate from start to finish—without the burden of the expense, delay, redtape, even thievery, so often associated with using a lawyer. Armed with *How To Probate and Settle An Estate Yourself Without The Lawyer's Fees,* you too should, in short, be able to perform the duties and responsibilities of an executor or administrator as well as anybody else—with or without the lawyers!

How To Use This Manual

A few words about the use of this guidebook. The "heart and soul" of this book—for a reader, especially, who is primarily concerned with actually probating and settling a decedent's estate— are *Chapters 5 or 6, then 7-A, 7-B, 7-C & 7-D.* These six chapters, together, deal with what could aptly be called the "nuts and bolts" of probating an estate upon a decedent's death, of managing and administering an estate until its settlement and distribution for the benefit of the rightful heirs and beneficiaries—the actual process of practically doing it.

However, before one can practically or effectively undertake the actual probate work, with the myriad of all the attendant tasks and duties involved thereof in the managing and settling of the estate, one would need to have had certain basic knowledge and information about the essential law and requirements on the major issues that need to be addressed, the necessary legal and technical procedures for going about it, etc.—matters which are addressed elsewhere in other chapters.

Thus, *Chapter 1* deals with the basic concepts of probate and estate settlement, and of the procedures of probate, as a helpful background material fundamental for kicking off and understanding the succeeding chapters. *Chapter 2* addresses the vital issue of the ideal human and other qualities that are desired of an effective estate executor, while *Chapter 3* immediately follows up with the basic steps that should be taken earlier on, the ideal conditions a will-maker or estate planner should be sure to leave a would-be estate administrator with, so as to ensure efficient management of the estate later—the basic matter of properly and timely ORGANIZING the estate long before hand. *Chapter 4* sums up the broad similarities in principles and procedures of probate and estate settlement that abound in all states across the country—designed, along with other chapters in the book, to enable persons in any particular state, other than New York, to be able to undertake probate work. *Chapter 8* deals with the settlement procedures for "small" estates, and *Chapter 9* deals with the procedures for "ancillary administration" (i.e., when a decedent's estate is located, in part or in whole, in another state), while *Appendices A and B* spell out, respectively, the basic rules of probate, and the laws of intestacy in no-will situations in all 50 and other states. And so on and so forth.

Granted, Chapters 5 or 6, and 7-A, 7-B, 7-C, & 7-D, are the most pivotal segment, as these sections, taken together and in that order, lay out a systematic, step-by-step procedure for properly probating a decedent's estate from start to finish—from the 'opening' of the estate in probate court and getting an executor or administrator appointed (in a will or no-will situation), to the assembling and evaluation of the estate affairs and property, the paying off of estate debts and administration expenses, the distribution of the balance of the estate to estate beneficiaries , and the making of final accounting to the court. However, as you yourself may quickly discover in reading through or using the guidebook, for you to be able to properly and competently undertake the probate tasks under *Chapter 5 or 6 through* 7-D, you need to have first mastered the *background materials* which are contained elsewhere in the manual, in other passages alluded to in the preceding paragraph above.

SO, THE ADVICE IS THIS: first of all, to begin with, read and comprehend all the "background" chapters, most importantly *Chapters 1 to 4* and *Appendices A to C,* to name just a few. Then, finally, go to the chapters that tie it all together for you, first to *Chapters 5 (for a will situation) or 6* (for a no-will situation), respectively, and SYSTEMATICALLY AND ORDERLY follow the procedures outlined therein to probate your decedent's estate. Then (after *Chapter 5 or 6),* simply follow next the succeeding chapters in their chronological order—*Chapters 7-A, 7-B, 7-C, & 7-D*—and again, follow the step-by-step procedures outlined in each chapter to complete and finalize your administration and settling of the estate.

A lot of times, you would probably not need all or some of the information provided in a given chapter; some information may be irrelevant or inapplicable in your particular situation. It's all here, though, just in case you need it!

Chapter 1
Probate Procedures And Estate Settlement: Let's Get The Background Information Straight, First

What happens when a person who made a Will dies? Who sees to it that what the testator provided for in the Will are carried out, and how? Or, what if the person dies without leaving a will, or an alternative instrument, such as a trust? How is his or her estate to be distributed? And to whom? And who sees to it that such distribution (and other affairs of the decedent) is carried out accordingly?

Issues like these—called probate proceedings in legal jargon—are the primary subject matter of this manual. Probate matters and procedures, proper, do not arise until the testator is actually dead and gone. *In this chapter, we shall address the basic pointers on the general principles of probate as a helpful background material for treating and understanding the rest of the book.*

A. What Is Probate?

In broad terms, probate proceedings are, in a word, the whole business of managing ("administering") and properly disposing of ("settling") the property and affairs of a dead person under the supervision of a 'Probate' or 'Surrogate' court. Basically, it involves the taking of legal custody, and the assembling of all the assets the dead person (the "decedent") might have owned or had interest in, the paying of the legitimate claims and obligations outstanding against him, and finally making a distribution of the balance left to those who are rightfully entitled to inherit from the decedent.

When a person dies and leaves some property of any kind behind, there's always this question: who is legally entitled to inherit the dead person's property—known as the "decedent's estate"? Often, it is not unusual to find a long list of relatives, real or otherwise, coming from near and far to lay claims to a share of the estate. This, say the professionals, is the fundamental reason why we must have this often lengthy, costly and agonizing process called "probate": for the court to assume a temporary supervision of the control and management of the decedent's estate to ensure that it is protected from possible misuse, and that the decedent's heirs, creditors, and others who are rightfully entitled to the estate would get it.

B. The Two Main Ways By Which A Decedent's Property Is Transferred

For our purposes in this manual, the two most relevant and important methods by which the property and affairs of a deceased person (his 'estate') may be transmitted, are: 1) by Will, and 2) by the law of Descent and Intestate Succession.

1) **By Will.** This is when a person, by means of a legally valid document known as a "Will," has designated the person(s) or institution(s) to which his (or her) property may go upon his death, and how his personal affairs are to be handled. A person who dies leaving a valid will is said to have died ***"testate."***

When the decedent's estate is to be transmitted by Will, the administration and probate proceedings regarding the estate are generally more simplified (and less costly); in contrast to what happens in a no-Will situation, the provisions of the Will are there to guide the executor along. The person appointed in the Will to handle the affairs of the estate—called the "Executor" or "Executrix"—would know, for example, where and how the decedent wishes to be buried, the nature and locations of his assets or indebtedness, who his beneficiaries are, what they should get, and the like. Following the instructions of the testator in his Will as closely as possible, therefore, the probate responsibilities of the executor ought to go faster and more smoothly.

2) By The Laws Of Intestate Succession (also known as the Law of Descent and Distribution). This is when the transfer of the decedent's estate has to be made according to the rules laid down by state law, usually because the deceased person left no valid Will. A person who dies without leaving a valid will is said to have died *"intestate."* The formula for distribution in intestacy situations for each state is outlined in Appendix B].

C. Does The Court Physically Administer Or Manage The Estate?

No. Strictly speaking, the probate function of the court is essentially supervisory—basically, the court supervises the work of the "executor" or "administrator," who is the one that actually and directly manages the affairs of the estate.

When the person who gets to do the actual administration of an estate is named by a Will, he is known as an EXECUTOR (an executrix, if a female). And when the court takes it upon itself to appoint a person to administer the estate, where the dead person died without leaving a Will, the man so appointed is known as an ADMINISTRATOR (an administratrix, if a female).

The general term "FIDUCIARY" or "PERSONAL REPRESENTATIVE" is often used to describe any person, male or female, acting in the capacity of an executor or administrator for an estate.

D. "Non-Probate Property": Certain Property Of The Decedent That Do Not Go Through The Probate Process

Not all property of a decedent passes through probate. Now, it is true that all property which a decedent owned or had an interest in would become part of his "estate" alright. However, *not* every property the decedent owned, or every property that is includable in his *estate,* would necessarily pass through the *probate* system, since there are certain kinds of property that pass directly to the designated beneficiaries without having to pass through probate.

Property of the kind which are not required to pass through probate are known as *"nonprobate"* assets, meaning that such assets can be transferred directly to their designated beneficiaries—and do not, therefore, need to go through probate and the attendant court formalities, legal expenses, and delays of the probate process. (In addition, you may own only a percentage or share of certain property, and with respect to such property, only that percentage or share which you actually own may you leave by your will). The kinds of property which qualify as non-probte property—and which are, therefore, NOT includable in the general assets that are probated—are as follows:

   1. Property Or Assets Which Have A Specifically Named Beneficiary
   This category consists or property or assets which have a specific beneficiary (or beneficiaries) designated in the instrument naming the parties to whom the proceeds directly go. It includes the following types of assets:
      • Proceeds from death or retirement benefits—life or accident insurance policies, plans, social security, retirement plans, IRA's and KEOGHS, and the like.
      • Proceeds from US Savings Bonds; they go directly to the payable-on-death beneficiaries designated in the bonds.
      • Payable-on-death bank accounts.

2. Certain Types Of Trusts:

Trust assets, whether the "revocable living" and "irrevocable living" types, qualify as non-probate assets, as such a gift is understood to be outright gift to be distributed <u>directly</u> to the designated beneficiaries by the appointed trustee.

3. Jointly-Held Property With right of survivorship.

Where any property (e.g., savings accounts, corporate bonds or stocks, or real estate) is owned by two or more persons as "joint tenants" or tenants-by-the-entirety, *with the right of survivorship,* that property will pass <u>directly</u> to the surviving partner 'by operation of law.' Hence, if a property is held in such a form, the decedent may not dispose of such property by will since it automatically goes to the surviving joint owner, and the executor may not include it in your own (the decedent's) estate.

> **NOTE:** This matter is very important and you should, as an estate executor, take strict note of this. The point you should note is that with respect to the category of property so far enumerated above (Items 1, 2 and 3), you (an executor or admnistrator) will not necessarily administer them or be responsible for them as an executor or administrator. Rather, your obligation with regard to those kinds of property will be primarily limited to assisting the designated beneficiaries in the best way you could in effecting the formal transfer of title or property to their names (see Chapter 7-C).

4. Exempt Property, Family Allowance Or Homestead.

In states or localities where a family exemption is allowed to the widow and the surviving children (such as in New York), that property that is an exempt property is not distributed as part of the estate but must be set aside outright for the family members concerned, as a way of ensuring that they are not abruptly cut off from support.

5. Property Or Assets Which The Decedent May Have Owned Only A Share Or Percentage Of

For this category of assets in which you may just own a certain share or percentage of, only that share or percentage which you (the decedent) actually owns, can be passed to the decedent's own beneficiaries, and is thus the ONLY part that gets counted as part of his (the decedent's) estate, or can legitimately be left by will to his beneficiaries.

This category will include the following types of assets or property:
- Decedent's specific partnership interest in a company (in such a situation, upon the decedent's death the partnership will often be dissolved and only his share of the partnership pursuant to the partnership agreement may be counted as part of his estate).
- Where property is held in "tenancy-in-common," usually denoting ownership by two or more parties who are not marital partners. (In such a situation, each party is deemed to own an equal proportional share of the property, and only that proportional share, and not the entire property, is counted as part of a decedent's estate.)

6. Decedent Spouse's Share Of Marital Property In Community Property States

Under the laws of the applicable 9 community property states, only community property owned by a marital couple are deemed to belong to both spouses in equal shares, and upon the death of one spouse, the surviving spouse is entitled to only his or her one-half of the community property. Thus, only the ONE-HALF of the decedent's community property is "owned" by him or her, and can be included as part of his estate.

Community property only applies to married persons in the following nine states that follow the marital "community property" system: Arizona, California, Idaho, Louisiana, Nevada, New Mexico, Texas, Washington, and Wisconsin. What property, exactly, qualifies as "community property" in these states? Simply put, all property, if any, acquired by either spouse (or both spouses), <u>during</u> the parties' marriage, except that acquired by gift or inheritance, is community property. (On the other hand, property owned by a spouse prior to the marriage and kept separate during the marriage, or property individually received during the marriage by him or her by gift or inheritance, is the "separate property" of that spouse owned by him or her only.)

In sum, if a decedent had been married and living in a community property state, the community property which he may dispose of by Will, or which is includable by the executor as part of the probate estate, is only one-half of the community property (and you can then add any separate property he may have, if any). Note, however, that people living in a community property state may also hold property in one or more of the other common forms, some of which are described in earlier passages above—by joint tenancy or tenancy by the entirety, or by tenancy-in-common. And, when such is the case, the usual rules of holding property in such forms will equally apply.

E. Grounds On Which The Terms Of A Will Could Be Contested or Disregarded

In most instances, the terms of the will, when there is one, would most likely be acceptable to the court as more or less final. However, there are some situations (by far fewer in number) when the terms of the Will may be set aside or be disregarded as invalid in assigning distribution rights.

One instance would be where a Will provides absolutely nothing for the surviving spouse, or for the decedent's (minor) children. The inheritance laws of most states provide for the spouse (the same for children in a few states) to receive a certain share of the estate, even if the Will were to provide otherwise. Such rights are known as the ***rights of "election," and of dower or courtesy.*** (See Appendix C for more details on this.)

Another instance would be where a Will proves (or is proven) to be invalid because of any number of reasons: undue influence, or fraud or duress used on the testator; mistakes in the signing of the Will, insanity or lack of testamentary capacity on the part of the testator because of weakened intellect; claims that the will does not comply with the statutory requirements or formalities required in the state (e.g., that it was not signed by the testator at the appropriate place or was not properly witnessed), etc. In such instances, the decedent will simply be thought of (in the eyes of the court) as one who died without leaving a Will, and the estate will therefore 'descend' (be distributed) according to the state's laws of Intestate Succession. (The Intestate Succession Laws for each of the 50 states are summarized in Appendix B).

A third instance would be where a decedent dies "partially testate" and "partially intestate"—that is, where, for example, some of the testator's property is either not mentioned in the Will, or is given to a beneficiary who dies before (or a few days after) the testator, and no 'residuary' provision or alternative person had been named to inherit the item. When such is the case, that portion of the estate to which partial intestacy applies will "descend" (be distributed) according to the state's laws of Intestacy Succession (see Chapter 6 and Appendix B).

Finally, those kinds of non-probate assets which have specifically named beneficiaries and/or are said to "pass by operation of law" (Section D (1), (2) & (3) above), are usually governed by the provisions of the "substitute Wills"— life insurance policy, pension contracts, trusts, and the like.

In practice, most will contests are made by disinherited children or close friends, and the most frequent reason for which wills are contested is based on the claim by contesting persons that they did not receive the inheritance they had expected. Frequently, such persons are disgruntled in that they somehow believe or expect (or were somehow led to believe) that they would be "remembered," or because they feel they are more closely related to the decedent than the beneficiaries named in the Will, and therefore more deserving of an inheritance.

THE GOOD NEWS THOUGH, IS THAT, IT'S GENERALLY DIFFICULT TO SET ASIDE A WILL. By and large, a Will cannot be set aside merely for the reason that someone is not happy with it's terms. A Will must be contested based on definite legal "grounds," and so long as a Will complies with certain basic requirements specified under each state's law for a valid will, it will be difficult for the court to invalidate it. Furthermore, it has been the general, traditional policy of the court to encourage people to have Wills, and consequently, as a practical matter, in most states persons who brave contesting the will bear a heavy legal burden, and the courts will not generally hold a will invalid—unless there's a strong and clearly convincing evidence that the given will does not represent the wishes of the testator.

F. At What Stage In The Probate Process May The Fiduciary Distribute The Estate Assets To The Beneficiaries

Generally speaking, the distribution of the estate's assets to those entitled to inherit them comes *last* in the administration process—that is, *AFTER* the fiduciary has first assembled and evaluated the assets of the decedent, determined the debts of the estate, if any, and paid them off, and after he shall have paid off the funeral expenses and administration expenses. Only then would the fiduciary be in a position to distribute whatever is left of the decedent's estate (if any).

As a rule, most states' laws provide that a fiduciary (an executor or administrator) need not pay out any inheritance until a specified time has passed from the time the Letters Testamentary (or Letters of Administration) was issued him. It is also commonly allowed—and recommended to executors by the author of this manual as good fiduciary practice—that the fiduciary not distribute estate assets to beneficiaries, UNTIL the legitimate estate expenses and creditors' claims have first been paid off, if applicable. (See Chapter 7-C, on p. 104, for more on this.)

G. Do I Pay Off The Decedent's Debts Or Obligations In Any Particular Order?

Generally speaking, yes. As a rule, probate laws commonly give first priority to paying off the *decedent's* **funeral expense** items—the costs of conveyance of the body to the place of burial, the costs of the funeral home, burial ceremonies and burial plot, the cost of a gravestone, where applicable, mourning clothes for the dependents of the deceased, and, at times, the cost of perpetual care of the cemetery plot, and the like.

The reason the executor is permitted to give first priority to payment of expenses of this kind is simple: it is almost universally considered to be in society's public interest that a deceased person be properly put to rest first, before one should go on to attend to other matters, whatever their urgency!!

After the funeral expenses, next come the **expenses incurred in administering the decedent's estate** in order of priority (rental fee for a safe deposit box, commissions to brokers and transfer agents for sale of securities, fees to appraisers, accountants, the executors or lawyers, clerical and postal service costs, and the like).

The decedent's debts take the third place in order of priority of satisfaction. Within this category, however, there is generally an order of priority for paying off debts of different kinds. A typical order is as follows:

1st: Debts entitled to a preference under the laws of the United States and of the State.
2nd: Taxes assessed on the property of the decedent before his death.
3rd: Court judgment and decrees entered against the decedent.
4th: All recognizances, bonds, sealed instruments, notes, bills, and unliquidated demands and accounts.

(See Chapter 7-B, pp. 97-8, for more on this.)

H. Do I Pay Out Legacies To Beneficiaries In Any Particular Order?

Yes. Legacies—i.e, gifts of personal, as opposed to real property, made by Will—are of two primary kinds: *"specific" legacies* and *"general" legacies*. A specific legacy is a gift of *specific* nature payable in property which is specifically identified and set apart; while a general legacy is a gift of a *general* nature payable out of the estate, but with no specific property identified or set aside in the Will for it. Specific legacies have to be satisfied first before general legacies, and where bequeathed assets need to be used to meet the expenses or debt obligations of the decedent, assets bequeathed as general legacies are the first to be applied. And within the general legacy category, those legacies designated as to the amount, must first be satisfied before the **"residuary legacy"** (i.e., before those legacies which constitute the remainder of the estate assets after the other legacies have been provided for) can be satisfied.

(See Chapter 7-C, p. 104 for more on this.)

I. Do I Sell Or Liquidate Estate Assets In Any Particular Order?

Yes. Generally, you do. In order to find the money to meet the obligations of the estate (funeral and administrative expenses, taxes, estate debts, etc.), the executor or administrator may have to "liquidate" (i.e., sell and reduce to cash) the decedent's assets—if it should become necessary to do so to fulfill vital estate obligations.

Under the laws of most states, all property of the estate, whether personal or real property, is chargeable with the decedent's debts and liabilities (except property which is specifically exempt by statute, such as a surviving spouse's homestead). The fiduciary must first sell only those items that are not necessary for the support and subsistence of the family of the deceased. Items which are *specifically* bequeathed to individuals are sold only if the sale of all other assets does not realize sufficient cash to meet estate obligations. Personal property is sold first; real property is usually sold only after the personal property is exhausted.

J. Who Inherits My Property If I Die Without A Will?

When a person dies **"intestate"** or without leaving a Will [or leaving an alternative instrument, such as a trust] disposing of his property, the laws of Intestate Succession (also called the Laws of "descent and distribution") take over and become the controlling formula by which the decedent's estate is distributed. Each state has specific written laws ("statutes") detailing the persons or classes of people entitled to inherit under conditions of intestacy. The intestate succession laws of the state in which the decedent was "domiciled" (i.e., where he was permanently resident) at the time of his/her death would govern. However, as a general rule, some persons who bear certain relationship to a decedent are almost always entitled to inherit from him or her under the laws of just about every state. They are, in their order of priority, the following:[1]

i) **The Spouse.** With a few rare exceptions—such as where a spouse has waived his or her rights of inheritance under a separation or antenuptial agreement, or where he/she had been found guilty of adultery, desertion, or failure to support the other spouse in certain states—the surviving spouse may not be disinherited by a decedent spouse, but has a primary right to a share of the decedent's estate. This right is said to belong to each spouse "by affinity" of the marital relationship, as opposed to a relationship by blood.

In addition to the normal distributive inheritance share of the spouse, the laws of most states also provide for a "family allowance" in money and property to be set aside for the support and maintenance of the surviving spouse and minor or disabled children until the estate is eventually distributed—specified household items or funds from the estate, the family home or apartment, and the like, depending on the particular state.

---

[1]See Appendix B for more detailed summary of the intestacy laws of each state.

ii) **Linear Descendants.** Next to the surviving spouse comes that class of the decedent's heirs who would inherit by virtue of "direct" (also called "linear") blood line. This is the class of people with the closest blood relationship to a decedent according to law and custom. This group includes the decedent's children, grandchildren, and parents in that order. Generally, the children and their descendants take a secondary status to the rights of the spouse. (When children survive their parent, then grandchildren do not, as a group, share in the grandparent's estate; they would be entitled to inherit from the grandparent's estate only if their parent was entitled to share in the estate, but was deceased.)

iii) **Linear Ancestors.** Next in the order of priority, would generally be the decedent's parents, who are said to be his "linear ancestors." (Linear ancestors may generally inherit in situations where the decedent leaves no surviving spouse, children or their ancestors.)

Then follows the **"collateral"** kindred of the decedent, such as his/her brothers and sisters or their descendants, or, where necessary, other so-called "next-of-kin" collateral persons who are still further removed from the decedent, such as the uncles, aunts, nephews and nieces, first cousins, and the like.

Finally, just what happens to a decedent's property when there's no person qualified or available to inherit his property under the laws of inheritance? It's simple: the law says that such property "ESCHEATS"—that is, it automatically passes to the state.

K. What Is A Spousal "Right Of Election"?

Under the doctrine of spousal 'election' contained in the laws of nearly every state, the terms of a decedent's Will are not necessarily the "final word" with respect to what the surviving spouse of the decedent could ultimately take. Where one spouse dies leaving a Will which either fails to provide anything for the surviving spouse, or provides a lesser amount than she or he thinks she is entitled to, the surviving spouse has the option ("the right of election") *to elect against the Will;* that is, he or she, as the case may be, may, instead, 'elect' to take the share provided under the state's law of election—which, though generally somewhat less than the share offered to a spouse under the intestacy inheritance laws, nevertheless guarantees that the surviving spouse is left with something reasonable rather than being totally disinherited. In short, the surviving spouse has the legal right to a specified share of the decedent spouse's estate, regardless of what the Will says!

The basic rationale behind such laws is to protect husbands and wives from otherwise being arbitrarily or unfairly disinherited by each other.

What is the specific amount to which a spouse is entitled? The amount differs from state to state in terms of the statutory provisions of each state, but typically it is one-third of the decedent's probate estate. (A summary of the spousal Right of Election for each of the 50 states is given in Appendix C, pp. 193-7.)

L. What Is The Spousal "Right Of Dower" Or "Curtesy"?

Dower is the right of a surviving wife to the use and enjoyment of any *real property* owned by the husband, while **curtesy** is the male equivalent, the right of a surviving hus*band* to a deceased wife's real property. The right usually lasts only for the duration of the survivor's life, and includes any rents and profits derived from the real property. This right is also referred to as the right to a life estate.
Most states which formerly had dower and curtesy laws under common law, have had the practice abolished in recent times. As of this writing, only 15 states still have some variations of dower and curtesy—Alabama, Arkansas, Hawaii, Iowa, Kansas, Massachusetts, New Jersey, Ohio, Rhode Island, Tennessee, Vermont, Virginia, West Virginia, and Wisconsin. And the number is constantly dwindling from year to year.

In general, except for a few states, the rights of dower or curtesy (where they exist) is usually IN ADDITION to the share taken under the laws of intestate inheritance (Appendix B). Only in a few states do the statutes provide for a choice to be made between the shares. (Notations are made in Appendix B for the few states still maintaining dower and curtesy.)

M. The 'Small Estate' Procedures: Estates Of Certain Size Need Not Go Through Formal Probate

Estates of certain sizes need not necessarily go through formal probate administration. Most states provide that, under certain conditions, the property of an estate falling under certain size categories may be disposed of without formal court "administration." This generally applies with respect to estates considered to be "small" estates. In New York, for example, a small estate procedure applies in any estate valued at $10,000 or less, with such estates exempt from having to go through a formal administration through the courts. (See Chapter 8 of this manual, pp. 132-4, for the detailed procedures of settling a small estate without a probate administration.)

Chapter 2
CAN YOU BE AN ESTATE EXECUTOR? HERE'S WHAT IT TAKES TO BE ONE

A. What Is An Executor?

Strictly put, an executor is a person (or corporation) who is expressly appointed by a testator (one who dies leaving a Will) to carry out the testator's directives made in his or her will. [If a female, the executor is called an Executress or Executrix]. In more general, practical terms, though, the term is used to describe someone who is legally responsible for managing, administering and settling a dead person's estate. Frequently, in probate or estate settlement work, the general term FIDUCIARY or PERSONAL REPRESENTATIVE OR ADMINISTRATOR is used to describe such a person, male or female, who is acting in the capacity of an executor of an estate. Hence, in this manual, these terms may often be used interchangeably.

B. The Significance Of Picking The Right Executor

In this chapter, we shall address the issue of what it takes to be a good and effective executor—the professional, temperamental, personal, psychological and other attributes and qualifications required of him. The basic objective is two-fold: on the one hand, to give the will or estate plan maker some clues and ideas as to what to look for in picking the appropriate candidates for appointment as executor. And, on the other hand, to give a person being considered for appointment as executor (or, more simply, who suddenly finds himself thrust in that position through death and unplanned change in circumstances) an idea as to whether he possesses the personal attributes to be able to handle the responsibilities, or, if not, what he'll at least need to have in order to be able to do so.

THE POINT CANNOT BE EMPHASIZED ENOUGH: CHOOSING THE RIGHT EXECUTOR IS PROBABLY THE SINGLE MOST IMPORTANT ELEMENT IN OVERALL DETERMINATION OF HOW WELL THE PROVISIONS OF A WILL WILL BE IMPLEMENTED, OR AN ESTATE ADMINISTERED OR SETTLED IN THE FINAL ANALYSIS. Why? The reason should be rather obvious: the executor's job is a critical one; he is the one who, in the end, is to actually see to it that the directives in your Will are implemented when you do die, the one who is to take over the control and management of your estate and affairs (payment of the bills, selling of property, making of the financial transactions and decisions, etc), and the one who is to actually make the distributions to your beneficiaries, and so on. On him (or her), more or less, will everything largely depend as to whether your estate is handled as you would have wished or not.

Hence, the critical importance of choosing the right person for the job cannot be overemphasized. Or, conversely, the critical importance for a person named or being considered to serve as an executor to be able to have some reasonable idea as to whether he has what it takes to handle the task, or should perhaps turn it over to someone else or seek professional help.

C. The Ideal Qualities Of An Ideal Executor

What are the ideal, personal qualities and attributes that an ideal estate executor or administrator should possess? What are the most desirable "personal" or "non-legal" qualities that he/she could have?

Aside from being a person of unquestioned character upon whom you (the testator or estate plan-maker) can completely rely on, the person chosen should preferably be a person you know and trust whose judgment you respect and who you know will respect your wishes. In addition, the person should be the type who has the level of financial and business experience and temperament, and the amount of time that will be required to be able to handle the estate responsibilities, bearing in mind the size or complexity of the estate and the provisions of the will thereof, if any. [Granted, though, as a rule, most will-makers (as well as trust-makers) almost automatically choose a close family member and/or principal beneficiary, such as a spouse or adult children, to serve as the executor.]

As outlined by Plotnick and Leimberg and other analysts in the field, the personal attributes and non-legal characteristics of a good executor, which constitute the major factors that should be used in selecting an executor, are many and varied and include the following:

- The "competence" of the proposed person in being able to undertake an executor's tasks
- The person's ability to appreciate and concentrate on "the best interests" of the estate beneficiaries, and lack of conflicts of interest
- Possessing personal knowledge of the beneficiaries' needs and the subject matter of the estate
- Experience in handling the inner workings or operations of the decedent's business, especially when the business is a specialized one
- Having management and investment knowledge of the kind that would put one in a "better position to step in and take control of the decedent's affairs"
- Having and being able to devote the amount of time necessary for discharging the duties and responsibilities of a personal representative
- The objectivity and impartiality of the person
- The physical proximity of the person to the estate assets and the beneficiaries.

However, the Plotnick and Leimberg team conclude, *of all the essential characteristics making for a good estate manager, in the final analysis the most fundamental one for a manager to possess, is the "human factor"—the proposed person's "competence in a general sense."* By this, they mean, essentially, the person's ability to learn fast and to learn and grow on and with the job, his ability to work with and get along with people, especially the estate beneficiaries.

Plotnick and Leimberg summed up their findings on the composite characteristics of a good estate executor or manager (or trustee), this way:

> "Knowledge of financial matters is not necessarily the most important qualification of an [estate or trust] executor. [This is so since] it is always possible for an executor, if lacking knowledge in certain areas, to learn more about the subject Selection of a person (or persons) who can firmly adhere to sound values is also important. Likewise, personal integrity and devotion to duty should be valued attributes, although these are often difficult to measure objectively. *That is why, in the final analysis, the human factor [the amount of personal effort and attention the party can bring to the task] plays such an important part in the evaluation of the executor's functions...*
>
> No list of standards, therefore, can be complete unless due consideration is given to the personal image of the executor as an incorruptible and caring individual in regard to the psychological as well as financial needs of the beneficiaries.
>
> Although it would seem obvious that an executor's "competence" must be paramount on any list of qualifications, this factor is often overlooked because of the sometimes emotional nature of the appointment.
>
> [Take this scenario for example]: Nancy, a dynamic and worldly business owner who ran an empire of interlocking businesses requiring the greatest amount of expertise, named her husband as her executor. Unfortunately, her husband could barely balance the family's checkbook. The results of Nancy's decision (based on emotion rather than logic) were disastrous. And the negative impact of her decision fell mainly on the spouse whom she had intended to protect.
>
> *Competence in a general sense is not necessarily measured by an awareness of all of the decedent's personal affairs or the intricacy of the decedent's business. A competent executor is one who can analyze the affairs as quickly as possible under the circumstances, determine what facets of the estate can be handled within the bounds of his or her knowledge and capabilities, and then secure professional assistance in those areas in which it is needed...*

> [In sum], Executors [should not be persons] who perform their duties in an objective vacuum without
> giving due consideration to the interests of the beneficiaries [for when they do, they would] often find
> that they have put out the fire only after the building has been destroyed...
> [Rather, the ideal candidate for the job is one who can recognize that] the executor's ultimate
> responsibility is to handle the estate and preserve and transfer its assets [to beneficiaries] in the most
> efficient manner possible under all attending circumstances."[1]

TRANSLATION: Sure, the other rather more "obvious" qualifications and questions for a good estate executor (e.g., having the appropriate business sense, the required ability and amount of time to devote to the responsibility and similar personal qualities and attributes mentioned above), are relevant and important; but, above all, the most fundamental and ideal personal quality required of an executor is his or her "competence"—his/her ability to act and decide on matters based on logic and rationality as to what would be in the best interest of the estate's beneficiaries, rather than on emotion; his/her ability to be truly dedicated, objective, and realistic, while also being caring and unselfish, once you (i.e., the testator) are gone!

D. The Ideal Executor Should Also Be Someone Who Knows Something About The Psychological Facets Of Death And Dying

a) The Role Of The Psychological Aspects Of Death And Dying In The Lives Of The Decedent's Survivors

To be sure, possessing such personal qualities and attributes as are enumerated in the preceding section is central in the making and make-up of an effective estate executor or administrator. However, according to experts, there is one other fundamental and essential quality an executor should have, or, at least, aspire to acquire, namely: *the special ability to work with people who are in a state of emotional stress, shock and mourning brought about by the loss of a loved one.*

Experts who hold to this view contend that having the skill and sensitivity to work with people who are in a state of emotional stress is essential because only by patience and understanding of the incredible pain and stress experienced by a decedent's survivors and loved ones can you really be sensitive to their deepest needs and best interests. One expert team, Plotnick and Leimberg, summed it up this way:

> "As executor, your most difficult task may be dealing with the survivors; [indeed] you may even be one
> yourself. Therefore, you must learn not only to face facts and figures, but also learn to face faces. A
> good executor should have the skill and sensitivity to work with people who are in shock, disorganized,
> and experiencing volatile emotions. These emotions may include guilt, loss, loneliness, and depression."[2]

b) The Five Stages Of Grief Experienced By The Dying Person And/Or His Survivors

According to Plotnick and Leimberg, there are two levels at which an executor will need to understand the "grief and awesome experience" experienced in a death situation: one, from the standpoint of the grief experienced by the dying person himself (or herself), and secondly, from the standpoint of the same emotion experienced by the survivors. Basically, for the dying person, there are five stages of grief he or she experiences: **1)** Denial (the initial it-can't-happen-to-me or this-can't-be-true reaction to the first inkling of the possibility of death, which is a common means by which a dying person deals with the uncomfortable fact of impending death); **2)** anger (the powerful 'why me' emotional trauma borne out of frustration that would often be directed at any available "convenient target," such as loved ones, doctors, friends, estate planning advisors, etc.); **3)** bargaining (the "Let me live one more year and I'll be good to my wife/husband/children" or "I'll denote money to my church/synagogue" plea); **4)** Depression (the response to the actual loss of health or use of part of the body that is often seen by the dying person as a prelude to the impending loss of life; and **5)** Acceptance (the final stage, characterized by absence of any emotions on the part of the dying person, as though he or she has finally come to terms ("acceptance") with the inevitability of death.

A dead person's survivors, it is said, often experience these same emotions and stages of grief often while the person is dying and, almost always, directly afterwards. For most substantial estates of a male decedent, for example, the widow (assuming there is one), suddenly thrust in the position of having to

[1]Plotnick & Leimberg, How To Settle An Estate, pp. 12-14.

[2]Plotnick and Leimberg, How To Settle An Estate (Consumer Reports Books of US, Yonkers, NY: 1991), p. 21. Much of the discussions in this segment is derived from this source, for which the author is deeply grateful.

take over many of the decedent's roles and tasks and to shoulder what could often be an overwhelming new responsibilities, is generally depressed, unhappy, and insecure, with her social life completely changed. (And, in situations when it is the man that survives—which happens far less often—he faces even more serious emotional problems, since it has been established that men seldom have the same kind of support system that women have to hold them up in such times of personal crisis). Survivors, men or women, would often experience guilt for what they did or did not do, or for the deceased person, or simply experience embarrassment or guilt for having lived while the deceased died; or they may feel anger for being "deserted" and left to face life's problems alone. And, perhaps the single most difficult and serious emotion of all among survivors, according to the experts, is a deep sense of loneliness and resentment at being left alone, with some studies of American widows showing that loneliness is the single most serious problem of widowhood among such women, followed by the financial pressure of raising children alone.[3]

In sum, the point is that the death of a person often leaves in its aftermath, some extreme emotional and financial problems and pressures for the loved ones and families left behind, which, in turn, often create unique psychological pressures. ***Hence, one vital but ideal quality of a good executor is the ability, skill and temperament to recognize and to be sensitive to the psychological aspects of death and dying.***

C) How This Knowledge Helps The Executor In Doing A Better Job

How can an executor properly utilize his knowledge and awareness of the psychological aspects of death and dying to do a better job of his responsibilities? How does having such skill or quality make him a better or more effective executor particularly to the estate's beneficiaries?

Generally speaking, an executor's awareness of the relevance of these issues would help him exercise essential patience and understanding with the decedent's survivors and the beneficiaries of the estate, and to better deal with the acts, reactions, or needs of such persons. For example, an alert executor who is fully aware that a dying individual would often take out his anger and frustration on his loved ones or any available, convenient targets for little or no real reason, will be quick to spot a testator who makes last-minute estate-planning decision primarily on the basis of his anger on a family member (or members), such as reduced legacies or total elimination of the heir(s) that is totally inconsistent with the testator's past desires or indications. But, even more importantly, an executor with knowledge of the role played by the psychological aspects of death and dying in the lives of a decedent's survivors, would be more particularly aware of the necessity of giving a decedent's survivors a feeling of control and a sense of usefulness and satisfaction by dent of meaningfully involving them in the decedent's unfinished business. Thus, primarily by involving the survivors in the important details regarding any unfinished business of the decedent and the settling of the estate affairs, and bringing them meaningfully into the decision-making process in such affairs, such an executor can, among other things, help revive and energize the spirits of the survivors and lift them from the usual symptoms of grief, pain, loneliness, and diminished sense of worth that is the classic lot for persons in such situation, into a position of better preparedness to overcome their loss and to go on with their own lives.

Again, as Plotnick and Leimberg succinctly put it:

> "As executor [knowledgeable in the role of the psychological aspects of death in the lives of the decedent's survivors], you can increase the family members' dignity by empowering them with as much control as possible. It is not enough to give survivors a voice; you must also give them a listener. Only then can they be active participants in the decision-making process. Hopelessness and depression are precipitated and exacerbated when individuals can't (or perceive they can't) act.
>
> Any steps you take to bring all family members into the decision-making process will relieve their feelings of helplessness. The death of a loved one will be experienced as less absurd, and may become more tolerable, if the family knows that the life of the deceased had meaning. So it is vital to do what you can to give the family a sense of pride in what the deceased accomplished...The more you can do to explain what comes next and how the family can take charge, the better off they will be."

---

[3]Accounts as cited by Plotnick and Leimberg, Ibid. pp. 23-4.

Chapter 3

ARE YOU GOING TO BE AN EXECUTOR FOR SOMEONE'S ESTATE? THEN BE SURE THE PERSON LEAVES YOU CERTAIN TOOLS & INFORMATION TODAY, TO HELP EASE YOUR TASK TOMMORROW

A. Why And How The Testator Should Help You Now To Simplify Your Job As Executor Tomorrow

If you are a testator making a Will (or a trustor preparing a trust), or an estate plan maker otherwise planning your estate, it's not just enough merely to make your Will and/or create your trust or other appropriate estate planning instruments. There is one other significant step you can—and should—take today while you are fully alive and well, to simplify for your appointed executor the task of carrying out his duties with greater ease and understanding: YOU'VE GOT TO ORDERLY ORGANIZE YOUR ESTATE FOR HIM (OR HER), AND GIVE HIM A FAIR IDEA OF THE DUTIES AND THE NECESSARY INFORMATION HE'D NEED TO DO THE JOB.

And if, on the other hand, you happen to be an executor or the administrator (or a trustee thereof) appointed by an estate plan maker to handle his or her estate, you had better be sure as well, that the person for whom you are to serve as the estate fiduciary provides you with these tools and facilities as they will help simplify your job and make life a lot easier for you!

How important is this step in facilitating the task of the executor, or in ensuring an easier or more effective settling of the estate, in the end? Extremely important, according to experts with vast field experience in the practical, day-to-day, nitty gritty tasks of estate settlement. In deed, some experts have gone so far as to contend that without this element—i.e., without a properly organized estate—to go with the Will, or the trust and/or other similar estate planning instruments, the efforts put into the preparation of such instruments shall have been woefully negated and wasted, in that one's estate executor, and heirs and loved ones would still not have escaped the much-dreaded pains, agony and expense of probate!

One widely respected and experienced expert, Henry W. Abts III, a hands-on professional estate planner and adviser who has created well over 2,000 living trusts and settled just as many estates in a lifetime of estate planning, maintains that with an organized estate (and a good Living Trust), it would "typically take less than one hour to settle an estate."[1] But, if the estate is not organized, he says, the result is the opposite: a "nightmare" in the settling of the estate.

---

[1]Abts, The Living Trust, p. 179.

Abts summed up the point rather sharply:

> "an organized estate facilitates a quick settlement and identifies what assets exist and where they are located.
>
> For most people, the biggest problem involved in settling an estate of a loved one is just being able to find all of the pieces. Even spouses do not always keep track of what the other spouse is accumulating.
>
> For example, many widows do not really know all of the stocks and bonds their husbands have purchased or all the pension benefits their husbands have earned over many years...
> Losing a loved one—especially a spouse—is a traumatic experience. People in mourning can think only of the loss and not of the many details that must be resolved to settle the estate...
>
> How large is the estate and where are the assets? Where is the deed to the house? Where are the checking and savings accounts and certificates of deposit? (The banks love to retain unclaimed accounts). Who was your last stock broker, and where are all those US Government savings bonds? [And so on and on].
>
> People "know" where their important papers are—until they go to retrieve them. I have watched both spouses, even in the most organized families, search high and low for missing documents. Imagine [then what would be] the dilemma if one spouse were removed. Similarly, trying to step in and assemble the estate of a...single person is a nightmare...
>
> Without organization, you have a nightmare; however, with organization, you create an orderly process for your surviving spouse, children, or other heirs. The orderly process allows the survivors to quickly identify your assets, legal documents, and distribution desires and then to settle your affairs— and then get back to living their own lives...[You do] not have to leave a jumble of jigsaw pieces as your legacy to your family..."[2]

In sum, the point is simple: if you are the will-maker or estate plan maker, you've got to be sure to ORGANIZE your estate and leave a reasonably organized estate for your would-be executor or administrator, with all the necessary documents and records, and the basic information concerning all facets of the estate fully assembled in one (or a few) known places and orderly organized for easy reference; and if you are a designated or prospective executor or administrator, you've got to prevail upon the estate plan maker, and insist that he (she) leave a well organized estate alongside any estate plan instrument (a Will, Trust, etc.) he might have also prepared.

> **NOTE:** For a prospective executor, before you ever agree that you'll be the executor, ask the testator or person who is proposing you for the job these basic questions: *how much overall estate planning and how much organizing of his estate and affairs has he done?*

B Some Steps You Must Take Now, To Organize Your Estate And Ease Its Administration & Settlement Later

To be sure, the subject of the appropriate devices and techniques by which to have a more orderly settling of an estate or a more simplified administration, or how to actually create such instruments, is a separate matter one step removed from the primary subject matter of this manual, and are clearly beyond the scope of the present manual. This is certainly not a book on estate planning. (Those who wish to delve into that subject in greater details may consult a sister volume to this manual also published by the same publisher, *"How To Properly Plan Your 'Total' Estate With A Living Trust, Without The Lawyer's Fees,"* by Benji O. Anosike.) However, in furtherance of the subject matter of this chapter, we shall give in this section a few pointers on the major methods and devices a testator or estate plan maker can use to assist his executor and make the task of estate administration easier for his executor. Basically, the techniques are two types: those that, through some estate planning, have the effect of shrinking the size of the "probate estate" so as to leave as little property as possible in the estate (and thus less work for the executor to do); and those techniques that are essentially designed to organize the information, records and the estate into an orderly, centralized, and readily accessible manner for the executor to be able to work with.

---

[2]Abts, pp. 149 & 151.

The following are the basic steps and methods:

1. *Prepare (take the time and be sure to actually do this) a detailed, information MASTER LIST or* WORKSHEET that will provide your executor all the essential information he'll require in administering the estate—information about the location of your records and documents, the property ownership documents and family records, and estate plan instruments, bank accounts, life, health, fire, liability and other insurance policies; real estate deeds; wills and trusts; stocks, bonds, and other securities; birth certificates, marriage licenses, and marital agreements; military service records; and Social Security information, etc.

2. *Make Advisers' List*
Make a list of important persons who the executor will need to contact or confer with upon your death, (their names, addresses and phone numbers—close family members relatives and friends, the clergy's insurance agents, brokers, accountants, attorneys, estate trustees, guardians, and other advisers.)

3. *Periodically review and update key dispositive documents*
Review and change your will, life insurance policies, and employee-benefit beneficiary designations, if appropriate and necessary. Check to make sure that all life insurance and disability premiums have been paid (and receipts or checks indicating payment have been appropriately filed away.)

4. *Consider making a revocable Living Trust as one of your Estate plan instruments.*
A revocable trust is one that can be altered, amended, revoked, or terminated at any time until the death of its creator. Placing property into a revocable *Living Trust* has many tremendous estate plan benefits, including providing for property management both during and after the lifetime of the estate plan maker; and it allows a smooth transfer of property to one's beneficiaries upon death.

But by far it's most important advantage is the ability to eliminate the much dreaded "agony of probate" with respect to the assets put in the trust—the cost, delay, and uncertainty involved in the probate process.

5. *Consider a living will and a Durable Power of Attorney and Medical Directive*
Assuming you desire that extraordinary means of life support be used or not be used to prolong your life, then be sure to draw up a document called a *Living Will* in which you'll formally express that desire. Furthermore, couple that with at least two other instruments that should go with the Living Will—a *Durable Financial and Medical Power of Attorney, and a Medical Directive* (to empower a "proxy" you would name with the right to act on your behalf in the event you were to become incapacitated or incompetent, but not dead.)

6. *If Applicable and Suitable for you, put your Property in other "Will Substitute" & "Non-Probate" Forms*
As already discussed more thoroughly in Chapter 1, certain types of property are not part of a dead person's estate, and hence putting one's property in such forms—e.g., joint tenancy ownership, a trust, pay-on-death bank accounts, proceeds of beneficiary-designated life insurance policies or employee retirement benefits, etc.—is a way of passing property <u>directly</u> to one's beneficiaries OUTSIDE an estate. The executor, in effect, would be spared the trouble of having to administer or settle such property as he will not normally be responsible for property that are held in such forms for it will not be considered part of the "decedent's estate." [See Chapter 1, especially Section D thereof (pp. 12-13) for more on this.]

7. *Leave a memo or letter of instructions.*
(This is a private, informal, nonlegal document you could leave with immediate relatives, explaining your wishes with respect to highly personal matters that should not be stated in a trust or publicly in the will, or that need to be handled immediately after death (such as funeral or burial arrangements); and should contain, as well, a list of names and phone numbers of the same financial advisors and others as are listed in Items #1 & 2 above, who can be relied on for advice and assistance.

8. Arrange for successor management or sale of business, if applicable.

If a business is involved, arrange for successor management and/or sale of the business. You can often do these more easily and profitably while the estate owner is alive than at a time when you are more likely to be emotionally distraught.

9. Establish domicile.

You (the testator) should establish a single domicile. This is to avoid death taxation by more than one state. You can do this by, for example, registering to vote in the desired state; applying for a driver's license in the desired state; transferring all bank accounts to the desired state; filing of your tax returns from the desired state; and living in the desired state for a period of at least more than 6 months each year. (If a decedent lived in two or more houses in different states in the course of one year, more than one state may attempt to tax his or her property)

10. Specify your marital status

Clearly and completely specify your current and past marital status (your complete marital history, in short). Clearly state, in written statement, preferably including your Will (and/or Trust, if applicable) the names, addresses, etc. of all your former and present spouses and divorces, if any, the dates and places of such marriage and divorces, etc. And, of course, be sure to put in the estate files the relevant records and documentations of the events. Furthermore, completely list each and every child (all of them) you ever had—legitimate or illegitimate, adopted, children by previous marriages, as well as any child(ren) that might have been left out of the Will. This way, you reduce any possible uncertainty, and hence make less likely any possible harassment or claims by persons who may otherwise claim they are entitled to some share of the estate.

11. Locate all relevant records & information in one known place.

Finally, you (the testator or estate plan-maker) must now arrange all the information and records you collected in an orderly manner. There's one good way to do this simply.

Here's what you do. Get a moderate sized, loose-leaf binder (or a file cabinet or drawer) with labelled dividers. Designate this by a name, say "THE ESTATE RECORDS BOOK". Now, carefully label the dividers to designate under each label or folder a separate subject matter or category of information. For example, one folder may hold tax returns and records, another could be for estate plan documents such as a will or trust, and so on. EXAMPLES: "Family Information," "Special Medical Care Needs," "Business Interests & Agreements," "Estate Plan Documents—Trusts, Wills, Durable Power of Attorney, Living Will, Etc.," "Real Estate," "Cash or Equivalent Funds," "Investments," "Loans," "Trustees & Successor Trustee," "Advisors & Trust Team," "The Final Operational Instruction For Settling The Estate," "Beneficiaries," etc.

Make a photocopy of each of the documents and records relating to your affairs. Then, selectively assemble and segregate and place these *photocopies* of the documents and records (just the photocopies) under the proper subheadings or labels. (With respect to the originals of the documents and records, put these away separately, preferably in a more secure but separate location away from the home, such as in a bank safe deposit box).[3] You'll probably wish to give a complete package of this information (The Estate Records Book) to the person whom you have chosen as your executor, or, at least, be sure that you clearly inform him or her as to the location and accessibility of the records book.

> NOTE: You must always view and treat this Estate Records Book, and all of the information and documentations that constitute it, as a "workbook"—that is, something that you should be working with on a continuous basis, adding to and deleting from, and changing and revising, constantly. Hence, you should keep the file handy and in a really accessible place.

---

[3]Laws vary from state-to-state on this, but many states allow the surviving spouse (and/or executor of a Will) prompt access to the box upon a spouse's death. However, a good practice would be to verify your state's policy in advance. It's simple to do: simply ask your bank whether the box will have to be "sealed" upon one's death.

Chapter 4
HOW TO PROBATE AND SETTLE AN ESTATE IN ANY PARTICULAR STATE IN THE NATION

A. There Are Broad Similarities In Probate Procedures Among All States

Each state has its own specific laws and procedures which govern probate and the settling of a decedent's estate with the given state (see Appendix A of the manual). However, here's the good news about this that is especially worthy of note for the readers of this manual: In general, the rules and procedures are basically identical from state to state in the broad principles which underlie the process.[1] The extent of the differences among state practices essentially relates merely to state-specific particulars that are inevitably unique to each state—matters such as the appropriate court for, or specific names by which the probate court is called in a given state, the specific titles of the forms needed to be filed in the proceedings, the particular sequence of events, the specific fees and amounts charged for probate filings in a particular state, and the like.

In the next few chapters (see chapters 5 & 6), we shall detail in more specific and elaborate terms, those procedures that are necessarily state-specific to a single state, the state of New York, *with one primary object in mind: namely, to employ this detailed elaborate treatment for illustrative purposes—as a "model" state whose procedures for probating and settling an estate are amply demonstrative of the general procedures all across the United States.*

New York State is particularly appropriate for illustrating the general principles in that the State's probate and estate settling requirements and procedures (outlined starting from Chapters 5 & 6) are fairly representative of the general procedures followed in most States. In deed, consequently, one truism can be fairly strongly asserted in this connection with all certainty: *if you are actually able to probate and settle an estate—or merely able to follow how to do so—in New York, you can just as easily do your probate and estate settlement in just about any other state. You would only need to use the same basic knowledge outlined in the next Chapters (and your God-given common sense!) to get it all done.*

B. Aids For Being Able To File In Your Particular State

In this Chapter, however, we shall outline the basic procedures generally involved in the undertaking of probate and estate settlement proceedings in any state or states in the United States. Furthermore, to further augment the information given in this Chapter for the benefit of readers who may wish to probate or settle an estate in other states other than New York, we also provide in Appendix A (pp. 152-177), a summary of the essential rules and information for probating and settling an estate in each of the 50 states and other jurisidctions. And, finally, on the same issue of attempting as best as we could to broaden the scope of this book to as wide a number of people and states as possible, a provision is made by the publisher to supply readers across several states with the legal forms usuable for probate filing or processing in individual states (Appendix I).

---

[1]In general, such procedures seek to approximate the Uniform Probate Code of 1969, which had the approval of the National Conference of Commissioners on Uniform State Law as well as the American and state bar associations.

C. Summary Of The Probate Process Generally

As stated above, whatever the state of your probate filing, the basic procedures of modern estate administration and settlement follow a closely similar pattern. What follows below in this chapter is a four-step summary of the general procedures in almost every state.

1. Locating The Will

If the deceased person left a Will, the Will (the true, signed, original copy) must first be located—in the testator's home, his safe deposit box, the office of the attorney who drafted the Will, if applicable, or, in certain states (such as Ohio and some others where a copy is required to be left with the court for safe-keeping), in the probate courthouse of the testator's county of residence.

The Will will generally name a person (or institution) who is to serve as the **"EXECUTOR"** or **"EXECUTRIX"** of the decedent's estate. In an overwhelming majority of cases (over 80 percent of all cases), the person designated as executor (or executrix) is likely to be a member of the testator's family, such as a spouse or child. But it could also be a trusted friend, or a corporation or a banking trust company, particularly where a large estate is involved.

2. Proving The Will Before The Judge And Getting An Executor Approved

In the very first step, called "opening the estate," the Will must first be "probated"—that is, presented before a probate surrogate court and 'proved' to be a valid and authentic document, truly made and signed by the deceased person himself. Usually it is the designated executor in the Will who files the petition with the court to have the Will probated.

Under the current procedures of most states, the preliminary probate (i.e., the 'proving') phase of a Will to the court is basically a simple matter, particularly in situations where these two conditions are met: i) where the executor can obtain sworn statements of confirmation (called "affidavits") from those persons who had witnessed the signing of the Will by the testator; and ii) where none of the heirs, or other persons who are required to be notified of the probate proceedings, raises any objections and are willing to give their (written) consent to the probate action. In such situations, the approach in many states (New York, Ohio, etc.) is often for the court to probate the Will "summarily," and confirm the appointment of the person named as executor or executrix. The party so confirmed as executor may be required to furnish "bond" (a kind of monetary pledge for the faithful performance of one's duties) if such a requirement had not been waived by the provisions of the testator's Will. **"Letters Testamentary"**—the formal document of authority authorizing the person to act as a court-approved executor—are then issued to the party by the court and he's ready to assume his responsibilities as executor.

3. Getting An 'Administrator' Appointed, Where No Will Exists

Now, if, on the other hand, the deceased person died intestate—that is, without having left a valid Will—any "interested person" may petition the court to have an **"ADMINISTRATOR"** ("administratrix" if female) appointed for the decedent's estate. (The term administrator is used as the equivalence of executor in an intestate situation.) With the court's approval of a person to serve as administrator, the court issues him with the **"Letters of Administration,"** the official instrument of an administrator's authority to act for the estate. The administrator would probably be required to furnish bond for the faithful performance of his duties, and with that, he (or she) is ready to begin the work of administering and settling the estate.

4. Undertaking The Actual Formal Administration And Settling Of The Estate

By whatever title the party who takes charge of an estate is called—"executor, " "administrator," "administrator with a Will Annexed," or what have you—such a person has basically the same special functions under the law, and is the "personal representative" or "fiduciary" of the affairs of the decedent's estate just as well.

It is after the above-described probate courtroom preliminaries are completed, that the actual, day-to-day administration or management phase of the estate is ready to be carried out. And, *essentially, when it comes to the actual administration phase of probate, the procedures do not differ much, whether it is one where a Will had been made, or one where none is available. In either instance, the fiduciary's responsibility, as an executor or administrator, is just about the same: to see to the winding down of the decedent's personal and financial affairs, finally ending in the distribution of the balance of the estate property.* Where a Will exists, the terms of the Will simply become the executor's guide for distribution; and where no Will exists, the formula laid down by the state's Intestate Succession Law [Appendix B] becomes, on the other hand, the administrator's guide for distribution.

D. The Duties Of The Estate Executor Or Administrator

The following summarizes the broad, overall duties of the fiduciary (whether an executor or administrator) in administering an estate, following the death of a decedent:

1. Locate The Will. It may have been placed in the testator's home, his safe deposit box, his attorney's or accountant's office, in the probate court clerk's office, or kept with the executor himself, etc.)

2. Carry out any special instructions in the Will concerning a funeral and burial arrangements, if any.

3. Probate the Will before the Probate or Surrogate Court — that is, submit it to the court with a certified copy of the decedent's death certificate attached, and show proof that what has been submitted is truly the   Will of the dead person, made and signed by him or her.

4. Be officially confirmed by the court to be the executor, and obtain his "Letters Testamentary" (the formal document of authority) to act as the executor for the decedent. (See a sample variant of the Letters Testamentary used in New York's Kings County at p. 63.)
Or, if the decedent died intestate (without leaving a Will), then have any interested person (e.g., a surviving spouse, next-of-kin, or a person having an interest in the estate) file a petition with the appropriate probate court to be appointed the Administrator for the decedent's estate and be granted Letters of Administration to handle the affairs of the estate.

5. Open the decedent's safe deposit box, if any, and make a record of its contents.

6. Ascertain all the personal or real property of the decedent and assemble them so that none would be lost, misused or overlooked; prepare an inventory of such property and have them properly appraised for their proper value.

7. Collect for the estate or the designated beneficiary, the proceeds of assets like life insurance, pension, dividends, interests, rents, veteran and social security benefits, rent or utility deposits, and the like, as applicable.

8. Ascertain all legitimate debts owed to the decedent, if any, and collect them.

9. Arrange (if applicable) to have the decedent's business or investments continued, liquidated, or sold — depending on the decedent's instructions in his Will.

10. Set aside any property that is exempt from administration for the benefit of the family or surviving spouse, or maintenance funds for the family (the "widow's allowance"), and provide it to the family to prevent undue financial hardship to the family during the estate administration period.

11. Publish or otherwise give proper notice to decedent's creditors for submission of their claims against the estate, if any.

12. Pay off the decedent's funeral expenses, the lawful debts, taxes or claims against his estate, and the expenses incurred in administering his estate. (In insufficient asset estates, he may have to sell certain estate assets to meet the estate obligations.)

Figure 4-1
SCHEMATIC ILLUSTRATION OF THE ESTATE EXECUTOR'S DUTIES IN THE PROBATE PROCESS

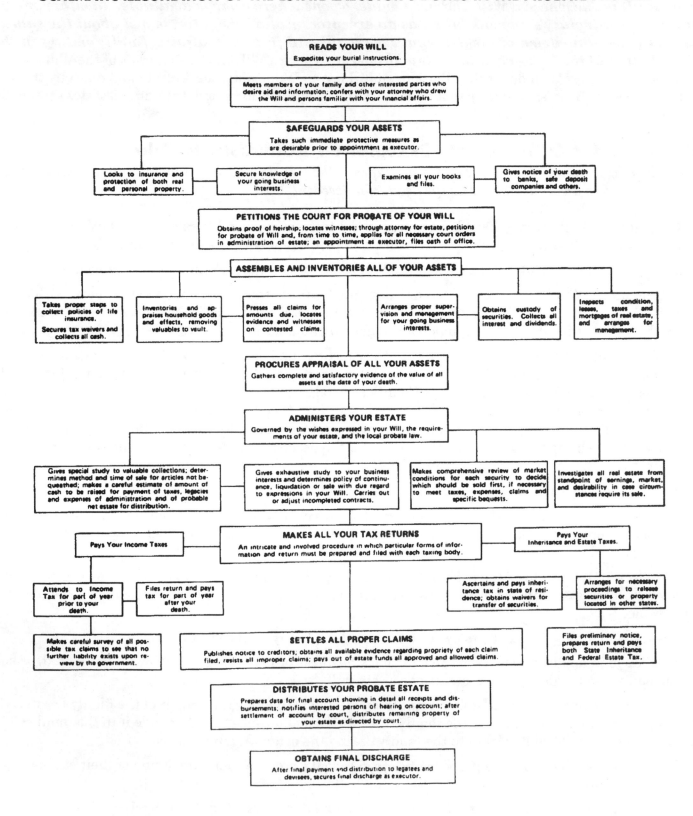

Reproduced, courtesy of Contemporary Books (Chicago), publisher of *The Living Trust*, by Henry W. Abts III, to whom the present author and publisher are deeply indebted.

13. Defend the estate in court, if anyone should contest the Will or sue the decedent's estate for whatever reason.

14. Assemble the beneficiaries of the estate, and distribute to them the balance of the estate (what is left after paying off the estate debts and administration expenses, etc.) in accordance with the provisions of the Will, or, if no Will was left, in accordance with the provisions of the State's Intestate Succession Law.

15. Submit a final accounting of his services—detailed statements of his receipts and disbursements for the estate—to the court, and obtain a formal discharge as executor.

E. How Long Does Probate And Estate Administration Take?

As a rule, lawyers who make a living out of probate work have long been reputed to have a habit of unnecessarily prolonging the probate proceedings way beyond what it should legitimately take. (They get paid, of course, according to the amount of time they could claim they spent on the "probate work"!!)

Edward E. Colby, a concerned California attorney and author of "Everything You've Always Wanted to Know About the Law But Couldn't Afford to Ask," makes this complaint of the probate court redtape: "The time factor is shocking and no one can explain any valid reason for (the) long delays."

Another of the many critics, Harper Hamilton of Boulder, Colorado, who is also an attorney and author, speaks harshly of the "probate rip off" involved in the typical probate process. Hamilton sums it up this way: "Typically, if any member of a family wanted to transfer property to other members — during lifetime — it can be done with the ease of signing a piece of paper…Simple, easy, a few minutes of your time. No big deal…But, hold it! Suppose he dies and the same property is to be transferred through the 'probate process.'? It will take the typical 'probate' matter one, two, three, five years to complete. You must bear unnecessary probate 'costs,' 'expenses,' delays, court proceedings, and on and on. Why is that?"

The point is that if you go by the "typical" lawyer-managed case, the probate process could take anywhere from as little as a few weeks or months in small-to-medium size estates, to several years. In the larger-than-average estates (those with a gross estate value of over $600,000), the time frame is generally measured in years. But we'd argue, though, that *as a practical matter, a period of one year[2]—if properly made use of—should generally be more than enough to complete the normal, average estate administration. This should especially be so where the relatives or beneficiaries readily cooperate with the executor and no unusual number of claims, litigations or contests arise.*

F. Procedures By Which You May Probate In Your Particular State

Briefly stated, to probate an estate in any state in the nation simply follow these steps:

1. Read the background chapter (Chapter 1) to get the preliminary background material you'd need.

2. Appendix A informs you on the essential rules particular to your desired state of probate filing.

3. With any luck, you should be able to obtain a supply of the applicable legal forms for the state of your interest from the publisher (Appendix I).

4. Follow essentially the same procedures as are outlines for New York's Probate (start from Chapter 5 or 6) to process your own probate and estate settlement case.

> NOTE: To order a supply of the appropriate blank forms necessary for probate filing in your state, see the Order Form on p. 239.

---

[2]The reason it should even be this long is that the probate laws of most states require a "minimum" waiting period of time (usually 6, 9 or 12 months) for completing probate of any kind. Hence, even if every required step is accomplished long before the minimum period, you may still have to wait out a period of time before you may conclude the probate process.

Chapter 5
"OPENING OF THE ESTATE" PART WHEN THERE IS A WILL. FIRST, GET THE WILL "ADMITTED TO PROBATE" AND HAVE THE DESIGNATED EXECUTOR CONFIRMED

ESTATE SETTLING PROCEDURES IN TESTATE (WITH WILL) SITUATIONS

In this Chapter, we go over New York's procedures for the so-called "TESTATE" situations (i.e., situations where there's a Will), starting here, first, with the court confirmation of the executor for the estate. That state's procedures in "intestate" (no Will) and "Small Estate" (no formal administration) situations, are gone over in Chapters 4 and 6, respectively.

The Surrogate's Court is the proper state court which handles all matters relating to probate and estate administration in New York. (Courts which handle estate matters go by various names in different states, such as "Probate," "Surrogate" or "Orphan's" court—see Appendix A on p. 152) There is one Surrogate's court located in each of New York's 62 counties. When somebody dies, New York would be the state that has the ORIGINAL jurisdiction over his estate, if one simple condition applies: if the deceased person's permanent residence (his "domicile") at the time of his death is determined to have been New York.

STEP-BY-STEP PROCEDURES FOR PROBATING A WILL

To probate a Will in a testate situation, just follow these simple 'STEPS' in the *exact* order in which they are listed below:

STEP **1**: LOCATE THE WILL

In a typical situation, at the death of a person, the family will make a diligent effort to locate the whereabouts of the dead person's will, if there is one, searching and inquiring around for it. Or, most often, some members of the family (usually the surviving spouse or children and the appointed executor of the Will) shall have already known where the decedent's will is located—it could have been kept in the testator's home, in the home of the designated executor or trusted relative or friend, in the office of the family or business attorney (who may, perhaps, have drafted the will), or in a safe deposit box,[1] etc.

---

[1]Under New York's procedures, there is a special procedure for examining a decedent's safe deposit box when one has reason to believe that the box might contain the decedent's last will, or his deed to a burial plot, and similar documents. Briefly, an "interested person" (a spouse, child, relative, etc.) makes out these two papers and submits them to the court clerk: "Petition to Open Safe Deposit Box" (sample Form P-10 on p. 55), and an "Order to Open Safe Deposit Box" (samples Form P-11 on p. 56). Upon the signing of the **Order** by the judge, you obtain a **"certified"** copy of the order from the clerk for service upon the safe deposit box company. Arrange (by phone) with the local New York State Tax Commission for its representative to meet with you at the office of the company on a designated date for the purpose of opening the box. Notify the safe deposit company (by phone also) of the date and place arranged.

On the appointment date, you deliver the certified copy of the Order (and the key to the box, if you have one) to the Tax Commission representative. The representative of the Tax Commission inventories and inspects the contents of the box as you and the company representative look on. If a will, deed, insurance policy, and similar documents are located in the box, they are turned over to the clerk of the court, and the box is resealed, until the entire contents are ready to be turned over later to a duly appointed executor or administrator of the estate.

If a will exists somewhere, one vital reason it's important that it be located _immediately_ after the decedent's death, is this: to make sure that, if the decedent shall have given some special instructions in the document for burying him (such as instructions for cremation or special religious services, etc.), those instructions could be timely complied with; such matters which are of the nature that they could not be postponed till the will could be formally probated or an executor appointed, are generally permitted to be carried out immediately.

STEP **2**: PREPARE THE NECESSARY PAPERS TO FILE FOR PROBATE

An essential preliminary order of business, even while the funeral activities are being carried out, is to hurry and have the will "probated"—that is, to have it formally "proved" in the appropriate court that the document is the genuine will of the deceased person actually made and signed by none other than him, and that he (she) was not of unsound mind at the time he signed it. THIS OUGHT TO BE DONE AS EARLY AS PRACTICABLE. Why? For this simple reason: the sooner you get the Will probated, the sooner will you (i.e., the executor) officially take office and begin to look after any unprotected or perishable properties that just might be going unattended, such as securities, cash or jewelry, and the like.

How do you initiate the probate process? You do so by filing a probate "petition" with the Surrogate's court. [In New York, any of the following "interested persons" may petition the court to probate a will: any person named as an executor or executrix, a beneficiary, guardian or trustee in the will; any creditor of the testator or any person(s) involved in a court action with the testator at the time; or any other "interested persons," such as the Public Administrator or a person who deems himself entitled to share as a beneficiary in the estate.]

A. Order (Obtain) The Necessary Forms For Filing Probate

To begin with, the first order of business is, of course to: GET THE NECESSARY FILING FORMS. HOW? For the added conveneince of the readers, **_Do-It-Yourself Legal Publishers_** makes available to its readership the _standard,_ fully pre-sorted, all-in-one package of forms—containing a complete set of the necessary forms for a New York State filing (the initial probate petition phase, as well as the probate accounting phase).

To order the Publishers' "all-in-one" standard forms (either for testate or for intestate situations), just complete the Order Form on p. 239 and send it away to the Publishers' Legal Forms Division at the given address therein.

NOTE: The applicable blank forms for probate filing for several other states may also be available from the publishers (see p. 239)

B. Then, Out Of The Forms Obtained, You Fill Out The Following

1. Form P-1, The **"Probate Petition,"** which is to be completed and _notarized_ in two places by petitioner. [Note that the format of this official form combines other subdivisions into its last page: (1) VERIFICATION; (2) OATH OF EXECUTOR; and (3) DESIGNATION OF CLERK FOR SERVICE OF PROCESS. (See pp. 42-4 for a sample preparation of the Petition form.)

2. Form P-2, The **"Original Citation (With Will)."** (See p. 45 for a sample preparation of this form.) Leave the "Affidavit of Service" part of this form blank for now, and complete it later in connection with "Step 4".

3. Form P-3, **"Waivers of Citation and Consent."** To be able to have an uncontested and relatively easier proceedings, this is a **_most necessary (and desirable) document to secure from ALL persons who are 'cited'_**—i.e., any person on whom the citation document is to be served. (See p. 47 for a sample preparation of this form.)

4. Form P-4, **"Notice of Probate."** (See p. 48 for a sample preparation of this form.)

5a. Form P-5A, **"Affidavit of Attesting Witnesses"**—this is to be signed and <u>notarized</u> by the two (or more) persons who had witnessed the signing of the will. (See p. 49 for a sample preparation of this form.)

OR

5b. Form P-5B, **"Deposition of Subscribing Witnesses"**—is to be signed and <u>notarized</u> by the two (or more) persons who had witnessed the signing of the will. (This form need not be necessarily filed until later in the proceedings, when it's time to have the "testimony" of the witnesses taken, "STEP 4" below on p. 35.) (See p. 50 for a sample preparation of this form.)

6. Form P-6, **"Renunciation of Appointment"**—this form is necessary only if a person named in the will as executor renounces his appointment and does not wish to serve. (See p. 51 for a sample preparation of this form.)

7. Form P-7, **"Affidavit Proving a Correct Copy of Will"**—to be filled in, signed and <u>notarized</u> by any two adults. (See p. 52 for a sample preparation of this form.)

8. Form P-8, **"Affidavit That No Party is in Military Service"**—to be signed and notarized by you, the petitioner. (See p. 53 for a sample preparation of this form.)

9. Form P-9, **"Decree Admitting Will to Probate"** (same as "Degree Granting Probate")—necessary ONLY in those counties in which the court itself does not prepare this paper on its own. (See p. 54 for a sample preparation of this form.)

NOW, OBTAIN ALSO THE FOLLOWING DOCUMENTS AND PAPERS, TO BE SUBMITTED TO THE COURT ALONG WITH THE PETITION PAPERS LISTED ABOVE:

    a. Original Copy of the Will
    b. A true zerox copy of the original Will
    c. A <u>certified</u> copy of the decedent party's death certificate.

> ***NOTE:*** If there are beneficiaries, potential or actual, under the Will's provisions who are minors (under 18 years in New York), or who are under legal disability or are judicially declared incompetents, the petitioner should, at this juncture, advise the parents or other persons who have legal custody of such a person, to do one of two things: either to apply, themselves, to have **"Letters of Guardianship"** issued to them, or to have another person apply for appointment as guardian for the minor or the incompetent. A special kind of guardianship, called 'guardian ad liem,' may also be necessary on occasion, when some yet un known minors or beneficiaries would have *ultimate* (not an immediate) share in the es tate—where, for example, the terms of a will which provides for the establishment of a trust further stipulates that the ultimate remainder of the trust assets is to go to lineal descendants of the immediate beneficiaries.
>
>   Whoever is appointed the guardian, if applicable (and *not* the executor or administrator), is the one who would have to represent the interests of such a minor or incompetent before the court. It is him that receives service of court papers on behalf of his 'wards' (the person who a guardian guards), and it is him that is supposed to (in theory, at least!) look after the distributive share of the estate to which the ward is entitled, etc. (Procedures for filing the petition for a guardianship appointment are outlined in Appendix F.)

STEP ■3■: FILE THE PETITION PAPERS WITH THE COURT CLERK

Now, you have completed and assembled all the petition papers and documents enumerated above, as applicable, to you. What do you do with them? You have to, quite simply, submit ("file") them to the probate court clerk (the office of the probate court clerk covering the county in which the decedent was last permanently domiciled).

The probate clerk will check over the submitted papers to make sure they are complete and properly filled out. And, assuming they are complete and in order, you'll be asked to pay the filing fee (currently ranges anywhere from $15 for an estate of up to $10,000 in value, to $450 for estates of $500,000 and over). If, on the other hand, the clerk should think there is some necessary information or paper that is missing or improperly filled out, the clerk will tell you so. In such instances, quietly ask the clerk to tell you *specifically* what needs to be corrected or supplied. Make a (written) record of what he says. Then go home, make the corrections or supply the missing documents required and resubmit the papers.

Once accepted by the clerk, the clerk will assign a "file number" to your case. Now, if it appears to the clerk (from the papers you submitted), that you, the petitioner, are the sole distributee of the estate, or that all persons who are beneficiaries, or are to be served with the "citation," have either waived the right to be cited (formally notified) or granted their written consent to the probate proceedings,[2] you know you pretty much have an **"UNCONTESTED"** probate case.

Clerk Either Sets Date For The Taking Of The Witnesses' Testimonies Or Issues A Citation For Service On The Parties.

If you have an uncontested case, the clerk will set the time and date at which the testimony of the required witnesses to the will are to be taken. (Under current practice, even this testimony-taking may entirely be waived as unncecessry, where the petitioner is able to submit properly signed and notarized statements ("affidavits") from those who had witnessed the decedent's signing of the Will at the time he/she did so. (Form 5B, Deposition of Subscribing Witnesses, shows a sample of such an Affidavit.)

The petitioner may not always have things that easy or smooth-running, however. Atimes, there just may be one (or more) persons who would prefer to hold out and withhold giving their consent. On such persons (if any), it would then be necessary to serve the "CITATION" paper officially (STEP 4 below). If such is the case, the clerk will formally issue you the citation document, and tell you the manner of service to be used in getting the document delivered to the parties, as well as the "return date" by which you must file proof with his office that the citation has been served.

STEP 4: SERVE THE PROBATE "CITATIONS" ON THE PERSONS REQUIRED, IF ANY

As is the case in a majority of probate filings, generally when there exists no contest among relatives of the decedent or other interested parties, it is usually not necessary to formally serve citations on any persons. Indeed, service of citation may probably not be necessary in your case. (Or, it may be).

It would usually not be necessary where: i) the petitioner is the sole distributee under the will; or ii) where all parties to a will have signed a proper statement consenting to, or waiving their right to get a citation (sample Form P-3, Waiver of Citation and Consent, is on p. 47).

Service (i.e., delivery) of citation on a person is simply the court's way of giving official notice to certain persons, to inform them that a probate petition has been presented to the court for its consideration. The citation (when served on a party) is said to be the legal force which "binds" or "joins" the cited party to whatever becomes the subsequent outcome of the probate proceedings. Hence, IT'S IMPORTANT THAT YOU MAKE SURE YOU LIST, IN FULL, UNDERLINE EACH AND EVERY PERSON OR ENTITY WHO OUGHT TO BE SERVED, AND THAT EACH OF SUCH PERSONS BE, IN FACT, SERVED.

a) WHICH PERSONS ARE TO BE SERVED? As a practical matter, the petitioner would not have to worry about this, for it is ordinarily the clerk of court who will (or, at least, should) fill in the necessary names into the citation sheet—or, at least, help the petitioner determine such names. So, whenever in doubt, you had better discuss it with the probate clerks who, as a rule, are not only very knowledgeable (often more so than the average lawyers themselves!), but also usually very helpful to petitioners in such

---

[2]Evidence of that is generally shown by the signing of the "Waiver of Citation and Consent" form by the party required to be cited.

matters. In any event, a safe rule of thumb, whenever you are not absolutely certain about a person's eligibility to be cited,[3] is to serve him the paper, anyway. Why not? You have nothing to lose by covering all reasonable possibilities!!

b) HOW DO YOU "SERVE" A CITATION ON A PARTY? It's this simple: you serve the citation document (the sample Form P-2 is on p. 45) by merely *delivering* or getting that piece of paper to the person listed on the face of that document, with a true copy of the Will attached.

THERE IS ONLY ONE CATCH INVOLVED IN MAKING A PROPER SERVICE OF A CITATION, THOUGH (or, in fact, in making a proper service of any legal paper, generally); the manner of getting the piece of paper to the persons who are to receive it must follow a certain simple but definite procedure *specifically* laid down by the law. *Here's the really central thing to remember:* where and when "personal" service is required by the court, the document MUST BE PHYSICALLY AND PERSONALLY HAND-DELIVERED DIRECTLY INTO THE HANDS OF EACH DESIGNATED PERSON WHO IS 18 YEARS OF AGE OR OLDER (unless, of course, the court authorizes the use of a different method of service). It may *not,* in other words, be simply mailed or just left in the person's mailbox or apartment (unless, of course, the authorized service is by methods other than "personal" service).

You may do the serving yourself; or you may have someone else (a relative, friend, co-worker—anybody over 18 yers of age) do it for you. Or, better still, for a fee of $25 to $45, you could hire a professional Process Server to do it for you. (Consult the local telephone directory for a listing under the heading "Process Server" or "Process Servers"). The local county Sheriffs and Marshals are often used, and they're often the most reliable and least expensive, especially when service is to be made in outlying counties and out-of-state locations.

To "serve" the citation (by personal delivery method), the individual who is to make the service will simply hand-deliver the paper (only copies of the original citation, not the original itself, may be served) to each of the persons listed and addressed on the citation form, with a copy of the will attached; it is not just mailed or left with someone else, when service by "personal service" method is designated. The paper is deemed to have been properly served by personally putting it directly into the hands of the person,[4] or, if he should refuse to accept it, by leaving it in his possession or control, such as dramatically dropping it on his desk or lap while he looks on and stating to him, "This is a citation for probate action on the estate of the deceased Mr. _____, Sir!

Then, here's the second important thing: to complete the service, the person who actually served the paper must do one more thing—he must, himself or herself, provide written proof that he did make the service. It's a simple requirement to meet: all he does is complete the back side of the original citation, Form 2-A, titled AFFIDAVIT OF SERVICE OF CITATION, for each of all the persons he served, and then have it <u>notarized</u> [he, himself, signs it in the presence of a Notary Public and gets it stamped by the notary]. (Sample preparation of this affidavit is on p. 46).

c) SERVICE BY METHODS OTHER THAN PERSONAL DELIVERY. Now, what if you don't know the whereabouts of a person who is to be served, or you can't get a hold of him (or her) to service him? Or, say you can't physically reach him, because he lives in another state or county? In such instances, you would have to serve the citation by one of the so-called "substitute" or "alternative" methods—***after you shall have FIRST applied, however, to the court and gotten its order of permission to use such a method.***

Such alternative methods of service may be any one of these: by mailing (certified or registered mail return receipt requested), or by 'nail and mail' substituted service, or by service on a designated agent, or by service upon a consular official, or by publication.

---

[3]In general, the following are entitled to a citation, unless any of them is the petitioner: i) all the distributees of the testator (his spouse, children or descendants of predeceased child, parents, brothers or sisters, and the like); ii) persons designated as executor, or as a beneficiary, trustee, or guardian either in the testator's Last Will, or in any other will of the same testator filed in the surrogate's court of the same county; iii) the testator himself, in any case where the petitioner alleges that the testator is merely "alleged" or "believed" to be dead (a rare case); iv) the State Tax Commission (applicable *only* in situations where the testator is not a domiciliary of the state); and v) the State's Attorney-General's office (applicable only where there are no known distributees available).

If a person required to be served should die after the testator but before the probate proceeding has been completed, or if such party has been served and then dies before the probate proceeding has been completed, his representative must be served in his place.

If you were applying for a service by publication, for example, you would need to prepare essentially three documents: i) *"Affidavit of Application for Service To Be Made by Publication"* (in which you detail, one by one, all the reasonable but exhaustive efforts you shall have made and the persons and sources of information you've checked regarding the parties being sought and the results thereof) [See Form P-12A, on pp. 57 for a sample of this form.]; ii) *"Citation To Be Published"* [See Form P-12B on p. 59 for a sample.]; and iii) *"Order for Service of Citation by Publication"* [See Form 12-C on p. 60 for a sample of this form.] (Service by mail is resorted to only after all other methods shall have been tried and have failed.)

Upon completion of these forms, you'll sign and notarize the Affidavit (Form P-12A) and submit all papers (with certified copies of the birth certificate and the Will attached) to the probate court clerk for presentation to the surrogate judge. If approved, the judge (surrogate) signs the *Order for Service of Citation by Publication.* You're now authorized to proceed with publication.

The first publication—if and when publication has been specifically applied for and authorized by the court—is required to be made under New York's procedures within 60 days of the filing of the probate petition. The citation paper, ONLY, is promptly sent to the editor of the designated paper, who must then publish it once a week for 4 successive weeks. Service is deemed to be complete on the 28th day after the first publication. (Allow at least 30 days between the first publication and the return date of the citation.) Upon completion, the publisher sends you an "AFFIDAVIT OF PUBLICATION" signed and notarized by the newspaper official, which you then file with the court as your proof of having made publication.

> **NOTE: Under New York's procedures, there is one exception where you can use the mailing method right away, without first having to seek or get the court's order of approval:** when more than 25 creditors are involved in an estate. The petitioner may simply mail a copy of the citation (by certified mail with return receipt requested) to each of the creditors, whether inside or outside the state, in such instances. Where creditors are less than 25 in number, however, service by mail may still be used but only with a prior court order authorizing it.

STEP 5: FILE WITH THE COURT CLERK YOUR PROOF OF HAVING SERVED THE CITATIONS

On (or, preferably, at least 2 days before) the day set by the clerk as the 'return date' for filing the proof of service of the citation with the court, you must (assuming service of citation had been applicable, of course) return to the clerk's office. You resubmit to the clerk the *original* copy of the Citation (Form P-2) with the *"Affidavit of Service of Citation"* on its back side (Form P-2A) fully completed and notarized by the person who had served the citation or citations. Now, if all of the required proofs are complete and show that all the required persons have been cited (or, if the issuance or service of citation had been either unnecessary, waived or dispensed with by the court), and if no objection to the probate has been filed with the clerk's office as of that date—which is usually the case in the overwhelming majority of probate cases—the clerk will mark the matter 'ready for decree' to admit the will to probate. The Will will be probated—subject only to a subsequent 'proving' of the Will.

4NOTE: To serve boards, commissions, counties, Park Districts, School or Sewage Districts and Towns, deliver the document to the chairman of the board, or to the President, Secretary, Clerk, Trustee or similar official thereof; to serve the City of New York, deliver to the Corporate Counsel or any other person designated by him to receive process; for other cities, deliver to the Mayor, comptroller, treasurer or counsel; to serve a court, deliver to any judge therein; to serve a domestic or foreign corporation or bank, deliver to an officer, director, managing or general agent; to serve a partnership, deliver to any partner; to serve a state, deliver to an Assistant Attorney General or the Attorney General within the state. Service of paper on a person in prison who fails to appear, or on an infant (under 18 years of age), may be completed by serving paper on the person's or infant's parent(s), guardian or custodian. If infant is 14 years of age or older, he too has to be served in addition to the parent(s), guardian or custodian. Judicially declared incompetents are served by service on the Committee appointed to look after them, and on the guardian ad Litem, if any.

And, where any of the parties required to be cited are under a disability (such as where he's an infant or incompetent), a **GUARDIAN AD LITEM**[5] may also have to be appointed or approved by the court then; the matter will still be marked for a decree, but subject to the "report" of the party so appointed as the guardian.

STEP 6: SEEK OUT & INVITE THE PERSONS WHO WITNESSED THE WILL-SIGNING FOR AN "EXAMINATION" BEFORE THE COURT

If you recall, the one professed central reason (and the main justification given in legal circles) for which we have to go through all these preliminary mountains of paperwork and runarounds involved in probating a will is this: just so that the decedent's will may be "proved" to the court to be a genuine and valid one. Hence, the next important order of business (after all the persons entitled to receive a citation notice have either been served or waived this right), is the conduct, by the court, of an "examination" of the persons who had been eye witnesses to the signing of the Will by the deceased person. The court clerk sets the date on which such examination of the witness(es) will be made.

What is the overall nature of this so-called **"examination"?** In theory, the basic rule which governs New York's procedures (indeed, the procedures of most states), is that at least TWO of the "attesting" witnesses to the will must be produced before the court and be "examined" (questioned) as to what they know about the will's genuineness, providing that such witnesses are (or can, with minimum ease, be made to be) within the state, and are competent and able to testify. However, as an accomodation to a growing public outcry for a more simplified probate system, the modern law of almost every state also provides that, should one or more of such witnesses not reside within the state, or be deceased or incompetent to testify, the court may, when proper application is made to it by the petitioner, allow that the testimony of such unavailable witnesses be done without.

As a practical matter, it turns out that what is actually required to satisfy the "examination" requirement of the court, is so simplified that it is easily met in the overwhelming majority of cases. For one thing, while the law talks of requiring a formal "testimony" of the witnesses under courtroom settings, in practice, the only testimony that is generally taken from the witnesses, especially when the proceedings are uncontested, takes the form of a standard pre-printed "affidavit" (or, where not available or properly made out, a "deposition" in place of that) made out by the witnesses and then submitted through the executor to the court.

a) Examination Procedures When The Two Witnesses Are Available.

If the executor has been able to obtain from at least two witnesses an *"Affidavit of Attesting Witnesses"*—same as sample Form P-5A on p. 49—and filed it with the clerk (usually done at the time of the initial filing of the probate petition papers), the necessary "testimony" and required *"proof"* of the will is just about met for most practical purposes.[6] However, where the Affidavit of Attesting Witnesses is not available (or is unacceptable to the particular court), then the court accepts in its place the "testimony" of the witnesses in the form of "depositions"—that is, a pre-printed, fill-in form containing pertinent questions to which the witness merely enters his answers and swears to its truthfulness (same as sample Form P-5B on p. 50). In such instances, the executor would obtain the blank deposition forms from the court clerk and simply have the witness(es) complete and <u>notarize</u> them. Upon resubmission of the completed deposition forms to the clerk, the clerk sets up an appointment with the witness(es) mentioned to ask a few further routine questions of them. (In about 99% of uncontested proceedings, it is the clerk of court—not the Surrogate's Judge—who actually conducts whatever examination there is to be made of witnesses!).

---

[5]See Appendix F for procedures for appointing guardians of various kinds.

[6]The two situations when this might not suffice are: i) when a party to the proceeding objects to the use of the affidavit; and ii) if the court should require that witnesses be produced for any other reason of its own.

These questions, usually asked by the clerk in an informal, out-of-the-courtroom setting, are typical:

"Mr/Ms Witness. Were you aquainted with the late Mr._____*(let's call him JOHN DOE)* of the city of _____, county of _____, state of New York?"

"For how long had you known the said decedent prior to the date of the propounded instrument (document)?"

"Please examine the instrument (Will) now produced and shown to you, and state whether or not you were present as a witness at the time that that instrument was executed (signed)?"

"Did you see the said John Doe that date, sign his Will on the _____ day of _____ 19___?"

"Did John Doe, the testator, say at the time that the document he was signing was his Last Will and Testament?"

"Was Mary Jones, the other witness who was present at the signing, and was she the one who also signed her name to Mr. Doe's Will?"

"Was Mr. Doe, in your opinion, of sound mind and memory and free from any restraint at the time he executed that instrument?"

"Was he, in your opinion, competent in every respect to make a Will at the time he executed that instrument?"

b) Examination Procedures When Only One Witness is Available.

It may happen that, for whatever the reason, you are unable to produce the required affidavits or depositions from the needed minimum of two attesting witnesses—absence of one witness from the state, death or later mental or physical incapacity or later incompetence of a witness, or mere inability by you to locate one of the witnesses, etc. If you face such a situation, there is a simple remedy open to you under the law: you may apply to the court to waive or forego the need for the "testimony" of the unavailable witness. If granted, then, the will would be probated based ONLY on the testimony of the ONE available witness (and that available witness may also be asked to identify the signature of the unavailable witness, in addition).

To make an application for the use of one witness, rather than two, follow this simple procedure:

First, prepare these two documents: i) **"Affidavit In Support of Application to Dispense With Testimony of Attesting Witness,"** in which you request that the testimony of such a person be dispensed with and give the reasons for such a necessity, such as the death, incapacity or disappearance of the witness (See Form 13A on p. 61 for a sample of such affidavit); and ii) an **"Order Dispensing With Testimony of Attesting Witness,"** to be signed by the authorizing judge (sample of form is Form P-13B). Then you *notarize* the affidavit, and submit the two documents to the clerk of court. Upon the court's approval of the application (when the Order is signed by the judge), the testimony of the one available witness (see section (a) above) will now suffice to probate the will.

c) Examination Procedures When <u>NO</u> Witnesses At All are Available.

In instances when both witnesses are merely absent from the state, the court may, if it likes, dispense entirely with the testimony of one witness (submit similar Affidavit and court order forms as in Section (b) above), but may require the taking of the testimony of the other witness "by commission."[7]

When *all* of the attesting witnesses are dead, incompetent, or unable to testify for reason of mental or physical incapacity or absence from the state, the will may still be probated, upon submission of aceptable written proof of the testator's and the attesting witnesses' handwriting—either by handwriting experts, or by any person or persons who are familiar with their signatures (plus any other facts available to prove the signatures).

The procedure is identical; you apply to the court for authorization by preparing and submitting these three papers to the court clerk: i) *"Affidavit In Support of Application to Dispense with Testimony of Attesting Witnesses"* (sample Form P-13A on p. 61); ii) an *"Order Dispensing with Testimony of Attesting Witnesses"* (sample Form 13B on p. 61); and iii) *"Deposition Proving Handwriting of Testator / Attesting Witnesses,"* to be completed and notarized by the handwriting expert or disinterested persons familiar with the respective witnesses' handwritings (sample Form P-13C on p. 62).

---

[7]Persons authorized to take testimony by commission are: an attorney of this state, or of the state in which the commission is to be taken.

STEP **7**: SERVE THE "NOTICE OF PROBATE" ON THE NECESSARY PERSON(S), IF ANY

The formal delivery ("service") of the document know as a NOTICE OF PROBATE to persons entitled to receive them, if any, is the next—and final—step in the Will "proving" phase of the probate proceedings under the New York's procedures. *The **Letters Testamentary*** will not be issued to an executor until proof of service of this notice is filed with the clerk. Unlike the situation with the Citation, whose service "enjoins" the person served to the authority of the local court, service of the *Notice of Probate* has no binding authority, but is purely informational in nature. It's merely meant to be "informational"—i.e., to advise the persons concerned about their potential interests in the estate, or of their status as alternate fiduciaries.[8]

Service of this document is a very simple matter. All you have to do is this: First, fill out the Notice of Probate form (sample preparation of Form P-4 on p. 48). Secondly, make photocopies of the Notice and mail a copy (petitioner may generally do this himself) to every one of the following persons: anyone named in the will or petition (as a beneficiary, trustee, guardian, or a substitute or successor executor, trustee or guardian) who has either not been served with a citation, or has not appeared or waived service of citation, as well as any minors or incompetents represented by a legal guardian.[9] Most preferably, do this mailing not less than 7 days BEFORE the date set by the court clerk for a decree to be signed or entered by the judge.

Finally, after the mailing, you complete the bottom part of the backside of the Notice of Probate (as in bottom part of Form P-4 on p. 48); have this part notarized and submit the two parts of the document to the court clerk as proof of your having carried out the notice-giving requirement.

STEP **8**: THE COURT ISSUES YOU THE "LETTERS TESTAMENTARY" CONFIRMING YOU AS EXECUTOR

Most wills are uncontested, and as with most states, the uncontested Will "proving" dimension of probate proceedings ends with the court's satisfaction that the Notice of Probate has been duly served on the proper parties. Thereafter, the surrogate judge signs the court order which formally "admits the Will to probate" (sample of *Decree Admitting Will To Probate* is on p. 54).

Upon the signing of the court order, the person or person(s) approved to serve as executor(s) [or .executrix(es)] should obtain from the clerk a few "certified" (i.e., stamped and official) copies of the **LETTERS TESTAMENTARY.**[10] This is the document that signifies officially that the court has approved the person named therein to act as the executor (sample Forms, P-14 & P-15, the Letters Testamentary, are on p. 63) *As an executor about to begin the actual administration of an estate, this is probably the most important document for you: you'll often need to show this document to the banks, to debtors, creditors, and other interested parties or companies before they may allow you to take possession of bank accounts, safe deposit box contents, personal or real property, etc., on behalf of the decedent's estate.*

---

[8]Note that persons entitled *only to* a Notice of Probate are not parties to the probate proceedings; they may become parties only if they have properly filed an objection to the appointment of the person designated to be executor.

[9]Note the following applicable rules under New York's procedures (SCPA 1409-1-2): When a decedent's will provides that an interest disposed of under the will shall not lapse but, instead, shall lapse to the issue of the primary beneficiary, then only the primary beneficiary (the parent) need be given notice of probate; furthermore, notice of probate need not be mailed to those persons whose names and addresses are unknown, if such is so indicated in the petition.

[10]This instrument, the Letters Testamentary, goes by various names in different states and jurisdictions, Certificate of Appointment, Letters of Administration, etc.

A FEW RELEVANT ISSUES BEFORE WE CONCLUDE THE WILL-PROVING & EXECUTOR APPOINTMENT PHASE OF PROBATE

Now, with the issuance of the Letters Testamentary, the "probate" or will-proving phase of the task is concluded for all practical purposes. You are now ready to begin the second, albeit the more important phase of your task as a court-appointed executor: the actual, PHYSICAL ADMINISTRATION OR MANAGEMENT, AND SETTLEMENT OF THE AFFAIRS OF THE ESTATE. But before we get to the procedures involved in that next phase (Chapter 7-A), there are a **few relevant facts you should have at the back of your mind:**

FIRST: What to do when the Will Fails to Name an Executor

If the testator's will had failed to name a person to serve as executor, or if the person named fails or is ineligible to act in that capacity for whatever reason (death, refusal to act, etc.), what do you do?

The law says that one or more other eligible persons may, in such a situation, apply to the court to have the **"LETTERS OF ADMINISTRATION c.t.a."** (Latin initials for 'with the will annexed') granted to them.

By New York's law, the following persons are to be granted such letters in this order: 1) either to the sole beneficiary under the will, or to his fiduciary, if such beneficiary dies after the testator; 2) one or more of the fiduciary beneficiaries, or to the fiduciary of the deceased ones, if any; and 3) if none of the above is available or willing to serve, then to any of the persons entitled to share as beneficiary in the estate or to the fiduciary of the deceased ones, if any. Letters may be granted, however, to anyone whatsoever who is otherwise eligible—if all the beneficiaries of the estate consent to his appointment (by signing the "Consent of Beneficiary of Will"—sample Form P-16 on p. 64).

The procedures for filing for the issuance of *Letters of Administration c.t.a.* are basically the same as those for granting Letters of Administration (Chapter 6). Basically, you obtain the following forms from the court clerk, complete them and re-submit them to the clerk: i) **Petition for Letters of Administration c.t.a.;** ii) **Consent of Beneficiary of Will c.t.a.;** iii) **Original Citation c.t.a.;** and iv) **Decree Granting Letters of Administration c.t.a.**

As with the procedures with respect to the regular Letters of Administration, if no valid objection is filed by anyone against the granting of the petition (after the whole process of citation serving shall have been undertaken), the judge will sign the decree granting the Letters of Administration c.t.a. to the petitioner.

SECOND: You May be Required to Post a Bond

Depending on the circumstances, you may be required to post a BOND with the court after you are confirmed by the court as executor. (It's like a kind of insurance to assure that you'll satisfactorily perform your duties as executor.[11])

If it should be required of you that you furnish a bond, the court will so inform you. Obtaining a bond (in the amount set by the court) should hardly be a problem: simply look up a surety company in your local Yellow Pages or telephone directory under the headings "Surety Bonds" or "Bonds-Surety and Fidelity." If you can come up with the company's charge (the "premium") for the coverage—which you are authorized, by the way, to pay out of the proceeds of the estate—your bonding policy will usually be issued you by the company in no time.

Persons serving in other fiduciary capacities, such as trustees, administrators, guardians, and the like, may often be required to furnish a bond also.

---

[11]Generally an executor (or trustee or guardian) under a will does not have to file a bond, if the will expressly prohibits this requirement. However, he will ordinarily be required to furnish bond, if the will expressly requires him to do so, and the value of the estate is in excess of $5,000, or the will makes no mention of posting bond at all.

Form P-1

Form UF-B-0 Revised

State of New York
Surrogate's Court: County of New York

Probate Proceeding, Will of

John James Doe,
···
Deceased.

Probate Petition

File No. ....

To the Surrogate's Court, County of New York

It is respectfully alleged:

(1) The name(s), domicile(s) (or, in the case of a bank of trust company, its principal office) and interest(s) in this proceeding of the petitioner(s) are as follows:

Name: David Edwards
Domicile or
Principal Office: 15 Probate Street
(Street and Number)

New York,   New York
(City, Village or Town)   (State)

Interest(s) of Petitioner(s):
(Check one)

☑ Executor(s) named in decedent's Last Will presented herewith
☑ Other (Specify) Testamentary Trustee named in decedent's Will.

(2) The name, domicile, date and place of death, and national citizenship of the above-named deceased are as follows:

(a) Name: John James Doe
(b) Date of death January 10th 1994
(c) Place of death New York county, New York
(d) Domicile Street 10 Death St.
    City, Town, Village New York
    County New York
    State New York
(e) Citizen (Subject) of U.S.A.

(3) The Last Will, herewith presented, relates to both real and personal property and consists of an instrument or instruments dated as shown below and signed at the end thereof, by the decedent and the following attesting witnesses:

December 21, 1993   David Owens
                                             Mary Jones
(Date of Will)   (Witnesses to Will)

Not Applicable   none
(Date of Codicil)   (Witnesses to Codicil)

(4) There is no other will or codicil of the decedent on file in the office of the court, and upon information and belief, there exists no will, codicil or other testamentary instrument of the decedent later in date to any of the instruments mentioned in paragraph (3) hereof, except NONE.

(5) The decedent left surviving:

(a) [X] Spouse (husband/wife).
(b) [x] Child or children; or descendants of predeceased child or children, natural or adopted.
(c) [ ] Father/mother.
(d) [ ] Brothers or sisters, either of the whole or half-blood; or descendants of such predeceased brothers or sisters.
(e) [ ] Grandfather/grandmother.
(f) [ ] Uncles or aunts.
(g) [ ] Descendants of predeceased uncles or aunts.

(Information is required only as to those classes of surviving relatives who would take the property of decedent if there were no will. The term "child or children" includes adopted as well as natural children. State number of survivors in each such class. Insert "X" in all subsequent classes. Insert "NO" in all prior classes.)

(6) The names, relationships and addresses of all distributees, of each person designated in the Last Will herewith presented as primary executor, of all persons adversely affected by the purported exercise by such Will of any power of appointment, of all persons adversely affected by any codicil and of all persons having an interest under any prior will of the decedent on file in the Surrogate's office, are hereinafter set forth in subdivisions (a) and (b): (If additional parties are to be added, attach schedule on sheet same length as petition).

(a) All persons and parties so interested who are of full age and sound mind, or which are corporations or associations, are as follows:

Name and Address	Relationship	Description of Legacy, Devise or Other Interest, or Nature of Fiduciary Status
Mary F. Doe, 10 Death St., New York, N.Y.	surviving wife	Gift of all tangible personal property & assets not otherwise devised by decedent to others; all real property; income of trust created under Article 6 of Will; donee of Power of Appointment.
John James Doe, Jr., 13 Third St., Bronx NY	Son	Gift of $20,000; 1993 Chevrolet Impala; income of trust under Article 6 of Will.
David Edwards, 15 Probate St., New York, N.Y.	Executor & Trustee	100 shares of General Motors Stock.

(b) All persons so interested who are persons under disability, are as follows:
(Please furnish all information specified in NOTE below.)

David Doe, 10 Death St., New York, N.Y.	Son	Gift of $15,000; income of Trust under Article 6 of Will; contingent remainderman of Trust under Article 6 of Will.

David is a minor, 17 years old, born 6/10/76; resides with mother, Mary F. Doe, the named testamentary guardian in decedent's Will.

(Note: In the case of each infant, state (a) name, birth date, age, relationship to decedent, residence address, and the person with whom he resides; (b) whether or not he has a general or testamentary guardian, and whether or not his father, or if dead, his mother, is living; and (c) the name and residence address of any guardian and any living parent. In the case of each other person under disability state (a) name, relationship to decedent, and residence address; (b) facts regarding his disability, including whether or not a committee has been appointed and whether or not he has been committed to any institution; and (c) the names and addresses of any committee, any person or institution having care and custody of him, and any relative or friend having an interest in his welfare. In the case of person confined as a prisoner, state place of incarceration. In the case of unknowns, describe such persons in the same language as will be used in the process. In each case give a brief description of the party legacy, devise or other interest as in paragraph (6) (a) hereof.)

(7) The names and domiciliary addresses of all substitute or successor executors and of all trustees, guardians, legatees and devisees, and other beneficiaries named in the Last Will herewith presented, other than those named in Paragraph (6), are hereinafter set forth in subdivisions (a) and (b): (If additional parties are to be added, attach schedule on sheet same length as petition).

(a) All such other legatees and devisees who are of full age and sound mind, or which are corporations or associations, are as follows:

Name	Address	Description of Legacy, Devise or Other Interest, or Nature of Fiduciary Status
Bernard Jones	120 Legacy St., New York, N.Y.	Gift of $1,000 under Will.
George G. Fuller	20 College Rd., Bronx N.Y.	Gift of $1,000 under Will.
Diana Merryman	2 Georgeton St., Jersey City, New Jersey	Substitute Executor & Trustee.

(b) All such other legatees, devisees and other beneficiaries who are persons under disability, are as follows: NONE.

(Please furnish all information specified in Note to paragraph (6) (b) hereof.)

(8) There are no persons, corporations or associations, interested in this proceeding other than those hereinabove mentioned.

(9) To the best of the knowledge of the undersigned, the approximate total value of all property constituting the decedent's gross testamentary estate is more than $ 300,000.... and less than $ 600,000....

(10) Upon information and belief, no other petition for the probate of any will of the decedent or for the granting of letters of administration on the decedent's estate has heretofore been filed in any Court.

WHEREFORE your petitioner(s) pray(s) (a) that process be issued to all necessary parties to show cause why the Last Will herewith presented should not be admitted to probate; (b) that an order be granted directing the service of process pursuant to the provisions of article 3 or the SCPA, upon the persons named in paragraph (6) hereof who are non-domiciliaries, or whose names or whereabouts are unknown and cannot be ascertained; and (c) that such Last Will be admitted to probate as a will of real and personal property and that letters issue thereon as follows:

(Check and complete appropriate request.)

☐ Letters Testamentary to.......David Edwards..

☐ Letters of Trusteeship to.......David Edwards..

Dated:.......I/20/94...

SIGNED: **X**...
(David Edwards)   (Petitioner)

....
(Petitioner)

| STATE OF NEW YORK | ss.: | **COMBINED VERIFICATION, OATH AND DESIGNATION** |
| County of _____ | | *(For use when a petitioner to be appointed executor is not a bank or trust company)* |

I, the undersigned ....David Edwards,..
being duly sworn, say:

(1) VERIFICATION: I have read the foregoing petition subscribed by me and know the contents thereof, and the same is true of my own knowledge, except as to the matters therein stated to be alleged upon information and belief, and as to those matters I believe it to be true.

(2) OATH OF EXECUTOR: I am over twenty-one (21) years of age and a citizen of the United States; I am not ineligible to receive letters. I am the executor(trix) named in the Last Will described in the foregoing petition and will well, faithfully and honestly discharge the duties of such executor(trix), and I shall duly account for all moneys or other property which may come into my hands.

(3) DESIGNATION OF CLERK FOR SERVICES OF PROCESS: I do hereby irrevocably designate the Clerk of the Surrogate's Court of New York County, and his or her successors in office, as a person on whom service of any process issuing from such Surrogate's Court may be made, in like manner and with like effect as if it were served personally upon me whenever I cannot be found and served within the State of New York after due diligence used.

My domicile is .15. Probate Street, New York, N.Y. 10010..........................

SIGNED: **X**...
(Signature of Petitioner)

On.................., 19......, before me personally came ....David Edwards..............
.... to me known to be the person described in and who executed the foregoing instrument. Such person duly swore to such instrument before me and duly acknowledge that ....David Edwards.. executed the same.

....
(Notary Public)

[Notary Public signs here & *fixes his official stamp thereto]*

Form P-2

UF Form A

[Enter here the names only of each & every person or institution that would seem deserving of being "cited" (notified) of this probate—generally (but not necessarily limited to) the parties listed in paragraphs 6(a), 6(b) (for whom citation has to be made through their guardians or custodians), 7(a) and 7(b) on p. 15 above. See footnotes on pp. 29 & 30 for a listing of the kinds of persons generally entitled to a situation.]

File No. _____ , 19 ____

CITATION (Will)

The People of the State of New York,
By the Grace of God Free and Independent,

To

MARY F. DOE ; JOHN JAMES DOE, JR. ; DAVID EDWARDS, who, as the Petitioner herein, already has notice of this proceeding and therefore need not be cited; DAVID DOE, a minor, being cited through MARY F Doe, his mother, the designated testamentary guardian; BERNARD JONES; GEORGE G. FULLER.

WALLACE DOE (decedent's adult son not mentioned in the Will); AGNES MANN (decedent's sister).

YOU ARE HEREBY CITED TO SHOW CAUSE before the Surrogate's Court, New York County, at Room 504 in the Hall of Records in the County of New York, New York, on _____ , 19 ____ at I0. A.M. why a certain writing dated ___December 2I,_____ , 1993.

which ha s been offered for probate by   DAVID EDWARDS,
residing at I5 Probate St., New York, N.Y. I00I0.
should not be probated as the last Will and Testament, relating to real and personal property, of
   John   James   Doe,   the , Deceased, who was at the time of his   death a
resident of I0 Death Street, New York city,   in the County of New York, New York.

Dated, Attested and Sealed, _____ , 19 ____

HON. _____

(L.S.)   Surrogate, New York County

_____
                                          Clerk.

Name of ~~Attorney~~ Petitioner, Pro Se.   DAVID EDWARDS   Tel. No. (2I2) _____

Address ~~of Attorney~~ I5 Probate St., New York, N.Y. I00I0

This citation is served upon you as required by law. You are not obliged to appear in person. If you fail to appear it will be assumed that you do not object to the relief requested. You have a right to have an attorney-at-law appear for you.

Form P-2A

Note.—If affidavit of service be made outside the State of New York, it must be authenticated in the manner prescribed by CPLR Sec. 2309 (c).

Affidavit of Service of Citation

State of New York

County of _____ ss:

_____Michael   Jacobs_____

of _700 Manhattan Rd., Brooklyn N.Y._, being duly sworn, says that   he is over the age of eighteen years; that   he made personal service of the within citation on the persons named below, whom deponent knew to be the persons mentioned and described in said citation, by delivering to and leaving with each of them personally a true copy of said citation, as follows:

On the _3o^th_ day of _January_ (_10.35 a.m._) , 1994
on _Mary F. Doe_
at _10 Death St. New York, N.Y. 10003_

On the_____ day of _____ , 19
on _____
at _____

On the_____ day of _____ , 19
on _____
at _____

On the_____ day of _____ , 19
on _____
at _____

On the_____ day of _____ , 19
on _____
at _____

Specify clearly time and place of service on each party served.

SIGNED: X _____
Michael Jacobs (Person making service of the citation(s) on the parties listed on the face of the Citation.)

Sworn to before me this

day of _____ , 19

_____
(NOTARY PUBLIC)

N.B.—Proof of service of the citation must be filed in the Probate Department not later than the second day preceding the return day of citation.

Form P-3

UP Form C

State of New York

Surrogate's Court, County of New York

NOTE: *This document needs to be made out by each & every person who agrees to waive (i.e., forgo) his/her being served with a citation. More than one person may use the same form.*

Probate Proceeding, Will of

JOHN JAMES DOE,

Deceased.

Waiver And Consent

January 21,   1994

To the Surrogate's Court, New York County:

MARY F. DOE, (for self & for DAVID DOE, minor)
the undersigned, being of full age and residing at   10 Death St., New York, N.Y.   10003

distributee of   JOHN JAMES DOE,   late of the County of New York, deceased,

do   hereby waive the issue and service of a citation in the matter of proving the Last Will

and Testament of said   John James Doe   , deceased, and consent that said

instrument   bearing date   12/21/'93

be admitted to probate forthwith. [The undersigned party having also received a copy of the said Will]

Dated,   January 21, 1994

[Names of consenting person (or, if more than one person is using this form, the persons) consenting.]

SIGNED: X   [Consenting person(s) signs here.]
X   (Mary F. Doe)

[Signatures of others—when more than one person are employing one form.]

X
X
X

STATE OF NEW YORK

COUNTY OF _____   } ss.:

On this_____ day of _____, 19__, before me personally came

Mary F. Doe   , to me known and known to me to be the

individual   described in and who executed the foregoing waiver and consent, and   they/he/she

acknowledged that they/he executed the same.

[Notary public signs & affixes his official stamp.]

(NOTARY PUBLIC)

N.B. — If the acknowledgment is taken outside the State of New York, a certificate of the officer's authority must be attached.

UF Form NP
State of New York
Surrogate's Court, County of New York

Form P-4

Probate Proceeding, Will of

JOHN JAMES DOE,

Deceased.

Notice of Probate

——————————————19——

Notice is hereby given that the Last Will and Testament of __John   James   Doe,__

late of the __city__ of __New York__, County of __New York,__ and State of New York has been offered for probate in the Surrogate's Court of the County of New York, that the proponent of said Will __David   Edwards__

residing at __15 Probate St., New York, N.Y.   10010__

and that the following are the names and post-office addresses of each person named or referred to in the said Will as substitute or successor executor, as trustee, guardian, legatee, devisee, or other beneficiary, as set forth in the petition herein, who has not been cited or has not appeared or waived citation; and as to such persons as are infants or incompetents, the names and post-office addresses of the persons to whom an additional copy of the Notice of Probate is required to be mailed; and that opposite the name of each such person is a characterization as to whether he is referred to in said Will as testamentary trustee or as guardian or as substitute or successor executor or as beneficiary.

[NOTE: Only the following need be included here: i) any adult "interested person" listed in the Petition who either does not qualify to be cited or would not waive citation; and ii) all infants and incompetents, through their legal guardians or custodians.]

Name	Post-Office Address	Nature of Interest or Status
David Doe, a minor child	c/o Mary F. Doe (child's mother) 10 Death St., N.Y. N.Y. 10003	beneficiary. Mother testamentary guardian.
Diana Merryman	2 Georgeton Street, Jersey City, N.J. 07670	Substitute Executor & Subst. Trustee.

Dated, ——————————— , 19 8 .

SIGNED: X——————————
David Edwards Attorney for Petitioner.

Office and Post Office Address __15 Probate St., New York, N.Y. 10010__

STATE OF NEW YORK   } ss.:
COUNTY OF

__David Edwards,__ , residing at __15 Probate Street,__
__New York, N.Y.__ , being duly sworn, says that he is over the age of __18__ years, that on the ——— day of ————————— , 19— , he deposited in the post office or in a post-office box regularly maintained by the government of the United States in the __Bronx, City__ of __New York__, State of New York, a copy of the foregoing Notice of Probate contained in a securely closed, post-paid wrapper directed to each of the above named persons, at the places set opposite their respective names.

Sworn to before me this——— day
of ————— , 19——

SIGNED: X———————
(Person who serves the Probate Notice)

——————
NOTARY PUBLIC

[This part is to be completed later in the proceedings, ONLY when and after the above-named parties shall have been served with the documents, if required.]

Form P-5A

T554 Affidavit of Subscribing Witness. Any County—Probate
UF Form M

NOTE: *Obtain one of this Affidavit (or its counterpart, instead) from EACH of the witnesses to decedent's will-signing—unless unable to do so.*

STATE OF NEW YORK

Surrogate's Court, County of ___New York___   2¹

Probate Proceeding, Will of

John James Doe,

_____ Deceased

Affidavit of Attesting Witness

_____ 19____

STATE OF NEW YORK, County of New York ss.: [Name of the witness concerned]

I, ___DAVID OWENS,___

residing at 12 St. Johns Street, Brooklyn N.Y. 11225   , New York,

being duly sworn as a witness in the above entitled matter make this affidavit at the request of the (attorney for) applicant to prove

the the will of ___John James Doe,___   , say:

I was acquainted with ___JOHN JAMES DOE,___   now deceased.

The subscription of the name of said decedent to *(a court-certified photographic reproduction of) the original instrument now

shown to me and offerd for probate as decedent's Last Will and Testament and bearing date ___December 21st 1993,___

was made by decedent at (name of hospital, institution or street address) ___his home, 10 Death St., Manhattan,___

New York on the ___21st___   day of ___December,___   19__93 in the presence of myself and

___Mary Jones___

the other attesting witness(s). At the time of making such subscription the said decedent declared the said instrument so subscribed

by decedent to be decedent's   Last Will and

Testament; and I thereupon signed my name as a witness at the end of said instrument, at the request of said decedent, and in

decedent's presence.

The said decedent at the time of so executing said instrument, was upwards of the age of eighteen years, and in my opinion

of sound mind, memory and understanding, not under any restraint or in any respect incompetent to take a will.

I also saw ___MARY JONES,___

the other attesting witness(es), sign ___her___ name(s) as witness(es) at the end of said instrument and know that

___she___ did so at the request and in the presence of said decedent.

___Jules Robertson,___ an attorney-at-law, admitted to practice in the State of New York, supervised

the execution of the said instrument in accordance with the statutory requirements of the Estate, Powers and Trusts Law.

X ___David Owens (The Attesting Witness)___

Sworn to before me this

_____ day of _____ 19__

_____
(Notary)

*Strike words within parenthesis if inapplicable.

Use BLACK ink only, as this sheet will be photographed.

Form P-5B

Form 710 40M 9-77

Surrogate's Court: County of Kings.

In the Matter of Proving
The Last Will and Testament
of

JOHN JAMES DOE   Deceased.

Deposition of Subscribing Witness

File No. ...., 19......

[Name of the witness who was a party to the decedent's will, signing event.]

State of New York, } ss.:
County of Kings,

MARY JONES, being duly sworn, deposes and says:—
I was acquainted with John James Doe, now deceased.
I was present and saw said deceased sign his name at the end of the paper writing or
(Court certified photocopy of the original paper writing)
now produced, shown me and offered for probate as his Last Will
and Testament, bearing date December 21st, 1993 . Said decedent, at the time of
such signing, declared said paper writing to be his Last Will
and Testament and requested DAVID OWENS,
the other subscribing witness, and me to sign our names as witnesses thereto. I thereupon
signed my name as a witness at the end of said paper writing in the presence of said decedent
and in the presence of David Owens
the other subscribing witness I saw David Owens
at the same time sign his name as witness at the end of
said paper writing in decedent's presence. Said decedent at the time was upwards of
eighteen (18) years of age, and in my opinion of sound mind, memory and understanding, not
under restraint, and in every respect competent to make a will. Deceased could read and
write the English language and was not blind and the said paper writing was the only one
executed.

That this affidavit is made at the request of David Edwards

Name of Executor, ~~Proponent or Attorney.~~

Witness sworn, examined and sub-
scribed this day of , 19 9 X MARY JONES (Witness)

(NOTARY PUBLIC OR THE PROBATE
COURT CLERK)

The original instrument or a court certified photocopy of the original instrument must be exhibited to
the witness at the time of execution of this deposition.

Form P-6

Renunciation of Executor and Waiver of Citation

SURROGATE'S COURT: COUNTY OF_____

Probate Proceeding, Will of   RENUNCIATION OF EXECUTOR
_____,   AND WAIVER OF CITATION
                      Deceased.   File No._____

I,_____domiciled at_____, New York, named as Executor in the Last Will and Testament of_____deceased, dated the_____ day of_____, 19_____, do hereby renounce the said appointment and all rights to Letters Testamentary in the estate of the said deceased or to act as executor under the said will, and I do hereby waive the issuance and service of a citation in the above entitled matter and consent that the said instrument be forthwith admitted to probate.

Dated:_____, 19_____

                                        Signature:_____
                                                [Type same Name beneath]

                                        Name (print)_____

                    SWORN TO BEFORE ME,
                    this_____day of _____19____

                    _____
                         (Notary Public)

Form P-7

UF Form 23

State of New York

Surrogate's Court, County of New York

Probate Proceeding, Will of

JOHN JAMES DOE,

Deceased.

**Affidavit Proving
a Correct Copy of the Will
Filed for Probate**

_____ 19____

State of New York }

County of New York } ss.:

We, ___Beatrice Rivera_____

and ___Laura Mullings_____ , being duly and severally sworn,

say, each for himself, that he has carefully compared the foregoing paper   with the original

thereof dated the _____21st_____ day of ___December_____ , 19 93 ,

about to be filed for probate, and that the same   is   in all respects a true and correct copy

of said instrument   and of the whole thereof.

SIGNED: X_____
Beatrice Rivera

X_____
Laura Mullings

Sworn to before me this   day of

____, 19

_____
(NOTARY PUBLIC)

Form P-8

FORM 780 15M 8-76 ——288

SURROGATE'S COURT, KINGS COUNTY

PROBATE PROCEEDING, WILL OF

JOHN JAMES DOE,

File No. ....19.......
Affidavit as to Persons in Military Service (Soldiers' and Sailors' Civil Relief Act of 1940— Approved by the President October 17th, 1940).

Affidavit that a Party is NOT in Military Service

STATE OF NEW YORK } ss.:
COUNTY OF _____ }

__David Edwards__, being duly sworn, deposes and

says:

That he resides at __15 Probate Street, NewYork, N.Y.__

and is the petitioner (or

(Strike out unnecessary allegation)

~~attorney for the petitioner)~~ in the above entitled proceeding.

That the following named persons, parties to this proceeding, were duly served with the citation issued herein, and none of them have appeared herein either in person or by attorney nor have any of them filed an answer to the petition.

Names | *Addresses*
Wallace Doe | 10 Gregory Lane, Queens N.Y. 11431

That he has made (or caused to be made) an investigation to ascertain if any of the above named persons are in the military service of the United States as defined by Section 101 of the Soldiers' and Sailors' Civil Relief Act of 1940, which Act he has read and with which he is familiar.

That the results of such investigation are as follows: __Wallace Doe is employed as Asst. Manager with Chemical Bank in Queens, and has been so employed on a full-time basis for the past 19 years, per Mr. Bankers, the personnel manager, in a telephone inquiry on 2/9/94.__

(To be used if affiant made the investigation)

~~That he caused an investigation to be made by~~

~~of~~ ~~whose~~

(To be used if independent investigation is made)

~~affidavit as to such investigation is hereunto annexed.~~

That from the facts set forth in this affidavit ~~(and the facts set forth in the accompanying~~

~~affidavit of _____)~~ I am convinced that none of the persons above-named are in the military service of the United States as defined in said Soldiers' and Sailors' Civil Relief Act of 1940, except

(Where any of the persons are in service, give details as to the Organization, Ship, etc., and present place of duty).

Sworn to before me this

day of _____ 19

(NOTARY PUBLIC)   X David Edwards

Form P-9

FORM 713 5M 8-76

At a Surrogate's Court held in and for the County of Kings, on the ___ day of _____ , in the year one thousand nine hundred and _____ .

Present. Hon. _____ **Judge of the Surrogate's Court**

In the Matter of Proving the Last Will and Testament of

JOHN JAMES DOE,

Deceased.

File No. _____, 19_____

Decree Granting Probate

SATISFACTORY PROOF having been made that jurisdiction has been obtained of all persons entitled to notice of this proceeding, and Edwin Long, Esq.

Guardian Ad Litem, having appeared in person for David Doe, minor, entitled to contingent remainderman of Trust established under Article six of decedent's Will;

And the witnesses to said Last Will and Testament David Owens & Mary Jones, having been sworn and examined, their examination having been reduced to writing, and filed, and it appearing that the said Will of John James Doe, duly executed, and that the Testator , at the time of executing it , was in all respects competent to make a Will, and not under restraint; and this Court being satisfied of the genuineness of the Will of John James Doe , and the validity of his execution; and the Probate thereof not having been contested;

IT IS DECREED, that the instrument offered for probate herein be, and the same hereby is admitted to probate as the Last Will and Testament of the said John James Doe, the deceased, valid to pass Real and Personal property, and that the said Will of John James Doe, and this Decree be recorded, and that Letters Testamentary be issued to the Executor, David Edwards, who may qualify thereunder, and that the said Executor, David Edwards, pay out of the assets of the estate to Edwin Long Guardian Ad Litem, the sum of ?? dollars as and for his compensation herein.

_____
Judge of the Surrogate's Court

Surrogate's Court: _____ County:

IN THE MATTER OF THE APPLICATION FOR
A SEARCH OF A SAFE DEPOSIT BOX FOR
THE WILL OF

John James Doe,

Deceased.

Petition to Open Safe Deposit Box

File No.................................19........

[Name of whoever is applying as the eligible "interested person" for access into the box.]

TO THE SURROGATE'S COURT OF THE COUNTY OF KINGS:

The petition of __Mary F. Doe,__
who resides at __10 Death St., New York, N.Y.__
respectfully alleges:

STATE RELATIONSHIP

That your petitioner is __the wife of the decedent__
of __John James Doe__ , Deceased, who died at __New York county,__
__New York,__ on the __10th__ day of __January__ , 19__84__ ,
and resided at that time at __10 Death St., New York, N.Y.__
a resident of the County of Kings. __New York.__

That the names of all persons who at the date of the deceased's death were distributees of the deceased by reason of being related to the deceased as spouse, child, issue of a deceased child, adopted child, issue of a deceased adopted child, father, mother, brother or sister of the whole blood or of the half blood or issue of a deceased brother or sister, or otherwise are as follows:

Name	*Relationship*
Mary F. Doe	wife
John James Doe, Jr.	son
David Doe	son
Wallace Doe	son

That the said deceased has a private safe in the vault of the __Chase Manhattan Bank,__
Company, a corporation doing business in the City of New York. That petitioner believes that said deceased may have left a Will or Codicil; a policy or policies of insurance issued in the name of said decedent and payable to a designated beneficiary or beneficiaries, and a deed to a burial plot in which said decedent is to be interred, in the said private safe, and requests that an order be made directing an officer of the said Company to permit __me and David Edwards,__
, in the presence of a representative of the Department of Taxation and Finance, to examine the said safe for the purpose of ascertaining if any of said papers or instruments be deposited therein, and if a Will or Wills or Codicil of said deceased be deposited therein, that the same be deposited in this Court; if such policy or policies of insurance be found, that they be delivered to the beneficiary or beneficiaries named therein, and if a deed to such burial plot be found that the same be delivered to your petitioner and that your petitioner be permitted to make a copy of any paper or papers found in said box bearing upon the desire of said deceased as to the disposal of h is remains, and your petitioner further prays that he permitted to make an inventory of the contents of said box.

Dated, ... 19........

X Mary F. Doe, ...
Petitioner.

Post Office Address : 10 Death St.,
New York N.Y.
10003

STATE OF NEW YORK
COUNTY OF KINGS } SS:

__MARY F. DOE__ being duly sworn, says that he is the petitioner named in the foregoing petition, that he has read the foregoing petition to by him/her and knows the contents thereof; and that the same is true of his/her own knowledge, except as to matters therein stated to be alleged on information and belief, and that as to those matters he/she believes it to be true.

Subscribed and sworn to before
me, this____ day of_____19__

Signed: X _____
Petitioner

Form P-11

Form 631A-3M-70632(78) ⊂━━━▷ 346

At a Surrogate's Court held in and for the County of Kings at the Courthouse, 2 Johnson Street, Brooklyn, in said County on the_____ day of 19 .

PRESENT:

HON. _____

IN THE MATTER OF THE APPLICATION FOR A SEARCH OF A SAFE DEPOSIT BOX FOR THE WILL OF

John James Doe,

Deceased.

Order to Open Safe Deposit Box

File No.................................19.........

Upon reading and filing the petition of _Mary F. Doe_,

verified on the _____ day of _____, 19_____, the _Chase Manhattan Bank_

_____ is hereby ordered and directed and hereby

authorized to allow _Mary F. Doe and Mr. David Edwards_ to open the private safe of

John James Doe, deceased, in the presence of the president or other

officer of the said safe deposit company and a representative of the State Tax Commission, and examine the contents of said safe for any last Will and Testament of said deceased or any codicil thereto, and without removing any other article therefrom, if any will or codicil be found therein, the said

_____Chase Manhattan Bank_____ is hereby ordered and
(insert name of bank)

directed forthwith to deliver the same personally or by registered mail to this Court, and it is further

Ordered that the petitioner be permitted to make an inventory of said safe deposit box; and it is further

Ordered that the petitioner be permitted to make a copy of any paper or papers found in the said safe deposit box bearing upon the desire of the deceased as to the disposal of h remains, and if a deed to a cemetery plot be found in the said safe deposit box, that the same be delivered to the petitioner; and it is further

Ordered that if any policy or policies of insurance issued in the name of said decedent and payable to a named beneficiary or beneficiaries be found in said safe deposit box, that the same be delivered to the beneficiary or beneficiaries named therein.

_____
SURROGATE

Form P-12A

SURROGATE'S COURT:
COUNTY OF_____

| [Add title of proceeding] |

Affidavit of Application for Service to be Made by Publication
[A sample]

File No._____

STATE OF NEW YORK)
COUNTY OF_____) ss.:

_____, being duly sworn, deposes and says:

1. That he is resident at No._____ _____Street, in_____ and that he is the petitioner in the above entitled proceeding, the same as the person designated as Executor herein in the Last Will and Testament of_____, deceased, which instrument was filed in the Clerk's Office of the Surrogate's Court,_____County, on the_____ day of_____ 19_____, and that he is familiar with all of the facts and circumstances heretofore had herein.

2. That this proceeding is brought for *[give the specific purpose]*.

3. That your deponent knew the late Mr._____, having been his friend and close companion for over 10 years during his lifetime. That at all times during the decedent's lifetime, in the course of conversations, I was informed by the said decedent, that he was a bachelor, and that he had no living heirs or kin or distributees.

4. That your deponent consulted with one Mr._____, a business partner and close associate of the decedent, as to whether the said decedent had any relatives, heirs at law, or kin, or distributees, in order to serve citation upon said persons, but was informed that he did not know of any such person or persons or the address or addresses, where they might be found.

5. That in order to find such person or persons, your deponent, having been informed that the said_____was a Citizen of the United States, did go on the_____day of_____, 19____, to the Board of Elections, and examined the book known as "Register of Voters Signature Copy," and found that the deceased registered and voted in the year____. The records, which purport to be information derived from the deceased, show that he was_____years of age, single, resided in the State of New York for____ years, _____years in the City of_____, born in_____, and became a citizen in_____.

6. That your deponent searched the records of the Naturalization Bureau,_____ County, between the years_____to_____, and found that one Mr._____ who may or may not be the same person as the deceased, became a citizen on_____19____, and which is recorded in Liber_____, page _____. I am informed by the Clerk in charge of said Books, that the record would only give the name of the witness who certified as to fitness, and no information as to the place of birth, residence, names of parents, or members of family. The Clerk would not permit your deponent to examine the said record unless I could furnish him with the name of the witness, and this name not being at your deponent's disposal, I could not examine the same.

7. That your deponent attempted to find persons of similar names as the deceased, and an examination of the_____Telephone Directory discloses there are about____listings with surnames of "_____."

8. That on the____day of_____19___, your deponent made a list of the names of persons listed in the said telephone directory of_____, whose surnames ended in "_____". Your deponent then caused to be prepared letters reading as follows:

Dear Sir:

Will you please be good enough to advise me as to whether or not you are in any wise related to one_____, deceased, late of No____ _____Place, where he resided for the past_____ years.

The said_____was born in the vicinity of_____, on or about the _____day of___19__.

Thanking you for any courtesy that you may show me in this matter, I am

Very truly yours,

9. That your deponent mailed copies of the above letter to the said persons, addressed to them at the addresses designated in the_____directories.

10. _____of the said persons sent replies to the above letter, but none of the said persons claimed or showed any relationship to the deceased

11. Several of the persons telephoned your deponent, and all of the said persons could not, and did not, claim any kinship to the deceased_____.

12. One of the said_____called at the office of your deponent on the ____day of____, 19__, and after a long conversation with said person, your deponent was unable to establish any kinship with the deceased.

13. That your deponent was informed by_____, that the deceased had several bank accounts, in ____ different savings banks, and in order to discover whether the bank records could furnish any information as to the decedent's relations, heirs, or next of kin, or distributees, your deponent went to the said banks, and the following is a report of what I discovered.

14. That on the____day of____19___, I went to the Savings Bank, located at_____Street and_____ Avenue in the city, and examined the card signed by the deceased, which is dated_____19___. The said card shows that the deceased gave the name of his father as "_____" and that of his mother as "_____." No further information, except that he resided at No.____ _____ Place,_____.

15. That on the ____day of ____19__, I went to the Savings Bank, located at _____Place and_____Street, and examined the card signed by the deceased on ____, 19___, which is the date the account was opened. The said card shows that the deceased was born in ____and gives no other information, but his address.

16. That on the_____day of_____ , 19___, I went to the_____Bank, which is located at _____ Avenue and_____Street. The person in charge of the card of account was by a coincidence named_____, to whom your deponent spoke, and who stated that he was not related to the deceased. Your deponent examined the card, and the only information was as above given as to name of father and mother, and that the deceased was born in_____.

17. That your deponent has inquired from_____as to whether he knows of any persons who are related to the said deceased, and was informed that he did not know of any such person. He advises your deponent that in conversations had with the deceased during his lifetime, he was informed that the deceased was born in the vicinity of_____.

18. That from the foregoing, it can be readily seen that your deponent has made diligent efforts and inquiry to find the heirs-at-law of the deceased but has been unable to find any person upon whom the citation can be served.

19. That no previous application for the relief herein prayed for has been made.

WHEREFORE, your deponent prays for an order granting that citation be served by publication.

SWORN TO BEFORE ME,
this _____ day of_____ 19___.

Signature:_____

[Type Name of same Deponent below the line]

_____
(Notary Public)

Form P-12B

Citation to Be Published

_____also known as_____, _____,and_____,—CITATION—
THE PEOPLE OF THE STATE OF NEW YORK, By the Grace of God, Free and Independent, to Attorney
General of the State of New York; The City of_____, Department of Hospitals; and to "Mary
Doe," the name "Mary Doe" being fictitious, the alleged widow of_____, also known as_____
deceased, if living and if dead, to the executors, administrators, distributees and assigns of "Mary Doe,"
deceased, whose names and post office addresses are unknown and cannot after diligent inquiry be ascertained by the petitioner herein; and to the distributees of_____ also known as_____,
_____,and_____deceased, whose names and post office addresses are
unknown and cannot after diligent inquiry be ascertained by the petitioner herein, being the persons
interested as creditors, distributees or otherwise in the estate of _____, also known as_____,
_____, and_____, deceased, who at the time of his death was a resident of No. _____ _____
Street, City of_____ , N.Y., send GREETING:

   Upon the petition of _[specify name of fiduciary]_ having his office at_____, Room_____, Borough
of_____, City and County of New York, as administrator of the goods, chattels, and
credits of said deceased:

   You and each of you are hereby cited to show cause before the Surrogate's Court of_____
County, held at_____, in the County of_____, on the _ day of_____19____, at 10 o'clock
in the forenoon of that day, why the account of proceedings of The Administrator of the _[specify name of
fiduciary]_, as administrator of the goods, chattels and credits of said deceased, should not be judicially
settled.

   IN TESTIMONY WHEREOF, We have caused the seal of the Surrogate's Court of the said County
of_____, to be hereunto affixed. Witness, Honorable_____, a Surrogate of our said
County, at the County of_____, the _____day of_____ in the year of our Lord one thousand
nine hundred and____.

_____
                                               Clerk of the Surrogate's Court

{Seal}

Form P-12C

Order for Service of Citation by
Publication—Unknown Distributees

Present: Hon._____, Surrogate.

┌─────────────────────────────┐
│   [Add title of proceeding] │
│   │
└─────────────────────────────┘

At a Surrogate's Court, held in and for the County of_____at_____, in said County, on the_____ day of_____ 19_.

Order for Publication

File No. _____

Upon reading and filing the petition of_____, verified on_____, 19____, the affidavit of_____, sworn to on the_____day of_____ 19__, and *[specify any other papers]*, and a citation having been duly issued in the above entitled matter, and the petitioner having produced proof to my satisfaction that the place or places of residence of all unknown next of kin and distributees of_____, deceased, if any there be, who and whose existence are unknown and cannot after diligent inquiry be ascertained and if any such heir at law or next of kin, or distributee has died subsequent to the death of_____, deceased, the unknown husbands, wives, widows, heirs at law, next of kin, distributees, legatees, and assignees, grantees, or persons, if any there be and whose names and places of residence and post office addresses are unknown and cannot after diligent inquiry be ascertained; and all other persons in any manner interested, directly or indirectly, in the estate of which the said_____died seized and possessed, who and whose names and places of residence are unknown and cannot after diligent inquiry be ascertained; the said_____ having been at the time of his death a resident of_____, and that personal service of the citation cannot with due diligence be made upon them within the State, and it appearing that the aggregate value of the interest in the estate of all persons to be served by publication amounts to more than $5,000, it is

ORDERED, that the service of the citation herein upon the said person or persons, and any and all unknown persons whose names or parts of whose names and whose place or places of residence are unknown, and cannot, after diligent inquiry be ascertained, and heirs at law, and next of kin of the said_____, be made by publication pursuant to CPLR 316, to wit: that the citation be published in two newspapers, to wit: The_____ and _____, being two newspapers printed and published in the County of _____, once in each of four successive weeks, which is the time I deem reasonable, and in the exercise of the discretion of the Court pursuant to SCPA 307(2)(a); and it is further

ORDERED, that the publication of the citation alone without the notice of the description of any real property affected by this proceeding (except to the extent the same shall be included in such citation), shall constitute full compliance with this order.

_____
Surrogate (Judge)

Form P-13A

Surrogate's Court—County of _____

In the Matter of Probate Proceeding, Will of: JOHN JAMES DOE, Deceased

Affidavit in Support of Application to Dispense With Testimony of an Attesting Witness

File No._____

STATE OF NEW YORK
COUNTY OF_____ss.:

David Edwards, being duly sworn deposes and says that:

1. I am the Executor named to the Will and petitioner herein and am domiciled at _15 Probate St., NYC._ On _____ 19____, I duly filed in this Court an instrument dated _Dec. 21, 1993,_ purporting to be the last Will of the above named decedent, together with a verified petition dated _1/20/94_ praying for the probate of the said Last Will.

2. Said Will was signed at the end thereof by the testator, and by me, _David Owens,_ and _Mike Johnson_ and _Mary Jones,_ as attesting witnesses

3. Said Mr. _Mike Johnson_ is a domiciliary of _____, and does not have any occasion to visit the United States or the State of New York.

4. The time which would be expended and the cost insurred in sending commission to take the testimony of the above-named attesting witness would cause undue expense, inconvenience, and hardship.

5. Petitioner and the said Mrs_____ are domiciled in _____ in the State of New York, and testified as attesting witnesses on _____ 19___.

6. No previous application has been made for the relief requested herein.

WHEREFORE, your deponent prays that an order be granted dispensing with the testimony of said _Mr. Johnson_ as an attesting witness.

SIGNED: [_Mike Johnson_]
[Type same Name below line]
Name (Print)_____

Sworn to before me, this _____ day of_____ 19___.

Form P-13B

At a Surrogate's Court held in and for the County of _____ at _____ on the _____ day of _____ 19_____.

Present: Hon. _____, Surrogate

[Add title of proceeding]

Order Dispensing with Testimony of Attesting Witness

On reading and filing the affidavit of Mr. _David Edwards,_ sworn to the _____ day of _____, 19___, and the affidavit of _____, sworn to the _____ day of _____ 19___, whereby it appears to the satisfaction of the Surrogate that _Mike Johnson_ one of the attesting witnesses to the paper writing dated the _21st day of Dec, 1993,_ puporting to be the Last Will and Testament of _John James Doe,_ the decedent above named, is permanently absent from the State of New York.

Now, on motion of _David Edwards,_ the above named petitioner herein, it is

ORDERED, that the testimony of _Mike Johnson,_ as an attesting witness on paper in the writing purporting to be the Last Will and Testament of _John James Doe_ dated _Dec 21, 1993,_ be and the same is hereby dispensed with.

_____
Surrogate/Judge

Form P-13C

SURROGATE'S COURT: COUNTY OF _____

In the Matter of Probate Proceeding, Will of: JOHN JAMES DOE,   Deceased

Deposition Proving Handwriting of Testator and/or Attesting Witness(es)

File No. _____

STATE OF NEW YORK
COUNTY OF _____ ss.:

[Name of the handwriting expert or person familiar with testator's signature], being duly sworn as a witness in the above-entitled proceeding, and examined on behalf of the petitioner to prove the said Will, says that he was for upwards of _____ years well acquainted with *[Enter name of the testator or attesting witness(es)]*, late of New York City, and with his manner and style of handwriting, having often seen him write, and that he verily believes that the signature *[name of the testator or attesting witness(es)]* subscribed as that of the testator to the instrument in writing now produced and shown to deponent purporting to be the Last Will and Testament of the said deceased, bear ing the date _____ day of *[Date of testator's signing of the Will]*, 19____, is the true, proper, and genuine signature and handwriting of the said testator.

Signed: X _____
Name (print) _____

Sworn to Before me,
this _____ day of _____, 19____.

_____
(Notary Public)

Form P-14

Letters Testamentary (Letters of Administration)

THE PEOPLE OF THE STATE OF NEW YORK

To:_____ David Edwards, of 15 Probate St., New York, NY _____

SEND GREETINGS:

WHEREAS, the Last Will and Testament of __John James Doe__, deceased, was duly admitted to probate by decree of the Surrogate's Court of _____ County on_____the_____day of_____, 19___, which decree directed the issuance to you of Letters Testamentary upon your qualifying according to law,

NOW, THEREFORE, KNOW YE that you are hereby authorized to administer the estate of the said deceased, subject to the jurisdiction and supervision of this court.

WITNESS Hon._____,a Surrogate of the County of _____this_____ day of_____19____.

_____
Clerk of the Surrogate's Court

Form P-15

Certificate of Letters Testamentary/Letters of Administration
(Short Form Version)

THE PEOPLE OF THE STATE OF NEW YORK

TO ALL TO WHOM THESE PRESENTS SHALL COME OR MAY CONCERN:

This is to certify that on the ____ day of _____ 19_____, LETTERS TESTAMENTARY of the Last Will and Testament of (Letters of Administration of the Estate of)
John James Doe
_____,

late of the County of _____ were duly granted and issued by the Surrogate of the County of_____ to _____, and that the same are still valid and in full force.

Dated, Attested and Sealed_____, 19_____.

Hon. _____Surrogate of_____County.

_____
Clerk of the Surrogate's Court

Form P-16

Consent of Beneficiary of Will
to Grant of Letters of Administration *c.t.a.*

SURROGATE'S COURT: COUNTY OF_____

Proceeding for Letters of Administration with the Will Annexed, Estate of *John James Doe*, Deceased

Consent to Grant of Letters of Administration *c.t.a.*

    I, the undersigned, of No._____ Street, _____, N.Y., being a beneficiary under the Last Will and Testament of _____*John James Doe*_____, the above named decedent, and under no legal disability, do hereby consent that letters of administration with the will annexed of the goods, chattels and credits of the said decedent, be granted to Mr. _____ of No. ____ _____ Street, N.Y., who is eligible to receive such letters of administration *c.t.a.*

Dated:_____, 19____.

Signature:_____
Name (Print):_____

Before me, on this day, _____, 19___,
appeared Mr._____,to me
known as same, who subscribed to and acknowledged the contents of the above document.

_____
(Notary Public)

Chapter 6
"OPENING OF THE ESTATE" PART IN A NO-WILL SITUATION.
FIRST, GET AN ADMINISTRATOR APPOINTED BY THE COURT.

ESTATE SETTLING PROCEDURES IN INTESTATE (NO-WILL) SITUATIONS

In the preceding Chapter 5, we dealt with the probate procedures involved in the so-called "TESTATE" situations—where the decedent dies leaving a valid Will. In this chapter, we shall cover the equivalent probate procedures in "INTESTATE"—that is, no will—situations, starting here, first, with the court approval of the administrator for the estate. Basically, the equivalent procedures in a no-will situation involve the whole business of getting the court to approve someone (called an "administrator" in a no-will situation, as compared to "executor" in a will situation), to administer the decedent's estate.

STEP-BY-STEP PROCEDURES FOR GETTING AN ADMINISTRATOR APPOINTED BY THE COURT

To get an administrator appointed and approved by the court under New York's court system, just follow these simple 'STEPS' in the exact order in which they are listed below:

STEP 1: PREPARING THE PETITION PAPERS FOR OBTAINING THE LETTERS OF ADMINISTRATION

Let's say, of course, that it has been pretty well determined that the decedent left <u>no</u> will behind. Then, even as all the funeral arrangements are being made, a proper person should hurry and apply to have an ADMINISTRATOR of the decedent's affairs offically appointed by the court. In deed, it is of utmost importance that this application be made very promptly, as early as possible. Why? For a very simple but significant reason: the sooner this is done, the sooner will the person appointed the administrator take office and begin to look after the decedent's estate and safeguard the unprotected or potentially perishable property, if any.

A. Determine Who Is Entitled To Receive Letters Of Administration To Serve As Administrator Of The Estate.

Generally, the right accrues to the decedent's next-of-kin: the surviving spouse, children, grandchildren, parents, brothers or sisters, in that order. Under New York's rules, for examples, letters of administration *must* ordinarily be granted to the following persons, in the order of priority listed below, if they are not otherwise ineligible or unqualified[1] at the time of the filing of the application: **i)** the surviving spouse; **ii)** the children; **iii)** the grandchildren; **iv)** the father or mother, the brothers or sisters; **v)** any other persons who are distributees and qualify; **vi)** the Public Administrator or the county treasurer; and **vii)** the petitioner for letters, whoever he/she may be.

By law, it is required that the above order of priority be strictly followed in appointing an administrator. However, in line with the modern philosophy in most states, the law also aims at speeding up the process; so it allows for letters to be granted to an eligible distributee or to a nondistributee, *providing* that ALL the distributees grant their consent to the proposed appointment. And, perhaps not surprisingly, the latter method turns out to be the method most frequently used among petitioners.

B. Order (Obtain) The Necessary Forms For Filing Probate

How do you initiate the petition? It's a simple matter. First, you've got to GET THE NECESSARY FILING FORMS for an "intestate" or no-Will petition. For the added convenience of the readers, ***Do-It-Yourself Legal Publishers*** makes available to its readership the *standard,* fully pre-sorted, all-in-one package of forms—containing a complete set of the necessary forms for a New York State filing (the initial probate petition as well as the probate accounting phases combined).

To order the Publishers' "all-in-one" *standard* forms (either for testate or for intestate situations), just complete the Order Form on p. 239 and send it away to the Publishers' Legal Forms Division at the given address therein.

> NOTE: The apppropriate blank forms for probate filing for several other estates may also be available from the publisher. (See p. 239).

C. Then, Out Of The Forms Obtained, You Fill Out The Following:

1. Form P-17, **"Petition for Letters of Administration,"** which is to be completed and *notarized* in two places by the petitioner. (See pp. 70-3 for a sample preparation of this form.) [Note that the format of this official form combines other subdivisions into its last page: (i) VERIFICATION; (2) OATH OF ADMINISTRATOR; and (3) DESIGNATION OF CLERK FOR SERVICE OF PROCESS].

2. Form P-18, **"Original Citation (NO WILL)"** (See p. 74 for a sample preparation of this form.) Leave the "Affidavit of Service" part of this form blank for now and complete it later in "Step 4."

3. Form P-19, **"Renunciation of Letters of Administintion & Waiver of Process."** To be able to have an uncontested and relatively easier probate proceedings, ***this is a most necessary (and desirable!) document to secure from ALL persons*** concerned—basically the distributees and all those listed to be "cited." (See p 76 for a sample preparation of this form.)

4. Form P-20, **"Order for Issuance of Citation."** (See p. 77 for a sample preparation of this form.)

5. Form P-21, **"Notice of Application for Letters of Administration."** (See p. 78 for a sample preparation of this form.)

6. Form 22, **"Decree Granting Letters of Administration"**—necessary *only* in those counties in which the court itself does not prepare this paper for you on its own. (See p. 79 for a sample preparation of this form.)

NOW, OBTAIN ALSO THE FOLLOWING DOCUMENT(S) AND PAPERS, TO BE SUBMITTED TO THE COURT ALONG WITH THE PETITION PAPERS LISTED ABOVE:

a. A <u>certified</u> copy of the decedent party's death certificate.

---

[1]To be eligible and to qualify, a person must be a "distributee" (a relative entitled to inherit) of the intestate decedent; if an alien, he must be a domiciliary of the state. Persons under the age of 18, or who have been adjudged incompetents, felons, or dishonest, are also ineligible to receive Letters of all types.

NOTE that certain persons, even if not eligible to receive letters of administration themselves, may nevertheless petition to have an administrator appointed—such as any person interested in the estate, a public administrator or county treasurer, a creditor of the decedent, or a court litigant against the decedent or his estate.

> ***NOTE:*** If there are beneficiaries, potential or actual, who are minors (under 18 years in New York), or who are under legal disability or are judicially declared incompetents, the petitioner should, at this juncture, advise the parents or other persons who have legal custody of such a person, to do one of two things: either to apply, themselves, to have the ***"Letters of Guardianship"*** issued to them, or to have another person apply for appointment as guardian for the minor or the incompetent. A special kind of guardianship, called 'guardian ad litem,' may also be necessary on occasion, when some yet unknown minors or beneficiaries would have an *ultimate* (not an immediate) share in the estate—where, for example, the terms of a will which provides for the establishment of a trust further stipulates that the ultimate remainder of the trust assets is to go to lineal descendants of the immediate beneficiaries.
>
> Whoever is appointed the guardian, if applicable (and *not* the executor or administrator), is the one who would have to represent the interests of such a minor or incompetent before the court. It is him that receives service of court papers on behalf of his 'wards' (the person who a guardian guards), and it is him that is supposed to (in theory, at least!) look after the distributive share of the estate to which the ward is entitled, etc. (Procedures for filing the petition for a guardianship appointment are outlined in Appendix F.)

STEP **2**: FILE THE PETITION PAPERS WITH THE COURT CLERK

(See the procedures outlined for the probate of Wills situations— 'Step Three' of Chap. 5 on pp. 34-5 above—and follow those same procedures. There's no testimony-taking requirement for an intestate situation; all references therein to 'testimony-taking' or 'witnesses' should obviously be ignored as inapplicable here, therefore.)

STEP **3**: SERVE THE PROBATE "CITATIONS" ON THE PERSONS REQUIRED, IF ANY

(See the procedures outlined for the probate of Will situations— 'Step Four' of Chap. 5 on pp. 35-7 above—and follow those same procedures.)

> NOTE: With respect to intestate service of citation, the following are generally required to be served: **i)** when petitioner is a distributee (i.e., a creditor), serve on all eligible distributees of any rank or priority who would otherwise have a right to letters of administration (except for those who have renounced or waived service); **ii)** when petitioner is *not* a distributee, serve on all eligible distributees and all ineligible domiciliary distributees who are incompetent or infants, if any; **iii)** when there are no eligible distributees, fiduciaries or commitees, a non-distributee petitioner must serve citation on the public administrator or county treasurer; **iv)** when the decedent is merely "alleged" or "believed" to be dead without certainty, serve citation also on the person alleged to be deceased (as well as on all of his presumptive distributees, of course). Service on a distributee who has *equal* right to letters of administration may be waived by the court (upon filing an Affidavit with the court asserting your inability to establish the distributee's whereabouts); however, service on a distributee who has a right to letters, if any, would still be required, usually by publication.
>
> Where some of the persons required to be cited are under disability (underage or incompetent), a GUARDIAN AD LITEM may also be required to be appointed and his report filed with the clerk before the letters may be issued. Procedures for appointing guardians of various kinds are in Appendix F, p. 229.

STEP 4: FILE WITH THE COURT CLERK YOUR PROOF OF HAVING SERVED THE CITATIONS

(See the procedures outlined for the probate of Wills situations—'Step Five' on pp. 37-8 above—and follow those same procedures.)[2]

STEP 5: SERVE 'NOTICE OF PETITION/APPLICATION FOR LETTERS OF ADMINISTRATION' ON THE NECESSARY PERSON(S), IF ANY

In intestate petition procedures, the court does not ordinarily require further service or filing of any more papers following its receipt of adequate proof that the citation has been fully served. Gernerally, if satisfied that no valid objections have been registered against the petition, the judge would usually sign the Decree Granting Letters of Administration to the petitioner (sample of the Decree is Form P-22 on p. 79).

However, sometimes certain courts or jursidictions may require one more formality before the judge may sign the Decree. It may require that a document, NOTICE OF PETITION/APPLICATION FOR LETTERS OF ADMINISTRATION (see Form P-21 on p. 78), be formally "served" (i.e., delivered) to certain persons the court may designate. In any event, in situations where and when this would be required to be undertaken by the court, the formal delivery ("service") of the NOTICE OF PETITION OR APPLICATION to persons entitled to receive them, if any, is the next—and final—step in the administrator appointment phase of the probate proceedings under New York's procedures. Under such a circumstance, the Letters of Administration will not be issued to an administrator until proof of service of this notice is filed with the clerk. Unlike the situation involved with service of the citation, which "enjoins" the person served to the authority of the local court, service of the Notice of Petition has no such binding authority, but is purely informational in nature. It's merely meant to be "informational"—i.e., to advise the persons concerned about their potential interests in the estate, or of their status as alternate fiduciaries.

Service of this document is a very simple matter. All you have to do is this: First, fill out the Notice of Petition form (sample preparation Form P-21 is on p. 78). Secondly, make photocopies of the Notice and mail a copy (petitioner may generally do this himself) to _every one_ of the following persons: anyone named in the petition (as a beneficiary, trustee, guardian, or a substitute or successor trustee or guardian) who has either not been served with a citation or has not appeared or waived service of citation, as well as any minors or incompetents represented by a legal guardian. Most preferably, do this mailing not less than 7 days BEFORE the date set by the court clerk for a decree to be signed or entered by the judge.

Finally, after the mailing, you complete the bottom part of the back side of the Notice of Petition (as in bottom part of Form P-21 on p. 78); have this part notarized and submit the two parts of the document to the clerk as _proof_ of your having carried out the notice-giving requirement.

STEP 6: THE COURT ISSUES YOU YOUR "LETTERS OF ADMINISTRATION" CONFIRMING YOU AS ADMINISTRATOR

Upon the signing of the court order, the person or person(s) appointed administrator(s) [or administratrix(es), if a woman] should obtain from the clerk a few "<u>certified</u>" (i.e., stamped and official) copies of the **LETTERS OF ADMINISTRATION**—the document which oficially represents the court's

---

[2]Where some of the persons required to be cited are under disability (underage or incompetent), a GUARDIAN AD LITEM may also be required to be appointed and his report filed with the clerk before the letters may be issued. Procedures for appointing guardians are in Appendix F.

Form P-15 on p. 63 as the Letters of Administration). *As an administrator about to begin the actual administraton of the estate, this is probably the most important document for you: you'll often need to show this document to the banks, debtors, creditors, and other interested parties or companies before they may allow you to take possession of bank accounts, safe deposit box contents, personal or real property, etc., on behalf of the* decedent's estate.

A FEW RELEVANT ISSUES BEFORE WE CONCLUDE THE APPOINTMENT OF THE ADMINISTRATOR PHASE OF PROBATE

Now, for all practical purposes, the initial phase of the procedures which has to do with the selection of an administrator, is completed. You are now ready to commence the second—and really the important—phase of an administrator's job: the *actual*, physical administration or management of the affairs of the estate. But before we get into the procedures involved in that second phase (Chapter 7-A, p. 80), **there are a few relevant facts you should have at the back of your mind:**

FIRST: What to do in the Event the Administratorship Becomes Vacant

Bear in mind that if the office of the designated administrator should become vacant later for whatever reason (such as resignation of a sole administrator, or his death, refusal to act or revocation of his letters, etc.), one or more other eligible persons may apply to the court to have **"LETTERS OF ADMINISTRATION d.b.n."** granted to them (d.b.n. are Latin initials for *de bonus non*).

The person(s) so appointed become(s) known as "administrator(s) d.b.n.," with exactly the same powers and responsibilities as the original administrator to continue the estate's administration. The procedures for applying for issuance of Letters of Administration d.b.n. are just about the same as those for granting plain Letters of Administration covered above in this chapter. Use the same petition forms[3] and the same procedures used for filing for plain Letters of Administration.

SECOND: You May be Required to Post a Bond

As an administrator (in contrast to an executor), you would almost certainly be required by the court to post a BOND with the court as a surety to assure that you will faithfully discharge your duties. If you should be required to do so, the court will so inform you. And obtaining a bond in the amount set by the court should hardly be a problem: simply look up a surety company in your Yellow pages or telephone directory under the headings "Surety Bonds" or "Bonds—Surety & Fidelity." Pay the company its charge or "premium" for the coverage (which is, of course, payable out of the proceeds of the estate), and you can be sure your bonding policy will be issued you by the bonding company in no time!!

---

[3]The only differing element here, which is rather minor, is that the petition for Letters of Administration d.b.n. should also add information as to the value of the estate as of the date of the administrator's death or the vacancy of his office.

Form P-17

Form 433-10M-70619(78) 346

BOND FILED IN THE SUM OF $........................

Surrogate's Court: County of ___Kings___

Proceeding for Letters of Administration.

Estate of :

JOHN JAMES DOE,

Deceased.

Petition for Letters of Administration

File No.........................19........

To the Surrogate's Court, County of ___Kings___

It is respectfully alleged:

(1) The name, domicile and interest in this proceeding of the petitioner, who is of full age, is as follows:

Name___John James Doe, Jr.___

Domicile___18 Third Street___
(Street and Number)

___Bronx, New York,___ ___N.Y.___
(City, Village or Town) (State)

Interest of Petitioner: (check one)

(X) Distributee of decedent, to wit:___oldest son___
(Relationship)

( ) Other (specify)___

Citizenship___U.S.A.___

(2) The following are the particulars respecting the above named decedent:

(a) Name___John James Doe___

(b) Date of Death:___January 10 1994___ Place of Death:___Brooklyn, New York___

(c) Domicile: Street___10 Death Street,___

City, Village or Town:___New York___

County:___Kings___ State:___New York___

(d) Citizenship___U.S.A.___

(3) Your petitioner has made diligent search and inquiry for a will of the decedent and has not found any and has been unable to obtain any information concerning any will of the decedent and therefore alleges upon information and belief that the decedent died without leaving any last will.

(4) Search of the records of this court shows that no application has ever been made for letters of administration upon the estate of the decedent or for the probate of a will of the decedent and your petitioner is informed and verily believes that no such application has ever been made to the Surrogate's Court of any other county of this State.

(5) The decedent left surviving:

(a) (X) Spouse (husband/wife).
(b) (X) Child or children, or descendants of predeceased child or children.
(c) ( ) Father/mother.
(d) ( ) Brothers or sisters, either of the whole or half-blood; or descendants of such predeceased brothers or sisters.
(e) ( ) Grandfather grandmother.
(f) ( ) Uncles or aunts.
(g) ( ) Descendants of predeceased uncles or aunts.

(Information is required only as to those classes of surviving relatives who would take the property of decedent if there were no will. The term "child or children" includes adopted as well as natural children. State number of survivors in each such class. Insert "X" in all subsequent classes. Insert "No" in all prior classes.)

(6) The decedent left surviving the following DISTRIBUTEES, whose names, degrees of relationship, domicile, post-office addresses and citizenship are as follows:

(a) The following who are of full age and sound mind:

Name	Relationship	Domicile and Post-office Address	Citizenship
Mary F. Doe	surviving wife	IO Death St., Brooklyn, N.Y.	U.S.A.
John James Doe, Jr.	son	I8 Third Street, Bronx, N.Y.	U.S.A.
Wallace Doe	son	IO Gregory Lane, Queens Village, New York, II43I	U.S.A.

[See Appendix B (pp. 118-121) for the kinds of persons to be listed here as distributees in a no-Will situation.]

(b) The following who are persons under disability:
(Please furnish all information specified in NOTE below.)

David Doe, a minor, age I7, born 6/IO/66; lives with mother, Mary F. Doe, at same address with decedent; no guardian or testamentary guardian.	son	IO Death St., Brooklyn, New York, II222	U.S.A.

NOTE: In the case of each infant, state (a) name, birth date, age, relationship to decedent, domicile residence address and the person with whom he resides; (b) whether or not he has a guardian or testamentary guardian and whether or not his father, or if dead, his mother, is living and (c) the name and address of any guardian and any living parent. In the case of each other person under disability, state (a) name, relationship to decedent and residence address, (b) facts regarding his disability, including whether or not he has been committed to any institution and (c) the names and addresses of any relative or friend having an interest in his welfare. In the case of person confined as a prisoner, state place of incarceration. In the case of unknowns describe such persons in the same language as will be used in the process. In each case give a brief description of the party's interest in the estate.)

(7) Decedent was the owner of and died possessed of certain PERSONAL PROPERTY, the value of which does not exceed the sum of __Four Hundred Thousand Dollars__ _$400,000_.

(8) Decedent died seized of REAL PROPERTY, in this state which is improved/unimproved (strike out one), the estimated value of which does not exceed $200,000

The estimated gross rents for a period of eighteen months is the sum of $ none (property is private home)

A brief description of each parcel is as follows:

two-floor, 11-room, frame house with finished basement and a two-car garage. Plot: half an acre.

(9) In addition to the value of the personal property stated in paragraph (7) hereof, the following right of action existed on behalf of the decedent and survived his death, or is granted to the administrator of the decedent by special provision of law, and it is impractical to give a bond sufficient to cover the probable amount to be recovered therein. (Write "None," or state briefly the cause of action and the person against whom it exists.) NONE

(10) There are no other persons than those mentioned hereinbefore who have an interest in this application or proceeding.

WHEREFORE your petitioner respectfully prays: (Check and complete all relief requested.)

(a) (✔) That process issue to all necessary parties to show cause why letters should not be issued as hereinafter requested;

(b) ( ) That an order be granted dispensing with service of process upon those persons named in Paragraph (6) hereof who have a right to letters prior or equal to that of the person hereinafter nominated therefor, and who are non-domiciliaries of whose names or whereabouts are unknown and cannot be ascertained;

(c) (✔) That a decree award Letters of Administration of the estate of the decedent to John James Doe, Jr., or to such other person or persons having a prior right as may be entitled thereto; and

(d) (✔) That the authority of the representative under the foregoing letters be limited with respect to none.

Dated: 1/20/94   SIGNED: X

John James Doe, Jr.

X _____
(Signature(s) of Petitioner)

STATE OF NEW YORK   } ss.:   Combined Verification, Oath and Designation (for use when petitioner is to be appointed administrator)

COUNTY OF.........................

I, the undersigned, the petitioner named in the foregoing petition, being duly sworn, say:

(1) VERIFICATION: I have read the foregoing petition subscribed by me and know the contents thereof, and the same is true of my own knowledge, except as to the matters therein stated to be alleged upon information and belief, and as to those matters I believe it to be true.

(2) OATH OF ADMINISTRATOR: I am over eighteen (18) years of age and a citizen of the United States; and I will well, faithfully and honestly discharge the duties of Administrator (trix) of the goods, chattels and credits of said decedent according to law. I am not ineligible to receive letters.

(3) DESIGNATION OF CLERK FOR SERVICE OF PROCESS: I do hereby designate the Clerk of the Surrogate's Court of Kings County, and his or her successor in office, as a person on whom service of any process issuing from such Surrogate's Court may be made in like manner and with like effect as if it were served personally upon me, whenever I cannot be found and served within the State of New York after due diligence used.

My domicile is..18 Third Street, Bronx N.Y. 10436
(State complete address)

SIGNED: X ....
John James Doe, Jr.

X ....
(Signature(s) of Petitioner)

On........................., 19......... before me personally came

John James Doe, Jr.

to me known to be the person described in and who executed the foregoing instrument. Such person duly swore to such instrument before me and duly acknowledged that he or she executed the same.

....
(Notary Public)

ATTORNEY

Name of Attorney.......none applicable.......   Tel. No..........................

Address of Attorney..........n/a

Form P-18

Form 439 3M 9-77

[Enter here the names only of each & every person or institution that would seem deserving of being "cited" (notified) of this proceeding—generally (but not necessarily limited to) the parties listed in Paragraphs 6(a) & 6(b) on p. 47. See footnotes on pp. 29 & 30 for a listing of the kinds of persons generally entitled to a citation.]

File No._____, 19____

CITATION (No Will)

The People of the State of New York,

By the Grace of God Free and Independent,

To:

MARY F. DOE; JOHN JAMES DOE, JR., who, as the Petitioner herein, already has notice of this proceeding and therefore need not be cited; WALLACE DOE; and DAVID DOE, a minor, being cited through MARY F. DOE, his mother.

A petition having been filed by John James Doe, Jr., who is domiciled at 18 Third Street, Bronx, New York 10436

YOU ARE HEREBY CITED TO SHOW CAUSE before the Surrogate's Court, Kings County, at the Court House, Civic Center, 2 Johnson Street, Brooklyn, New York, on _____ 19__ , at 9:30 A.M., why a decree should not be made awarding Letters of Administration of the estate of

JOHN JAMES DOE,

Deceased, who at the time of his death was domiciled at 10 Death Street, _____

Brooklyn, in the County of Kings, State of New York.

Dated, Attested and Sealed, _____ 19__ .

HON. BERNARD M. BLOOM

Surrogate.

(L. S.)

_____

Clerk.

Name of Attorney Petitioner, Pro Se. JOHN JAMES DOE, Jr. Tel. No. (212)

Address of Attorney 18 Third Street, Bronx, N.Y. 10436 (Apt. 3)

This Citation is served upon you as required by law. You are not obliged to appear in person. If you fail to appear it will be assumed that you consent to the proceedings, unless you file written objections thereto. You have a right to have an attorney-at-law appear for you.

Note.—If affidavit of service be made outside the State of New York, it must be authenticated in the manner prescribed by CPLR 2101, 2309.

Form P-18A

Note.—If affidavit of service is made outside the State of New York, it must be authenticated in the manner prescribed by Section 2309 CPLR.

AFFIDAVIT OF SERVICE OF CITATION

State of New York

ss.:

County of..

Michael Jacobs

of.... *100 Manhattan Rd., Brooklyn N.Y.* ....being duly sworn, says that he is over the age of eighteen years; that he made personal service of the within citation on the persons named below, whom deponent knew to be the persons mentioned and described in said citation, by delivering to and leaving with each of them personally a true copy of said citation, as follows:

Specify clearly time and place of service of each party served.

On the *30th* day of *January* 1994, on *Mary F. Doe* at *10 Death St., Brooklyn N.Y.* @ *10.35 a.m.*

On the.................day of...........................19...., on..............................
at..

On the.................day of...........................19...., on..............................
at..

On the.................day of...........................19...., on..............................
at..

On the.................day of...........................19...., on..............................
at..

SIGNED:
_____
Michael Jacobs (Person making service of the citation(s) on each of the parties listed in the citation - pp._____ above)

Sworn to before me on the
.... day of............... 19....

_____
(NOTARY PUBLIC)

Form P-19

Form 438-20M-70620(78) ⟨⟩ 346

Surrogate's Court, County of Kings

[Obtain one of this document from EACH of the distributees consenting to grant this waiver.]

Proceeding for Letters of Administration,

Estate of

JOHN JAMES DOE,

....

Deceased. File No..

Renunciation of Letters of Administration and Waiver of Process

The undersigned, being of full age and a distributee of the decedent above-named being related as

.........the wife..........and whose domiciliary address is..IO Death Street,................
State relationship   Street and Number

..........Brooklyn,...New York,.....................
City, Village or Town   State

hereby personally appears in the Surrogate's Court of Kings County and :

(1) renounces all rights to Letters of Administration upon the estate of said decedent,

(2) waives the issuance and service of process in this matter, and

(3) consents that such Letters of Administration may be granted by the Surrogate to any other person or persons entitled thereto without any notice whatsoever to the undersigned.

Dated :...   X Mary F. Doe...

State of..⎫
                                                                  ⎬ ss. :
County of..⎭

On...19...., before me personally came

.......................Mary F. Doe...,

to me personally known to be the same person described in and who executed the foregoing instrument, and

to me such person duly acknowledged that he or she executed the same.

_____

(Notary Public)

Form P-20

Order For Issuance of Citation upon Application for Letters of Administration

At a Surrogate's Court, held in and for the County of _Kings_, at _____, in the City of _New York_, on the _____ day of _____, 19____.

Present: Hon. _____, Surrogate.

Proceeding for
Letters of Administration, Estate of:
John James Doe,
      Deceased.

ORDER
File No._____

On reading and filing the petition of _John James Doe, Jr.,_ verified the _____ day of _____, 19___, praying for the appointment of _John James Doe, Jr.,_ as _Administrator_ of the goods, chattels and credits of _John James Doe_, deceased, it is

ORDERED that a citation issue to_____returnable on a day therein designated then and there to show cause why the prayer of said petition should not be granted and why the said _John James Doe, Jr.,_ should not be appointed _Administrator_ of the goods, chattels and credits of _John James Doe_, deceased.

_____
Surrogate (Judge)

Form P-21

Notice of Application for Letters of Administration

Proceeding for Letters of Administration,

Estate of

JOHN JAMES DOE,

Deceased.

Notice Is Hereby Given:

(1) That an application for letters of administration upon the estate of _____ JOHN JAMES DOE _____, deceased, has been made by _____ John James Doe, Jr., _____ petitioner, whose post-office address is 18 Third Street, Bronx N.Y. 10436

(2) That each and every name of the intestate known to the undersigned is: JOHN JAMES DOE; sometimes known as JOHNNY DOE.

(3) That petitioner prays that this Court awards letters of administration to John James Doe, Jr.

(4) That a decree will be made directing the issuance of letters of administration to John James Doe, Jr.

(5) That the name and post-office address of each and every distributee set forth in the petition and known to the undersigned are as follows:

(a) Distributees who have been duly *cited*, have *waived* citation, or have *appeared* in this proceeding:

Name of Distributee	*Post-Office Address*
Mary F. Doe	10 Death St., Brooklyn NY 11222
John James Doe, Jr.	18 Third St., Bronx N.Y.
Wallace Doe	10 Gregory Lane, Queens Village, New York, 11431
David Doe	10 Death St., Brooklyn, NY 11222

(b) Other distributees:

Name of Distributee	*Post-Office Address*

[Enter any other distributees who either: i) was NOT or did NOT qualify to be cited; or ii) have NOT signed a citation waiver; or iii) never responded.]

That the undersigned does not know of any other distributees of said decedent.

That letters of administration will be issued on or after the _____ day of _____, 19___.

X _____
Signature of petitioner or attorney

18 Third Street
Street Address

Bronx, N.Y. 10436
City-Town-Village; — State

Dated: _____ 19___.

STATE OF NEW YORK } ss.:
COUNTY OF }

[Name of the person serving the papers]
.... residing at 18 Third St., Bronx .... N. Y.,
[The server's address]

being duly sworn, deposes and says that deponent is over the age of eighteen years; that on
[Name of the party served]
...................................., 19___, deponent deposited in a letter box or other official depository under the exclusive care and custody of the United States Post Office Department, located at
[Address of the P.O. at which mailed]
.... a copy of the foregoing Notice of Application for Letters of Administration, contained in a securely closed postpaid wrapper, directed to each of the persons named above in Paragraph 5(b), respectively, at the post-office address indicated opposite the name of each such person.

SIGNED: X _____
(Person who serves the NOTICE paper on parties)

Sworn to before me this

_____ day of _____, 19___.

....
(Notary Public, State of New York)

[This part is to be completed later in the proceedings, ONLY when and after the above-named parties shall have been served with the documents, if required.]

Form P-22

At a Surrogate's Court held in and for the County of _Kings_, at _____ _2 Johnson Street_ _____, in the City of _New York_, on the _____ day of _____ 19__.

Present: Hon. _____, Surrogate.

Decree Granting Letters of Administration

Proceeding for Letters of Administration, Estate of: JOHN JAMES DOE, Deceased

DECREE
File No. _____

On reading and filing the verified petition of *[Name of the proposed administrator]* and a citation having been duly issued and returned with proof of due service upon all persons required by law who have not waived or appeared herein, and no objections having been filed *[or, and_____, having appeared in her proper person (or by_____, her attorney), and having filed objections and the Proofs and allegations of the parties having been heard, and the Surrogate, on_____19_____ having made and filed his decision in writing]*, and it appearing that _John James Doe_, is dead,

Now, on motion of _John James Doe Jr._, the Petitioner herein, it is

DECREED, that Letters of Administration of the Goods, Chattels and Credits which were of said. _John James Doe_, deceased, be awarded to the said Petitioner upon his qualifying and filing a bond in the sum of _____ ($_____) Dollars.

_____
Surrogate (Judge)

Chapter 7-A

Assembling And Evaluating The Estate's Affairs And Property: Phase One Of The Actual Estate Administration's Four-Phase Process

THE FOUR PHASES IN THE ACTUAL ADMINISTRATION OF THE ESTATE PROPER

As is listed below, there are essentially FOUR distinct phases in the administration and estate settling proper, of an estate. Never mind all the tedious paperwork and the seeming seriousness and importance involved in just getting an administrator appointed, or getting a will "admitted to probate" (Chaps. 5 & 6). The plain fact of the matter is this: notwithstanding all that fuss, that phase of the procedures is really only the preliminary part—in fact, the relatively less relevant or substantive part—of what your job would be all about as an executor or administrator. Hence, it is only after those preliminary formalities have been finished with that you truly get into THE ACTUAL ESTATE ADMINISTRATION OR ASSET MANAGEMENT FUNCTIONS proper.

Take a proper note of this fact first: *that whether an estate is being administered under a condition of testacy or of intestacy, the actual procedures of administering any estate does not actually differ much. In each of the two instances, the personal representative of the estate, whether he be formally called by the name "executor" or "administrator," has basically the same job: the job of assembling the decedent's assets, paying off the lawful debts and expenses of his estate, and distributing the balance, if any, to those entitled to them. The only real difference, which is really one of procedure rather than substance, is this: that in a testate situation (where a will exists), the terms of the Will generally become the executor's guide for the settlement and distribution of the decedent's estate; while in an intestate situation (where no will exists), the settlement and distribution formula would generally be those laid down by the state's Intestate Succession Laws which then become the administrator's guide for the distribution, instead.*

That part of probate which involves the actual administration and settlement of the estate, proper, fall into FOUR basic phases:
   (a) assembling and evaluation of estate property;
   (b) satisfaction of administration expenses and estate debts;
   (c) distribution of balance of estate to beneficiaries; and
   (d) formal accounting of the fiduciary's stewardship to the court and closing of probate.

For greater clarity to the reader, the procedures involved in the actual administration of the estate are organized into FOUR sub-chapters—the present chapter 7-A, and the next three sections, sub-chapters 7-B, 7-C, and 7-D. Each of these sub-chapters is devoted to one of the above-stated principal phases of the probate administration.

The presentation in every one of these sub-chapters is intended to cover the widest possible situations of frequent or potential relevance in the administration of estates. Hence, although that should be rather obvious, readers are expressly reminded that not every item listed or covered in these chapters would necessarily be applicable in the particular estate you administer; indeed, many items may not be applicable to the average estate. Frequently, determination of what may be relevant is a matter for the personal judgment of the fiduciary.

We begin below (as the fiduciary will also be expected to do) with the ASSEMBLING AND EVALUATION OF THE ESTATE. As in previous chapters, the basic format here is to list the items in an orderly, systematic order.

PHASE ONE
OF THE ESTATE ADMINISTRATION:
THE ASSEMBLING AND EVALUATION PHASE

ACTION 1: CHANGE DECEDENT'S ADDRESS, IF NECESSARY

One essential objective you (i.e., the fiduciary) should accomplish quickly is to ensure that it is you—and not an unauthorized person—that would be getting the correspondence or other messages intended for the decedent. The right course of action would depend largely on the circumstances.

If you live in the same household as the decedent, for example, or if there are still some (dependable) members of the decedent's family, say his surviving spouse or adult children, left in the decedent's house, you may leave the address unchanged and simply advise the parties to safeguard for you any correspondence meant for the decedent. In any event, if you should see a need to change the decedent's address for whatever reason, just bear in mind that getting that done is a simple matter. You may visit the decedent's local post office (the branch which covers his address) with your Letters of Appointment and fill out an 'address change' form, or you may just address a short letter to the post office to request the changeover (with a copy of your Letters attached, of course).

SAMPLE LETTER

Dear Postmaster:

I have been duly appointed executor (or administrator) of the Estate of the late Mr. _____ *(say, John Doe),* who resided at _____*(his/her address)*_____. (See copy of my court-approved Letters Testamentary/of Administration attached hereto). Pursuant to my responsibilities in this matter, please have all future messages and correspondence for the late Mr. Doe forwarded to me at this address: No. 127 Hancock St., Apt. 4, Brooklyn, N.Y. 11216.

Sincerely yours,

Signed:_____

ACTION 2: INVENTORY THE DECEDENT'S HOMEPLACE

In theory, the "proper" practice to follow in the administration of an estate calls for a search to be conducted through the decedent's residence and a detailed, painstaking inventory taken of his personal belongings and records. That's the theory of it!! It turns out, however, that as a practical matter, such in-depth inventory of the household is hardly ever undertaken in most estates, except for cases involving unusually affluent households.

As a rule, it is only personal items of high value or unique nature (such as jewelry, paintings, rare books, antiques, and the like) that get inventoried and detailed in the inventory sheet. And the balance of the household property is lumped together under catch-all categories. (An example would be to enter something like this in the inventory sheet: *"Five rooms of household furniture and furnishings estimated to value $2,000; one dining room of miscellaneous dishes and linen, and a kitchen of regular cooking utensils estimated to value $500."*)

There is no set rule or procedure. In a typical case where a decedent dies leaving a spouse or children to whom he has most probably bequeathed his property, anyway, it would obviously be ridiculous to go rummaging through every nook and corner of the house in search of items. But, in general, you should use your discretionary judgment in determining when an extensive inventory would or would not be necessary.

The format of an inventory need not be elaborate or complicated. Usually, it is advisable to have one (or more) members of the decedent's family, preferably a primary beneficiary, present while the inventory is being taken. It's enough to write (or type) out the list of the items legibly, on a properly captioned and identified sheet of paper. Upon completion of the listing, the inventory sheet must be signed and dated by each of the parties present at the inventory.

The initial caption and identifying information on an inventory sheet might read something like this:

THE ESTATE OF JOHN DOE, DECEASED

Inventory of the contents of the decedent's household, taken at:_____on this date_____, with the following persons present as witnesses of the said inventory: Edward Lewis, Executor, Mrs. Jane Doe, wife of decedent.

ACTION 3: INVENTORY THE SAFE DEPOSIT BOX, IF APPLICABLE

The procedure which you (i.e., the executor or administrator) follow here would depend largely on what your state is. Basically, for states which do not require that the box be sealed, the executor (or administrator) would be the one entitled to enter and remove the contents of the box, generally upon presentation of his Letters of Appointment. However, for states which have an inheritance tax which exceeds the federal tax credit (New York is one such state), the executor would often arrange to coordinate his entry into the box with the responsible officials of the state taxing authorities.

Under New York's procedures, for example, while an executor could merely examine the contents of a safe deposit box without presenting a tax waiver, the State Tax Commission would not release its contents to the executor, or any bank accounts (if in excess of $2,000), stocks and bonds, or the proceeds of life insurance on the decedent's life (if in excess of $20,000), unless a waiver clearing the estate of any state tax liability had first been obtained from the commission. (See footnote on p. xxx for the procedures involved in obtaining a New York tax waiver.)

In any case, as in the procedures for inventorying the homeplace (Action 2 above), all that is involved in a safe deposit box inventory is the making of as complete and descriptive a listing of the box contents as possible; credible or independent persons who observe the inventory taking should sign the inventory sheet as witnesses.

The following format will serve most purposes of the average safe deposit box inventory writeup:

ESTATE OF JOHN DOE, DECEASED

Inventory of the contents of Deposit Box No._____, kept with the Bankers Trust bank, 200 Lane St., Brooklyn, N. Y., on this date *[date of the inventory]*, with the following persons present as witnesses of the said inventory: Edward Lewis, Executor, and_____.

Cash—$900 in U.S. money, found in an envelope in decedent's top dresser drawer
Jewelry—1 silver necklace; 1 gold studded ring

Savings passbook with the Bankers Trust—passbook #4167 with a balance of $10,160 per entry made on 1/17/94

$500 U. S. Series E Bonds registered in the names of John Doe and Agnes Doe. Serial No. 4396778 due 10/96

$5,000 U.S. Treasury Bill, 5%, No, 24396778 due 10/15/95

200 shares of American Tel and Tel stock, registered in the name of John Doe, Reg. No. 2439

100 shares of IBM, registered in the name of Mrs. Jane Doe

Real Estate Deed from Richard Miller to John Doe and Jane Doe, as joint tenants with rights of survivorship, for decedent's place of residence at No. 10 Hill St., Manhattan. Note for satisfaction of mortgage dated 10/20/92 and signed by Richard Miller.

Life Insurance Policy with the Metropolitan Life Co., Policy #49876, face value of $90,000, registered in the name of John Doe. Beneficiary Agnes Doe.

Miscellaneous personal papers, including school certificates, birth and marriage certificates, and the like, representing no apparent financial value.

The undersigned hereby certify that they were present, on the_____day of_____ 19___, at the inventory of the contents of the safe deposit box described above, and that the foregoing listing is a complete, true and accurate inventory of the said box.

Signed by: 1. _____
2. _____
3. _____

ACTION 4: EXAMINE DECEDENT'S PERSONAL PAPERS, TAX RETURNS, BANK AND BROKERAGE STATEMENTS, ETC., AS APPLICABLE, FOR CLUES

It should be obvious that an executor cannot even begin to search out or to assemble a decedent's assets (much less take official control of them!) unless he knows where to look to find the assets, in the first place. So, where do you look? Well, one common source of securing good leads as to the possible nature and location of assets which might otherwise be unknown or lost to the estate, is the decedent's personal papers and records. A close scrutiny of the decedent's last or last two tax returns (copies of which are obtainable from the IRS when not available at home), would, for example, give helpful hints as to his sources of income and the nature and extent of his asset holding. Looking through cancelled checks (and other records) for the past one of two years will also be most helpful.

In general, the decedent's personal papers should indicate, or at least shed some light on, the nature and extent of assets owned by him, such as life insurance policy, retirement plans, deeds, bank accounts, etc. The same should be true for any debts owed by (or to) the decedent, evidenced by notes payable, mortgage notes, and the like.

Consider sending a short LETTER OF INQUIRY to certain selected banks or stock brokers, when warranted (see sample Form P-24, "Executor/Administrator's Letter of Inquiry," on p. 85). How do you decide whether or not you should do this, or even which institutions ought to be contacted? Simply, it should depend on what the information at your disposal suggests—from the contents of the Will, from your personal knowledge of the decedent's dealings, from your examination of the decedent's papers, from your discussions with his business associates or family members, and the like. If the circumstances should suggest the possibility, even if remote, that the decedent may have been engaged in an unfinished business, you might be better off filing an inquiry with that institution anyway.

Brokerage accounts of any type, whether of "regular" or "margin" type, should either be closed or transferred to the decedent's estate as soon as possible. Contact the stock transfer agent or the stock division of the banks or brokerage houses holding the decedent's stocks or bonds and have them send any future dividends and interests due on the securities directly to your official fiduciary address.

ACTION 5: CHECK ON EMPLOYMENT-RELATED BENEFITS PAYABLE TO DECEDENT

You (the fiduciary) should always contact the employer of the decedent, whenever paid employment is applicable to the decedent, to determine whether there are any wages, accrued vacation time pay or fringe benefits to which the decedent is entitled, e.g., life, health or accident insurance plans; retirement, pension or profit-sharing plans; stock option plans; deferred compensation or union benefits, and the like.

When a decedent has any employment-related benefits coming to him, there would likely be two main questions of relevance you'll need to address. The first one is: are the benefits to be paid to the decedent's estate, or, as is more common, directly to a named beneficiary? Basically, look to the terms of the will or the employment contract for the answer to this question.

The second likely issue would be how (in what manner or form) to take the payment so as to maximize the tax advantages on it. In general, when employment benefits are paid or payable to the employee's beneficiaries, it is the **beneficiaries** themselves that get taxed on the proceeds as in*come* to them as of the time of their receipt of the payment (except, perhaps, for that portion of the benefits, if any, which derive from the employee's own contributions, and for the proceeds of group life insurance, which, like other life insurance, are normally exempt from income tax). (Under certain special conditions provided for by the income tax law, however, up to $5,000 of certain types of employment benefits received by a beneficiary are excludable from the recipient's taxable income after the death of the employee.) Almost all employee benefits, except benefits which accrue from "qualified" plans, will be subject to the federal estate tax (Appendix D). Finally, whenever an employer takes it upon himself to make, and makes payment of the benefit directly to the surviving spouse or children of the decedent employee, the payment, particularly if relatively small in amount, may be treated as a "gift" and thus not taxable to the recipient.[1]

In general, payments received from a revocable employee trust (as opposed to those which are payable or received directly from individuals), are taxed as income. For payments made from pension, profit-sharing or stock option plans, the single most important thing to look for is this: does the particular plan fall under the "qualified" plan category under the IRS code (Section 401(a) and 403(a) of the Code)? Briefly, a "qualified" plan gets special income and estate tax advantages (principally the advantage of not being subject to the federal estate tax[2]); an unqualified plan does not.

Of importance to you, of course, is, how do you determine whether the decedent's employment benefits come under the "qualified" or "unqualified" category? There's one simple way of finding out: *don't spend even a minute of your precious time trying to figure it out yourself from the IRS code text; just go directly to the decedent's personnel officer and ask!* He should (and often does) know this information off hand. Of course, you can always talk to your tax accountant in the final analysis. (Indeed, because of the significant tax advantages associated with having a qualified plan in recent times, most "funded" pension plans and "deferred" profit-sharing plans are nearly always certain to be of the "qualified" type nowadays!!)

---

[1] In New York, any such direct payment in the amount of less than $1,000 would qualify as an exempt "family allowance" which, under the state law, would pass directly to these beneficiaries anyway.

[2] The exceptions where such advantages do not accrue, are where any portion of the employment benefits derive from the employee's contributions to the plan, and with respect to any benefits that are payable to an employee's "estate."

Form P-24

Executor/Administrator's Letter of Inquiry Concerning Assets of the Decedent

Name: *[Executor/Administrator's]*, Executor/Administrator,

The Estate of_____, Deceased

To: *[Name & Address of Brokerage, bank or other institution]*

Address:_____

Date:_____

RE: Estate of _____, Deceased

Account Nos_____

Dear Sir/Madam:

I am the Executor (or Administrator) duly appointed by the court, of the Estate of the late Mr(s)_____, who died on _____ 19___. [See copy of the court-issued Letters Testamentary (Letter of Administration) attached hereto.]

It is my understanding, and/or I have cause to believe from information and the decedent's records, that the said late Mr(s)_____, kept some accounts (the following accounts) with your bank (brokerage firm): _____.

Please confirm, in writing, the following information as they remain currently outstanding with your institution on the decedent:

1. All accounts of decedent (including every asset owned, loan or other liability owed by him).
2. Type of account (checking, savings, IRA, personal loan, mortgage, etc.); the exact name or names in which each and every account is titled
3. Date on which each account or transaction was first opened or contracted
4. Balance in each account as of this date_____
5. Name of the beneficiaries or co-owners named in the account with the decedent, if any
6. Name and account number(s) of safe deposit boxes kept by the decedent with your institution, if any

Thank you very much for taking the time to attend to this matter.

Cordially yours,

_____
Edward Lewis,
Executor, Estate of John Doe, Deceased

ACTION 6: FILE FOR DECEDENT'S SOCIAL SECURITY, VETERANS & OTHER GOVERNMENT ENTITLEMENTS OR CIVIL SERVICE BENEFITS

Under various Federal and state laws and programs, various benefits are often available to survivors of persons who worked during their lifetime. Such programs include Survivors Insurance administered federally under the Social Security Administration, the Veterans Administration Agency's veterans' insurance, and various special insurance plans for civil servants who served in local, state and national government—e.g., federal social security, medicare, medicaid, Railroad Retirement.

With respect to social security entitlements, for example, cash benefits (which could be either lump-sum or monthly, depending on the circumstances) may be paid to: 1) the dependent unmarried child of a retired or disabled worker entitled to benefits, or an insured worker, if the child is: under age 18, or age 18 or over but under a disability which began before age 18, or age 18 or over but under age 22 and attending school full-time; 2) the widow of a deceased insured worker, if the widow is 60 years of age or over; 3) the widow of an insured worker, regardless of her age, if she is caring for a child of the deceased under age 18 or disabled; 4) the dependent widower of a deceased insured worker at age 62 or over; and 5) the dependent parents of a deceased insured worker at age 62 or over.

Basically, as executor you are to see if any payments are due the decedent which have not yet been paid, and then contact the appropriate government agency to collect the payment. Applying for any of these benefits, whatever the type (or just making an inquiry about the decedent's eligibility to receive one), should be a simple matter. You only need call, write or visit the local district office of the agency which administers the program involved to get the details about the procedures for filing the necessary forms or claims application. (The addresses and telephone numbers are generally listed in the local telephone directories under the heading "Government.") Then, have the surviving spouse, or if unavailable or unable to do so, then the executor, to fill out and file the necessary application forms and follow through until the payments are received. Certified copies of the marriage certificate, birth certificates of minor children, the decedent's death certificate, and the fiduciary's Letters of Appointment, should also be attached to ensure speedier determination on the application.

ACTION 7: CHECK ON DECEDENT'S LIFE & OTHER FORMS OF INSURANCE

Life insurance proceeds are always paid (and payable) _directly_ to the beneficiary named in the insurance policy, regardless of what the Will says. When the insurance policy stipulates that the proceeds are payable to third parties other than the insured (such as to the decedent's spouse or children), such proceeds do not have to be administered or distributed by the executor; such proceeds are said to "pass outside" the decedent's probate estate, meaning _directly_ to the beneficiaries named. (Nothing, of course, prevents an executor from volunteering to help out a willing beneficiary in collecting his entitlement from the insurance company.)

On the other hand, however, the proceeds are treated as part of the decedent's estate which will then make it subject to being administered or distributed by the executor (or administrator), under any of the following situations: i) when the policy is payable to the insured person (i.e., the decedent) himself; ii) to his "estate" or "personal representative," or the "executors or administrators of the estate"; or iii) if there is no named beneficiary in the policy. And in such a case when the proceeds are to accrue to the decedent's estate, it would, of course, be the executor's responsibility to file the claims. For estate tax purposes, proceeds which are payable to persons other than the decedent or his estate are said to be "gifts" to the recipients and are not includable in the decedent's estate.[3]

---

[3]This will generally include instances when the decedent did not effectively own the policy—when he is neither the insured, nor the designated beneficiary—but was, however, the one who paid the premium. Under certain other conditions (usually when the decedent was the owner of a policy taken out on the life of another), the proceeds are includable in the decedent's estate for tax purposes, but _only_ to the extent of the "replacement value" of the premium paid (obtain the 'replacement value' figure from the company's underwriters).

How do you file claims with an insurance company? It is a fairly routine operation. All you do is call up the company or its local agent and request a complete set of the company's claims forms.[4] Upon completion, you re-submit the forms to the company (attach **certified** copies of the death certificate and your Letters of Appointment, and photopcopies of the insurance policy). Thereafter, the insurance company representative will contact you (and/or the beneficiary named in the policy) with the procedures and information for getting possession of the proceeds.

ACTION 8: COLLECT ALL DEBTS OWED TO OR DUE THE DECEDENT, IF ANY

Make all diligent search for any debts or monies that might be owed the decedent by anybody or entity. As an executor, it is your duty—and you have the legal authority—to demand such payments from any persons or entities. And if and when someone who owes the decedent won't pay up, you can seek collection remedy for that through the probate court process, or sue separately in another court to collect .

Collectible debts may include the following: monies borrowed by decedent's relatives, friends or business partners, incomes or payments due, such as royalties or dividends or interests, rental income due, tax refunds due, and so on.

ACTION 9: OPEN A SEPARATE BANK ACCOUNT FOR THE ESTATE

One strict rule governing the conduct of fiduciaries of all descriptions (whether they be executors, administrators, trustees, guardians, or what have you), is that they may not indulge in the sin of 'comingling'—i.e., the mixing of the estate funds or property with their own. An act of comingling, if it should occur, is viewed with the utmost seriousness—and suspicion—by the courts and the beneficiaries or distributees alike, and may involve the fiduciary in serious criminal penalties, aside from his being subject to a discharge as fiduciary.

Hence, one of the earliest official actions you should take as an executor or administrator immediately following your appointment, is to close out any existing bank accounts of the decedent and, in its place, open a separate account exclusively for the estate. Open the estate bank account in a bank located in the city or county in which the probate is filed. (It should be a most easy thing to get done. Which bank officer wouldn't be thrilled to land some relatively lucrative new business for his bank!? Just remember, though, to ask for one of those newer types of accounts which combine savings and checking account features together. This way, you shall have made sure that any 'excess cash' is probably 'invested' to earn income at all times for the benefit of the estate.)

Whatever estate monies you receive or come by must go into the estate account you have opened. And it is from this account that you must draw checks to pay all estate debts and expenses. As much as practicable, make all payments by checks, with all estate checks drawn or withdrawals made, signed in your official fiduciary capacity. As you proceed in the probate proceedings, keep accurate, day-to-day records and files of the financial disbursements or receipts on all amounts, big and small, and make brief notes (or keep accounting ledgers) of such transactions, where necessary. You'll need these records at the end: when it comes time to render your formal accounting to the court (Chapter 7-D).

Also, if the decedent owned any Certificates of Deposit with any banks you should also transfer them into the estate account. But, first, check on the maturity dates and the interest rates of the CD's and inquire with the bank officials about it. If there is a substantial penalty for an early withdrawal, or there is no immediate need for you to cash in the certificates in the decedent's name that are paying a significantly higher interest rate than the savings account, you may want to let the CD remain in its current status until it matures.

---

[4]You may also want to obtain IRS Forms 712 or 938, "Life Insurance Statement," at the time, for aid in filing the estate tax returns later in the proceedings. As a rule, the insurance companies will furnish you (as well as the beneficiaries directly) this form, but only if requested to do so in writing.

ACTION 10: DETERMINE WHICH ASSETS ARE "PROBATE ESTATE" ASSETS & WHICH ARE NOT

One important determination you are likely to make at some point is to determine which decedent property comes within his "probate estate"[5]— meaning that part of the decedent's total assets that is distributable according to the terms of the Will or the applicable laws of distribution. The reason this is important to you is simple: *it is the "probate" assets (and such assets only) that an executor (or administrator) is legally empowered to control and administer,* and any other assets owned or held in the name of the decedent (the 'non-probate estate') are said to "pass directly" to their beneficiaries, and hence would NOT have to pass through or be administered by the executor or the court. Thus, if you can have a good knowledge of what part of the estate you are officially responsible for administering, you will then be in a better position to plan your work, assigning greater immediacy to such assets.

Here comes the important question for you, then: **how do you determine which assets belong to the decedent's 'probate estate'?** The formula is this simple: exclude from the decedent's total estate all those properties which "pass directly" from the decedent to their beneficiaries; whatever is the remainder thereafter, is the "probate estate."

THE FOLLOWING ARE THE MAJOR KINDS OF SUCH PROPERTY WHICH 'PASS DIRECTLY' TO THE BENEFICIARIES:

A) Property With Designated Specific Beneficiaries:

i) Insurance. The proceeds of life insurance policies are ordinarily payable in the manner provided by the policies—that is, directly to whoever is/are named as beneficiaries. Unless the policy designates the decedent himself, or his estate, as the beneficiary (or no beneficiary is named or surviving), the proceeds would, therefore, NOT be includable in the decedent's probate estate.

ii) Annuities and Employee Benefits. Annuities, pension and employee benefits under varied pension or profit-sharing plans, are generally *NOT* included in the probate estate, whether the benefits are payable to the employee (the decedent) himself, or to his spouse or dependents.

iii) Social Security. Social security and pension benefits payable under federal law do not become part of the probate estate.

B) Trust Property of Various Types

Property of a trust established by the decedent in which he continued to exercise the right (or merely reserved the right) to name himself the beneficiary or trustee of the trust, or in which he continued to exercise effective control of the trust during his lifetime, would NOT be part of the decedent's probate estate (unless the trust had been terminated, or had been revoked by the decedent prior to his death).

C) Jointly-held property:[6]

'Joint tenancy' property (i.e., property held in the name of the deceased and one other person or persons) with the "right of survivorship" provisions, pass directly to the remaining surviving joint owner or owners. A variety of assets, such as stocks, bonds, bank accounts, savings and loan accounts, are often held in this manner. When real property is likewise held in joint names by a married couple, it is called "tenancy by the entirety." When two or more parties—who are usually, but not always, married to each other—hold title to a real or personal property, but *without* the survivorship provision, then ONLY that *undivided* ownership share that belongs to the decedent becomes "probate estate" property, while the undivided share belonging to the surviving parties remains theirs.

---

[5]NOTE: that the term decedent's "probate estate" is different from his "gross estate,'" and the two should not be confused. Gross estate is relevant essentially in federal and state estate tax assessment situations, and certain property rights and items owned or controlled by a decedent during his lifetime may be treated as part of the decedent's "gross estate" for tax purposes,while not being includable as part of his "probate estate." (See Appendix D on pp. 200-2 for more on the composition of the "gross estate".)

[6]NOTE that while jointly-held property in marital situations can pass direct to the beneficiary (i.e., to the surviving spouse), it is taxed *entirely* to the estate of whichever is the second spouse to die, and not at all to the estate of the first spouse to die.

D) "Set Off" Or "Exempt" Property For Family

Most states provide for certain property left by a decedent to be set aside to provide "minimum" support for his family during the duration of the settlement of the estate.[7] Whenever such property 'set off' is provided for under the state's estate laws, such property passes *directly* to the surviving family members and does not become part of the probate estate.

E) Property Which The Decedent May Have Owned Only A Share Or Percentage Of

Just that share or part of a property which the decedent owns, is 'probate estate'—e.g., his specific partnership interest in a company; or in a property held in a "tenancy-in-common" ownership arrangement. The other share or part which the decedent does not own in such situations goes *directly* to the other surviving co-owners.

F) Decedent's Share Of Marital Property In A Community Property State

Only one-half of any such property, if any, which are marital community property in the nine community property states, qualify as the decedent's probate estate. The 9 applicable states are: Arizona, California, Idaho, Louisiana, Nevada, New Mexico, Texas, Washington and Wisconsin.

[For more on the kinds of property which form the "probate estate," see also Section D of Chapter 1, at pp. 12-13, titled "Non-Probate Property: Certain Property of the Decedent That Do Not Go Through the Probate Process"].

ACTION 11: TERMINATE ALL UNNECESSARY EXPENSES BEING INCURRED BY THE ESTATE

If warranted by the circumstances (say, for example, that no adult member of the decedent's family continues to live in the decedent's residence), you should contact the utility companies and have the lights, telephone, cooking or heating gas supply, etc., terminated or transferred to a survivor's name. This should be done as early as practicable. It's probable that the decedent may have left a deposit with the utility companies; such should, of course, be reclaimed for the estate.

If the decedent lived in a rented house or apartment, it is advisable that you make efforts to inventory the household property and warehouse it rapidly (or distribute it to the beneficiaries); if family members would continue to occupy the accomodation, you should have the lease and rental charge transferred to their names right away.

All accounts or contractual obligations for which no clear need or benefit now exists for continued retention, such as checking accounts, charge accounts, credit cards, and the like, should be closed out forthwith to save the estate from further interest charges and expenses.

In instances where the insurance policies being paid for by the decedent had been taken out on a property (an automobile, a house, etc.) which now passes directly to a survivor through joint tenancy, you should arrange to cancel (or merely transfer) the decedent's policy—preferably, after having advised the surviving beneficiary to acquire his own insurance and allowing him reasonable time to do so.

An automobile, even when parked away and left unused, is one property that not only loses value rapidly through its depreciation, but is also capable of running up expenses or involving an estate in unpredictable traffic difficulties with the law. If a car is left behind by the decedent, you should make a rapid determination regarding its disposition—if specifically willed to someone, transfer the title to the beneficiary's name as soon as you are able to determine that the balance of the estate would be solvent; if it's a part of the general ("residuary") estate, put it up for sale and get cash for it right away.

---

[7]For New York, for example, such exempt property (to which only the decedent's surviving spouse and children under age 21 are entitled under the state's law), includes the following: all housekeeping items up to $5,000 in value; certain books, family items and cash not exceeding $1,000 in value; and domestic animals, farm machinery, one motor vehicle and one tractor, not exceeding $5,000 in value.

ACTION 12: GET ADEQUATE INSURANCE COVERAGE ON ESTATE PROPERTY, WHERE NECESSARY

One very important obligation of an executor (or administrator) is to manage and safeguard the estate assets with the utmost prudence—with the kind of prudence that would ordinarily be expected of a reasonable, prudent businessman or woman. Fiduciaries who fail to live up to this standard may generally be held personally liable in the courts by the estate beneficiaries or creditors.

Hence, where warranted by the nature of the estate assets, and where adequate funds are available to meet the premium payments, it may not be prudent to let a pre-existing insurance coverage lapse; or, perhaps, it may even be advisable that an entirely new policy be taken out where none had existed before. It's all a matter for you, as executor, to use your best judgment to determine.

First, determine whether an insurance coverage is both necessary and financially feasible for particular estate assets. And if it is, then you must ensure that such assets are adequately covered—both, that is, in terms of the variety of the coverage you buy (casualty and liability, theft, fire, collision/comprehensive, storm, flood, or what have you), and in terms of the variety of assets you cover (real and personal property, jewelry, rare or antique objects, automobiles, etc.).

Assuming an estate property is half-way "insurable" by normal insurance carrier standards, getting a company to issue you an insurance policy on any amount desired should be a very simple matter. Just about all you have to do is call a reputable insurance company (with your check for the premium charge ready, of course!) and the company's salesmen and policy experts will take it from there.

ACTION 13: DETERMINE WHAT TO DO WITH THE DECEDENT'S BUSINESS, IF APPLICABLE

If the decedent owned a going business or was a principal partner in one, a decision would need to be made either to continue it, or to liquidate or sell it. In New York, as in almost any other state, there would be no real problem for the executor where there is a will which gives such executor power to sell assets and specific instructions on whether to continue or to dispose of the testator's business.

When the decedent makes no such provisions in his will, however, or where he leaves no will at all, the decision on the fate of the business is the executor's to make, based generally on the surrounding relevant circumstances at the particular time.

To begin with, a good deal of the choice of what to do with the business would depend, usually, on the particular legal structure of the decedent's business: i.e., on whether it is a "sole proprietorship," or a "partnership," or a "corporation." If it's a sole proprietor (i.e., a business which is owned by only one person, in this case the decedent), then it is the decedent's estate that automatically becomes the owner of the assets of the business and is responsibie for its debts. And, generally speaking (indeed, unless otherwise provided for in the will), a sole proprietorship business is usually liquidated as soon as practicable; this way, you are more likely to realize the maximum market value for the business, especially where the decedent was the key person without whom the daily management and operations of the business would not be practicable.

Now, if the decedent's business is a partnership—defined, for our purposes here, as one owned by more than one person—and the capital invested by the decedent, and/or the personal services he provided is the primary income-producing factor for the company, the Partnership is, by most rules of law, usually terminated on the death of the partner. The surviving partners are then required (under most partnership agreements and the general rules of law) to liquidate the business and make an accounting to the estate of the deceased partner. However, if the decedent's will or partnership agreement should provide against discontinuation, or if the decedent's estate or beneficiaries are able to strike up a mutual agreement for a different arrangement, the executor may have still other options.

For businesses which are a corporation, the general considerations which go into choosing whether it should be sold or continued are based on two main factors, among others: i) if the personal services the decedent provided the company were the primary income producing factors behind the company's operations, a sale at his death is often desirable; ii) if, on the other hand, the primary income producing factor for the company was the capital investment provided the company by the decedent, continuation of the business may be preferable, so long as continued competent management can be assured. When the corporation involved is of the "closely held," "one man" or "family" corporation type—that is, a corporation in which the decedent is the sole stockholder or the controlling stockholder—the corporation continues as a separate entity after the decedent's death, but becomes, in effect, a property of his estate.

Here are some helpful steps for an orderly handling of the administration of a decedent-owned business:

a) If the decedent left a will, follow the specific instructions in the will, if any, on whether to liquidate, sell or continue the business.

b) Examine the Partnership Agreement or the Buy-Sell Agreement (for corporations), if any. And if there are provisions therein for having the surviving partners or stockholders buy the decedent's business interest in the event of death or resignation, those provisions should generally be followed.

c) Contact the officers and managers of the business; attempt to allay any concerns they may entertain as to the fate of the business or their own futures in it. Designate competent and reliable persons to take charge of running the company's operations, even if for a short period.

d) If warranted by the circumstances, change or tighten up the internal company rules for financial control; require that any monies paid out on behalf of the company (say, for amounts in excess of certain magnitudes), may now have to be authorized or countersigned by you or your designated representative, for example.

e) If seemingly warranted, have the officers and employees bonded against potential theft or mismanagement.

f) If the decision is to continue the business, one major difficulty the business is likely to encounter, as customers and creditors typically hold back with caution at first (especially if the decedent is the key man in a proprietorship or family enterprise situation), is this: shortage of the necessary liquid funds to tide the business over the initial period of uncertainty. More often, though, a more urgent reason for needing liquidity might be to pay the administration expenses (especially the family's living expenses) and estate taxes,[8] as applicable.

If you can find the money to pay these out of other assets of the estate, it would be great. But if you can't, the cash may have to be taken out of the business, where possible.

g) If the decision is to discontinue or sell the business, the best market may be found within the business itself—the surviving partners of the decedent, his fellow stockholders through an employee stock ownership or exchange plan, a corporate pension plan, if any, or possibly a family foundation, etc.

And what's the price to sell? The general rule is to use the 'fair market value' criteria as the test of the acceptable price to sell: defined as the net amount which a willing buyer would pay to a willing seller for an item. For publicly traded securities, the fair market value is easy to determine—it's the stock market quotation on the stock; for stocks of a closely held corporation or interest in an unincorporated business, the price at which a business is sold within a reasonable time after the owner's death will usually be accepted as establishing its true value—provided the sale is an "arm's length" transaction (i.e., a genuine, bona fide sale that is neither "forced" nor based on obviously unreasonable terms, say rushed sale made to the sons of a deceased owner.)

---

[8]NOTE: There are two ways you may possibly look into (or ask your tax accountant) by which you may pay taxes out of the business without having to impair its capital: i) Redemption of stock. Under the so-called "Section 303 redemption" rule of the IRS code (it's concerned with making a distribution in cash or property by a corporation to its shareholders out of its earnings but for the specific purpose of paying estate taxes), the estate can, in effect, take the tax money out of the surplus of the corporation without incurring the usual level of income tax liability. Briefly, the applicable rule is that if the value of the decedent's stock exceeds 50% of the value of his "adjusted gross taxable estate," the stock can be redeemed without it being considered a dividend—which is usually taxed at a higher rate to stockholders as ordinary income. The stock redemption is limited, however, to the extent by which the amount received does not exceed the taxes, funeral, and administration expenses incurred. ii) Installment Method. Usually the Federal estate taxes, when applicable, must be paid within 9 months after the death of the estate owner. But under this special provision of the tax laws, the executor is permitted to pay that portion (and only that portion) of the federal tax which is attributable to the value of the business interest in up to 10 annual installments, *providing* that the value of the business interest exceeds 35% of the value of the gross taxable estate or 500% of the value of the net taxable estate. Any balance of the tax for anything beyond the value of the business interest would still be payable within the regular 9 months. The installment provision is available to all types of business structures in which: a) the decedent's capital interest or voting power is not less than 20%; or b) there are 10 or fewer partners or stockholders.

ACTION 14: HAVE THE ESTATE PROPERTY APPRAISED

An important duty of the executor, which logically comes after he has identified and assembled the assets comprising the decedent's estate, is to put a value on the assets assembled. Aside from any other uses, asset evaluation is generally necessary for tax purposes; whether an estate will be liable for an estate tax, and what the amount of tax will be, will depend largely on the assessed value of the "taxable estate." [Procedures for estate taxation are set forth in Appendices D & E.]

But, even more importantly, making sure to obtain a written valuation and appraisal of the assets owned by the decedent as of the date of his (or her) death is regarded as one of the most significant functions the executor must acccomplish for this reason: this is necessary in order to establish, in writing, a new "cost basis" (evaluation) of the estate assets as a basis for substantiating a new "stepped up" cost basis of the assets to the IRS when you or the inheritors eventually sell the property.[9]

Do you have to get an official appraiser appointed by the court to do the evaluation, or do you do it by yourself? It all depends. Basically, what to do would depend on two factors: i) on the nature of the assets involved, and ii) on the rules followed by your local court (get this information from your local court clerk). While the courts of certain states reserve to themselves the exclusive right to appoint the appraisers, others permit the executor (or his representative) to suggest persons to be appointed by the court. And yet many others allow the executor the exclusive right to appoint the appraisers. New York's methods fall under the last category; the appointment of an official appraiser to value all assets in the estate is not required.

The following steps are recommended in the appraising of estate assets:

i) If your jurisdiction is one that permits the executor either to suggest an appointee for the appraiser's job or to make the appointment himself, just make sure you pick only those persons with established professional reputation and competence. (Professional estate appraisers, who may do the evaluation for a fee, are listed in your local telephone directory under the heading "Appraisers.")

ii) Determine whether a formal appraisal is at all necessary in the first place, depending on the kind and quantity of assets comprising the estate. (Inquire with the court clerk.) When formal appraisal is necessary, sort out those properties on which you can place a value yourself and differentiate such property from those which should be assigned to expert appraisers to appraise.

iii) To save the estate some appraisal fees (which can often run into considerable sums even for modest-sized estates), determine[10] the values yourself for those assets whose values are readily ascertainable (e.g., listed stocks or bonds, whose value can be ascertained from a stock broker or from price quotations in the newspapers; personal property such as household furniture or automobiles; and even real property[11]). Then employ (or merely consult) an expert appraiser to determine the value of only that property which is of specialized nature (e.g., works of art, jewelry, stamp or coin collections, antiques, business interests, and the like).

---

[9]A "stepped-up" cost basis for an asset enables you (the inheritor) to keep the value of the asset at the same amount, thus minimizing the taxable gain attributable to the asset for months, or possibly years later, when the property is eventually sold. Thus, the written valuation provides a valid documentation for the asset's current market value for determining stepped-up valuation.

[10]The formal rules for determining the values of assets (at their 'fair market values') are outlined in the form for the federal Estate Tax return (IRS Form 706) and the instructions which accompany that return. This form, which is obtainable from your local IRS office at no charge, should be readily consulted in your valuation work.

[11]For real estate valuation, you may call upon a local realtor or real estate broker in the same neighborhood. A notarized statement (an "affidavit") from a licensed broker in the area in which the property is located will generally suffice with most courts; the realtor gives his valuation of the property based on what an equivalent property sold for within the recent past, the probable repair cost, tax assessment values by local property tax authorities, etc. And, to obtain the current market value of financial securities (stocks, bonds, etc.)., simply look up the price quotations in the newspaper on or near the date of death. Then, put the newspaper page bearing the price quotation (the whole page with the date thereof intact) in your estate settlement file. Or, alternatively, simply get a written note from a licensed stock broker, listing the price quotation for the securities as of the date of death.)

ACTION 15: GET A TAX IDENTIFICATION NUMBER; FILE THE DECEDENT'S AND THE FIDUCIARY'S INCOME TAX RETURNS

A. The Important Thing To Worry About As An Executor

True, as an estate executor or administrator you are responsible for seeing to it that the decedent's final federal and state and local income and estate taxes are filed, as applicable. BUT HERE'S THE PRACTICAL ADVICE ON WHAT TO DO: *do not get yourself lost in the fancy details of the mechanics and arithmetic of estate tax preparations and filings.* There are many many other functions you can better devote your energies to as executor. Rather, you should better concern yourself with two aspects that are, in this author's view, of more fundamental and actual relevance to the tasks required of you as an executor: namely, the question of determining whether the estate involved is of such size and value as to require having a tax return filed, in the first place; and, secondly, having a broad overview of the principles involved and the essentials to look for in estate taxation.

The point to be made here is that, as a practical matter, the mechanics of physically preparing the necessary tax return forms for an estate is a fairly simple and routine matter—certainly far less complex or involved than you might ordinarily be led to think. For one thing, other than Form 706, (the U.S. Estate Tax Return), which is agreed by almost all to be the most complex of all the estate tax returns, the tax return forms involved in the average estate case are fairly easy and straightforward to complete. All you generally need do is follow carefully the explicit instructions given in the IRS "publication" and "Instructions Booklet" which come with the forms, and you shouldn't have much trouble completing the returns. Secondly, IRS tax accountants and tax return preparation experts frequently stand ready to figure out the tax liability (or tax credits) for you on request. But even most importantly, the point is that you have a better option other than to physically prepare the tax forms yourself; you should, rather, just do what many executors/administrators and most practicing estate attorneys do, anyway: simply hand over the returns to a professional tax accountant to complete for you for a modest fee!!

Here, therefore, we'll concern ourselves not so much with the mechanics of physically filing out the estate tax returns, but with the broad overview of what to concern yourself with, the general principles and procedures governing estate taxations.

B. Getting A Tax I.D. Number & Filing The Decedent's Income Tax Returns

Every estate (or trust) must have an "employer identification number" (also known as the "tax identification number"). The significance of this number is that once obtained, it is the number that the executor (or administrator) would use for the purposes of identifying the decedent's estate in his filing of IRS Form 1041 (the Fiduciary Income Tax Return) for the estate. Getting this number assigned to you is a simple matter: just obtain Form SS-4 from the IRS office, which you fill out and resubmit to the IRS and they'll assign you the number. (A separate employer ID number is required for each estate and each trust, where applicable.)

For the moment, in this section, we shall address only the "income"-oriented category of taxes that may have to be filed for (or be payable by) the decedent or his estate. [The other category of taxes, such as the federal estate or state death taxes, will be treated in the next section, under ACTION 16].

There are principally two income type of tax returns (or tax payments) that are most relevant to you as an estate executor or administrator. They are:

    i) IRS Form 1040; and
    ii) IRS Form 1041

i) Form 1040—This is the Federal return required to be filed with the IRS on the decedent's behalf for his (the decedent's) own personal tax return for his last year of life (as differentiated from the return for the income of his estate, which is Form 1041). The return simply covers the decedent's income, if any, *for that portion of his last year up to the date of his death.* The tax rates, forms, and due dates are exactly the same as those for personal income taxes.

Now, as the executor of the estate, you should note (and also explain that to the surviving spouse, if applicable) that the surviving spouse has a right still to file a JOINT income tax return (Form 1040) for that year in which the spouse died, if the couple were usually filing joint returns prior to the decedent spouse's death. He (she) should also be told to be sure to keep strict record of the decedent spouse's last medical and funeral expenses, as those expenses can be deducted from the surviving spouse's own taxable income, and the funeral expenses deducted for estate tax purposes.

ii) Form 1041—This return is to be arranged by the fiduciary to be filed with the IRS (usually after the decedent's final Form 1040 had earlier been filed). A decedent's estate becomes a separate, independent taxable entity of its own upon the death of the decedent. Hence, this return (U.S. Fiduciary Income Tax Return or IRS Form 1041) is meant to cover the tax due on the income earned by the decedent's <u>estate</u>, if any income was so earned. The returns (one for the state and another for the federal) are required of just about every estate, big or small.[12] You have the option, as an executor or administrator, to elect to file this either on a fiscal year basis, or to file for the balance of the year of death and for subsequent calendar years.

The forms for each of the required final tax returns are readily obtainable from a local IRS office. [See "How To Get IRS Forms and Publications" on p. 207]. As stated above, the completion of these particular forms are essentially an uncomplicated and routine affair. Just about all you would have to do to do a good job of it is to follow the official instructions in the booklet which accompanies the forms. Or, alternatively, as suggested above, the easiest course would be to simply turn the matter over to a tax accountant, preferably the one who prepares the decedent's income-tax returns, for a nominal fee, payable out of the estate, or you may consult with a tax return preparation assistant at an IRS district office. Helpful necessary data for the filing of the return could be gathered from examination of the decedent's prior tax returns, cancelled checks, and the like.

ACTION 16: FILE FOR THE FEDERAL ESTATE & STATE DEATH OR INHERITANCE TAXES, IF APPLICABLE

As an estate executor (or administrator), another type of taxes you are also responsible for in seeing to its payment, where applicable, are the federal estate tax and "death" taxes imposed by states (state estate and inheritance taxes).

These taxes, and the filing of the tax returns for them, are more fully discussed in Appendices D & E. For the present discussion, we shall only enumerate the principal taxes in the category for which the returns should be filed, as applicable, and/or the taxes paid. They are:

(i) Federal Estate Tax—Form 706, "U.S. Estate Tax Return," would have to be filed with the IRS, but only if you (the executor) determine that the decedent's "gross estate"[13] at the time of his death, is in <u>excess</u> of $600,000 for a single person, or in excess of $1.2 million for a married couple. If and when it is large enough to require the filing of this form, then it must be filed within 6 months of the death, and any taxes due must be paid within 9 months.

This form (IRS Form 706) is, in truth, a lengthy and highly complex tax return—the most forbidding of all estate tax forms.[14] The good news about it, though, is this: you don't even have to file it, if there is no federal estate tax payable; no Form 706 is necessary, if no estate tax is owed or payable! *(Caution:* whenever you are to find that the filing of this form is applicable, hire a tax accountant and let him handle it; this is one instance when it would be advisable and worth your getting a professional help!) One relatively inexpensive option would be to seek the services of a tax consultant or accountant, or a tax return preparation assistant at an IRS office.

---

[12]In strict terms, the specific requirements are that this form (Form 1041) is to be filed if: 1) the estate has a gross annual income in excess of $600; or 2) if it has a beneficiary who is a non-resident alien.

[13]See Appendix D at pp. 200-2 for more on what and what comprise the "gross estate" and how it is defined or calculated.

[14]Here's an idea of the complexity of Form 706: with its various supporting schedules, it is over 30 pages long; the official instructions for completing it are 22 pages long, and the IRS publication 448, "Federal Estate and Gift Taxes," is about 40 pages long.

ACTION 17: FILE INVENTORY AND APPRAISEMENT REPORT WITH THE COURT

There are two occasions during probate proceedings when the decedent's estate is required to be evaluated for tax purposes: first, when it is evaluated for the purposes of filing the Federal Estate tax return, and second, when it is done for filing the state tax return. Aside from these, however, it is not unusual—in fact, it is usual—for the executor to find that he would probably have to file other valuation or "inventory" reports with the probate court [usually at the preliminary stages of the proceedings, say at the time the first application is made to probate the will or administer the estate, or within a stipulated time (60 days is usual) from the date of the executor's appointment .

When there are such additional preliminary valuations of the estate assets required in a case, such valuations are usually an approximation; as a rule, later valuations (say for tax purposes) may develop a higher or lower value, or may remain unchanged.

If the court in your jurisdiction requires a non tax-related preliminary valuation, just prepare a comprehensive inventory of the estate assets using the format developed from ACTION Items 2 and 3 above ("Inventory of Decedent's Homeplace" and "Inventory of the Safe Deposit Box," respectively), and the values developed from ACTION Item 14 above (" ... Estate Property Appraised").[15] The courts of some localities do supply the official forms for filing the necessary inventory report, when required.

---

[15]NOTE that the "non-probate estate" assets (jointly held property, life insurance proceeds, pension benefits, and the like) may either be segregated in the listings, or completely excluded, with a clear notation made therein to that effect.

Chapter 7-B
PHASE TWO OF THE ADMINISTRATION PROCESS: PAYING OFF ADMINISTRATION EXPENSES & ESTATE DEBTS

After the estate fiduciary has collected the estate assets together and inventoried them (the subject of the preceding sub-chapter 7-A), the next phase of the probate administration work is the *PAYMENT* phase—the paying of the debts and obligations of the decedent or his estate, if any.

The following steps are recommended for an orderly handling of this phase of the administration by the fiduciary. **As much as possible, these steps should be followed in the order in which they are listed below:**

STEP 1: GIVE NOTICE TO CREDITORS TO PRESENT CLAIMS

Almost every jurisdiction requires that a "notice" of some sort be given to the creditors of a decedent, to inform them of the probate proceedings and invite claims, if they have any. In each instance, the basic purpose is identical: namely, to give the creditors (or potential claimants) a fair opportunity to present their claims so that they can at least be considered for possible payment. In practice, the only things that vary with different states are the nature and method by which such notice is required to be given, and the time limits within which creditors must present their claims to the executor.

New York's procedures (discussed in details herein for the purpose of illustrating the general practices) are typical. The state's time limit within which the creditors are to present their claims to the executor, is seven (7) months from the date of the issuance of the Letters of Appointment to the fiduciary. This is the time limit applicable in situations where the fiduciary does not publish the notice. Where publication is used, however, this time limit is shortened to three months—from the date of the first publication.

After the allowed time limit—seven or three months, as the case may be—has run out, the fiduciary is considered legally released from any *personal* liability to any creditors who have not filed claims; he may, thereafter, make "good faith" payments to creditors who have filed valid claims by that time and distribute the balance of the estate to the beneficiaries of the estate.[1]

Under New York's rules, a published notice to creditors is merely permissible but is not mandatory. As a practical matter, because of the extra trouble and expense often involved in giving the notice by means of publication, this method of giving notice to creditors is generally not commonly used in most states, including New York. However, for those who may, for whatever reason, wish to go the publication route, we give below the court procedures as done under the New York State practice.

---

[1]NOTE: Ordinarily, a fiduciary is not obligated to go to extraordinary lengths to flush out a decedent"s claimants or creditors. Nevertheless, he is said to have a "minimal responsibility" to look for claimants in the first place, and to know of those who presumptively should be known. Hence, fiduciaries should, when possible, examine the books of the decedent's business, inquire with relatives, employees and associates, as to claimants or debtors known to them. And when potential claimants are known, such persons should be sent notices even merely as a sign of "good faith."

NOTE: Experience has, nevertheless, shown that unless a fiduciary who is to make use of the publication method is prepared to file with the court the initial petition for publication *immediately* after the Letters are granted, it would serve a better practical purpose, anyway, to just wait out the 7 month period and forget about making a publication.

To serve notice by the publication method, you must first apply to the court for an order giving you authorization to do so. Forms designated by the following titles (and often obtainable from the court clerk's office) are to be completed and filed with the court clerk: **i)** *"Petition for Designation of Newspapers in Which to Publish Notice of Creditors."* [see a sample Form P-25 on p. 99]. **ii)** Either *"Notice to Creditors to Present Claims"* [see a sample Form P-26 on p. 99] or *"Notice of Appointment, Notice To Creditors & To Unknown Heirs"* [see a sample Form P-27 on p. 100]; and **iii)** *"Order Designating Newspapers in Which to Publish Notice to Creditors."* [see a sample Form P-30 on p. 102].

When the judge signs the Order (Form P-30), meaning that the publication is authorized to be done, you immediately contact the newspaper he designates in the order and have the editor insert the notice in the paper once a week for *3* consecutive months.

Creditors who wish to file claims of whatever kind with the fiduciary, would do so in writing (sample Form P-28 on p. 101, *"Claim Against Estate,"* may be used for this). And with certain types of claims, you may use your discretion to require a sworn affidavit from the claimant certifying that the claim is justly due, and that it had not been previously paid. (Sample Form P-29 on p. 101, *"Affidavit In Support of Claims Against Estate,"* may be used by creditors for this.)

Whenever you are faced with a disputed claim for or against the estate, you must bear in mind that **you have an option—and the power, under the law—to make a reasonable judgment thereof as to either go through a court litigation for it, or to compromise the claim.** When you allow a claim in any instance, you are to give notice of such allowance to the claimant (sample Form P-31 on p. 102, *"Notice of allowance of Claim,"* may be adapted for this). If you reject a claim, in whole or in, part, you must also give a written notice of the rejection to the claimant *promptly* (adopt sample Form P-32 on p. 103), *"Notice of Rejection of Claim,"*), or the claim will be considered an allowed claim. Furthermore, Notices of Rejection are required to be "served" by mail on each claimant involved, and *promptly* too. (An Affidavit of Service may be reqired by the court to be filed for each notice mailed, as written proof showing that each party was actually served.)

Any objections to the rejection of claims (which happen to still remain unresolved by you in the end) are reserved to be given a final determination and settlement by the court—usually, during the time of the fiduciary's final accounting to the court.

STEP 2: PAY OUT CLAIMS ACCORDING TO A PROPER ORDER OF PRIORITY

Every claim of whatever kind, whether they are for funeral, medical, administrative, tax, creditors' claims or what have you, are claims which must be filed with and confirmed to the executor before it could ever be paid. As soon as the claims have been properly assembled, the executor evaluates each and every one regarding its validity and amount. Their legitimacy established, the claims may be paid off as rapidly as the availability of funds permits. However, **before you (the executor) make any payments, there's one rule you must first follow: be careful to follow the appropriate "order of priority"** *among the creditors.* Fundamentally, though, this rule is really relevant only with respect to instances where the assets of the estate do NOT look comfortably *adequate* to meet the known claims against the estate.[2]

New York's prescribed order of preference for paying off claims and debts, is typical of the applicable order in almost every other state:

i) Funeral expenses, cost of administration and cost of the decedent's last illness. These are all said to be "pre-existing and superior obligations" which are entitled to first priority satisfaction. Note that the attorney's fees , as well as the executor's or administrator's commissions, are classified among administration expenses. So, unless you elect to "waive" a fee for your services as an executor, you might as well make sure you yourself get paid for your services at the appropriate time![3]

Under the laws of just about every state (see Appendix A), an estate executor or administrator is entitled to a fee or commission for the services he or she renders on behalf of the estate. He (she) may, however, voluntarily "waive" (give up) that right to the fee, or to a part of it. As a rule, executors who are also the principal or substantial beneficiaries of an estate usually waive the executor's fee, as they figure that the property is coming to them, any way. One disadvantage of collecting a fee under such a circumstance, is that you'll then have to pay income tax on it; however, if on the other hand, you were to collect the pay-out in the form of estate distribution as a beneificary, you'll collect it totally free of income tax.

ii) Debts owed to Federal and state governments or agencies—estate and inheritance taxes, income taxes. and the like. (State and Federal estate tax computation procedures are in Appendices D & E, pp.198 + 204. Where the estate taxes are required by the terms of the will, or by the state law, to be apportioned to certain beneficiaries, such payments should be charged against the respective inheritance shares of the parties.)

iii) Next in the order of priority are **taxes assessed on the decedent's property** prior to his death.

iv) Judgments and decrees awarded against the decedent come next, subject to the priority of each of them to the others.

v) General debts—i.e., the recognized debts and obligations of the decedent, come last.

Whenever you pay off any claims (or settle or dispose of them in any other way), make sure you obtain an appropriate voucher or a *notarized* release from the parties paid or otherwise settled (sample Form P-33 on p. 103, *"Release upon Payment of Claims/Distribution by Fiduciary,"* may be adapted for this). Make all money payments by check, and promptly make a notation in the check book (or in a ledger) for each check drawn, giving information about the purpose for which payment was made. (You'll

---

[2]As a practical matter, where the size of assets is clearly sufficient to meet all legitimate claims, the issue of following a special order of priority in satisfying claims is irrelevant. It wouldn't matter in such circumstances who you pay first (or even whether you waited out the statutory 7-month period or not before making payments), since everybody's claim would ultimately be satisfied anyway!

[3]Get the rates of the fiduciary's **commission** for your jurisdiction and the basis on which it is to be computed from your local court clerk's office. To get your commission money for the executor's commission (or for the attorney's fee) for services rendered—the amount is usually set by law or based on a percentage of the probate estate handled—you will often have to pay or allow yourself the commission and then report the payment (accurately) in your final accounting to the court. Or, as is done in a fewer number of jurisdictions, you would file the usual application ("petition") with the court requesting an order allowing you the fee. See Appendix A for each state's commission rate information.

Form P-25

Petition For Designation Of Newspapers In Which To Publish Notice To Creditors To Present Claims

SURROGATE'S COURT: COUNTY OF_____

> In the matter of the Petition of
> _David Edwards,_
> as Executor of _John James Doe,_
> Deceased, for an Order to Designate
> Newspaper(s) in Which to Publish Notice
> to Creditors to Present Claims

PETITION
File No._____

TO THE SURROGATE'S COURT,   COUNTY OF_____

The petition of _David Edwards,_ residing at _15 Probate St.,_ County of _New York_ State of New York, respectfully states upon information and belief:

1. _John James Doe_ died on _Jan 10, 1994,_ a resident of the county of _New York,_ State of New York, leaving a Last Will and Testament dated _Dec 2, 1993,_ which was duly admitted to probate by the Surrogate's Court of _New York_ County, on_____, 19___. Letters Testamentary thereon were issued to petitioner on_____, 19_____.

2. There are no other persons than those mentioned hereinbefore who have an interest in this application or proceeding.

WHEREFORE, petitioner prays for an order of the Surrogate of _New York_ County designating the newspapers in which to publish Notice to Creditors of said deceased, to present their claims, according to law.

Dated:_____19____

X_____
                                    Petitioner
                                    P.O. Address

[Verification]   SWORN TO BEFORE ME
on this _____ day of _____, 19____.

Form P-26

Notice To Creditors To Present Claims

Pursuant to an order of Hon._____, Surrogate of the County of _____, dated_____, 19____.

NOTICE is hereby given, according to law, to all persons having claims against _John James Doe,_ late of the City of_____, County of _New York,_ to present such claim(s), with the vouchers thereof, to the undersigned, Executor of the Last Will and Testament of said _John James Doe,_ at the office of the said _Executor_ herein, at No. _15 Probate Street,_ City of _New York,_ on or before the _____ day of _____ 19 ___.

Dated: _____ NY ____ 19___

Signed: _____
Executor of the Last Will and Testament of:
Estate of _John James Doe_
P.O. Address _19 Probate St, NY, NY._
Tel No. (enter)

Form P-27

Notice Of Appointment, Notice To Creditors & To Unknown Heirs'

TO ALL PERSONS INTERESTED IN THE ESTATE OF _____, Deceased.

Notice is given that _____ was on _____*(date)*_____ appointed personal representative of the estate of _____, who died on _____ (with) (without) a Will.

There was a prior small estate proceeding *(Delete last sentence if inapplicable)*
Further information can be obtained by reviewing the estate file in the office of the Register of Wills or by contacting the personal representative or the attorney.

All persons having any objection to the appointment (or to the probate of the decedent's will) shall file their objections with the Register of Wills on or before the _____ day of _____ 19___.

[The above paragraph should be deleted where the initial appointment of a personal representative is made under judicial probate]

Any person having a claim against the decedent must present the claim to the undersigned personal representive and file it with the Register of Wills, with a copy to the undersigned on or before the earlier ot the following dates:
(1)   Nine months from the date of the decedent's death; or
(2)   Two months after the personal representative mails or otherwise delivers to the creditor a copy of this published notice or other written notice notifying the creditor that the claim will be barred unless the creditor presents the claims within two months from the mailing or other delivery of the notice. A claim not presented or filed on or before that date, or any extension provided by law, is unenforceable thereafter. Claim forms may be obtained from the Register of Wills

_____

_____

Personal Representative

True Test Copy

Name and Address of Register of Wills for

_____

_____

Name of newspaper designated by personal representative_____
PUBLISH THREE TIMES

Form P-28

Claims Against Estate

SURROGATE'S COURT: COUNTY OF_____

[Add title of proceeding]

File No._____

To *[name of personal representative]*, Executor under the Last Will and Testament of _John James Doe_, deceased.

You are hereby notified that there is due to me from the estate of _John James Doe_, deceased, the sum of _____ ($_____) Dollars, for goods sold and delivered and services rendered as follows:

[concisely state facts forming basis of claim].

Dated:_____, 19____

[Signature of Creditor]

[Address of Creditor]

Form P-29

Affidavit In Support of Claim Against Estate

SURROGATE'S COURT: COUNTY OF_____

[Add title of proceeding]

AFFIDAVIT
File No._____

STATE OF NEW YORK
COUNTY OF_____

_____, being duly sworn, deposes and says:

1. That I reside at _____County, State of_____

2. That the annexed claim against _John James Doe_, Deceased, is just and true, and that the several claims for goods sold and delivered and for services, rendered therein charged for were actually delivered and furnished to the said _John James Doe_.

3. That I know of no offsets and of no evidence of indebtedness.

4. That no part of said claim has been paid, and the full amount thereof in the sum of _____ ($_____) Dollars is now actually due and owing to the deponent.

5. That I hold no security.

Signature: _____

[Type Name of same Deponent beneath]

Sworn to Before me, this_____day of_____ 19_____.

Form P-30

Order Designating Newspaper(s) In Which To Publish Notice To Creditors To Present Claims

At a Surrogate's Court, held in and for the County of_____ at_____, in said County, on the_____ day of_____ 19___.

Present: Hon._____, Surrogate.

[Add title of proceeding]

ORDER
File No._____

An application having been made by petition of _David Edwards_, Executor of the estate of the above named deceased, duly verified on the_____ day of_____, 19___, praying for the designation of newspapers in which to publish notice to creditors to present their claims against the estate of said deceased, it is

ORDERED, that the said executor insert a notice once in each week for 3 consecutive months in the following newspapers published in the County of_____,_[specify names of newspapers designated]_, and requiring all persons having claim against said deceased, _John James Doe_, to present the same to the petitioner, care of _David Edwards_, at No. _15 Probate Street_, County of _New York_, State of New York, on or before a day specified in said notice, which shall be at least 3 months from the date of first publication of the said notice.

_____
Surrogate (Judge)

Form P-31

Notice Of Allowance Of Claim

SURROGATE'S COURT: COUNTY OF_____

Probate proceeding, Estate of: _John James Doe_,
Deceased.

File No._____

PLEASE TAKE NOTICE that the undersigned, Executor of the Last Will and Testament of _John James Doe_, the above named decedent, does hereby admit and allow your claim against of the estate of said decedent, dated_____ 19___, in the sum of_____ ($_____) Dollars for _[specify nature of claim]_.

Dated:_____, 19___

Signed:_____
Executor of the Last Will and Testament of:
John James Doe, deceased

To: _[His/Her name & address]_
Claimant

Form P-32

Notice of Rejection of Claim

SURROGATE'S COURT: COUNTY OF_____

[Add title of proceeding]
RE: Estate of <u>John James Doe</u>,
                  deceased

File No._____

PLEASE TAKE NOTICE, that the undersigned, Executor of the Last Will and Testament of the above named decedent, hereby rejects your claim against the estate of said decedent dated _____, _____, in the sum of _____ ($_____) Dollars *[state nature of claim]*, for the following reasons: *[state reasons for rejection, e.g., claim has already been paid, statute of limitations bars claim, etc.]*.

Dated:_____, 19___.

Signed:_____
                          Executor of Last Will and Testament of:

                         _____

To: *[enter his/her name & address]*
    Claimant

Form P-33

Release Upon Payment of Claim or Distribution by Fiduciary

RELEASE

KNOW ALL MEN BY THESE PRESENTS, that I, [claimant's name], for and in consideration of the sum of _____ ($_____) DOLLARS, duly paid and delivered to me by [executor's name], Executor of the Last Will and Testament of [decedent's name],Deceased, the receipt of which is hereby acknowledged, do hereby remise, release and forever discharge the estate of said [decedent's name], Deceased, his heirs, executors and administrators, of and from all causes of action, suits and liabilities whatsoever, arising out of the certain claim against the estate of said [decedent's name], Deceased, for all goods sold and delivered during the period _____, 19___ to _____, 19___, duly presented to said executors by notice of claim dated _____, 19___.

IN WITNESS WHEREOF, I have hereunto set my hand and seal on this ____ day of ____ 19___

(Acknowledgment) (TO BE NOTARIZED)

Signed:_____
                        Type same claimant's name
                           beneath line)

Chapter 7-C

PHASE THREE OF THE ESTATE ADMINISTRATION PROCESS: DISTRIBUTING THE BALANCE OF THE ESTATE TO BENEFICIARIES

DISTRIBUTION OF THE ESTATE ASSETS

After the executor or administrator has paid off or otherwise settled the financial obligations of the estate (the subject of the preceding Chapter 7-B), the next phase of business for the executor (or administrator), is *DISTRIBUTION*—to distribute the balance of the decedent's estate (if any), to those entitled to them.

The following systematic steps are recommended to the fiduciary in order to guard against the possibility of making payments or distributions that may later need to be returned to satisfy some prior claims:

ITEM 1:

As soon as you can see your way clear enough to be able to determine when the making of distributions is likely to be commenced, notify the beneficiaries of your plan to make distributions. Do so by a brief letter, or by personal contact or conversation, depending on what is convenient or what is the state's legal requirements on this, if any.

Basically, you'll officially inform each person of his or her inheritance entitlement, and request the parties to expect distribution at an appointed date, time, and place to which you invite them to assemble.

ITEM 2:

As a general rule—unless you have otherwise absolutely ascertained that sufficient estate assets will remain to meet all estate obligations and legacies—you should withhold paying out any legacies, at least until the period specified by your state's law for filing and proving claims has elapsed (7 months in New York).[1] This way, you will be protected from the possibility of personal liability to some yet unknown creditors or beneficiaries who may possibly show up later. [See the required time period to wait for in your state in Appendix A].

ITEM 3:

If the decedent died testate (i.e., leaving a Will), examine the contents of the will closely; the directions in it for disposition of assets should be your basic guide for deciding who should get what item. If, on the other hand, the decedent died intestate (i.e., without having left a will), turn to the law governing intestacy distribu-

---

[1]We presume here, of course, that all the outstanding debts and obligations of the estate shall have already been satisfied earlier.

tions in the decedent's state; that should be your basic guide for deciding who should get what in the estate.[2] (Summary of intestacy laws for all states in the Union are outlined in Appendix B, pp. 178-192).

ITEM 4:

As discussed in an earlier section of the manual (see "What is a spousal 'right of election'?" in Section K of Chapter 1 at p. 17), under the laws of various states, the widow (or widower) has what is known as the "right of election"—that is, the right *either* to accept what is given to her under the terms of the will, *or, alternatively,* to "elect" (choose) to take that distributive share which the law says a spouse may take in place of the will's share.[3] (Election usually becomes a possibility where a surviving spouse feels that the inheritance the Will provides him/her is less than he/she would have gotten had the testator died without a will.)

Should the issue of election arise in the estate you handle, first check your state's statutes (see Appendix C) to determine whether or not the right of election is applicable therein, and if so, the alternative shares permissible to the surviving spouse may be given. Then, in order to make the election, you are to have the spouse file a written election application with the probate court within the time specified under the state law. As a rule, election must be indicated and officially filed with the court within the time specifically prescribed under the law, and failure to do so within that time results in permanent loss of the the surviving spouse's right to take in place of the will.

ITEM 5:

In making distributions governed by the terms of a will, the pay-out order of priority is to *pay out the* **"specific"** *legacy or bequest provisions first, before paying out the* **"general"** *legacies or bequests—that* is, to first pay out those gifts which are designated in specifically identified property.[4]

What happens if a testator designates a specific legacy to a beneficiary but the beneficiary dies before the death of the testator, or the beneficiary is, in some way, incapable of taking under the will (say, because it was lost or destroyed, or the testator sold it or otherwise disposed of it before death)? Then, in such a case, the legacy is said to **"lapse"**—i.e., to fail because it can no longer be exercised by reason of the decedent's death. In such a case, providing the testator expressly provides for alternative treatment in the event of such a contingency, the bequest is satisfied out of the "residue" of the estate. Thus, for example, the children of a designated beneficiary who predeceases the testator may simply be substituted as the takers of what the testator has attempted to give the deceased legatee.

But, here's a slightly different situation—the case of an **"ADEMPTION."** An ademption is a removal or extinction of a legacy by the testator, a taking away. In the case of an ademption, the testator removes the legacy or withdraws its disposition by some act clearly indicating an interest to revoke it, say, by the testator deliberately giving away the devised property during his life to another person, or the existence of attendant circumstances that render it impossible to effect the transfer of payment as directed by the will. In other words, in this situation, *the decedent's intent* would be the controlling factor. In the case of a gift deemed to be "adeemed," the named beneficiary is not entitled to any other property from the estate in place of the specified legacy. For example, suppose a testator provided in her will, "I give and bequeath my 1993 Cadillac Deville to my daughter Jane," but a few months later, before she died and after making her will, the testator had an open disagreement with Jane and sold the car or gave it away to a second daughter. That gift to Jane would be deemed "adeemed"—intentionally removed or taken away with apparent intent to revoke the legacy!

General legacies or bequests (i.e., gifts payable out of the estate assets, but for which NO specific property or assets was designated in the will) should be paid <u>second</u>, after the specific ones have been paid.

---

[2]NOTE: In certain states, the administrator of an intestate estate would first have to file a formal "petition" with the court for an Order to Determine Heirs, before he may physically distribute the assets to beneficiaries.

[3]Another variant of this is the right of dower or curtesy, whereby the spouse may elect between the share taken "by dower or by curtesy," on the one hand, and a certain distributive share, or intestate share on the other hand. The statutes of those states which allow dower or curtesy—the states are few in number—provide which share shall be taken in situations when an election is not made. See Appendix C for a listing of the states which still maintain the rights of dower or curtesy.

NOTE, however, that in many instances where a spouse is named as the beneficiary of a trust under the terms of a will, the surviving spouse would also lose her right to the trust property—if she elects to take against the will.

[4]A provision in the will, such as this Will, will suffice "I bequeath my 1993 Cadillac Deville to my daughter, Jane, and in the event that she does not survivie me, then to her chidren, and in the event that the bequest is unavailable at the time, then an alternative equivalent property should be provided her out of my residuary estate."

(As a rule, if it had been necessary to use or liquidate bequeathed assets to meet estate expenses or the decedent's debt obligations, general legacy items shall have been the first to be applied.)

Even within the general legacy category, you should also differentiate between two basic types of property in making pay-outs: between those legacies that are named as to amount, and those that constitute the remainder of the estate assets thereafter (the so-called "residuary" legacies). *General legacies which are designated as to specific amounts are first satisfied before the residuary legacies.*

ITEM 6:

On occasion, a disagreement may arise among beneficiaries over who is to get what specific tangible items. (This possibility is often more likely where there is more than one beneficiary who is entitled to share in non-specific bequests or the residue of an estate under the terms of a will.)

If you should have a disagreement among your beneficiaries or distributees, you should always seek to compromise. (Or, alternatively, you may simply sell the residuary items at their fair market values and apportion the cash to beneficiaries as a part of the balance of the estate.) *Negotiation and amicable agreements among the parties (where achievable), spares you, as well as the beneficiaries themselves, the possibility of time-consuming, costly rounds of hearings before a judge that could well eat up the assets at issue in the end.*

> NOTE: As with most jurisdictions, including New York, it is to the court that any disputes or unresolved issues over claims are reserved for eventual settlement "as justice shall require." Typically, the objecting party (say, a beneficiary who objects to his distributive share of the estate, or a creditor who contends that he has not been paid) would formally file a protest petition with the court (and serve a copy of same on the fiduciary) asking for an opportunity to present his objection on the occasion set for the fiduciary to render his judicial settlement or "accounting"—a meeting before the surrogate judge, at which the estate fiduciary renders an accounting of his stewardship. The judge would then set a hearing on the protest petition at which he would hear the evidence presented and then attempt to determine the rights of the objecting parties. Only after that—after the objections shall have been satisfactorily decided upon and settled by the judge—would the court sign the final order discharging the fiduciary from his term of office.
>
> *NOW, THEN, HERE'S THE POINT: if you can get your creditors and distributees to cooperate and to accept your disposition of the estate (preferably by having them give you a notarized statement of their consent to the distribution), you would not have to go through a hearing. In deed, you may not even have to submit to an accounting, for, in such instances, the court would often sign the final decree without requiring such formalities!!*

ITEM 7:

Whenever you make distributions, make sure you obtain proper receipts from the recipients. Or, if distribution is for money, always make payments by check and retain the cancelled check as a receipt. You could simply type or write up a voucher (a form note or letter) with a sufficient description of the items distributed and have it signed by the respective recipients. For certain persons, you may consider obtaining a written, notarized release from them for distributions you make to them (Form P-33, *"Release Upon Payment of Claim/Distribution by Fiduciary,"* sampled on p. 103, may be adapted for this purpose.)

For distributions to a distant or out-of-town beneficiary, the bequest could be more safely delivered to the beneficiary through the local bank of the decedent's estate to its correspondent bank in the beneficiary's locale. Then, proper instruction will be given for the correspondent bank to obtain necessary receipts from the beneficiary before the inheritance is released to him or her.

NOTE: If your distributees include any minors (under 18 for New York, and no more than 21 for any state), or persons who are legally disabled or incompetent, you must distribute their entitlements not directly to them,but through their guardians. Such guardians, where one is necessary, shall have been appointed by the Court earlier in the proceedings—usually at the initial petition stage for the probate of the will or appointment of an administrator. (Procedures for obtaining Letters of Guardianship from the court are in Appendix F.)

Chapter 7-D

The Fourth And Final Phase Of The Estate Administration Process: Making Final Accounting To The Court

ACCOUNTING TO COURT

The fourth phase—and final duty—of the fiduciary in probate administration in most jurisdictions, is the ACCOUNTING phase—to make an "accounting" of his stewardship as the estate fiduciary and file a report of it with the court.

Each state prescribes the specific printed forms for rendering the required accounting to the court, but the forms are generally alike in their essence, with necessarily the same basic data frequently required. In general, such forms call for summary statements of all estate assets which came under the control or management of the fiduciary, of assets sold, claims and administration expenses paid, and the amounts already distributed or to be distributed to those entitled to the residuary estate. A complete set of the typical forms used under New York's procedures is made available to its readership by ***Do-It-Yourself Legal Publishers*** (see p. 239 for the ordering information). Readers could either order the accounting forms alone, or as part of the package of the initial probate petition forms.

Here are the typical "accounting" procedures under New York's court requirements:

STEP 1: You Obtain, Complete & Submit The Proper Accounting Forms To The Accounting Court Clerk

The required forms, under the New York system, are:

i) Form P-34, at pp. 110-2, **"Account of Proceeding of Exectutors/Administrators"**—to be signed and notarized by the fiduciary involved. New York's procedures call for one type of Account form to be used for an estate WITH a trust provision involved, and a slightly different type for one WITHOUT a trust provision.

ACCOUNT OF EXECUTORS/ADMINISTRATORS form for an estate *WITH* a trust is reproduced on pp.110-2; it is fully filled out in the manual (along with the applicable schedules) for the purposes of giving the readers a fairly standard sample illustration. A sample copy of an Account form for an estate WITHOUT a trust provision is reproduced blank and uncompleted on pp. 129, for the readers' added overview.

An important integral part of the Account form are the matching **"Schedules"** which the fiduciary must prepare (or, for a nominal fee, have his accountant prepare for him) to go with the form. The SCHEDULES (see pp. 113-9) are, simply, a detailed elaboration and item-by-item breakdown of the "SUMMARIES" (the total figures) contained in the account form (p. 110 below). You simply follow the account form [pp. 110-2 (or, pp. 129-131, if a non-trust estate)], and systematically prepare each schedule to match with the respective schedule headings therein, supplying in each schedule the information called for by the "instructions" set forth for that schedule.

    i) Form P-35, **"Petition for Voluntary Accounting,"** to be signed and *notarized* by the fiduciary (or fiduciaries). (Sample preparation of this form is on pp. 120-2).

    ii) Form P-36, **"Citation/Notice (of Accounting)"**—sample preparation of this form is on p. 123 .Leave back of the form blank, and complete that part, the "Affidavit of Service" part, later when service of the citation (where required) is completed.

    iii) Form P-37, **"Affidavit of of Regularity,"** to be signed and *notarized* by the fiduciary. (Sample preparation of this form is on p. 124).

    iv) Form P-38, **"Waiver (and Consent) to Citation":** one original could be signed and *notarized* by all "interested persons" to the accounting proceeding who approve of or at least do not wish to object to the fiduciary's work (the clerk will help you determine such persons). (Sample preparation of this form is on p. 125.)

    v) Form P-39, **"Decree (Order) Settling Account of Executor/Administrator,"** prepare and leave for the signature of the judge, if petition is approved. (Sample preparation of this form is on p. 126).

    Fill out, as well, the last or back page of this form—captioned *"Notice of Settlement,"* reproduced at bottom of p. 128)

NOTE THE FOLLOWING:

1) When a will provides for a TRUST—i.e., when the testator makes a provision that some designated property shall be set aside and managed for the benefit of a designated person(s)—it is generally the executor of the estate who bears the responsibility for accounting for both the segregated trust assets (the principal as well as the income), and the balance of the estate (the non-trust assets). And this is still so, whether it is the executor himself or some other different person that is appointed by the testator to serve as the administrator ("trustee") of the trust.

    Hence, in rendering an accounting for an estate with trust provisions, a careful distinction is made in the accounts, differentiating between transactions that are applicable to the principal (same as the 'corpus') of the trust, and those that are applicable to the income (and expenses) from such assets as of the date of the decedent's death. Hence, as could be seen from the sample accounts forms (especially the "Summary" sections, pp. 112 and 113 respectively), *the executor's account is modified slightly when a TRUST is involved, primarily with regard to differentiating between the principal and the income parts in the summaries and schedules.*

2) You have, of course, just as much right to choose to prepare by yourself each and every one of the papers required in the formal accounting. Generally, the instructions contained in the official forms used for the accounting are detailed and explicit enough that anyone who simply follows those instructions can usually assemble the necessary accounting figures and supporting data to complete the forms and their matching "schedules." And if you are in the habit of doing your own tax return, you'll probably enjoy making up these accounts schedules by yourself, anyway.

    You ought to know, however, that as a practical matter, this is one job most executors or administrators—as well as the probate lawyers alike—would rather not do themselves; traditionally, such persons assign the preparation of the final accounting papers to estate accountants, the recognized specialists in this aspect of probate, for a relatively nominal fee. *So, be aware of the fact that when in need, you may just do what the lawyers do: have an accountant take care of these final papers for you!!*

STEP **2** : SERVE ACCOUNTING CITATION ON PARTIES, IF NECESSARY

Upon your filing the above papers with the surrogate's court clerk, the clerk then sets a date for a "hearing" to be held on your accounting petition—i. e., a date for the fiduciary's formal presentation of the accounting report in court. The clerk will also approve the fiduciary's NOTICE ("citation"), and issue copies of the document to the fiduciary for service to be made on all interested persons, such as creditors, legatees, next of kin, etc. [Those whose claims or bequests may have been granted or settled, or those who may have signed Form P-38, the *"Waiver of Citation"* paper for the fiduciary (Item IV in "Step 1" above), may not need to be served with this citation.]*

The fiduciary then gets the citations served on the parties, as required, and files the Affidavit of Service with the clerk.

*NOTE that most distributions, especially the 'general' bequests of set dollar amounts and legacies of specific items, are almost always paid and satisfactorily settled long before the formal accounting. Hence, in most accountings, it is usually those who are either entitled to the residue of the estate or have not yet been paid, that have any real need for a formal notice of the accounting since it is they, more than other parties, who need to have an opportunity to appear in court and register their displeasures, if any.

STEP **3** : ATTEND THE COURT ACCOUNTING HEARING

On the date set by the court for the formal accounting hearing session, the fiduciary makes his appearance as directed. Now, if any legitimate objections have been registered with the court by any interested person(s) by this time, the judge will hold a hearing to determine the merits (or demerits) of the objecting parties' claims.

Typically, however, no objections shall have been raised or filed. *In the vast majority of cases, especially if involving small and medium-sized estates, all interested distributees and creditors shall have signed a statement—the "Waiver to Citation" form—generally agreeing to the stewardship of the fiduciary.* In such instances, where no valid objections[1] to the accounting exist, the court may dispense with the accounting requirement entirely; it would generally sign the decree (see Form P-39) granting the executor or administrator the payment of his fiduciary commission and discharging him from further responsibilities on behalf of the estate.

With the court's signing of its decree of discharge, you may finally go home and rest assured in satisfaction of a job well done. And a well deserved congratulations at that, too!!

> **NOTE,** finally, that in estates with trust provisions, it will be the executor's moral (though not necessarily legal) obligation to see to it that the person designated as the trustee files a petition with the court for Letters of Trusteeship—usually when the assets of the trust are ready for segregation, which may be before or after completion of the administration of the estate. This way, upon securing his letters of trusteeship, the trust assets would be turned over to the trustee for his continued management in accordance with the terms of the trust.

---

[1]"Valid objection" grounds for which a fiduciary's accounting may be rejected by the court, would generally be a breach of the fiduciary's duties, or an improper distribution or expenditure (e.g., a finding by the court that an administrative expense for which the fiduciary has been credited was an improper one). In instances of such a finding, the court would reject such expenditures or distributions and direct that a proper one be made. Additionally, the fiduciary may also be held personally liable for a breach of duty.

Form P-34

Form 37-A

16961-75 (C.S.) ➝ 94

Uniform Form of Account

ACCOUNT FOR EXECUTORS WHERE TRUST INVOLVED
SURROGATE'S COURT — COUNTY OF NEW YORK

ACCOUNTING OF

David Edwards,

as Executor

File No. _____ 19___

ESTATE OF John James Doe,

Deceased

TO THE SURROGATE'S COURT OF THE COUNTY OF NEW YORK:

The undersigned does hereby render the account of proceedings as follows:

Period of account from (date?)

to (date?)

This is a final account.

The instructions concerning the schedules need not be stated at the head of each schedule. It will be sufficient to set forth only the schedule letter and heading.

For convenience of reference, the schedule letter and page number of the schedule should be shown at the bottom of each sheet of the account.

PRINCIPAL
Schedule A
Statement of Principal Received

INSTRUCTIONS. This schedule must contain an itemized statement of all the moneys and other personal property constituting principal for which each accounting party is charged, together with the date of receipt or acquisition of such money or property. If real property has been sold by the executors, this schedule must set forth the proceeds of sale of such property.

Schedule A-1
Statement of Increases on Sales, Liquidation or Distribution

INSTRUCTIONS. This schedule must contain a full and complete statement of all realized increases derived from principal assets whether due to sale, liquidation, or distribution or any other reason. It should also show realized increases on new investments or exchanges. In each instance, the date of realization of the increase must be shown and the property from which said increase was derived must be identified.

Schedule B
Statement of Decreases Due to Sales, Liquidation, Collection,
Distribution or Uncollectibility

INSTRUCTIONS. This schedule must contain a full and complete statement of all realized decreases on principal assets whether due to sales, liquidation, collection, or distribution, or any other reason. It should show decreases on new investments or exchanges and also sales, liquidations or distributions that result in neither gain nor loss. In each instance, the date of realization of the decrease must be shown and the property from which said decrease was incurred must be identified. It should also report any asset which the fiduciary intends to abandon as worthless, together with a full statement of the reasons for abandoning it.

Schedule C
Statement of Funeral and Administration Expenses Chargeable to Principal

INSTRUCTIONS. This schedule must contain an itemized statement of all moneys chargeable to principal and paid for funeral, administration and other necessary expenses, together with the date and the reason for each expenditure.

Where the will directs that all inheritance and death taxes are to be paid out of the estate, credit for payment of same should be taken in this schedule.

Schedule C-1
Statement of Unpaid Administration Expenses

INSTRUCTIONS. This schedule must contain an itemized statement of all unpaid claims for administration and other necessary expenses, together with a statement of the basis for each such claim.

Schedule D
Statement of All Creditors' Claims

INSTRUCTIONS. This schedule must contain an itemized statement of all creditors' claims sub-divided to show:

1. Claims presented, allowed, paid and credited and appearing in the Summary Statement, together with the date of payment.
2. Claims presented and allowed but not paid.
3. Claims presented but rejected, the date of and the reason for such rejection.
4. Contingent and possible claims.

5. Personal claims requiring approval by the court, pursuant to SCPA 1805.

In the event of insolvency, preference allowed various claims should be stated and the order of their priority.

Schedule E
Statement of Distributions of Principal

INSTRUCTIONS. This schedule must contain an itemized statement of all moneys paid and all property delivered from principal to the legatees, trustees, surviving spouse or distributees of the deceased, the date of payment or delivery thereof, and the name of the person to whom payment or delivery was actually made.

Where estate taxes are required to be apportioned and payments have been made on account of said taxes, the amounts apportioned in Schedule H against beneficiaries of the testamentary estate shall be charged in this schedule against the respective individual's share.

Schedule F
Statement of New Investments, Exchanges and Stock Distributions

INSTRUCTIONS. This schedule must contain an itemized statement of (a) all new investments made by the executor with the date of acquisition and cost of all property purchased, (b) all exchanges made by the executor, specifying dates and items received and items surrendered; and (c) all stock dividends, stock splits, rights and warrants received by the executor, showing the securities to which each relates and their allocation as between principal and income.

Schedule G
Statement of Principal Remaining on Hand

INSTRUCTION. This schedule must contain an itemized statement showing all property constituting principal remaining on hand, including a statement of all uncollected receivables and property rights due to the estate.

INCOME

Schedule A-2
Statement of All Income Collected

INSTRUCTIONS. This schedule must contain a full and complete statement of all interest, dividends, rents and other income received, and the date of each receipt. Each receipt must be separately accounted for and identified, except that where a security has been held for an entire year, the interest or ordinary dividends may be reported on a calendar year basis.

Schedule C-2
Statement of Administration Expenses Chargeable to Income

INSTRUCTIONS. This schedule must contain an itemized statement of all moneys chargeable to income and paid for administration, maintenance and other expenses, together with the date and reason for each such expenditure.

Schedule E-1
Statement of Distributions of Income

INSTRUCTIONS. This schedule must contain an itemized statement of all moneys paid and of property delivered out of income to the beneficiaries, the date of payment or delivery thereof and the name of the person to whom payment or delivery was actually made. If more convenient, distributions of income to any one beneficiary may be reported, by the calendar year.

Schedule G-1
Statement of Income on Hand

INSTRUCTIONS. This schedule must contain a statement showing all undistributed income.

Schedule H
Statement of Interested Parties

INSTRUCTIONS. This schedule must contain the names of all persons entitled as legatee, devisee, trustee, surviving spouse, distributee or otherwise to a share of the estate or fund, with their post-office addresses and the degree of relationship, if any, of each to the deceased, a statement showing the nature of and the VALUE or approximate VALUE of the interest of each such person.

Also a statement that the records of this court have been searched for powers of attorney and assignments and encumbrances made and executed by any of the persons interested in or entitled to a share of the estate and a list detailing each power of attorney, assignment and encumbrance, disclosed by such search, with the date of its recording and the name and address of each attorney in fact and of each assignee and of each person beneficially interested under the encumbrance referred to in the respective instruments, and also whether the accounting party has any knowledge of the execution of any such power of attorney or assignment not so filed and recorded.

Schedule I
Statement of Estate Taxes Paid and Allocation Thereof

INSTRUCTIONS. This schedule must contain a statement showing all estate taxes assessed and paid in respect of any property required to be included in the gross estate of the decedent under the provisions of the Tax Law or under the laws of the United States. Final New York Estate Tax receipt or an order of exemption from tax must be presented with the decree settling the final account unless the accounting party proceeds under S C P A 1804(3). This schedule must also contain a computation setting forth the proposed allocation of taxes paid and to be paid and the amounts due the estate from each person in whose behalf a tax payment has been made and also the proportionate amount of the tax paid by each of the named persons interested in this estate or charged against their respective interest, as provided in E P T L 2-1.8.

Where an allocation of taxes is required, the method of computing the allocation of said taxes must be shown in this schedule.

Schedule J
Statement of Computation of Commissions
INSTRUCTIONS. This schedule must contain a computation of the amount of commissions due upon this accounting.

Schedule K
Statement of Other Pertinent Facts and of Cash Reconciliation
INSTRUCTIONS. This schedule must contain a statement of all other pertinent facts affecting the administration of the estate and the rights of those interested therein. It must also contain a statement of any real property left by the decedent which it is not necessary to include as an estate asset to be accounted for, a brief description thereof, the gross value and the amount of mortgages or liens thereon at the date of death of the deceased. A cash reconciliation must also be set forth in this schedule so that verification with bank statements and cash on hand may be readily made.

SUMMARY

The following is a summary statement of ___John James Doe's___ Estate ___ account:

PRINCIPAL ACCOUNT

CHARGES:

Amount shown by Schedule "A" (Principal received)	$229,715	
Amount shown by Schedule "A-1" (Realized Increases on principal)	$ 69.00	
Total principal charges		$ 229,784

CREDITS:

Amount shown by Schedule "B" (Realized decreases on principal)	$ -0-	
Amount shown by Schedule "C" (Funeral and administration expenses)	$ 6,569.55	
Amount shown by Schedule "D" (Creditors' claims actually paid)	$ I,520.63	
Amount shown by Schedule "E" (Distributions of principal)	$ 207,7I5	
Total principal credits		$ 2I5,805.I8
Principal balance on hand shown by Schedule "G"		$ I3,978.82

INCOME ACCOUNT

CHARGES:

Amount shown by Schedule "A-2" (Income collected)	$ 22,865.53	
Total income charges		$ 22,865.53

CREDITS:

Amount shown by Schedule "C-2" (Administration expenses)	$ -0-	
Amount shown by Schedule "E-1" (Distributions of income)	$ 22,865.53	
Total income credits		$ 22,865.53
Balance of undistributed income remaining on hand as shown in Schedule "G-1"		$ -0-

COMBINED ACCOUNTS

Principal remaining on hand	$ I3,978.82
Income remaining on hand	$ -0-
Total on hand	$ I3,978.82

The foregoing principal balance of $ I3,978.82 consists of $ I3,978.82 in cash and $ -0- in other property on hand as of the ?? day of ____ ??, 19 ??. It is subject to deduction of estimated principal commissions amounting to $ II,I05.98 shown in Schedule J, and to the proper charge to principal of expenses of this accounting. -0-

The foregoing income balance of $ -0- consists of $ -0- in cash and $ -0- in other property on hand as of the ?? day of ____ ??, 19 ??. It is subject to deductions of estimated income commissions amounting to $ -0- shown in Schedule J, and to the proper charge to income of expenses of this accounting.

The attached schedules are part of this account.

SIGNED: X ____

Executor

AFFIDAVIT OF ACCOUNTING PARTY

STATE OF NEW YORK }
COUNTY OF } ss.:

being duly sworn, says: that the foregoing account contains according to the best of my/our knowledge and belief a true statement of all my/our receipts and disbursements on account of the estate and of all moneys or other property belonging to the estate which have come into my/our hands or been received by any other person by my/our order or authority for my/our use and that I/we do not know of any error or omission in the account to the prejudice of any creditor of, or person interested in, the estate.

Sworn to before me this..day of

_____ 19........ X

_____

(Notary Public)

_____

Page One (of Schedules)

Schedule A
Principal Received

Item	Date	Source	Amount/Value
1.	1/25/94	Emigrant Savings Bank Acct. #2055-24	$155,400
2.	1/25/94	Hamilton Savings Bank Acct. # 174601	$ 40,600
3.	2/4/94	Amalgemated Life Ins. Co.	$ 5,519
4.	2/4/94	Jewelry Appraisal	$ 8,591
5.	2/10/94	Cash on hand	$ 4,105
6.	2/10/94	1993 Chevrolet Impala	$ 9,500
7.	2/10/94	100 Shares of General Motors Corp. Stock	$ 6,000
			$ 229,715

Note: This statement is exclusive of all assets and property deemed to be non-estate items, such as jointly-held real property, decedent's personal household effects, and the like.

Schedule A-1
Increases of Sales, Liquidation or Distribution

Date	Item	Gain/Loss
2/15/94	Sale of Jewelry	+ $69.00
	Total	$69.00

Schedule B
Decreases Due to Sales, Liquidation, Collection, Distribution or Uncollectibility

N O N E

Page Two (Schedules)

Schedule C
Funeral & Administrative Expenses Chargeable to Principal

Item	Paid to	Purpose	Amount
1.	Niebey Chapel	Headstone for plot	$1,000
2.	Niebey Chapel	Funeral expenses, decedent	300
3.	Beth Daniel Cemetery	Perpetual Care	600
4.	Robert Blaikie & Co.	Bond 12/21/93-3/21/94	400
5.	Surrogate's Court	Probate filing fee	100
6.	Fiduciary Income Tax	1993	700.88
7.	Fiduciary Income Tax	1994	1,500.73
8.	Bureau of Vital Records	Death Certificate	12.50
9.	Surrogate's Court	Filing Bond	40.50
10.	Prudential Savings Bank	Safe Deposit Box entry fee	42.50
11.	Surrogate's Court	Filing box opening petition	7.00
12.	Beth David Cemetery	Filing Fee	4.00
13.	S.A. Holston	Jewelry Appraisal	25.00
14.	Surrogate's Court	Copy—Letters Testamentary	6.00
15.	Executor	Tolls & gasoline—1994	154.29
16.	Bank of New York	Service Fees	202.00
17.	Michael I. Kessman, CPA	Preparation of Fiduciary Tax Returns	300.00
18.	New York State	Fiduciary 1993	102.26
19.	New York State	Fiduciary 1994	161.89

$6,569.55

Page Three (Schedules)

Schedule C-1
Unpaid Administration Expenses

Proposed Payee	Purpose	Amount
David Edwards	Executor's requested commission per computation in Schedule J below.	$11,105.98
	Total:	11,105.98

Schedule D
All Creditors' Claims

1. Claims presented and paid:

   A. Rent due on apartment maintained by decedent in NY City 12/93-1/94 (Rumal Realty Co.) $665.63

   B. Funeral bill for prior deceased daughter, Pauline Doe 855.00

2. Claims presented but not paid: NONE .... -0-

3. Claims presented but rejected: NONE .... -0-

4. Contingent and possible claims: NONE .... -0-

5. Personal claims requiring Court approval pursuant to Section 1805 of SPCA: NONE

TOTAL: $1,520.63

Schedule E
Distributions of Principal made

Item	To Whom Distributed	Date	Amount/Value
Cash	David Edwards, as Trustee, for trust fund under terms of Article 6 of decedent's Will	1/17/94	$80,000
Cash	John Doe Jr., decedent's son, per terms of Will	2/24/94	20,000
1993 Chevy Impala	John Doe Jr.	2/24/94	9,500
100 Shares Gen. Motors Stock	David Edwards, legatee under Will	2/24/94	6,000
Cash	Mary F. Doe, for David Doe, a minor legatee son	2/24/94	15,000
Cash	Bernard Jones, testamentary legatee	2/24/94	1,000
Cash	George G. Fuller, testamentary legatee	2/24/94	1,000
Cash	Mary F. Doe, surviving wife	2/24/94	75,715
			207,715

Note: Estate taxes are not required to be apportioned; they are to be paid out of the estate.

Page Four (Schedules)

Schedule F
New Investments, Exchanges & Stock Distributions

N O N E

Schedule G
Principal Remaining On Hand

Cash on hand in Bank of New York, Acct. #PA-616-133125 $13,978.82

TOTAL: 13,978.82

Schedule A-2
Statement of All Income Collected

Interest collected on principal on deposit in Estate checking-plus account #PA-616-133125 in the Bank of New York from opening date of Dec. 23rd, 1993:

1994:	$529.00	
Sub Total		$529.00

Interest collected in Treasury Bill investment of principal through the Bank of New York:

1993:	$1,608.46	
1994:	3,876.83	
Sub-Total		$5,485.29

Interest earned on decedent's account at Hamilton Savings Bank while waivers were pending:

1992:	$2,021.06	
1993	$2,098.64	
1994:	$2,208.82	
Sub-Total:		$6,328.52

Interest earned on decedent's account at Emigrant Savings Bank, converted into JOHN JAMES DOE TRUST after decedent's death:

Dec 20, 1993-June 19, 1994		$10,522.72
Sub-Total:	$10,522.72	

Total Interest............................$22,865.53

Page Five (Schedules)

Schedule C-2
Adminstration Expenses Chargeable to Income

N O N E

Schedule E-1
Distribution of Income

A. Income from JOHN JAMES DOE (testamentary) TRUST:

Item	To Whom Distributed	Amount/Value
Cash	Mary F. Doe, surviving wife	$5,261.36
Cash	John James Doe, Jr., son	2,630.68
Cash	Mary F. Doe, for David Doe, a minor	2,630.68

B. Income from non-Trust estate account, as listed in Schedule A-2 above:

Cash	To Mary F. Doe, surviving spouse of decedent	12,105.81
	TOTAL:	$22,865.53

Schedule G-1
Statement of Income on Hand

N O N E

Schedule H
Statement of Interested Parties

Name	Relationship	Address
Mary F. Doe	Surviving Wife	10 Death St., NY, NY
John James Doe, Jr.	Son	18 Third St., Bronx, NY
David Edwards	Executor/Trustee Legatee	15 Probate St., NY, NY
David Doe	Minor Son, Mother as Guardian	10 Death St., NY, NY
Bernard Jones	Legatee	120 Legacy St., NY, NY
George G. Fuller	Legatee	20 College Rd., Bronx, NY
Department of Taxation	Taxes	2 World Trade Center, NY, NY
Fidelity & Deposit of Maryland	Surety	110 William St., NY, NY
UNKNOWN	UNKNOWN	UNKNOWN

Fiduciary's Statement: The records of this Court have been searched for powers of attorney and assignments and encumbrances made and executed by any of the persons interested in or entitled to a share of the estate. And no such powers, assignments or incumbrances were found. Your peititoner has NO knowledge of the execution of any such power of attorney or assignment so filed or recorded.

Signed:_____

Page Six (Schedules)

Schedule I
Estate Taxes Paid & Allocation Thereof

The Estate is below the minimum taxable estate both for the Federal government and the New York State, and, hence, no estate tax is due. A copy of the Form ET-90, filed with the NY State to finalize this Estate, is attached herewith, however, for information purposes only. (*PETITIONER: attach such Form ET-90 to conform with the statement made, if so made.*)

Schedule J
Computation of Commissions

Principal received	$229,715.00
Gains on sale	69.00
Interest earned (Income collected)	22,865.53
TOTAL ESTATE:	252,649.53

$100,000 X 5%	=	$ 5,000.00
$152,649.53 X 4%	=	$ 6,105.98
TOTAL COMMISSION		$11,105.98

Schedule K
Statement of Other Pertinent Facts & Cash Reconciliation

This application for a final accounting is being made by David Edwards, the party appointed Executor of the estate of the decedent on _(Date),_ by the Honorable _(Judge's Name)_, the Surrogate of _____ County.

The order approving the Petitioner as Executor did not prohibit Petitioner from making any distributions or from paying the fees for professional services by accountants, appraisers, etc. Distributions were accordingly made, and fees for professional help paid.

At the time of his death, the decedent had basically four (4) assets comprising his estate: a bank account with Emigrant Savings Bank; an account with the Hamilton Savings Bank; the residential property where decedent resided with this surviving wife; and personal property such as automobile, and jewelry on deposit in a safe deposit box at Emigrant. All of the said assets were held in the name of the decedent only, except for the real property which was held in joint names with his surviving wife, Mary F. Doe.

Initially, the administration and settlement of the estate was delayed for some time due to the NY State Tax Commission having misplaced their file on the estate. The safe deposit box was originally inventoried as part of a Will search on January 11, 1994. The confirmation of the Court as to your Petitioner's representation of the estate as Executor came some three (3) months later. In the interim, the Tax Commission's file vanished.

Page Seven (Schedules)

After your petitioner assembled the original assets, closed out the lease on the separate apartment maintained in the city by decedent with a minimal payment, your Petitioner initiated exhaustive inquiries with the State of New York, attempting to get back into the safe deposit box for inventory purposes. For about three months the State objected to this on the grounds that it did not wish to accept the carbon copy of the original box-opening report that was in your Petitioner's possession; the State wanted, but could not find the original document. Finally, the State abandoned their search and accepted our document, opened a new file, and permitted your Peititoner to reinventory the box and take possession of its jewelry contents, which were thereupon appraised and sold, ET-90 form prepared reflecting no tax due, and this accounting was prepared.

Your petitioner administered (and is hereby accounting for) all other assets of the decedent, except the household items and personal effects of decedent and the jointly held real property, all of which your Petitioner considered non-estate assets, and hence conveyed the control and/or possession of that over to the surviving wife. (The real property is an 11-room, 2-garage, frame house; value approx. $150,000-$200,000; no mortgage outstanding or known liens thereon.)

Pursuant to the provision of decedent's Will, your Petitioner segregated out and used part of the bank deposit funds to set up THE JOHN JAMES DOE TRUST to benefit the persons designated in the Will (the Wife, Mary; and sons, John Jr. and David); the balance of the estate were accordingly distributed to the beneficiaries, as designated in the decedent's Will.

During the period of your Petitioner's administration of the estate, the greatest care was taken to maximize interest earned. All ready cash was deposited into a "NOW" style checking acount. The bulk of principal cash was constantly invested and reinvested in short-term Treasury investments. All remaining funds are currently on deposit in the bank.

Cash Reconciliation

Schedule A		$229,715.00
Schedule A-1		69.00
Scheulde A-2		22,865.53
		252,649.53
Less:		
Schedule C		6,569.55
Schedule D		1,520.63
Schedule E		207,715.00
Schedule E-1		22,865.53
		238,670.71

Balance: 13,978.82 (reconciles with balance-on-hand in Schedule G above).

Form P-35

SURROGATE'S COURT
COUNTY OF <u>New York</u>

Accounting of

DAVID EDWARDS,

as EXECUTOR **of**

The Estate of JOHN JAMES DOE,

Deceased

PETITION FOR A
VOLUNTARY ACCOUNTING

by Executor of Will
(with Trust Provisions)
or by Trustee

To the Surrogate's Court of the County of <u>New York</u>:

(1) The petition of <u>David Edwards</u>
residing at <u>15 Probate Street, New York, N.Y.</u>

respectfully states :

(2) The decedent died on <u>January 10th 1984</u> , and at the time of his
death was a resident of <u>10 Death Street, New York, N.Y. 10003</u>

(3) Letters of <u>Testamentary</u> (or, if more applicable, enter "LETTERS OF ADMINISTRATION")
were granted to your petitioner(s) by the Surrogate's Court of New York County, New York, on the <u>??</u>

____ day of _____<u>??</u>_____ , 19____

(4) More than seven months have elapsed since the issuance of said letters or

~~The time for presentation of claims, as fixed by a notice duly published, has expired~~

(5) The names and post-office addresses of all persons interested in the Estate or Trust Fund to whom

process must issue pursuant to the provisions of SCPA 315 and SCPA 2210, are as follows:

Name and Post-Office Address	Relationship	Nature of Interest
Mary F. Doe, 10 Death St. New York, N.Y.	surviving wife	testamentary beneficiary
David Doe (same address as above)	minor son	testamentary beneficiary
John James Doe, Jr., 13 Third St., Bronx N.Y.	son	testamentary beneficiary

If any persons, or their names, residences and post-office addresses be unknown, the petition must substantially set forth the facts which show what efforts have been made to ascertain the same and a general description of the parties, showing their connection with the decedent and their interest in the matter. SCPA 304

Name and Post-Office Address	Relationship	Nature of Interest
Bernard Jones, 120 Legacy St., New York, N.Y.	legatee	$1,000
George G. Fuller, 20 College Rd., Bronx N.Y.	legatee	$1,000
Wallace Doe, 10 Gregory Lane, Queens Village, Queens N.Y.	son	none stipulated in decedent's will

That all of the above-named persons in Paragraph 5 are of full age and of sound mind,

EXCEPT David Doe,

who   is an   infant   over the age of fourteen years, residing with the mother, Mary F. Doe, at the address set forth above.

and

who is an   Infant   under the age of fourteen years, residing with

and

who   NONE   incompetent   and whose committee is

residing at

(6) By virtue of the provisions of SCPA 315 it appears to be unnecessary to serve process on the following persons whose interest is being represented by persons hereinabove named:

Name and Post-Office Address	Relationship and By Whom Represented	Nature of Interest
David Doe, 10 Death St., New York, N.Y.	minor son of decedent, and of Mary F. Doe, the mother & testamentary guardian.	beneficiary of estate & trust fund

(7) The following legatees have been paid as shown by their acknowledged releases filed herewith: Mary F. Doe, for herself and for the minor son, David Doe; John James Doe, Jr.; David Edwards; Bernard Jones; George G. Fuller.

All of said above mentioned persons in paragraphs 6 and 7 are of sound mind; and all are of full age, **EXCEPT** David Doe.

State whether or not the infant has a general or testamentary guardian, and the name, relationship, and post-office address of the person with whom such infant resides. SCPA 304

who   is an   infant over the age of fourteen years, residing with his mother, Mary F. Doe., who is named in decedent's Will as David's testamentary guardian.

— and —

Erase unnecessary allegations.

who —————————— infant under the age of fourteen years, residing with

— and —

If any person named be an adjudged, or an alleged incompetent, state the facts regarding his incompetency, and the name and post-office address of a relative or friend having an interest in his welfare; also the name and post-office address of the committee, if any, and the name and post-office address of the person or institution having the care or custody of the incompetent. SCPA 304

who ————————— incompetent and whose committee is residing at

(8) There are no other persons than those above mentioned interested in this proceeding except as there might be a person or persons of the class mentioned in paragraph 6 whose name or existence is unknown to your petitioner(s).

(9) There is no accounting proceeding now pending.

(10) Your petitioner(s) **is** desirous of rendering to said Surrogate's Court an account of probate proceedings, and therefore prays that the account be judicially settled,

and that the persons above mentioned and all necessary and proper persons be cited to show cause why such settlement should not be had and for such other and further relief as the Court may deem just and proper.

Dated, _____ 19 ___

Signed X _____
Petitioner(s)

City, County and State of New York, ss.:

DAVID EDWARDS, _____

the petitioner (s) named in the foregoing petition, being duly sworn, depose and say that

he has   read the foregoing petition subscribed by him and know the contents thereof; and that the same is true of HIS own knowledge, except as to the matters therein stated to be alleged on information and belief, and that as to those matters HE believe it to be true.

Sworn to this _____ day
of _____, 19 ____.

X _____
Petitioner (s)

_____
(Notary Public)

SURROGATE'S COURT **CITATION**
County of New York

THE PEOPLE OF THE STATE OF NEW YORK

By the Grace of God Free and Independent

T0 ....

In the Matter of the Judicial Settlement of the
Account of Proceedings of

DAVID EDWARDS,

.... Executor (or Administrator) of

JOHN JAMES DOE,
                                    Deceased

[The names of the person (or persons) who are decedent's creditors, heirs, legatees, devisees, beneficiaries, distributees, who would NOT give you a signed accounting citation waiver (the form on p. 51), go here.]

being the persons interested as creditors, legatees, devisees, beneficiaries, distributees, or otherwise in the estate

of .... John James Doe ...., deceased,

who at the time of his death was a resident of .... 10 Death St., New York, N.Y. 10003

Send Greeting:

Upon the petition of .... David Edwards, Executor, *[Name of the Executor or Administrator, as applicable.]*

residing at .. 15 Probate St., New York, N.Y. 10010

You and each of you are hereby cited to show cause before the Surrogate's Court of New York County, held at the Courthouse in the County of New York, on the ..(leave blank, Clerk fills in).... day of

.................................., 19......, at nine-thirty o'clock in the forenoon of that day, why the

account of proceedings of .... David Edwards

.... Executor of the Estate of John James Doe, ... should not be judicially settled.

Dated, Attested and Sealed, ...(leave blank)............., **19**....

(L.S.)   HON.

David Edwards
Attorney for Petitioner(s)   Surrogate, New York County

15 Probate St., New York, N.Y. 10010
Address   Chief Clerk

(enter)
Tel. No.

This Citation is served upon you as required by law. You are not obliged to appear in person. If you fail to appear it will be assumed that you consent to the proceedings, unless you file written objections thereto. You have a right to have an attorney-at-law appear for you.

State of New York

County of .... } ss.:

PROOF OF SERVICE OF ACCOUNTING CITATION

David Edwards

of 15 Probate St., New York, NY ...., being duly sworn, says that he is over the age of eighteen years; that he made due service of the within citation in the above-entitled special proceeding on the persons named below, whom deponent knew to be the persons mentioned and described in said citation, by delivering to and leaving with each of them a **true copy of said citation**, as follows:

On the .... day of ...... (date when service is made) ...., 19......

on ...... (names of the party or parties served) ....

at ...... (addresses at which the parties are served?) ....

[Name of the person who actually served the accounting citation.]

Sworn to before me this .... day of

.................................., 19...... }   SIGNED: ....

(NOTARY PUBLIC)   (Person Serving the Account Citation)

124

Form P-37

In the Matter of ACCOUNTING of
DAVID EDWARDS, as

EXECUTOR of

JOHN JAMES DOE,

Deceased.

File No. _____

Affidavit of Regularity

State of New York }
County of _____ } ss.:

__David Edwards__ , *being duly sworn, says*

Executor
that he is the ~~attorney~~ *for the* __Estate of JOHN JAMES DOE,__

herein: That all the parties
to this proceeding have been duly cited or have duly waived the issuance and service of a
citation herein and consented to the entry of a decree or order herein, & the manner and form
by which each party was cited, *or offered a waiver of same, was as follows:*

I. *By service of a copy of the citation issued herein upon the following persons in the*
manner prescribed by SCPA 307 (1), as more fully appears by the proof of service thereof, made
in the manner and form prescribed by law and filed herein on the _____ *day of*
_____ *, 19___ , viz.:*

(Name) **(When)** **(Where)**

[Enter, only for persons upon whom you were required to serve an acct. citation, the
names of the parties served, the dates and addresses at which served. For any persons
who have signed a waiver & consent statement (p. 106) for you, however, DO NOT
enter them here, but use Paragraph III below to list those.]

[Enter the date when Proof of Service of Acct.
Citation (p. 104) was filed in court, if any.]

Non-residents, etc.

II. *By service thereof pursuance of an order made herein on the* _____ *day of*
_____ *, 19___ , under SCPA 307 (2) as more fully appears by the*
proof of service thereof, made in the manner prescribed by law and filed herein on the
day of _____ *, 19___ , viz.: On*

[Enter in this paragraph the names of the parties served out of state, and dates & ad-
dresses at which served.]

[Date when the Proof of
such service was filed in court.]

[If service of acct. citation was made out of state, enter
the date of the court order authorizing it.]

Parties who waive
or consent.

III. *Personally or by attorney by duly executed waivers of the issuance and service of*
the citation herein and a consent to the entry of a decree or order and filed herein on the _____
day of _____ *, 19___ , by*

[Enter here the dates when waivers of acct. citation (p. 106)
from anyone was filed with the court, if any.]

IV. *That no notice of appearance has been filed herein, except by* _____

[Enter in this paragraph the names of the parties, if any, who sent you a Notice of Ap-
pearance (notice of their intention to appear or to oppose your accounting). If none,
enter: NONE.]

That all of the persons named above are of full age and are of sound mind, excepting those
hereinbefore stated to be otherwise, and comprise all the parties, as deponent verily believes, who
have any interest in this proceeding.

Sworn to before me this _____

day of _____ *, 19___ .*

SIGNED: X _____
Executor/Administrator

(NOTARY PUBLIC)

N. B.—Where a person cited is an infant, a lunatic, an habitual drunkard, or for any cause mentally incapable adequately
to protect his rights, it must so appear in the foregoing affidavit. The age of the infant must also be stated.

Form P-38

Surrogate's Court
County of New York

ACCOUNTING OF

David Edwards

as Executor

of

John James Doe

Deceased

Waiver of Citation
(Accounting)

File No.................... 19........

[Enter here the names of every heir, distributee, fiduciary, beneficiary, etc., who agrees to sign, or signed this accounting waiver form for you.]

To the Surrogate's Court of the County of New York:

Mary F. Doe, for herself and as Testamentary Guardian for David Doe, a minor; John James Doe, Jr.; Bernard Jones; George G. Fuller.

[Enter "distributees," "heirs," "next-of-kin," "creditor," "beneficiary," as applicable.]

the undersigned, being...the whole persons interested as...heirs, distributees, & beneficiaries

in the estate or fund of.......John James Doe......................, deceased, do hereby appear in person and waive the issue and service of a citation in the above-entitled matter, and consent that a decree be made settling the account of said.....David Edwards.........................

as Executor...

Signed: I. X................

2. X

3. X

4. X

Dated...}

................................, 19....}

State of..

County of......................................} ss.:

[Names of the parties granting the waivers?]

On this..day of..,19........ before me came Mary F. Doe, John James Doe, Jr., Bernard Jones and George G. Fuller, to be known, and known to me to be the individuals described in and who executed the foregoing waiver and consent, and acknowledged to me that they executed the same.

....
(Notary Public)

N. B.—Certificate of authorization of notary is required if waiver is acknowledged in a foreign country. Real Property Law § 311

Form P-39

FORM 073 5M 8-74 ◄══► 288

At a Surrogate's Court held in and for the County of ___??___

at the Courthouse in the Civic Centre, 2 Johnson Street,

in the Borough of ___M___ County of ___?___, City of

New York, on the _____ day of _____

in the year 19_____.

Present, Hon. NATHAN R. SOBEL, Surrogate.

Accounting of :

DAVID EDWARDS, as Executor of

JOHN JAMES DOE,

Deceased.

File No. _____19_____

Decree Settling Account of Executor/Administrator

[Enter date on which the accounting petition was filed with the court.]

David Edwards, as Executor of Estate of John James Doe, deceased,
having on the ___?___ day of _____ 19___ , presented and filed

account and a petition praying that the same may be judicially settled;

State
Incidental
Relief

furthermore: that the Court allow petitioner a commission of $II,ID5.98
as Executor's commission, and for such other relief as may be just and
proper in the discretion of the Court.

[Use this paragraph to enter the relief wanted for any outstanding obligations still to be paid—e.g., accountant's or appraiser's fees, executor's/administrator's commission, disposition to be made of the final balance still remaining, etc.]

(Affidavit of regularity to be submitted)

And more than seven months having expired since the issuance of Letters **Testamentary**
(or, LETTERS OF ADMINISTRATION, as the case may be)

And the Court having obtained jurisdiction of all the necessary and proper parties to
this proceeding;

And the Surrogate having examined the said account and found the same correct, DOTH ORDER, ADJUDGE AND DECREE, that the said account be and the same is hereby judicially settled.

The following is a SUMMARY STATEMENT of, the said Account as judicially settled, made and recorded pursuant to the Statute in such case made and provided, that is to say:

The said Estate of JOHN JAMES DOE, is _____ charged with:

Amount shown by Schedule "A"
(Principal received) .... $ 229,715

Amount shown by Schedule "A-1"
(Realized increases on principal) .... $ 69.00

Amount shown by Schedule "A-2"
(Income collected) $22,865.53

     Total charges .... $ 252,649.53

The said _____ Estate of John James Doe, is _____ credited with:

Amount shown by Schedule "B"
(Realized decreases on principal) .... $ -0-

Amount shown by Schedule "C" (include "C-2" if Trust Acct)
(Funeral and administration expenses) .... $ 6,369.55

Amount shown by Schedule "D"
(Creditors claims actually paid) .... $ 1,520.63

Amount shown by Schedule "E" (or "E" & "E-I")
(Distributions to legatees, distributees, etc.) $230,580.53

     Total credits .... $ 238,670.71

Balance on hand shown by Schedule "G" ("F", if a non-Trust account) . $ 13,978.82

    The foregoing balance of $13,978.82 _____ consists of $ 13,978.82 _____ in cash and
$ _____ -0- _____ in other property on hand as of the _____ day of _____ ??? _____, 19 _____.

And it is hereby further ORDERED, ADJUDGED and DECREED that said David Edwards, the Executor, _____ do and _____ is _____ hereby ordered and directed to pay out and dispose of the said balance so remaining in _____ his _____ hands as aforesaid as follows:

That _____ he _____ do retain the sum of $11,105.98 (Eleven Thousand, one Hundred and Five 98/100)————————————Dollars

($ 11,105.98 _____) as and for _____ his _____ lawful commission to which he, as Executor of the Estate, entitled on this accounting.

That he do retain further the sum of NO _____

                                                                        Dollars

($ none), which sum is hereby allowed to _____ as and for _____

reasonable Costs and other Expenses in this proceeding.

That he do then pay unto the following parties, these legacies, bequests, or inheritance share: the sum of $2,872.84, to Mary F. Doe, dec

I) the sum of $2,872.84, to Mary F. Doe, decedent's surviving spouse, that being the balance still remaining with the Executor upon his deduction of his commission ($11,105.98) from the estate's Principal on Hand of $13,978.82;

2) .... *[Enter here, provision(s) by which to dispose of the final balance of the estate funds or property still to be left in your hands, if any.]*

3) ....

ENTER: _____

                    Surrogate (Judge)

(The Back Cover of the Decree Form)

NOTICE OF SETTLEMENT

Sir: PLEASE TAKE NOTICE that a decree Settling Account of **David Edwards**, as Executor, of which the within is a true copy, will be presented for settlement to:

HON. NATHAN R. SOBEL, Surrogate at the Courthouse, 2 Johnson Street, Brooklyn, New York.

on the _____ day of _____ *[Clerk fills in]* M.

Dated _____ 19 ___

at _____ 19 ___

Yours, etc.

Executor/Petitioner: David Edwards

Attorney for

Office and Post Office

Address 15 Probate St., N.Y., N.Y. 10010

To: _____

Attorney for _____

[The names & addresses of each interested person, (or their attorneys, if any) are to go here, as required by the court.]

Form P-34-A

R 564—Account of Executors and Administrators
Official Form: 9-1-67.

Surrogate's Court, County of

ACCOUNTING OF

as

ESTATE OF

Deceased.

ACCOUNT OF

EXECUTORS AND ADMINISTRATORS

File No._____ 19___

TO THE SURROGATE'S COURT OF THE COUNTY OF

The undersigned does hereby render the account of proceedings as follows:

Period of account from   to

This is   a final   account.
        an intermediate

The instructions concerning the schedules need not be stated at the head of each schedule. It will be sufficient to set forth only the schedule letter and heading.

For convenience of reference, the schedule letter and page number of the schedule should be shown at the bottom of each sheet of the account.

Schedule A

Statement of Principal Received

INSTRUCTIONS. This schedule must contain an itemized statement of all the moneys and other personal property constituting principal for which each accounting party is charged, together with the date of receipt or acquisition of such money or property. If real property has been sold by the fiduciary, this schedule must set forth the proceeds of sale of such property.

Schedule A-1

Statement of Increases on Sales, Liquidation or Distribution

INSTRUCTIONS. This schedule must contain a full and complete statement of all realized increases derived from principal assets whether due to sale, liquidation or distribution or any other reason. It should also show realized increases on new investments or exchanges. In each instance, the date of realization of the increase must be shown and the property from which said increase was derived must be identified.

Schedule A-2

Statement of All Income Collected

INSTRUCTIONS. This schedule must contain a full and complete statement of all interest, dividends, rents and other income received, and the date of each receipt. Each receipt must be separately accounted for and identified, except that where a security has been held for an entire year, the interest or ordinary dividends may be reported on a calendar year basis.

Schedule B

Statement of Decreases Due to Sales, Liquidation, Collection, Distribution or Uncollectibility

INSTRUCTIONS. This schedule must contain a full and complete statement of all realized decreases on principal assets whether due to sale, liquidation, collection or distribution, or any other reason. It should also show decreases on new investments or exchanges and also sales, liquidations or distributions that result in neither gain nor loss. In each instance, the date of realization of the decrease must be shown and the property from which said decrease was incurred must be identified. It would also report any assets which the fiduciary intends to abandon as worthless, together with a full statement of the reasons for abandoning it.

Schedule C

Statement of Funeral and Administration Expenses

INSTRUCTIONS. This schedule must contain an itemized statement of all moneys chargeable and paid for funeral, administration and other necessary expenses, together with the date and the reason for each expenditure.

Where the will directs that all inheritance and death taxes are to be paid out of the estate, credit for payment of same should be taken in this schedule.

Schedule C-1
Statement of Unpaid Administration Expenses

INSTRUCTIONS. This schedule must contain an itemized statement of all unpaid claims for administration and other necessary expenses, together with a statement of the basis for each such claim.

Schedule D
Statement of All Creditors' Claims

INSTRUCTIONS. This schedule must contain an itemized statement of all creditors' claims subdivided to show:

1. Claims presented, allowed, paid and credited and appearing in the Summary Statement, together with the date of payment.

2. Claims presented and allowed but not paid.

3. Claims presented but rejected, the date of and the reason for such rejection.

4. Contingent and possible claims.

5. Personal claims requiring approval by the court, pursuant to SCPA 1805.

In the event of insolvency, preference allowed various claims should be stated and the order of their priority.

Schedule E
Statement of Distributions Made

INSTRUCTIONS. This schedule must contain an itemized statement of all moneys paid and all property delivered to the legatees, trustees, surviving spouse or distributees of the deceased, the date of payment or delivery thereof, and the name of the person to whom payment or delivery was actually made.

Where estate taxes are required to be apportioned and payments have been made on account of said taxes, the amounts apportioned in Schedule H against beneficiaries of the testamentary estate shall be charged in this schedule against the respective individual's share.

Schedule F
Statement of All Personal Property Remaining on Hand

INSTRUCTIONS. This schedule must contain an itemized statement showing all personal property remaining on hand, including a statement of all uncollected receivables and property rights due to the estate. The schedule must further show the date and cost of all such property that was acquired by purchase, exchange or transfers made or received, together with the date of acquisition and the cost thereof.

Schedule G
Statement of Interested Parties

INSTRUCTIONS. This schedule must contain the names of all persons entitled as legatee, devisee, trustee, surviving spouse, distributee or otherwise to a share of the estate or fund, with their post-office addresses and the degree of relationship, if any, of each to the deceased, a statement showing the nature of and the value or approximate value of the interest of each such person.

Also a statement that the records of this court have been searched for powers of attorney and assignments and encumbrances made and executed by any of the persons interested in or entitled to a share of the estate and a list detailing each power of attorney, assignment and encumbrance, disclosed by such search, with the date of its recording and the name and address of each attorney in fact and of each assignee and of each person beneficially interested under the encumbrance referred to in the respective instruments, and also whether the accounting party has any knowledge of the execution of any such power of attorney or assignment so filed and recorded.

Schedule H
Statement of Estate Taxes Paid and Allocation thereof

INSTRUCTIONS. This schedule must contain a statement showing all estate taxes assessed and paid in respect of any property required to be included in the gross estate of the decedent under the provisions of the Tax Law or under the laws of the United States. Final New York Estate Tax receipt or an order of exemption from tax must be presented with the decree settling the final account. This schedule must also contain a computation setting forth the proposed allocation of taxes paid and to be paid and the amounts due the estate from each person in whose behalf a tax payment has been made and also the proportionate amount of the tax paid by each of the named persons interested in this estate or charged against their respective interest, as provided in EPTL 2-1.8.

Where an allocation of taxes is required, the method of computing the allocation of said taxes must be shown in this schedule.

Schedule I
Statement of Computation of Commissions

INSTRUCTIONS. This schedule must contain a computation of the amount of commissions due upon this accounting.

Schedule J
Statement of Other Pertinent Facts and of Cash Reconciliation

INSTRUCTIONS. This schedule must contain a statement of all other pertinent facts affecting the administration of the estate and the rights of those interested therein. It must also contain a statement of any real property left by the decedent which it is not necessary to include as an estate asset to be accounted for, a brief description thereof, the gross value and the amount of mortgages or liens thereon at the date of death of the deceased. A cash reconciliation must also be set forth in this schedule so that verification with bank statements and cash on hand may be readily made.

THE FOLLOWING IS A SUMMARY STATEMENT OF THIS ACCOUNT:

CHARGES:

Amount shown by Schedule "A"
(Principal received) _____ $_____

Amount shown by Schedule "A-1"
(Realized Increases on principal) _____ $_____

Amount shown by Schedule "A-2"
(Income Collected) _____ $_____

     Total charges _____ $_____

CREDITS:

Amount shown by Schedule "B"
(Realized decreases on principal) _____ $_____

Amount shown by Schedule "C"
(Funeral and administration expenses) _____ $_____

Amount shown by Schedule "D"
(Creditors' claims actually paid) _____ $_____

Amount shown by Schedule "E"
(Distributions to legatees, distributees, etc.) _____ $_____

     Total credits _____ $_____

Balance on hand shown by Schedule "F" _____ $_____

The foregoing balance of $_____ consists of $_____

in cash and $_____ in other property on hand as of the _____ day of _____,

19____. It is subject to deduction of estimated principal commissions amounting to $_____
shown in Schedule I and to the proper charge to principal of expenses of this accounting.

The attached schedules are part of this account.

_____

_____
                    Executor Administrator

STATE OF NEW YORK, COUNTY OF _____ SS.:   **AFFIDAVIT OF ACCOUNTING PARTY**

                  being duly sworn, says: That the foregoing account contains according to the best of my/our knowledge and belief a true statement of all my/our receipts and disbursements on account of the estate and of all moneys or other property belonging to the estate which have come into my/our hands or been received by any other person by my/our order or authority for my/our use and that I/we do not know of any error or omission in the account to the prejudice of any creditor of, or person interested in, the estate.

Sworn to before me this _____ day of

_____   _____
          19_____

_____

Chapter 8

SETTLEMENT OF "SMALL" ESTATES: PROBATE PROCEDURES WHEN NO COURT ADMINISTRATION IS REQUIRED

Many states now have a simplified procedure whereby an estate which is considered a "small" estate is excused from formal administration proceedings, irrespective of whether the decedent left a will or not. This procedure, also known as **"summary"** administration, is the practice followed in New York. Here, under a procedure termed the "Settlement of Small Estates Without CourtAdministration," the estates of persons who die intestate or testate, whether the decedent be a New York resident or otherwise, may be settled _without_ having to go through a formal court administration.

CONDITIONS FOR SMALL ESTATE ADMINISTRATION

Whatever the state involved, an estate may qualify for summary or small estate administration only if it meets certain conditions set by the state. Generally, it is required that _the probate estate's total value not exceed_ a certain designated maximum amount, and that it not include any solely owned real property of the decedent.

In general, the permissible maximum dollar value of estates for eligibility ranges anywhere from $5,000 to $60,000, and may be lower or higher, depending on the state in question. _**It should be noted, however, that one common feature of the small estate law of most states is that it is generally provided that in calculating the decedent's estate for the purposes of determining whether the estate qualifies as a "small estate," certain designated major assets which are otherwise includable in the decedent's "gross estate," are to be excluded and not be considered.**_ For example, only the decedent's so-called "non-probate" assets (Chapter 1, Section D & Chapter 7-A, "Action 10")—i.e., only his/her _solely_-owned probate assets—are generally counted; and any assets the decedent might have held in some form of joint ownership with another person, or in trust, may not be counted for the purpose of determining the minimum value. "Community property" states allow one-half of the value of the community property to be deducted from the probate estate when the decedent is a spouse.

Thus, after allowing for all the usual permissible deductions to be taken, it is generally customary that what would have really been a "large" estate will still qualify for administration nevertheless.

To qualify for "small estate" treatment under the New York State rules, for example, all that is required is that the decedent have PERSONAL property having a gross value of no more than $10,000, and which is located within the state. In computing the value of such personal property for the $10,000 limitation, none of the following property, if owned by the decedent, is included: interests in jointly held bank accounts or in jointly owned real or personal property or assets of any types; trust accounts or U.S. savings bonds POD. [This is so, since they are the "non-probate assets" which, as you'll recall from the previous discussion in Chapters 1 and 7-A (pp. 12 and 88),are said to pass <u>directly</u> to their inheritors "by operation of law," and not by intestacy or the contents of any will]. In addition, any real property owned by the decedent is also excluded from inclusion, and the small estate procedure may be used regardless of the value of the real property owned by the estate.

As with most other states which have this provision, New York's procedures for filing under small estate provisions are simple and far less time-consuming or costly. **New York's "small estate" procedures fall into these few basic STEPS:**

STEP 1: FILE PETITION WITH THE COURT FOR A "VOLUNTARY ADMINISTRATOR" TO BE APPOINTED

The person who settles or administers the estate falling under New York's "small estate" category is called by the designation **"VOLUNTARY ADMINISTRATOR."** So, the first order of business to kick off the procedures in this instance, would be to apply to the decedent's domiciliary county's Surrogate's Court to have a Voluntary Administrator appointed.

Who is eligible for appointment as a voluntary administrator? In general, the surviving spouse of the decedent has *the first* right of appointment. However, where there is no surviving spouse, or where he/she gives up the right to act or is unable to act for whatever reason, then the right is given to any competent, adult domiciliary of the state within any of these categories who applies and qualifies: the decedent's children, grandchildren, parents, brothers or sisters, in that order.

To commence the proceedings, order the petition forms for a "small estate" filing from the Publisher. See the Order Form on p. 239 for your order-placing information.) You'll be sent a multi-page form titled **"Affidavit in Relation to Settlement of Estate under Article 13."** (See Form P-40 on p. 135 for a sample preparation of this form.) You complete this form at your earliest convenience and have it *notarized* (by you). Then you resubmit this affidavit to the court clerk with the following documents: i) a "certified" copy of the decedent's death certificate; and ii) a copy of the decedent's Will, where the decedent died testate.

As a rule, upon your presentation of these papers to the clerk, he is not supposed to ask too many questions of your application. (And, usually, he doesn't!) No special formality is required: there's no "citation" required, no issuance of any court order, no giving of bond by the approved administrator, and the like. The clerk simply files away your application and assigns your case a "file number" upon your paying the nominal filing fee of $1.00. The clerk then issues you two basic documents: i) a "certified" copy of the affidavit you had filed with him;[1] and ii) a short CERTIFICATE OF THE COURT. (This second document, which simply shows that the required affidavit has been filed with the court by the voluntary administrator and that the administrator has the court's authorization to act in that capacity as a voluntary administrator, is what you would often have to furnish to various persons or institutions with whom you'll deal, as proof of your authority to act on behalf of the decedent's estate.)

STEP 2: VOLUNTARY ADMINISTRATOR PERFORMS HIS REQUIRED "SUMMARY" ESTATE SETTLEMENT DUTIES

Having got a voluntary administrator appointed, the next order of business is, of course, for the voluntary administrator to carry out his duties. Basically, a voluntary administrator has more or less the same rights, powers, duties and liabilities as a conventional executor or administrator with respect to the personal (but not necessarily with respect to the real) property of the estate.

---

[1] It is also the clerk who must, on his own, mail a postcard notice of the proceeding to each distributee listed in the affidavit, if any.

Briefly, you would, as a voluntary administrator, seek to do the following:

1. Sue to recover the decedent's property withheld from you, if any, or to collect debts and enforce contractual claims owned by the decedent (permissible only when the amount involved, together with all other non-exempt assets of the estate, does not exceed the $10,000 limit).

2. Collect and reduce all the decedent's assets to your possession and liquidate such assets (i.e., sell for cash) to the extent necessary and possible.[2]

3. Open a separate bank account exclusively for the estate, and deposit all estate monies received by him therein; sign all checks drawn on or withdrawals made from such account in the name of the estate in your official fiduciary capacity.

4. Pay the decedent's funeral expenses, and the administration expenses and debts of the decedent, out of the assets available.[3]

5. Distribute the balance of the assets, if any, to the person or persons entitled to inherit them (either under the provisions of a will, or under the intestate succession laws of the state—Appendix B).

6. Submit to the court an account of all personal property of the decedent you received and disbursements you made.

STEP 3: SUBMIT AN ACCOUNTING REPORT OF YOUR ACTIVITIES TO THE COURT

The final duty of the voluntary administrator would be to submit an accounting of his stewardship to the court. He is required to account *ONLY* for any *PERSONAL* property of the decedent which he received or disbursed, since his powers do not ordinarily extend to the administration of real or jointly-held personal property under New York's procedures.

Fulfilling the requirement for an accounting under the "small estate" procedures is, again, a much more simplified matter. The voluntary administrator does not have to render any lengthy formal "accounting." All he's required to do is to submit the following pieces of information to the clerk of court: i) the certified copy of the *"Affidavit in Relation to Settlement of Estate, under Article-13"* on which the necessary endorsements by the proper parties have been entered (last page of Affidavit, as on p. 137 of this manual); and ii) an attached, *notarized* statement of the estate assets collected, and all receipts, disbursements and distributions made thereof (the third page of the affidavit form, subheaded *"Report and Accounting Settlement of Estate without Administration,"* as on p. 137 of this manual). Also, attach all receipts and cancelled checks for all estate transactions undertaken, where available.

Now, for all practical purposes your functions as a voluntary administrator of the small estate have been well concluded!

---

[2]Whenever the voluntary administrator pays or collects any assets, claims, or indebtedness on behalf of the estate, it is required that he issue (or obtain) receipts for same. In addition, the voluntary administrator must have the party paying an indebtedness or delivering any estate property to him endorse the amount of the payment made or describe the property surrendered, on a certified copy of the court-endorsed affidavit. It is this affidavit, containing all such endorsements, that the voluntary administrator would submit back to the court as his official "accounting" (Step Three herein on p. 134) at the conclusion of his functions.

[3]Generally, the payment of certain debts owed to a deceased person, such as those represented by bank accounts, insurance proceeds, employee death benefits and unpaid wages or retirement obligations, may be made *directly* to the persons who are entitled to receive them without court administration. New York's laws (SCPA 1310-2) permit that the surviving spouse may, by filing a proper affidavit with the court (Form SCPA 1310-2/3 "Affidavit to Obtain Payment of Debt Owed to Creditor without Administration," obtainable from the court clerk's office), receive a payment of not more than $3,000 *of* the debt owed to the decedent immediately after his death. Another payment of debt owed to the decedent, not to exceed $5,000, may, at the expiration of 30 days after the decedent's death, be obtained by the surviving spouse or children of the decedent.

Form P-40

FORM 402 3M 8-76 [●] 2⁸9

Surrogate's Court, County of <u>New York</u>

In the Matter of the Estate

of

JOHN JAMES DOE,

.

Deceased.

Affidavit in Relation to Settlement of Estate Under Article 13, S C P A

File No.............................., 19

INSTRUCTIONS: In completing this form, answer each question. This may be done in some instances by crossing out words in parenthesis and in other instances by inserting the required information.

STATE OF _____ }

COUNTY OF _____ } ss.:

[Name of whoever is the "interested person" who is making the petition for a Small Estate Administration.]

I, _____ John James Doe, Jr. _____ domiciled at

<u>18 Third Street, Bronx, city of New York,</u> State of New York,

being first duly sworn, depose and say:

I am the _____ son _____ of _____ John James Doe, _____, deceased,

and make this affidavit pursuant to Article 13 of the Surrogate's Court Procedure Act.

1. The name of the deceased is: <u>John James Doe</u>
2. Deceased died intestate on <u>January 10th</u>, 19<u>84</u> at <u>New York, N.Y.</u>
<u>home</u>, <u>10 Death Street</u> <u>New York county & city</u>
(Place of Death)   (Street and Number)   (City or Town)
State of <u>New York</u>

3. At the time of death, deceased was domiciled at:
<u>10 Death Street, Manhattan, New York city,</u>, State of New York.

4. Deceased died: (Check applicable line)

__X__ Intestate (without a will)

_____ Testate (with a will which is filed with this affidavit).

5. Search of the records of the court show that no application has been made in the estate of the decedent for voluntary administration, letters of administration or probate of a will and your affiant is informed and verily believes that no such application has ever been made to any other surrogate's court of this state.

6. The value of the entire personal property, wherever located, of the decedent hereinafter listed, exclusive of joint bank accounts, trust accounts, U.S. savings bonds POD and jointly owned personal property, does not exceed $5,000.

7. The names and addresses of the decedent's distributees under the New York law and their relationship to him are as follows:

Name	Address	Relationship
Mary F. Doe & David Doe	10 Death St., New York, N.Y.	wife & minor son
John James Doe, Jr.	18 Third St., Bronx NY	son
Wallace Doe	10 Gregory Lane, Queens Vlg. Queens	son

8. The names and addresses of all beneficiaries in the will of deceased filed herewith and their relationship to him are as follows: no will applicable.

Name	Address	Relationship

(If more space is needed, add a sheet of paper.)

9. The following, exclusive of joint bank accounts, trust accounts, U.S. savings bonds POD and jointly owned personal property, is a complete list of all personal property owned by the decedent, either standing in his own name or owned by him beneficially and including items of value in any safe deposit box:

Items of Personal Property
Separately Listed

Value of
Each Item

[Give each item's (or group of identical items') current estimated market or resale value.]

[List here the non-jointly owned personal property items, one by one, as applicable.]

(If more space is needed, add a sheet of paper.)

10. All the liabilities (names of creditors and amounts) of the decedent known to me are as follows:

[Supply the answer required, as best known to you. If none, enter: NONE.]

11. I undertake to act as voluntary administrator of the decedent's estate and to administer it pursuant to Article Thirteen of the Surrogate's Court Procedure Act.

In doing so, I agree to reduce all of the decedent's assets to possession; to liquidate such assets to the extent necessary; to open an estate bank account in a bank of deposit or savings bank in this state in which I shall deposit all money received; to sign all checks drawn on or withdrawals from such account in the name of the estate by myself as voluntary administrator; to pay the expenses of administration, the decedent's reasonable funeral expenses and his debts in the order provided by law; and to distribute the balance to the person or persons and in the amount or amounts provided by law. As voluntary administrator, I shall file in this court an account of all receipts and of disbursements made.

12. I understand that this proceeding is no determination of the estate tax liability, if any, in the event that the decedent had any interest in real property in this state or any joint bank accounts, trust accounts, U.S. savings bonds POD, jointly-owned or trust property.

13. If letters testamentary or of administration are later granted, I acknowledge that my powers as voluntary administrator shall cease and I shall thereupon deliver to the rightful executor or administrator a complete statement of my account and all assets and funds of said estate in my possession.

X *John James Doe Jr.*
_____
Affiant (Person applying to
serve as Vol. Administrator)

SUBSCRIBED AND SWORN to before me this _____ day of _____ 19___

[Notary Public signs here & affixes his official stamp thereon.]
_____
Notary Public

REPORT AND ACCOUNT IN SETTLEMENT OF ESTATE
WITHOUT ADMINISTRATION UNDER ARTICLE 13, SCPA

120

The undersigned, heretofore appointed as the voluntary administrator of the above entitled Estate, reports and accounts as follows:

1. There has come into my hands the following personal property of the deceased which is on hand or has been converted into cash in the amounts indicated:

[Items from among items in Paragraph 9 above (p. ___), which you liquidated into cash (or retained "as is"), and the amount so realized.]

(If more space is needed, use back of this page or add a sheet of paper.)

The total value thereof does not exceed ~~Three~~ **TEN** Thousand Dollars.

2. All of said personal property has been disbursed or distributed as follows:

[Supply the information—name of each distributee & the amounts (or the property) he/she received.]

Returned herewith are receipts or canceled checks showing the payment of expenses of administration and such disbursements or distribution.

3. No part of the estate of the decedent remains in my hands.

X _John James Doe Jr._
Voluntary Administrator

STATE OF _____ }
COUNTY OF _____ } ss.:

John James Doe Jr. being duly sworn, deposes and says:
I have read the foregoing Report and Account and know the contents thereof; the matters and things therein stated are true as of my own knowledge; the foregoing Account is in all respects just and true and contains a full, particular and true account of all money and property of the deceased coming into my possession; and the administration expenses, disbursements and distribution shown have been actually made for the purposes and reasons therein stated.

X _John James Doe Jr._
Affiant (Voluntary Administrator)

SUBSCRIBED AND SWORN TO before me this _____ day of _____ 19___.

_____
Notary Public

Chapter 9
ANCILLARY ADMINISTRATION:
PROBATE PROCEDURES WHEN DECEDENT'S ESTATE IS LOCATED IN A "FOREIGN" STATE

When a domiciliary (i.e., a permanently resident person) of a particular state dies leaving an estate located either within that given state or outside of it; or when a domiciliary of another state dies leaving property within this (i.e., New York) state, New York's courts may have some legal right to exercise authority over the administration of such an estate in either of both situations. Normally, when a person dies leaving property in more than one state, the decedent's domiciliary state at the time of his death is the primary place where the court proceedings concerning the probate of his will or the intestate administration of his estate is undertaken. This domiciliary state then becomes the principal or **"ORIGINAL"** jurisdiction for the administration of the decedent's estate.[1] However, an "ancillary" administration (i.e., a lower-level, supplementary administration) will also have to be instituted in *each* of the other states or countries (the non-domiciliary states) where the decedent left property.

If it should happen that a decedent for whom you serve as a principal or domiciliary executor or administrator, was a New York domiciliary who owned real or personal property in another state, it would be your additional responsibility to arrange for an "ancillary" administration of the decedent's "foreign" (non-New York) assets to be undertaken.

There are a few "foreign" states (i.e., "foreign" to the domiciliary state) where it is possible for the principal executor or administrator in the domiciliary state to act on the estate's behalf in the foreign state—upon his meeting certain eligibility requirements, of course. In general, though, for most practical purposes, you will probably have to arrange to get a resident of the foreign state appointed and approved by that state's local court as a so-called **ANCILLARY ADMINISTRATOR,** thereby qualifying him to represent the interests of that part of the decedent's overall estate which is located in the said foreign state.

You may contact a trusted relative, friend or acquaintance, who is a resident of that foreign state to handle the ancillary administration for you there. The selected person doesn't have to be an attorney. But, if you so prefer, you may select a practising attorney in the area. (It's easy to do. Just check the state or national legal directory for a listing of the registered attorneys within the given state. Contact several of them, preferably by writing, and get several quotations. Then make a choice. However, before you give a go-ahead to a final choice, make sure you entered into a written agreement with that lawyer fully spelling out the extent of his duties, fees, and timetable for payments and for completing the work, etc.)

[1]When a non-domiciliary of New York directs in his will that the will be probated in New York under New York's law, such a will can be admitted to New York, provided it is properly executed in accordance with New York's requirements and that the decedent's property is located within New York.

STEP-BY-STEP PROCEDURES FOR SETTING UP AN ANCILLARY ADMINISTRATION

What are the procedures for setting up an ancillary administration in a given foreign state? The details of such procedures differ, of course, from state to state. But, fortunately, the broad basic principles which govern them are almost the same in just about every jurisdiction.

Assume a situation where New York is a "foreign" state—meaning that the decedent is a domiciliary of another state—but that he left behind an estate (in part or in whole) located in New York State.

Here would be the ancillary administration procedures in New York:

STEP 1: SELECT THE PERSON TO BE APPOINTED ANCILLARY ADMINISTRATOR

If the decedent left a will in which he expressly appointed a given person to serve as the executor of his property within the foreign state, or in which he expressly appointed a person to administer all of his property wherever located, then consider nominating such a person (even if he's one and the same person as the executor) to serve as the ancillary administrator.

In situations involving intestate (no will) administration, select a resident of the foreign state, whether a lay person or an attorney—preferably a reliable next-of-kin or relative of the decedent, or a friend or acqaintance of average intelligence thereof—to serve.

STEP 2: PREPARE & FILE THE ANCILLARY ADMINISTRATION PETITION PAPERS WITH THE NEW YORK COURT'S CLERK

Under New York's law (it is the same procedure with most other states), the petition for ancillary probate or ancillary letters of administration, may be made by any creditor, or a person interested in the estate (a beneficiary, distributee, etc.), or a public administrator or such other official. The petitioner need not necessarily be the one serving as the domiciliary executor or the person applying for appointment as the ancillary administrator, or be even eligible for such an appointment.

The following petition forms used in New York are typical:

FOR TESTATE (WITH WILL) SITUATIONS:
1. Form P-41, *"Petition for Ancillary Probate"* (sample blank copy of form is on pp. 142-4).
2. Form P-42, *"Citation Upon Application for Ancillary Probate"* (sample blank copy of form is on p. 145).
3. Form P-43, *"Decree Admitting Will to Ancillary Probate"* (sample blank copy of form is on pp. 146-7).
4. Form P-44, *"Designation of Person to Receive Ancillary Letters"* (sample blank copy of form is on p. 148).

FOR INTESTATE (NO-WILL) SITUATIONS:
1. Form P-45, *"Petition for Ancillary Administration"* (sample blank copy of form is on pp. 149-150).
2. Form P-46, *"Citation Upon Application for Ancillary Letters of Administration"* (sample blank copy of form is on pp. 148).
3. Form P-47, *"Decree Granting Ancillary Letters of Administration"* (sample blank copy of form is on p. 151).
4. Form P-44, *"Designation of Person to Receive Ancillary Letters"* (sample blank copy of form is on p. 148).

NOTE: These forms are obtainable from the Publisher's legal forms division. See p. 239 for form ordering information.

Upon completion of the petition papers, the petitioner submits them to the New York Surrogate's Court clerk in the county in which the property is located. Certified copies of the will (when applicable), and of the death certificate and the original Letters Testamentary or Letters of Administration from the domiciliary state, should also be attached along with the fee charged for the filing.[2]

The clerk assigns a "file number" to the case. If found necessary that certain persons be cited, he'll issue petitioner such citation papers and set a "return date" by which proof of completion of their service on the necessary parties is to be filed with the clerk's office.

STEP 3: SERVE THE CITATIONS UPON THE REQUIRED PERSONS, IF ANY

(See the procedures outlined in the probate of will situations—'Step Four' of Chapter 5 on p. xxx—and follow those same procedures. Those required to be served in the present instance, however, are the following: the State Tax Commission; all creditors or persons claiming to be creditors who reside within the state; and, depending on the court's directive, any other person(s) who may either be entitled to letters themselves or to nominate others to receive one, may have to be served.)

STEP 4: FILE WITH THE COURT CLERK THE PROOF OF SERVICE OF CITATION

(See the procedures outlined in the probate of wills situations—'Step Five' of Chapter 5 on pp. xxx—and follow those same procedures.)

STEP 5: THE COURT ISSUES PETITIONER HIS "ANCILLARY LETTERS OF ADMINISTRATION"; HE PERFORMS HIS ESTATE SETTLEMENT DUTIES

Upon the court's approval of the petition, the judge will sign the court order of approval and issue the appointed person the *ANCILLARY LETTERS OF PROBATE (or ANCILLARY LETTERS OF ADMINISTRATION).* This document represents the court's authorization of the person to act in that fiduciary capacity within the given foreign state (New York in our example here)

Thereafter, the next order of business is, of course, for the ancillary administrator to carry out his duties. Generally speaking, an ancillary administrator has more or less the same rights, powers, duties and liabilities as a conventional executor or administrator *within* the foreign jurisdiction for which he is authorized to act.

Briefly, you would, as an ancillary administrator, seek to do the following:

i) Protect the interests of beneficiaries, distributees and creditors who are domiciled *within the* foreign state for which you are appointed.

ii) Sue to recover property withheld from you within the state, if any, or to collect debts or enforce a contractual claim owned by the decedent within the state.

---

[2]Foreign courts often require some documentary proof that there is, in fact, an administration of the estate actually taking place in the decedent's domiciliary state before they may grant ancillary approval. Submission of these original letters would generally be deemed a sufficient proof of that.

iii) Collect and reduce to your possession the decedent's assets within the state, and liquidate such assets for cash, as may be directed by the local court.

iv) Open a separate bank account exclusively for the estate and deposit all estate monies received by you in that account; sign all checks drawn on or withdrawals made from such account, in the name of the estate in your official fiduciary capacity.

v) Pay, as directed by your state's court, the debts of the decedent due to creditors domiciled within the state, and the administration expense incurred in the course of your official duties.

vi) Transmit any remaining assets, upon completing payment of all legitimate debts and expenses, to the "original" jurisdiction—the state or country where the domiciliary letters were granted. There, the principal executors (or administrators) of the estate in the domiciliary state may now dispose of any such transmitted assets according to the laws of that domiciliary state.

Form P-41

Form 719—5M—4-72 ANC. TEST. PET.   13676-72   94

SURROGATE'S COURT
COUNTY OF KINGS

IN THE MATTER OF THE APPLICATION FOR
ANCILLARY LETTERS TESTAMENTARY AND
ANCILLARY PROBATE PROCEEDINGS OF
THE LAST WILL AND TESTAMENT OF

_____ (full name of the deceased person)

Late of ___(a non New York State Address)___

State of ___(a "foreign" - i.e. non-New York - State)___

_____
                                    Deceased.

**Petition For
Ancillary Probate**

TO THE SURROGATE'S COURT OF THE COUNTY OF KINGS:

The petition of ___(name of the person applying)___

residing at _____ State of _____

respectfully showeth that your Petitioner is the Executor named in the Last Will and Testament

of _____

_____, deceased.

That said decedent was, at the time of h___ death, a citizen of the United States and a domiciliary of County of _____, State of _____, and departed this life in _____, State of _____

_____ day of _____, 19___, possessed of PERSONAL PROPERTY located within the County of Kings, State of New York, having an estimated value of $_____.

That said decedent died seized of REAL PROPERTY situated in the County of Kings, State of New York. That said real property is improved / unimproved. A brief description of each parcel is as follows:

That the estimated value of such real property and improvement is $_____.

That heretofore and on the _____ day of _____, 19___, a will of real and personal property made by said decedent was duly admitted to probate or established

a competent court within the State of _____ where the decedent was domiciled as aforesaid, and the said will was executed in the State of _____, and in the manner prescribed by the Laws of the said state.

That said will is filed and recorded in the ....

.... *the same being the proper office therefor, as prescribed by the laws of said State of* .... *and the said will, with the proofs and the records thereof, remain in said court. That the probate of said Last Will and Testament is not subject to contest under the laws of the said state of* ....

That on the .... *day of* .... *19* ...... *letters testamentary upon the estate of said deceased were duly issued by said court to* .... *as* .... *Execut........... named in said will and who is presently the duly qualified and acting Executor of said estate.*

That a copy of the will, the decree admitting it to probate and said letters testamentary are hereto annexed, authenticated in the manner prescribed by SCPA 1614.

That Petitioner has made diligent search as follows, to wit, by ....

....

....

(State Amount of Debts Due by Decedent.) *to discover whether any creditors or persons claiming to be creditors of the decedent reside within this State, and he is also familiar with the financial affairs of the decedent, and he knows of his own knowledge that there are no creditors of the decedent with the State of New York except* ....

....

That the following persons are entitled to Ancillary Letters or are entitled to designate an appointee for such letters (set forth names, addresses and status of such persons):

That the amount of security given on the original appointment of said .... *was* ....

That no previous application for ancillary letters testamentary or for ancillary probate on the said Last Will and Testament has been made in this or any other Surrogate's Court of this State.

That there is no estate tax assessable upon this estate.

That there are no other persons than those hereinbefore mentioned interested in this proceeding.

Your Petitioner therefore prays that said exemplified copies be recorded and that said Last Will and Testament be admitted to ancillary probate in this court and that ancillary letters testamentary be issued to h____ upon h____ qualifying as prescribed by law, and that a citation issue directed to the creditors herein named and generally to all creditors of the decedent within the State to show cause why such letters should not issue without a bond.

Dated _____, 19____

SIGNED: X _____ Petitioner.

STATE OF NEW YORK
COUNTY OF KINGS   } ss.:

_____

the Petitioner named in the foregoing petition, being duly sworn, deposes and says that ___he has read the foregoing petition subscribed by h____ and knows the contents thereof; and that the same is true of h____ own knowledge, except as to the matters therein stated to be alleged on information and belief, and that as to those matters ___he believes it to be true.

SIGNED: X _____ Petitioner.

Sworn to this _____ day

of _____ 19____

_____

Form P-42

Citation Upon Application for Ancillary Probate

File No._____, 19_____.

CITATION

The People of the State of New York,
By the Grace of God Free and Independent;

TO:　　[NOTE: *This citation must be issued to the State Tax Commission, to all domiciliary creditors or domiciliaries claiming to be creditors, and to such other persons entitled to Letters or to designate an appointee as the court, by order, directs.*]

[Names of the person (or persons) to be cited.]

A Petition having been duly filed by _____, who is domiciled at _____,

You Are Hereby Cited To Show Cause before the Surrogate's Court, _____ County, at _____ _____ in the County of _____ on _____, 19___, at ___M, why a decree should not be made in the estate of _____, lately domiciled at _____, in the County of _____, State of _____, admitting the Last Will and Testament of said decedent dated _____, 19___, to ancillary probate in said Court based upon its probate in the said State of _____, and granting ancillary letters thereon to _____, the person named as executor therein.

Dated, Attested and Sealed, _____, 19___

_____
Surrogate

_____
Clerk

Form P-43

Form 19-A   5M-5-71-12480 (C.S.) ⟨≡⟩ 94

At the Surrogate's Court in and for the County
of Kings, at the Court House in the Civic
Center, 2 Johnson Street, Brooklyn, N. Y.,
on the_____ day of_____, 19____

Present:

Hon. _____

Surrogate

In the Matter of the Application for Ancillary
Probate of the Last Will and Testament of

(the full name of the deceased person)

Late of (a non- New York State address)

State of (a "foreign" i.e. non-New York - State)

Deceased

Decree Granting (Admitting Will To) Ancillary Probate

_____19_____

A copy of the record of the will of_____(the decedent's name)____

_____

_____, deceased,

late of the_____of_____

State of_____, and of the judgment, decree or order

of the _____Court of_____within

said state, entered the_____ day of_____, 19____, duly

admitting the same to probate (and of the letters testamentary issued thereon to

_____

the execut or (-rix) in said will named), authenticated as prescribed by statute,

having been filed in this court on the_____ day of_____, 19_____

(together with an instrument duly executed by the said Executor, named

authorizing (name of such person being so authorized ?)

to receive ancillary letters testamentary upon the estate of said deceased)

and the said (name of the person to be appointed to serve in N.Y.)

_____

having therewith presented to and filed in this court   h is verified petition praying for a decree awarding ancillary probate, and the Surrogate having ascertained to his satisfaction that there are/are no creditors or persons claiming to be creditors of the said decedent residing within the State of New York as follows: _____

_____

_____

_____

Now, on motion of _____ ,the Executor

~~attorney~~ for said Estate of _____

It is Ordered and Decreed that the said will be admitted to ancillary probate and ancillary letters testamentary be issued to the executor named in said will

_____

_____

_____

_____

_____ upon h taking and subscribing the statutory oath or affirmation and qualifying as prescribed by law, and

Note—Provide for bond when one is required

It is Further Ordered and Decreed that none of the property of the decedent shall be removed from this state until sufficient evidence has been given to the State Tax Commission to enable it to ascertain the estate tax herein.

ENTER: _____

Surrogate (Judge)

Form P-44

SURROGATE COURT: COUNTY OF _____

[Add title of proceeding]

Designation of Person To Receive Ancillary Letters

File No._____

I, the undersigned, _____, Public Administrator of the City of _____ and County of _____, State of _____, the sole acting domiciliary Administrator of the Estate of _____, also called _____, deceased, having my office at _____, State of_____, having been duly appointed administrator of the said decedent's estate by the _____ Court of the State of _____ for the City of _____ and County of _____, on the _____ day of _____ 19___, and still acting as such administrator, do now hereby designate and authorize _____, of No.____ _____ Street, in the City of _____ and State of New York, to apply for and receive Ancillary Letters of Administration upon the Estate of _____, also called _____, deceased, in the Surrogate's Court, _____ County , New York, and I do further authorize the said _____ to do and act in connection with the said estate and the matters mentioned above as fully and effectively as I could do it if personally present, and I do further waive the issuance of service of process upon me in connection with the ancillary proceeding to be commenced herein, and I do further consent to the entry of a decree issuing Ancillary Letters of Administration to the said _____.

Dated: _____ 19____

Signature_____

[Type Name]

[Acknowledgment]

Form P-46

Citation Upon Application for Ancillary Letters of Administration

CITATION

File No. _____, 19____.

THE PEOPLE OF THE STATE OF NEW YORK,
BY THE GRACE OF GOD FREE AND INDEPENDENT,

To: *[names of the person (or persons) to be cited]*

A petition having been duly filed by _____, who is domiciled at _____,

YOU ARE HEREBY CITED TO SHOW CAUSE before the Surrogate's Court, _____ County, at _____ in the County of _____, on _____ 19___, at _____ M., why a decree should not be made in the estate of _____, lately domiciled at _____, in the County of ___, State of ___, granting ancillary letters of administration on the said estate of said _____, deceased, to the above named petitioner.

Dated, Attested and Sealed, _____ 19___.
[L.S.]

_____
Surrogate Clerk

Name of Petitioner_____ Tel. No._____
Address of Petitioner_____

This citation is served upon you as required by law. You are not obliged to appear in person. If you fail to appear, it will be assumed that you do not object to the relief requested. You have a right to have an attorney-at-law appear for you.

Note: If affidavit of service be made outside the State of New York, it must be authenticated in the manner prescribed by CPLR 2101, 2309.

Form P-45

Form 40

FORM

Kings County Surrogate's Court

In the Matter of the Application for
Ancillary Letters of Administration
on the Estate of

(full name of the deceased person)
_____Deceased.

Petition for Ancillary Letters of Administration

File No._____ _____19_.

TO THE SURROGATE'S COURT OF THE COUNTY OF KINGS:

See
Sections
160, 161
and 162
S. C. A.

The petition of (party asking to receive the Ancillary Letters)
residing at_____State of_____
respectfully showeth that your Petitioner is (relationship or connection to decedent)
of said deceased.

That said deceased was at the time of h___ death a resident of
and departed this life in_____ on the_____day of
19____, having personal property within this county, to wit:
_____

The said deceased at the time of h___ death was_____seized of improved or unimproved real
estate in this state, consisting of_____

That heretofore on the_____day of_____
19____ Letters of Administration on the estate of said decedent were duly granted to____
by____
a competent court in the State of_____
where the decedent so resided as aforesaid, a copy of which letters, authenticated as prescribed by
section 45 of the Decedent Estate Law is attached hereto and made a part hereof.

That your petitioner is the_____
person entitled to the personalty of the decedent under the laws of___
proof of which is herewith submitted.

The Petitioner has made diligent search as follows, to wit, by_____
_____
_____

to discover whether any creditors or persons claiming to be creditors of the decedent reside within
this State and he is also familiar with the financial affairs of the decedent, and he knows of his own
knowledge that there are no creditors of the decedent within the State of New York, except_____
_____

That the amount of security given on the original appointment was_____
That the amount of personal property in this State left by the decedent does not exceed in value
_____dollars.

That no previous application for letters or ancillary letters of administration has been made in
this or any other Surrogate's Court in this State.

Your Petitioner therefore prays that the said Surrogate issue a citation according to law, and
issue ancillary letters of administration to h___ upon h___ qualifying as prescribed by law.

Dated, the_____day of_____, 19____

The State
Tax Com-
mission
must be
cited
or its
waiver
obtained
on every
application
for
ancillary
letters.

X_____
Petitioner.

STATE OF_____ _____COUNTY OF_____ ___ _____ss.:

_____ _____ ___ __ _ ___ _____the above-named Petitioner

being duly sworn, say:__ __ ___ __ _____ __ __ I have read the foregoing

Petition and the same is true to my own knowledge, except as to the matters therein stated to be

alleged on information and belief, and as to those matters I believe it to be true.

Sworn to,

before me this_____ ___ _____.day___

of __ _____ ___ __ .19___

X _____ _____ _____

Notary Public.

STATE OF___ _____ _____COUNTY OF___ _____ _____ss.:

_____ _____ _____ ___.a citizen of the United States and

over twenty-one years of age, do solemnly swear and declare that I will well, faithfully and honestly

discharge the duties of Ancillary Administrat_____ ___ ....of the Goods, Chattels and Credits which

were of_____ _____ ___ _____ _____deceased, according to law.

Sworn to,

before me this_____ _____ _____.day.___

of ___ . ___ _____.19___

X _____ _____ _____

Notary Public.

Designation under S.C.A. §95.

I,___ _____ _____ _____ _____about to be appointed

the Ancillary Administrat ___ ___ ___in this proceeding, residing at No_____

do hereby designate the Clerk of the Surrogate's Court of the County of Kings, and his successor in

office as a person on whom service of any process issuing from said Court in this proceeding or in any

other proceeding which shall affect the estate of the said ___ __ ___ _____

_____ _____ ___ _____ _____ _____deceased,

may be made in like manner and with like effect as if it were served personally upon me, whenever I

cannot be found and served within the State of New York after due diligence used.

X _____ _____ _____

STATE OF___ ___ _____COUNTY OF_____ ___ _____ss.:

On this_____ _____.day of_____ _____ ___ _____, 19___, before me personally

came_____ _____ _____ _____ _____

to me known and known to me to be the individual_____described in and who executed the foregoing

instrument and___he_____ _____ ___acknowledged to me that___he___.executed the same.

Notary Public.

Form P-47

At a Surrogate's Court held in and for the County of Kings, on the

day of_____ _____ _____ in the year 19____.

Present,

_____, Surrogate.

In the Matter of the Application for
Ancillary Letters of Administration
on the Estate of

_____ Deceased.

Decree Granting Ancillary Letters of Administration

A copy of the record of the proceedings for Letters of Administration on the Estate of

_____

late of the_____ of _____

and State of_____ _____ deceased, and of

the Letters awarded by the _____ Court of

_____ within said State, entered the

_____ day of_____ _____19____, duly

appointing

Administrator of said estate, authenticated as prescribed by statute, having been filed in this court,

on the_____ _____ _____ day of _____ _____ 19____,

(together with an instrument duly executed by the said_____ _____ _____

authorizing_____ _____ _____ to receive

ancillary letters of administration upon the estate of said deceased) and the said _____ _____

having therewith presented to and filed in this Court ___h.___ verified petition praying for a decree

awarding to ___h.___ ancillary letters of administration on said estate.

Now, on motion of_Mr/Mrs _____

~~attorney~~ for said **Ancillary Letters of Administration** . Petitioner

IT IS ORDERED and DECREED that ancillary letters of administration on the Estate of

_____

_____deceased,

issue to the said_____upon ___h.___ filing a bond in the sum of $____ __

and otherwise qualifying according to law. And it is further

ORDERED, ADJUDGED and DECREED that none of the property be removed from this

State without first giving the State Tax Commission sufficient evidence to enable it to ascertain the

tax due thereon.

_____
Surrogate. (Judge)

Appendix A
SUMMARY OF BASIC PROBATE RULES IN ALL 50 & OTHER STATES*

As stated in Chapter 4 above, the broader probate and estate settlement procedures of most states are basically identical, and the differences from one state to another usually relate merely to the specific peculiarities particular to each state.

Broadly, the probate principles and procedures detailed in this manual for the State of New York (see, especially, Chapters 5,6,7-A,7-B, 7-C, 7-D) are fairly representative of the general principles and procedures of most states. And *if you are able to merely follow the New York procedures, you can rest assured that you can just as equally probate an estate in just about any other state in the nation — simply by using the same basic knowledge outlined in those chapters.* Given in this Appendix below, for the benefit of those who live or want to probate an estate in other states, are the bare essentials and summary rules for doing so in all 50 states and other U.S. territories.

INTRODUCTION TO UNDERSTANDING THIS APPENDIX

The following notes will help you understand the terms and concepts in the appendix. Other terms and concepts not specifically defined are explained in the text, as well as in the Glossary of Relevant Terms in Appendix G. The information provided under *statutes,* gives the code section for the state wherein you can look up your state probate law. (Always be sure to check the latest updates contained at the pocket section at the end of each volume). The term *"P.R."* is an abbreviation for "personal representative" (i.e., executor or administrator) of the estate. The P.R. (personal representative) category explains when a person living outside of the state where probate occurs can be appointed as a personal representative. A personal representative named in the will qualifies, regardless of his or her state of residence. But some states require the personal representative to appoint a person (an agent) living within the state to receive correspondence and legal notices.

In brief, *"unsupervised"* refers to an informal probate procedure that requires little or no supervision, and *"supervised"* refers to a formal procedure (hearing, notice requirement, etc) that require court approval at major steps.

With regard to the information provided under the caption *"Administration,"* the words in parentheses which come after *"unsupervised"* or *"supervised,"* are the terms used by each state to describe its version of unsupervised or supervised administration, while the term *"Administration Unnecessary"* refers to estates for which a streamlined procedure can be used, and for which often a signed release form (an *"affidavit"*) can replace full administration — something very similar to the *"small estate"* or *"summary"* procedures outlined in Chapter 8 of the manual. These three terms refer to the three basic types of administration used to probate estates. (See the Glossary of Terms, Appendix F, for explanation of these terms.)

Under the *Proving Will* caption, *"witness"* refers only to a person who witnessed and signed the will of the decedent. A will may often be proved by either formal or informal procedures. The formal proof of a will does

---

*The following data was largely compiled in March, 1990. Since state laws and court rules may change at any time, you should verify the most current status of the information given for your state with the probate registrar before proceeding with probate. And/or, since much of this information comes from your state's probate code, you may also check your state's latest probate law in the local public library. Most of the material, as updated , is current as of 1993.

not imply that formal administration must be used, or visa versa. A will may be subjected to a formal proof even in unsupervised (or *"informal"*) administration. Self-proved will refers generally to where the will involved is shown to have been properly executed by the testator and then *notarized* by the witnesses.

- •*Admin. Notice* ("Administration Notice"), when listed, refers to the first notice of the initiation of probate.
- •*P.R. Notice* indicates the time and method required for notifying all interested persons of the appointment of the personal representative.
- •*By Affidavit* refers to a procedure for small estates by which an inheritor can collect certain property simply be signing an affidavit.
- •UPC—stands for Uniform Probate Code.
- •*Creditor Notice* refers generally to publishing a notice in a newspaper to inform creditors about the decedent's death the appointment of a P.R., and the deadline within which they may file claims, if any.
- •*Spouse's Automatic Share* refers to the rights allowed a spouse under the state law to receive property automatically when the other spouse dies, and the amounts thereof. (See Glossary of Relevant Terms in Appendix G). Note that automatic share is separate and apart, and absolutely different from, the *Spouse's Intestate Share* (Appendix B), or the *Spouse's Right to Election* (Appendix C).

ALABAMA: PROBATE COURT
Statutes: Code of Alabama (1978), Title 43, Chapters 2-1 to 8-298
Administration: (1) Unsupervised (Informal); (2) Supervised (Formal); (3) Summary: For estates under $3,000 consisting solely of personal property.
Holographic Wills: Not recognized
Proving Will: By one witness or by proof of the handwriting of the testator and one of the witnesses. Self-proved wills are recognized. Wills are generally submitted within 30 days after death.
Appraisals: Real property: by tax assessment. Personal property: Estimated by PR. Privately hired appraisers are optional.
Claims: Must be presented within six months after appointment of Executor (or Administrator).
Accountings: Not required. If requested, due 12 months after appointment of executor, and annually thereafter until estate is disposed. Notice of final settlement must be given by newspaper publication once each week for three consecutive weeks, unless waived by consent from all interested parties.
Executor: Nonresidents may not be appointed.
PR Notice: To all interested parties by certified mail within one month after appointment of PR and at least ten days prior to hearing on probate petition.
Creditor Notice: By newspaper publication once each week for three consecutive weeks, due within one month after appointment of PR.
Inventory: Not required. If requested by interested party, due within two months after appointment of PR.
Contests: Due within six months after admission of will, filed in circuit court.
PR Fees: up to 2 1/2% of receipts and 2 1/2% of disbursements, additional 2 1/2% for real property sold. Realtor's commissions are charged separately.
Attorney's Fees: No statutory provision.
State Tax: Credit Estate Tax.
Tax Due: 15 months after death.
Notes: Alabama is a UPC state.
Spouse's Automatic Share Rights: Homestead up to $6,000, personal property up to $3,500 and family expenses during administration; allowance for family living expenses up to 1 year if estate is solvent.
Order of Priority of Claims/Debts: (1) Funeral Expenses, (2) administrative expenses, (3) expenses during last sickness, (4) taxes owed before deceased's death, (5) any debts to deceased's employees from the year of death, and (6) all other debts.

ALASKA: SUPERIOR COURT
Statutes: Alaska Statutes (1988), Title 13
Administration: (1) Unsupervised (Informal); (2) Supervised (Formal): by petition of interested party and court agreement; (3) Summary: If estate (minus some real estate claims) totals less than sum of the spouse's exemptions plus administration, funeral and last illness costs; (4) Administration Unnecessary: For estates under $6,000 probate court settles estate. By Affidavit, may collect personal property if estate (minus real estate claims) is less than $15,000, if inheritor applies at least 30 days after death an no P.R. application is pending.
Holographic Wills: Recognized
Proving Will: Informal: Properly witnessed wills are accepted without further evidence. *Formal:* By affidavit or testimony of one witness. Self-proved wills are recognized. Wills must be submitted within three years of death.

Admin. Notice: Informal: No notice required. *Formal:* To all interested parties by regular mail 14 days before hearing.

Appraisals: Privately hired appraisers may be employed.

Claims: Due within four months after first newspaper publication, or within three years after death if no notice to creditors was published.

Accountings: Informal: By sworn statement of PR. *Formal:* By a final accounting.

PR: Nonresidents may be appointed.

PR Notice: To all interested parties by regular mail within 30 days after appointment of PR.

Creditor Notice: By newspaper publication once each week for three consecutive weeks.

Inventory: Due within three months after appointment of PR. Sent to all interested parties who request it. May also be filed with court.

Contests: Should be file at or before formal hearing. Formal: Appeals must be filed before order approving distribution, or 12 months after order admitting will, whichever is first. Informal: an appeal must be filed within six months of closing, or 12 months after order admitting will, whichever is first.

PR Fees: Reasonable compensation.

Attorney's Fees: Reasonable compensation, usually hourly rate.

State Tax: Credit Estate Tax.

Tax Due: 15 months after death.

Notes: Alaska is a UPC state.

Spouse's Automatic Share Rights: Homestead up to $27,000; personal property up to $10,000, and reasonable family expenses during administration up to 1 year.

Order of Priority of Claims/Debts: (1) Administrative expenses, (2) funeral expenses, (3) debts and taxes with preference under federal law,(4) expenses during last sickness, (5) debts and taxes with preference under state law, and (6) all other debts.

Community property or common law state? Common Law.

ARIZONA: SUPERIOR COURT

Statutes: Arizona revised statutes (1980), Title 14, Chapter 1102, Title 33, Chapter 601

Administration: (1) Unsupervised *(Informal)*; (2) Supervised *(Formal)*: by petition of interested party and court agreement; (3) Summary; (4) Admin. Unnecessary: For estates under $30,000 where 30 days have elapsed since death and no P.R. has been elected.

Holographic Wills: Recognized

Proving Will: Informal: Properly witnessed wills are accepted without further evidence. *Formal:* By affidavit or testimony of one witness. Self-proved wills are recognized. Wills must be submitted within three years of death.

P.R.: Nonresidents may be appointed.

P.R. Notice: To all interested parties by regular mail within 10 days after appointment of P.R.

Creditor Notice: By newspaper publication once each week for three consecutive weeks upon appointment of P.R.

Inventory: Due within 3 months after appointment of P.R. Sent to all Interested parties who request it. May also be filed with court.

Appraisals: By privately hired appraisers.

Claims: Due within 4 months after the first newspaper publication, or within 3 years after death if no notice was published.

Accountings: Due 12 months after appointment of P.R., and annually thereafter until estate is closed.

Contests: Should be filed before or at formal Will hearing. Informal: an appeal must be filed within 6 months of closing, or 12 months after order admitting will, whichever is first. Formal: Appeals must be filed before order approving distributions, or 12 months after order admitting will, whichever is first.

P.R. Fees: Reasonable compensation.

Attorneys Fees: Reasonable compensation. Itemized statement of work frequently filed.

State Tax: Credit Estate Tax.

Tax Due: 9 months after death.

Spouse's Automatic Share Rights: Half of community property; homestead up to $12,000; personal property up to $7,000; and reasonable family expenses up to 1 year if solvent.

Order of Priority of Claims and Debts: (1) Administrative expenses, (2) funeral expenses, (3) debts and taxes with preference under federal law, (4) expenses during last sickness, (5) debts and taxes with preference under state law, and (6) all other debts.

Notes: Arizona is a UPC and community property state. One-half of the property acquired during marriage is owned by the surviving spouse.

ARKANSAS: PROBATE COURT

Statutes: Arkansas Statutes Annotated (1987), Title 28, Chapters 24-101 to 48-305.

Administration: (1) Supervised *(Formal)*; (2) Admin. Unnecessary: Generally for estates solvent under $50,000 after debts and spouse's exemptions where 45 days have elapsed since death and no P.R. has been appointed.

Holographic Wills: Recognized

Proving Will: By testimony of two witnesses, by proof of the signatures of the decedent or witnesses, or by other evidence. Self-proved wills are recognized. Wills must be submitted to court within five years after death.

P.R.: A nonresident is required to appoint a resident agent.

P.R. Notice: To all interested parties by regular mail.

Creditor Notice: Estates over $1,000, by newspaper publication once each week for two consecutive weeks. Estates under $1,000, by posting notice to creditors in the courthouse.

Inventory: Due within 2 months after appointment of P.R.

Appraisals: Real estate that is sold is usually professionally appraised. P.R. usually appraises the estate.

Claims: Due within 2 months after appointment of P.R.

Accountings: Due 12 months after appointment of P.R., and annually thereafter until estate is closed.

Contests: Generally due before order approving final distribution. Must be made within five years after admission of will.

P.R. Fees: First $1,000—10%, next $4,000—5%, above $5,000—3%, additional fees allowed for substantial duties in handling real property.

Attorneys Fees: First $5,000—5%, next $20,000—4%, next $75,000—3%, next $300,000—2.75%, next $600,000—2.5%, 2% of the balance. Additional fees for extraordinary services upon petition.

Tax Due: 9 months after death.

Spouse's Automatic Share Rights: Homestead up to $2,500; personal property up to $1,000. Half of all community property. Allowance for family and living expenses up to $500 for two months. Furnishings reasonably necessary for family.

Order of Priority of Claims and Debts: (1) Administrative expenses, (2) funeral expenses, last illness expenses and wages due to deceased's employees, and, (3) all other debts.

Community property or common law state? Common law.

CALIFORNIA: SUPERIOR COURT (PROBATE DIVISION)

Statutes: West's Annotated California Codes (1980), Probate Code Vols: 52-54, Secs. 1-1700.

Administration: (1) Unsupervised *(Independent or Informal);* (2) Supervised *(Formal);* (3) *Summary:* for estate under $60,000, less debts, if spouse and/or minor children survive decedent; (4) Non-probate transfer (section 650): for estates consisting entirely of community property passing entirely to surviving spouse, spouse collects all property left by will or intestacy. One hearing verifies property rights and dispenses with administration. (5) Admin. Unnecessary: For estates of personal property only, under $30,000 (excluding owed wages and motor vehicles).

Holographic Wills: Recognized

Proving Will: Informal: By testimony of one witness, or by proof of the handwriting of the testator and that of one witness. Self-proved wills are recognized.

P.R.: Nonresidents may be appointed.

Admin. Notice: To all interested parties by regular mail within 10 days before hearing on will.

P.R. Notice: Combined with Admin notice.

Creditor Notice: Called Notice of Death. By newspaper publication 3 times in minimum of a 10 day period.

Inventory: Due within 3 months after appointment of P.R.

Appraisals: By P.R. and an inheritance tax referee.

Claims: Due within 4 months after appointment of P.R. (one year for out-of-state claimants who did not receive notice).

Accountings: Due 12 months after appointment of P.R. , 18 months if federal estate tax is filed.

Contests: Due within 120 days after will admitted.

P.R. Fees: First $15,000—4%, next $85,000—3%, next $900,000—2%, above $1,000,000—1%, additional fees for extraordinary services.

Attorneys Fees: Follows P.R. schedule.

Tax Due: 9 months after death.

Spouse's Automatic Share Rights: Half of all property acquired during the marriage, use of home for 60 days after filing inventory and reasonable family allowance during administration, or for long period at the court's discretion.

Order of Priority of Claims and Debts: (1) Administrative expenses, (2) funeral expenses, (3) expenses of last illness, (4) family allowance, (5) wages, (6) mortgages and other liens not already secured, (7) judgments, (8) all other debts.

Community property or common law state? Community Property.

Notes: California requires a tax referee to appraise property. Information is available from State Inheritance Tax Referees Association. Direct descendents (children and grandchildren of children who have died) automatically receive their intestate portion of the estate unless mentioned by name in a will.

COLORADO: PROBATE COURT (DENVER); DISTRICT COURT (ALL COUNTIES).

Statutes: Colorado Revised Statutes (1979), Title 15.

Administration: (1)Unsupervised *(informal);* (2) Supervised *(formal):* by petition of interested party and court agreement; (3) Summary; (4) Admin. Unnecessary: For estates under $20,000 and without real property; inheritor may, by filing affidavit, collect such property.

Holographic Wills: Recognized.

Proving Wills: Informal: properly witnessed wills are accepted without further evidence; *Formal:* by affidavit or testimony of one witness; Self-proved wills are recognized. Wills must be submitted within three years of death.

Admin. Notice: Informal: no notice required; *Formal:* to all interested parties by regular mail 14 days before hearing.

P.R. Nonresidents may be appointed.

P.R. Notice: Informal: to all interested parties by regular mail within 30 days after appointment of P.R.; Formal: to all interested parties by regular mail ten days before hearing.

Creditor Notice: By newspaper publication once each week for three consecutive weeks.

Inventory: Informal: not required. Formal: Due within 90 days after appointment of P.R.

Appraisals: By P.R.

Claims: Due within four months after first newspaper publication, or within one year after death, if notice was not published.

Accountings: Informal: by sworn statement of P.R.; *Formal:* final account due no sooner than six months after appointment of P.R.

Contests: Informal: due within three years of closing statement; *Formal:* generally due before order allowing distribution of estate.

P.R. Fees: Reasonable compensation, usually hourly rate.

State Tax: Credit Estate Tax.

Tax Due: 9 months after death.

Spouse's Automatic Share Rights: Half of all community property; personal property: $7,500; and reasonable family living expenses during administration; if estate is insolvent, up to 1 year.

Order of Priority of Claims & Debts: (1) Those with property held by the deceased as a fiduciary or trustee; (2) administrative costs; (3) funeral expenses; (4) debts and taxes with preference under federal law; (5) last illness expenses; (6) debts and taxes with preference under Colorado law, and; (7) all other debts.

Community property or Common Law State? Common law.

CONNECTICUT: PROBATE COURT

Statutes: Connecticut General Statutes Annotated, Title 45.

Administration: (1) Supervised *(Formal);* (2) Admin. Unnecessary: for net estates under $20,000 (transfer by affidavit).

Holographic Wills: Not recognized if written and signed in Connecticut. Recognized if written and signed in any other state that does recognize holographic wills.

Proving Wills: By testimony, statement or affidavit of witnesses, or proof of signatures. Self-proved wills are recognized. Wills must be submitted within 30 days after death.

P.R.: Nonresidents may be appointed.

P.R. Notice: To all interested parties by regular mail.

Creditor Notice: By newspaper publication within ten days after court orders notice to creditors.

Inventory: Due within two months after appointment of P.R. (four months by petition).

Appraisals: Check with your local Registrar of Wills.

Claims: Due by date determined by the court; usually 3 to 12 months after first newspaper publication.

Accountings: Final account due 12 months after appointment of P.R.

Contests: Before or during proof of will. Appeal: By new trial to superior court within 30 days of order (within 12 months if notice of order not received).

P.R. Fees: First $10,000 — 5%; next $40,000 — 3%; next $200,000 — 2.5%; next $750,000 — 2%; next $1,000,000 — 1.5%; above $2,000,000 — 1%; minimum fee $200.

Attorney Fees: Reasonable compensation, but in practice 5-7% of estate value.

State Tax: (1) Inheritance Tax; (2) Credit Estate Tax.

Tax Due: Nine months after death.

Spouse's Automatic Share Rights: Limited. Court sets family living expenses and may allow use of the family car during the administration of the estate.

Order of Priority of Claims & debts: (1) Funeral and administrative expenses; (2) last illness expenses; (3) taxes due to the United States or the State of Connecticut; (4) wages due to the deceased's employees within three months of the date of death; (5) certain other preferred claims, and; (6) all other debts.

Community property or common law state? Common law.

Note: Connecticut probate information is available by contacting: Probate Administration, 805 Maine Street, West Hartford, CT 06017.

DELAWARE: COURT OF CHANCERY (OFFICE OF REGISTER OF WILLS)

Statute: Delaware Code Annotated, Title 12.

Administration: (1)Supervised *(Formal);* (2) Summary: for estates consisting mostly of jointly owned property; (3) Admin. Unnecessary: for estates consisting solely of personal property under $12,500 if 30 days have elapsed since death and no P.R. has been appointed (transfer by affidavit).

Holographic Wills: Not recognized.

Proving Wills: By testimony of one witness, or by proof of signatures of testator and witnesses, or by other sufficient proof. Self-proved wills are recognized. Person with custody of will must submit it to Register of Wills within 10 days of knowledge of death.

P.R.: A nonresident may be appointed.

P.R. Notice: By posting notice in county courthouse within 40 days after appointment of P.R.

Creditor Notice: Estates over $10,000 require newspaper publication once each week for three consecutive weeks.

Inventory: Due within three months after appointment of P.R.

Appraisals: Usually done by P.R. Privately hired appraisers are optional.

Claims: Due within 6 months after appointment of P.R. Claims arising after decedent's death due within 6 months after they arise.

Accountings: Final account due within one year after appointment of P.R. Extensions permitted by petition. Notification of closing to all interested parties must be mailed before filing account.

Contests: Due before the hearing to prove the will. Appeal: filed in Court of Chancery within 6 months after admission of will, by anyone not present or cited to appear at the original proof of will.

P.R. Fees: For estates between 0-$5,000 — $250 plus 11.3% over $2,200; for estates between $100-200,000 — 4.5%; for estates $5,000,000 and over — 2.8%. *(Note:* Delaware bases fees on all personal property, one half jointly held property, and one half of all other real estate, regardless of whether or not it is sold. A complete breakdown of fees is available through the Register of Wills office.)

Attorney's Fees: Follows P.R. schedule. Combined Attorney and P.R. fees shall not exceed percentage maximums.

State Tax: (1) Inheritance tax; (2) Credit Estate Tax.

Tax Due: Nine months after death.

Spouse's Automatic Share Rights: Living expenses up to $2,000.

Order of Priority of Claims and Debts: (1) Administrative expenses; (2) funeral expenses; (3) last sickness expenses; (4) wages due to deceased's employees for one year prior to death; (5) state taxes; (6) rent due for one year prior to death, (7) various contracts and obligations for payment of money, delivery of goods, and so forth; and (8) all other debts.

Community property or common law state: Common law.

DISTRICT OF COLUMBIA: SUPERIOR COURT (REGISTER OF WILLS — PROBATE DIVISION)

Statutes: District of Columbia Code, Titles 18-20.

Administration: (1)Unsupervised *(Abbreviated or informal);* (2) Supervised *(Standard or Formal);* (3) **Summary:** For estates under $10,000 (probate office supervises administration); (4) Admin. Unnecessary: For estates consisting solely of two or less motor vehicles if all debts and taxes are paid.

Holographic Wills: Not recognized.

Proving Will: Informal: Properly witnessed wills are admitted without further evidence (without notice to all interested parties). *Formal:* By affidavits of witnesses. Wills are submitted within 90 days of death.

Admin. Notice: Informal: No notice required. *Formal:* To all interested parties by registered mail and newspaper publication once each week for two consecutive weeks.

P.R.: Nonresidents may be appointed by designating the Registrar of Wills as resident agent.

P.R. Notice: To all interested parties by regular mail.

Creditor Notice: By newspaper publication once each week for three consecutive weeks and by publication in the Washington Law Reporter.

Inventory: Due within 90 days after appointment of P.R.

Appraisals: Real estate: By privately hired appraiser listed with the Registrar if sold during probate. By tax appraisal, if not sold. Personal property: By court appointed appraiser.

Claims: Due within 6 months after first newspaper publication of appointment of P.R.

Accountings: Due within one year and one day after first newspaper publication of appointment of P.R. and every 9 months thereafter until estate is closed.

Contests: Due within 6 months after newspaper publication of appointment of P.R.

P.R. Fees: Reasonable compensation, based on the hours spent and complexity of the issues.

Attorneys Fees: Follows P.R. fee schedule.

State Tax: (1) Inheritance tax; (2) Credit Estate Tax.

Tax Due: 18 months after death.

Spouse's Automatic Share Rights: Allowance for $10,000 in family living expenses before debts but after $750 in funeral costs.

Order of Priority of Claims and Debts: (1) Family allowance up to $10,000, (2) back rent, (3) District of Columbia judgements, and (4) all other debts.

Community property or common law state? Common law.

Notes: All real estate is included in the probate estate. By consent of all interested parties, the full court audit may be waived and replaced by a quicker "cursory review."

FLORIDA: CIRCUIT COURT

Statutes: Florida Statutes Annotated, Chapters 731-738.

Administration: (1)Supervised *(Formal);* (2) Summary *(Family Administration):* For estates having only personal property (i.e., without real estate) under $60,000; (3) Summary: Generally for estates under $25,000, or when decedent died more than 3 years ago.

Holographic Wills: Not recognized.

Proving Will: By oath of one witness, by oath of the P.R. named in the will or by oath of a disinterested person. Self-proved wills are recognized.

P.R. A nonresident relative of the decedent may be appointed.

P.R. Notice: to all interested parties by certified mail.

Creditor Notice: By newspaper publication once each week for two consecutive weeks.

Inventory: Due within 60 days after the appointment of P.R.

Appraisals: By P.R. or privately hired appraiser.

Claims: Due within 3 months after first newspaper publication. Claims not rejected within 4 months after first newspaper publication are automatically accepted.

Accountings: Final account due within 12 months after appointment of P.R. Extensions by court permission.

Contests: Due within 3 months after first newspaper publication.

P.R. Fees: Reasonable compensation.
Attorney Fees: Reasonable compensation.
State Tax: Credit estate tax.
Tax Due: 9 months after death.
Spouse's Automatic Share Rights: Household property, cars and appliances up to $10,000. Lifetime use of real property; personal effects of the deceased up to $1,000; $6,000 allowance in family living expenses during the administration of the estate.
Order of Priority of Claims & debts: (1) Administrative expenses, (2) $3,000 funeral expenses, (3) debts and taxes with preference under federal law, (4) last illness expenses for the 60 days preceding death, (5) family allowance, (6) debts after death due to continuation of the deceased's business to the extent of the business's assets, and (7) all other debts.
Community property or common law state? Common law.
Notes: Florida is a modified UPC state.

GEORGIA: PROBATE COURT
Statutes: Code of Georgia Title 24, Sections 101+, Title 113, Sections 101+
Administration: (1)Unsupervised *(Informal)*; (2) Supervised *(Formal)*; (3) Admin. Unnecessary: For estates where all interested parties consent and all debts are paid.
Holographic Wills: Not recognized (but occasionally admitted).
Proving Will: Informal (without notice): By testimony of one witness (becomes conclusive after seven years). *Formal:* Hearing after notice to all interested parties by personal service and newspaper publication. Will must be submitted within a reasonable time after death.
P.R.: Nonresident may be appointed if his or her interest is equal to or greater than all other beneficiaries combined.
P.R. Notice: To interested parties in Georgia by personal service at least ten days prior to formal proof of will.
Creditor Notice: Within 60 days after appointment of P.R. by newspaper publication, once each week for four successive weeks.
Inventory: Informal: None. Formal: Due within four months after appointment of P.R.
Appraisals: Usually done by P.R.
Claims: Due within three months from last newspaper publication date.
Accountings: Informal: Half page closing statement. Final account due if requested by any interested party. Formal: Not sooner than 6 months   after appointment of P.R., if requested by an interested party. Due within 12 months after appointment of P.R.
Contests: Filed in probate court. Appeal filed in superior court.
P.R. Fees: Reasonable compensation by law, but in practice, up to 2.5% of money received and 2.5% of money paid out. Additional fees allowed for extraordinary services.
Attorneys Fees: No statutory provision.
State Tax: Credit estate tax.
Tax Due: 9 months after death.
Spouse's Automatic Share Rights: The court determines allowance for family living expenses, of no less than $1,600.
Order of Priority of Claims & Debts: (1) One-year's support for deceased's family, (2) funeral expenses, (3) administrative expenses, (4) taxes or other debts due to the United States or Georgia (5) debts due by deceased from having been a trustee or other type of fiduciary, (6) judgements, mortgages, and liens against items of specific property, (7) debts for rent, (8) general judgments against the deceased, (9) open accounts, and (10) all other debts.
Community property or common law state? Common law.
Notes: The Georgia State Bar Association publishes a general guide on Georgia probate. After proof of will, informal administration is handled completely outside of court. Administration is unnecessary when there is no will and, by petition, all heirs agree, not to probate the estate. The petition should name all the hiers-by-law, list the amounts and descriptions of all property, show that all heirs have agreed to a specific division of the property. The probate judge then orders that all estate assets be transferred automatically to the designated heirs. The judge publishes a notice to creditors, and if no objections arise from the creditors, and all estate debts are paid, assets directly transfer upon the probate judge's order.

HAWAII: CIRCUIT COURT
Statutes: Hawaii Revised Statutes, Title 560, Sections 2+
Administration: (1) Unsupervised *(Informal)*; (2) Supervised *(Formal)*: For all estates over $40,000; (3) Summary: For estates under $20,000; (4) Admin. Unnecessary: Estates under $5,000 (transfer by affidavit without a P.R.).
Holographic Wills: Not recognized.
Proving Will: Informal: properly witnessed wills are accepted without further evidence. *Formal:* by affidavit or testimony of one witness. Self-proved wills are recognized. Wills must be submitted within five years of death.
Admin. Notice: Informal: No notice required. *Formal:* To all interested parties by regular mail 14 days before hearing date.
P.R.: Nonresident may be appointed only if immediate family member.
P.R. Notice: With notice of administration.
Creditor Notice: By newspaper publication once each week for three successive weeks at least 10 days before hearing on will.
Inventory: Due within 30 days after appointment of P.R.
Appraisals: Appraiser usually appointed by the registrar or court.
Claims: Due within four months after first newspaper publication.
Accountings: Final account due within two years after appointment of P.R.

Contests: Should be filed before or at formal will hearing. Formal: appeals must be filed before order approving distribution, or 12 months after order admitting will, whichever is first. Informal: an appeal must be filed within six months of closing, or 12 months after order admitting will, whichever is first.

P.R. Fees: Reasonable compensation, but in practice: First $15,000 — 4%; next $85,000 — 3%; next $900,000 — 2%; next $2,000,000 — 1.5%; above $3,000,000 — 1%. Additional 5-7% charged on income of estate.

Attorneys Fees: Reasonable compensation, but practice follows P.R. fee schedule.

State Tax: (1) Inheritance Tax; (2) Credit Estate Tax.

Tax Due: 18 months after death.

Notes: A probate manual is available through "Hawaii Continuing Education." Ask your Registrar of Wills about it. Hawaii is a modified UPC state.

Spouse's Automatic Share Rights: Homestead: $5,000; personal property: $5,000 and allowance for family living expenses during administration of the estate.

Order of Priority of Claims and Debts: (1) Administrative expenses; (2) funeral expenses, (3) up to $6,000 in family allowance, (4) homestead allowance, (5) exempt property, (6) debts and taxes with preference under federal law, (7) last-illness expenses, (8) debts and taxes with preference under Hawaii law, and (9) all other debts.

Community property or common law state? Common law.

IDAHO: DISTRICT COURT (MAGISTRATE'S CIVIL DIVISION)

Statutes: Idaho Code (1978), Titles 14 and 15, Chapters 2-500+, 3-101+

Administration: (1) Unsupervised (*Informal*); (2) Supervised (*Formal*): by petition of interested party and court agreement; (3) Summary; (4) Admin. Unnecessary: for estates under $6,000, probate court settles estate.

Holographic Wills: Recognized.

Proving Will: Informal: Properly witnessed wills are accepted without further evidence. *Formal:* by affidavit or testimony of one witness. Self-proved wills are recognized. Wills must be submitted within 3 years of death.

Admin. Notice: Informal: No notice required. *Formal:* to all interested parties by regular mail 14 days before hearing.

P.R. A nonresident may be appointed.

P.R. Notice: to all interested parties by regular mail within 30 days after appointment of P.R.

Creditor Notice: by newspaper publication once each week for 3 consecutive weeks, upon appointment of P.R.

Inventory: due within 3 months after appointment of P.R.

Appraisals: Privately hired appraiser may be employed.

Claims: due within 4 months after first newspaper publication.

Accountings: Informal: by sworn statement of P.R. Formal: by a final accounting, due no sooner than 6 months after appointment of P.R.

Contests: Should be filed before or at formal will hearing. Formal: appeals must be filed before order approving distribution, or 12 months after order admitting will, whichever is first. Informal: an appeal must be filed within 6 months of closing, or 12 months after order admitting will, whichever is first.

P.R. Fees: Reasonable compensation.

Attorneys Fees: Reasonable compensation.

State tax: (1)Inheritance tax; (2) Credit estate tax.

Tax due: 9 months after death.

Spouse's Automatic Share Rights: Half of community property. Homestead: $4,000 if there are no dependent children living with spouse, or if there are, it is $10,000. Personal property: $3,500; allowance for living expenses during the administration, and court may increase the allowance if requested by the executor.

Order of Priority of Claims & Debts: (1) Administrative expenses, (2) funeral expenses and last illness expenses (3) debts and taxes with preference under federal law or Idaho law, and (4) all other debts.

Community property or common law state? Community property.

Notes: Idaho is a UPC and community property state. One-half of the property acquired during marriage is owned by the surviving spouse. Informal administration may not be initiated until 30 days after death.

ILLINOIS: CIRCUIT COURT

Statutes: Illinois Annotated Statutes, Chapter 25, Paragraph 24+; Chapter 140 ½, Paragraph 1

Administration: (1) Unsupervised (*Independent*); (2) Supervised (*Formal*): For estates under $150,000; (3) Summary: For estates under $50,000; (4) Admin. Unnecessary: For estates under $25,000 (transfer by affidavit).

Holographic Wills: Not recognized.

Proving Will: Informal: Properly witnessed will automatically admitted without notice. *Formal:* By two witnesses, or by other competent evidence (statements or affidavits). Self-proved wills are recognized. Wills must be submitted 30 days after appointment of P.R.

P.R. Nonresidents are required to appoint a resident agent.

P.R. Notice: To all interested parties by regular mail.

Creditor Notice: By newspaper publication once each week for three consecutive weeks, beginning 14 days after appointment of P.R.

Inventory: Filed in court within 60 days after appointment of P.R. Copies also sent to all beneficiaries.

Appraisers: By P.R. or privately hired appraiser.

Claims: Due within six months after appointment of P.R.

Accountings: Due within six months and 60 days after appointment of P.R. Annual account due 12 months and 30 days after appointment of P.R.; also due as requested by court. Copies sent to all beneficiaries.

Contests: Due within six months after will is admitted to probate.

P.R. Fees: Reasonable compensation by law, but in practice: First $25,000 —5%; next $750,000 —3.5%-4.5%; next $50,000 — 3%-3.5%; next $150,000 — 2.5%-3%; next $750,000 — 2%-2.5%; above $1,000,000 — 1.5%.

Attorneys Fees: Reasonable compensation.

State Tax: (1) Inheritance tax; (2) Credit estate tax.

Tax Due: Ten months after death.

Spouse's Automatic Share Rights: Homestead: $7,500. Allowance for 9 months of living expenses up to $10,000; plus $2,000 for each minor or adult dependent.

Order of Priority of Claims: (1) Funeral expenses and administrative expenses, (2) surviving spouse's or children's award, (3) debts due to the U.S. Government, (4) last-illness expenses and any wages due to the deceased's employees from four months prior to death but no more than $800 per employee, (5) money and property held in trust by the deceased which cannot be traced, (6) debts due to the state of Illinois or any political subdivision, and (7) all other debts.

Community property or common law state? Common law

INDIANA: PROBATE COURT (VIGO AND ST. JOSEPH COUNTIES) CIRCUIT OR SUPERIOR COURT (ALL OTHER COUNTIES).

Statutes: Burns Indiana Statutes Annotated, Title 29.

Administration: (1) Unsupervised *(Informal):* for solvent estates if all interested parties consent; (2) Supervised *(Formal);* (3) Summary; (4) Admin. Unnecessary: for estates under $8,500 if 45 days have elapsed since death and no P.R. has been appointed (transfer by affidavit). *(Note:* Probate judges in some counties do not recognize unsupervised administration. Check with your local Registrar of Wills.)

Holographic Wills: Not recognized if written and signed in Indiana. Recognized if written and signed in a state that does not recognize holographic wills.

Proving Will: Informal only; by testimony of one or more witnesses, by proof of handwriting of testator or two witnesses. Self-proved wills are recognized. Wills must be submitted within three years of death.

P.R.: Nonresident may be appointed only as co-P.R. with a resident.

P.R. Notice: to all interested parties by regular mail.

Creditor Notice: by newspaper publication once each week for two successive weeks.

Inventory: due within 60 days after appointment of P.R.

Appraisals: Privately hired appraiser may be employed.

Claims: due within five months after first newspaper publication.

Accountings: due within one year after appointment of P.R. and annually thereafter until estate closed.

Contests: due within five months after the will is submitted for probate.

P.R. Fees: Reasonable compensation; usually one-half of the percentages allowed attorneys.

Attorneys Fees: Reasonable compensation, but law courts frequently establish a percentage basis for attorney compensation. Check with your county Probate Registrar for the specific percentage used. *(General guidelines:* first $5,000—10%; next $55,000—5%; $60,000 - $500,000—3%; above $500,000—2%.)

State tax: (1) Inheritance tax; (2) Credit estate tax.

Tax Due: Twelve months after death.

Spouse's Automatic Share Rights: $8,500 in personal property; if there is less than $8,500 in personal property real estate may be used to make up the difference.

Order of priority of Claims: (1) Administrative expenses, (2) funeral expenses, (3) allowance to spouses or children, (4) debts and taxes with preference under federal law, (5) last sickness expenses, (6) debts and taxes with preference under Indiana law, and (7) all other debts.

Community property or common law state? Common law.

IOWA: DISTRICT COURT

Statutes: Iowa Code Annotated, Title 32, Ch. 633

Administration: (1) Supervised *(formal);* (2) Summary: For estates under $30,000; (3) Admin. Unnecessary.

Holographic Wills: Not recognized.

Proving Will: By oral or written testimony of at least one witness; or by proof of the signatures of the testator and witnesses. Self-proved wills are recognized. Will must be submitted within five years after death.

P.R.: Nonresident may be appointed in some cases.

P.R. Notice: To all interested parties and creditors by newspaper publication once each week for two consecutive weeks upon the appointment of P.R.

Inventory: Due within 60 days after appointment of P.R.

Appraisals: Estimated by P.R. unless inheritance tax division requests appraisal (performed by one of their division's appraisers).

Claims: Due within six months after second newspaper publication.

Accountings: Final account and settlement due within three years of appointment of P.R.

Contests: Due within six months after second newspaper publication.

P.R. Fees: Reasonable compensation by law, but in practice: First $1,000 — not more than 6%; next $4,000 — 4%; above $5,000 — 2%.

Attorneys Fees: Same as P.R. fee schedule.

State Tax: (1) Inheritance tax; (2) Credit estate tax.
Tax Due: 12 months after death.
Spouse's Automatic Share Rights: Living expenses for 1 year and some personal property.
Order of Priority of Claims and Debts: (1) Court costs, (2) other administrative expenses, (3) funeral expenses, (4) debts and taxes with preference under federal law, (5) last-illness expenses, (6) debts and taxes with preference under Iowa law, (7) debts to any of the deceased's employees for services within 90 days of death, and (8) all other debts.
Community property or common law state? Common law.
Notes: The sale of real estate and the closing of the estate require hearings, and notice to all interested parties 20 days before hearings on each, unless waived in writing.

KANSAS: DISTRICT COURT

Statutes: Kansas Statutes Annotated Chapter 79, Subject Sections 101, 501, 601.
Administration: (1) Unsupervised *(informal);* (2) Supervised *(formal);* (3) Summary.
Holographic Wills: Not recognized.
Proving Will: By testimony of two witnesses; or by evidence of signatures.
P.R.: Nonresidents may be appointed in specific cases.
P.R. Notice: To all interested parties and creditors within ten days after filing petition for probate.
Creditor Notice: By newspaper publication once each week for three consecutive weeks.
Inventory: Due within 30 days after appointment of P.R.
Appraisals: Called "valuation." By P.R. or private appraiser, depending on local practice.
Claims: Due within six months after first newspaper publication.
Accountings: Final account and settlement are due nine months after appointment of P.R. and annually thereafter until estate is closed.
Contests: Due within nine months after the first newspaper publication.
P.R. Fees: Reasonable compensation, but in practice: First $10,000 — 5%; next $15,000 — 4%; next $25,000 — 3%; next $50,000 — 2%; and above $100,000 — 1%.
Attorneys Fees: Reasonable compensation.
State Tax: (1) Inheritance tax; (2) Credit estate tax.
Tax Due: Nine months after death.
Spouse's Automatic Share Rights: Personal property or cash up to $7,500; lifetime use of decedent's real estate up to 1 acre within urban limits, and 60 acres within farm land if no taxes are owed on it.
Order of Priority of Debts and Taxes: (1) Funeral expenses, (2) last sickness expenses and administrative costs, (3) judgements against the deceased rendered during the deceased's lifetime, and (4) all other debts.
Community property or common law state? Common law.

KENTUCKY: DISTRICT COURT (UNCONTESTED PROCEEDINGS), CIRCUIT COURT (CONTESTED PROCEEDINGS).

Statutes: Kentucky Revised Statutes, Chapters 394.000 - 395.000
Administration: (1) Supervised *(formal);* (2) Admin. Unnecessary: (a) dispensing by agreement: for estates without debts or claims, if all beneficiaries agree. (b) for estates under $5,000 where spouse survives decedent and applies. Both (a) and (b) require creditor notice by newspaper publication once each week for 6 consecutive weeks.
Holographic Wills: Recognized.
Proving Will: Informal: by testimony or statements of one witness or by proof of the handwriting of the testator. Additional proof may be required. Formal: upon request of interested party, proof as court requires. Self-proved wills are recognized. Wills are generally submitted within 2-3 months after death.
Admin. Notice: To all interested parties at least 5 days before hearing on probate petition. Estates under $1,000 require no notice.
P.R.: A nonresident is required to appoint a resident agent. Nonresident relatives of decedent require no resident agent.
P.R. Notice: Combined with admin. notice.
Creditor Notice: Clerk of circuit court publishes appointment of P.R. each month.
Inventory: Due within 2 months after appointment of P.R.
Appraisals: By P.R.
Claims: Due within one year after appointment of P.R. or within 3 years after death if no P.R. is appointed.
Accountings: Due not sooner than six months, but before 2 years after appointment of P.R. Annually thereafter until estate is closed.
Contests: Filed in circuit court within 2 years after district court order admitting will.
P.R. Fees: Up to 5% of estate value and income; additional fees for extraordinary services by petition.
Attorneys Fees: Follows P.R. schedule. Attorney also acting as P.R. can only receive a total of 5% of estate value. Additional fees for extraordinary services by petition.
State Tax: (1) Inheritance tax; (2) Credit estate tax.
Tax Due: 18 months after death.
Spouse's Automatic Share Rights: half of all community property; half of the decedent spouse's separate personal property and living expenses up to $7,500 after administration, funeral and last illness costs; half of the real estate owned by decedent spouse at death, plus lifetime use of one third of other real estate.

Order of Priority of Claims and Debts: (1) Administrative expenses, (2) funeral expenses, (3) debts and taxes with preference under federal and Kentucky law, and (4) all other debts.
Community property or common law state: Common law.
Notes: Specific information on Kentucky probate (used by Registrar of Wills) is available from the Liberty National Bank in Louisville, KY.

LOUISIANA: DISTRICT COURT
Statutes: Louisiana Statutes Annotated, Code of Civil Procedure (1980), Articles 2811-3462; Civil Code, Articles 871-1465
Administration: (1) Supervised *(formal);* (2) Admin. Unnecessary: for estates consisting solely of personal property under $50,000, if the only inheritors are spouse, siblings or issues.
Holographic Wills: Recognized
Proving Will: Informal: by oath of a Notary Public and one witness; by oath of two credible persons who recognize the decedent's Notary's, or witness's signature. *Formal:* upon petition of any interested party. Self-proved wills are recognized.
P.R.: A nonresident is required to appoint a resident agent.
P.R. Notice: Not required but frequently mailed to all interested parties.
Creditor Notice: As required by court order (usually by newspaper publication prior to estate closing).
Inventory: Due upon appointment of P.R.
Appraisals: Court appoints two appraisers.
Claims: Presented to P.R. before or at the final hearing to settle the estate.
Accountings: Due 12 months after appointment of P.R. and annually thereafter until estate closed.
Contests: Usually made by petition for formal proof of will. Appeal by separate trial.
P.R. Fees: Generally 2.5% of the inventory, but may be increased by the court upon petition.
Attorneys Fees: No statutory provision.
State Tax: (1) Inheritance tax; (2) Credit estate tax.
Tax Due: Nine months after death.
Spouse's Automatic Share Rights: At least half of the community property.
Order of Priority of Claims and Debts: (1) Funeral expenses, (2) charges imposed by law, (3) last illness expenses, (4) servant's wages for the last year and current year, (5) amounts due retailers for family provisions for six months prior to death and rent due to innkeepers or boarding houses for one year prior to death, (6) clerk's salaries, if any, and (7) all other debts.
Community property or common law state? Community property.
Notes: Louisiana is a community property state. One half the property acquired during marriage is owned by the surviving spouse.

MAINE: PROBATE COURT
Statutes: Maine Revised Statutes Annotated, Title 18A, Sections 1-101 to 5-614; Maine Rules of Court, Rule 4
Administration: (1) Unsupervised *(informal);* (2) Supervised *(formal);* (3) Summary; (4) Admin. Unnecessary: for estates under $10,000 (transfer by affidavit).
Holographic Wills: Recognized.
Proving Will: Informal: properly witnessed wills are accepted without further evidence. *Formal:* by affidavit or testimony of one witness. Self-proved wills are recognized. Wills must be submitted within three years of death.
P.R.: Nonresidents may be appointed.
P.R. Notice: To all interested parties by regular mail within 30 days after appointment of P.R.
Creditor Notice: By newspaper publication once each week for two successive weeks within 30 days after appointment of P.R.
Inventory: Due within three months after appointment of P.R.
Appraisals: Privately hired appraiser may be employed.
Claims: Due within four months after first newspaper publication.
Accountings: Informal: by statement of P.R., no sooner than six months after appointment of P.R. Formal: due after filing deadline (four months after first newspaper publication).
Contests: Should be filed before or at formal will hearing. Formal: Appeals must be filed before order approving distribution, or 12 months after order admitting will, whichever is first. Informal: An appeal must be filed within six months of closing, or 12 months after order admitting will, whichever is first.
P.R. Fees: Reasonable compensation, but in practice up to 5% of estate value (less for large estates).
Attorneys Fees: Reasonable compensation, usually based on an hourly rate.
State Tax: (1) Inheritance tax; (2) Credit estate tax.
Tax Due: 12 months after death.
Spouse's Automatic Share Rights: Homestead up to $5,000; personal property up to $3,500 and living expense allowance during term of administration.
Order of Priority of Claims and Debts: (1) Administrative expenses, (2) funeral expenses, (3) debts and taxes with preference under federal law, (4) expenses during last sickness, (5) debts and taxes with preference under Maine law, and (6) all other debts.
Community property or common law state? Common law.
Notes: Maine adopted most of the UPC in 1981.

MARYLAND: ORPHAN'S COURT (CIRCUIT COURT IN MONTGOMERY AND HARTFORD COUNTIES)

Statutes: Annotated Code of the Public General Laws of Maryland, Estates and Trusts Title 4, Sections 4-101+.

Administration: (1) Supervised *(formal)*; (2) Summary: for estates under $20,000.

Holographic Wills: Recognized only if made outside U.S. by persons serving in military, but void after one year after discharge.

Proving Will: Informal: (or Administrative): properly witnessed wills proved without notice. *Formal (or Judicial):* by request of interested party or court.

P.R.: A nonresident is required to appoint a resident agent.

P.R. Notice: Names and addresses of all interested persons, and copies of creditor notice sent to Register of Wills by certified mail within 20 days after appointment of P.R. Register sends out notice (which is usually waived by consent of all interested persons).

Creditor Notice: By newspaper publication once each week for 3 consecutive weeks. The first is generally due within 20 days after appointment of P.R.

Inventory: Estimate of inventory due with filing of petition for probate. Full inventory due within 3 months after appointment of P.R.

Appraisals: Real estate (if sold): by privately hired appraiser. Personal property: by privately hired or court appointed appraiser.

Claims: Due within 6 months after appointment of P.R.

Accountings: Due within 6 months after appointment of P.R., and every 6 months thereafter until estate is closed.

Contests: Due within 6 months after first newspaper publication.

P.R. Fees: For personal property: first $20,000 — 10%; above $20,000 — 4%. Real property if sold: 10% of value.

Attorneys Fees: Reasonable compensation. Attorney and P.R. fees jointly shall not exceed P.R. fee schedule. But in practice attorneys use percentages allowed P.R.

State Tax: Inheritance tax.

Tax Due: 15 months after death.

Spouse's Automatic Share Rights: Allowance for living expenses up to $2,000, plus $1,000 for each unmarried under 18.

Order of Priority of Claims and Debts: (1) Fees due to the registrar of wills, (2) administrative expenses, (3) funeral expenses not to exceed $2,500, (4) executor's, real-estate agents, and attorneys fees, (5) family allowance, (6) taxes due by the deceased, (7) last-illness expenses, (8) up to three months back rent owed by deceased, (9) wages, salaries, and commissions due for services performed for three months prior to death, (10) any Maryland old-age assistance claims, and (11) all other debts.

Community property or common law state? Common law.

Notes: Maryland's formal procedure is done entirely by mail.

MASSACHUSSETS: PROBATE AND FAMILY COURT

Statutes: Massachussetts General Laws Annotated Ch. 190-206.

Administration: (1) Supervised *(Formal);* (2) Summary: For estates consisting solely of personal property under $15,000 (excluding motor vehicle).

Holographic Wills: Not recognized.

Proving Will: By testimony or affidavits of two witnesses or by written consent of all interested parties. Self-proved wills are recognized. Will must be submitted within 30 days after knowledge of death.

Admin. Notice: To all interested parties by registered mail or personal service (depends on your county) at least 14 days before hearing on will.

P.R.: A non-resident is required to appoint a resident agent.

P.R. Notice: Combined with Admin. Notice.

Creditor Notice: By newspaper publication once each week for 3 consecutive weeks.

Inventory: Due within 3 months after appointment of P.R.

Appraisals: Real property: Privately hired appraiser. Personal property: By P.R.

Spouse's Automatic Share Rights: Living expenses and use of home for 6 months. In certain situations use of home up to $100,000 until death or remarriage.

Order of Priority of Claims or Debts: (1) (Last-illness expenses, funeral expenses, and administrative expenses. (2)debts with preference under federal law, (3) public rates, taxes and excise duties, and (4) miscellaneous other small claims and all other debts.

Community Property or Common Law State: Common Law

Claims: Due within 4 months after appointment of P.R. All claims considered valid unless P.R. disclaims them by notice within 4 months and 60 days after appointment of P.R.

Accountings: Due 12 months after appointment of P.R. and annually thereafter until estate is closed.

Contests: Made at hearing on probate petition. Appeal: due within 30 days after admission of will.

P.R. Fees: No stautory provision, generally 5% of estate value.

Attorneys Fees: No stautory provision, generally 5% of estate value.

State Tax: (1) Estate Tax, (2) Credit Estate Tax.

Tax Due: 9 months after death.

Notes: Review of attorneys fees by the court can be requested by an interested party (routinely requested).

MICHIGAN: PROBATE COURT

Statutes: Michigan Compiled Laws Annotated, Sections 600.801+, 700.12+.

Administration: (1) Unsupervised (*Independent or Informal*); (2) Supervised (*Formal*) (3) Summary: For intestate estates up to maximum of $20,000 if spouse or minor children survive decedent, or for estates under $5,000; (4) Admin. Unnecessary: For estates consisting solely of vehicles valued under $10,000 (transfer by affidavit).

Holographic Wills: Recognized.

Proving Will: Informal: By consent of all interested parties. *Formal:* By testimony of persons with knowledge of signing of will. Holographic wills are admitted by proof of the handwriting of the testator. No provision for self-proved wills. Wills generally submitted within 90 days of death.

Admin. Notice: Informal: None if waived by all interested parties. Formal: To all interested parties by personal service 5 days before hearing on will, or by registered mail 10 days before hearing and by newspaper publication for 3 weeks.

P.R.: Nonresident may be appointed.

P.R. Notice: Informal: None if waived by all interested parties. *Formal:* To all interested parties by personal service 5 days before hearing on probate petition, or by registered mail 10 days before hearing and by newspaper publication for three weeks.

Creditor Notice: By one newspaper publication at least 10 days before claims hearing date is set (hearing date for claims is set 2-4 months after first publication).

Spouse's Automatic Share Rights: Homestead up to $10,000; personal property up to $3,500; allowance for living expenses during term of the estate adminstration, or for 1 year if the estate is insolvent.

Order of Priority Of Claims & Debts: (1) Administrative expenses, (2) funeral expenses, (3) family allowances and homestead exemptions, (4) certain claims against the estate, such as last-illness expenses and debts due to the federal government or the State of Michigan, and (5) all other debts.

Community property or Common Law State: Common Law.

Inventory: Informal: None if waived by all interested parties. Formal: Due within 60 days after appointment of P.R.

Appraisals: Real property: By privately hired appraiser or double tax assessment. Personal property: Estimated by P.R.

Claims: Due within 18 months after claims hearing date if the estate is open. Claims are barred if the estate is closed.

Accountings: Informal: None, if all interested parties agree. Formal: Due 12 months after apointment of P.R. and annually thereafter until estate is closed.

Contests: Due prior to the hearing for probate. Appeal: Filed in court of appeals within 21 days of the probate order.

P.R. Fees: Reasonable compensation, but in practice: First $1,000—5%; next $4,000—21/2 %; above $5,000—2%. Additional fees for extraordinary services.

Attorneys Fees: Reasonable fees.

State Tax: (1) Inheritance Tax; (2) Credit Estate Tax.

Tax Due: Nine months after death.

Notes: Michigan is a UPC state. Michigan's version of informal probate requires no inventories or accounts if all interested parties consent.

MINNESOTA: PROBATE COURT (DIVISION OF COUNTY COURT, EXCEPT HENNEPIN AND RAMSEY COUNTIES).

Statutes: Minnesota Statutes Anotated, Ch. 524-528.

Administration: (1) Unsupervised (*Informal*); (2) Supervised (*Formal*); (3) *Summary:* Generally for estates under $30,000; (4) *Admin. Unnecessary:* For estates under $6,000, probate court settles estate.

Holographic Will: Not recognized.

Proving Will: Informal: Properly witnessed wills are accepted without further evidence. *Formal:* By affidavit or testimony of one witness. Self-proved wills are recognized. Wills must be submitted within three years of death.

P.R.: Nonresident may be appointed.

P.R. Notice: Informal: By regular mail to all interested parties upon appointment of P.R.; *Formal:* By regular mail to all interested parties 14 days before hearing on will.

Creditor Notice: By newspaper publication once each week for two consecutive weeks.

Inventory: Due three months after appointment of P.R. Sent to all interested parties who request it; may also be filed with court.

Spouses's Automatic Share Rights: Personal property up to $9,000; one automobile; lifetime use of homestead if there are living children or issue of deceased children; allowance for living expenses during administration of the estate up to 18 months for solvent estate or 12 months for insolvent estate.

Order of priority of claims or debts: (1) Administrative expenses, (2) funeral expenses, (3) debts and taxes with preference under federal law, (4) last-illness expenses, (5) medical expenses from up to one year preceding deceased's death, (6) debts and taxes with preference under Minnesota law and (7) all other debts.

Community Property or Common Law State: Common Law.

Appraisals: Usually done by P.R.

Claims: Due within four months after first newspaper pubication of within three years of death if no notice was published.

Accountings: Informal: Closing statement sent to all interested parties. Formal: Final account is due 18 months after appointment of P.R

Contests: Should be filed before or at formal will hearing. Formal: Appeals must be filed before order approving distribution, or 12 months after order admitting will, whichever is first. Informal: An appeal must be filed within six months of closing or 12 months after order admitting will, whichever is first.

P.R. Fees: Reasonable compensation.
Attorneys Fees: Reasonable compensation.
State Tax: (1) Estate Tax; (2) Credit Estate Tax.
Tax Due: 9 months after death.
Notes: Minnesota is a UPC state. Formal administration usually requires use of an attorney.

MISSISSIPPI: CHANCERY COURT

Statutes: Mississippi Code Annotated Title 91.
Administration: (1) Supervised *(Formal)*.
Holographic Wills: Recognized.
Proving Will: Informal:(without notice): By testimony of one witness, or by affidavit of witness. *Formal.:* By petition of any interested party. Holographic wills proved by affidavits of two disinterested persons. Self-proved wills are not recognized.
P.R.: Nonresident may be appointed.
Admin. Notice: To creditors and all interested parties by newspaper publication once each week for three consecutive weeks, within a reasonable time.
Inventory: Due within 90 days after appointment of P.R.
Appraisals: Normally by three court-appointed appraisers.
Spouse's Automatic Share Rights: Lifetime use of homestead up to $30,000 and 150 acres, plus allowance for living expenses for 1 year.
Order of Priority of Claims & Debts: (1) Last-illness expenses, funeral expenses, and administrative expenses, and (2) all other debts.
Community Property or Common Law State: Common Law.
Claims: Due within 90 days after notice by newspaper publication.
Accountings: Due 12 months after appointment of P.R. and annually thereafter until estate closed.
Contests: Due within two years after probate if will informally proved (without notice).
P.R. Fees: Up to 7% of estate value.
Attorneys Fees: Reasonable compensation.
State Tax: Estate Tax.
Tax Due: Nine months after death.

MISSOURI: CIRCUIT COURT (PROBATE DIVISION)

Statutes: Vernon's Annotated Missouri Statutes Ch. 472-474
Administration: (1) Unsupervised *(Independent or Informal):* If requested by will or consented to by all interested parties. (2) Supervised *(Formal);* (3) Summary: For estates under $15,000 if 30 days have elapsed since death and no P.R. has been appointed.
Holographic Wills: Not recognized.
Proving Will: By testimony of 2 witnesses; by testimony of one witness and proof of the handwriting of the other witness(es); by other competent evidence. Self-proved wills are recognized. Will must be submitted to court within 3 years.
P.R.: Nonresidents may be appointed.
P.R. Notice: To all interested parties by regular mail, upon appointment of P. R.
Creditor Notice: By newspaper publication once each week for 4 consecutive weeks, at least 4 weeks in advance of final closing.
Inventory: Due within 30 days after appointment of P.R.
Spouse's Automatic Share Rights: Homestead up to half of the estate or $7,500, whichever is less; some personal property; automatic or reasonable living expenses for 1 year.
Order of Priority of Claims & Debts: (1) Court Costs and fees. (2) administrative expenses. (3) exemptions and allowances, (4) funeral expenses (5) debts and taxes with preference under federal law, (6) last-illness expenses and servants' wages, (7) debts and taxes with preference under Missouri law (8) judgments rendered against the deceased during his or her lifetime, and (9) all other debts.
Community Property or Common Law State: Common Law.
Appraisals: By P.R. or privately hired appraiser.
Claims: Due within 6 months after first newspaper publication.
Accountings: Final account due exactly 6 months after first newspaper citation. Notice to all interested parties must be mailed within 15 days before final settlement.
Contests: Due within 6 months after first newspaper publication.
P.R. Fees: First $5,000—5%; next $20,000—4%; next $75,000—3%; next $300,000—2%; next $600,000—2 1/2%; above $1,000,000—2%.
Attorneys Fees: Follows P.R. fee schedule.
State Tax: Credit Estate Tax.
Tax Due: 9 months after death.
Notes: By statute, Missouri is the only state in which attorneys must be hired to probate estates, to include making all court appearances. State is a modified UPC state.

MONTANA: DISTRICT COURT

Statutes: Montana Code Annotated Title 72.

Administration: (1) Unsupervised (*Informal;* (2) Supervised (*Formal):* By petition of all interested parties and court agreement; (3) *Summary;* if estate, minus debts, totals less than $7,500.

Holographic Wills: Recognized.

Proving Will: Informal: Properly witnessed wills are accepted without further evidence. *Formal:* By affidavit or testimony of one witness. Self-proved Wills are recognized. Wills must be submitted within three years of death.

P.R.: Non-resident may be appointed.

P.R. Notice: To all interested parties by regular mail within 30 days after appointment of P.R.

Creditor Notice By newspaper publication once each week for three successive weeks within four months after death.

Inventory: Due within three months after appointment of P.R.

Spouse's Automatic Share Rights: Homestead up to $20,000; personal property up to $3,500 and allowance for living expenses during administration (only up to 1 year where the estate is insolvent).

Order of Priority of Claims & Debts: (1) Administrative expenses, (2) funeral expense and last-illness expenses, (3) U.S. estate taxes and Montana estate and inheritance taxes, (4) debts with preference under federal and Montana laws (5) any other federal taxes or Montana taxes, and (6) all other debts.

Community Property or Common Law State: Common law.

Appraisals: By privately hired appraiser or P.R.

Claims: Due within four months after first newspaper publication.

Accountings: Final account due within 15 months after appointment of P.R.

Contests: Should be filed before or at formal will hearing. *Formal:* Appeals must be filed before order approving distribution, or 12 months after admitting will, whichever is first. *Informal:* An appeal must be filed within six months of closing, or 12 months after order admitting will, whichever is first.

P.R. Fees: By practice: First $40,000—3%; above $40,000—2%. Minimum fee: $100.

Attorneys Fees: Up to 1 1/2 times the compensation allowed to the P.R.

State Tax: (1) Inheritance Tax; (2) Credit Estate Tax.

Tax Due: 18 months after death.

Notes: Montana is a UPC state.

NEBRASKA: COUNTY COURT

Statutes: Revised Statutes of Nebraska, Ch.30 Sections 2201-2326

Administration: (1) Unsupervised (*Informal);* (2) Supervised (*Formal):* By petition of interested party and court agreement; (3) *Summary;* (4) Admin. Unnecessary: For estates under $10,000.

Holographic Wills: Recognized.

Proving Will: Informal: Properly witnessed wills are accepted without further evidence; *Formal:* By affidavit or testimony of one witness. Self-proved wills are recognized. Wills must be submitted within three years of death. P.R.: Nonresidents may be appointed.

P.R. Notice: To all interested parties by regular or certified mail within 30 days after appointment of P.R.

Creditor Notice: By newspaper publication once each week for three consecutive weeks.

Inventory: Due within 60 days after appointment of P.R .

Spouse's Automatic Share Rights: Homestead up to $7,500; personal property up to $5,000; allowance for living expenses during the administration (up to only 1 year where the estate is insolvent).

Order of Priority of Claims or Debts: (1) Administrative expesnses, (2) funeral expenses, (3) debts and taxes with preference under federal law, (4) last-illnes expenses, (5) debts and taxes with preference under Nebraska law, and (6) all other debts.

Community Property or Common Law State: Common Law.

Appraisals: Privately hired appraisers may be employed.

Claims: Due within two months after first newspaper publication.

Accountings: Informal: By sworn statement of P.R.; *Formal:* By a final accounting.

Contests: Generally within 30 days of admission (or rejection) of will.

P.R. Fees: Reasonable compensation.

Attorneys Fees: Reasonable compensation.

State Tax: (1) Inheritance Tax; (2) Credit Estate Tax.

Tax Due: 12 months after death.

Notes: Nebraska is a UPC state. Informal probate is one of the easiest in the country.

NEVADA: DISTRICT COURT

Statutes: Nevada Revised Statutes (1979), Title 12 (Ch. 133-156).

Administration: (1) Supervised (*Formal);* (2) Summary: For estates under $100,000; (3) *Admin. Unnecessary:* For estates under $10,000 if 40 days have elapsed since death without appointment of P.R. (transfer by affidavit). In some cases, it could be where estate does not exceed $25,000.

Holographic Wills: Recognized.

Proving Will: By affidavit of witnesses; by testimony of witnesses; by other satisfactory evidence.

Admin. Notice: To all interested parties by certified mail at least 10 days before hearing on will.

P.R.: Nonresident may be appointed.

P.R. Notice: With notice of administration.

Creditor Notice: By three newspaper publications after appointment of P.R., with at least 10 days passing between first and last publication.

Inventory: Due within 60 days after appointment of P.R.

Appraisals: Privately hired appraisers may be employed.

Spouse's Automatic Share: Half of the community property; homestead; some personal property and, at the court's discretion, allowance for living expenses.

Order of Priority of Claims or Debts: (1) funeral expenses, (2) last-illness expenses, (3) family allowance, (4) debts with preference under federal law, (5) up to $600 in wages for services to deceased in the 120 days prior to death (6) judgments and liens against the deceased and (7) all other debts.

Community Property or Common Law State: Community Property.

Claims: Due within 90 days after first newspaper publication (within 60 days if estate is under $60,000).

Accountings: First account is due 30 days after judge acts on claims. Final account due upon closing of estate.

Contests: May be made at any time within six months after will is admitted to probate.

P.R. Fees: First $1,000—6%; next $14,000—4%; above $5,000—2%.

Attorneys Fees: Reasonable compensation, but in practice up to 5% of estate value.

State Tax: None.

Notes: Nevada is a community property state. One-half of the property acquired during marriage is owned by the surviving spouse.

NEW HAMPSHIRE: PROBATE COURT

Satutes: New Hampshire Revised Statutes Annotated Titles 56 and 57 (Ch. 547-569).

Administration: (1) Supervised *(Formal);* (2) *Summary:* For estates under $5,000; (3) Admin. Unnecesary: For estates consisting solely of wages, salaries, or commissions under $500, if a spouse survives decedent.

Holographic Wills: Not recognized.

Proving Will: Informal: By testimony of one witness, without notice. *Formal: Upon petition of any* interested party. Self-proved wills are recognized. Wills are usually submitted within 30 days of death.

P.R.: A nonresident is required to appoint a resident agent.

P.R. Notice: To all interested parties within 60 days after appointment of P.R., by certified mail.

Creditor Notice: By newspaper publication within 15 days after appointment of P.R., once each week for two consecutive weeks.

Inventory: Due within three months of appointment of P.R.

Appraisals: Real Estate: tax-assessed value; Personal Property: court-appointed appraiser.

Spouse's Automatic Share: Use of home for 40 days after death, plus allowance for living expenses during the administration which will be deducted from the spouse's inherited share.

Order of Priority of Claims & Debts: (1) Administrative expenses, (2) funeral expenses, (3) widow's allowance, (4) unpaid taxes, (5) last-illness expenses, and (6) all other debts.

Community Property or Common Law State: Common Law.

Claims: Due within six months after appointment of P.R. If estate is insolvent, 1-3 commissioners are court appointed.

Accountings: Due 12 months after appointment of P.R. and annually thereafter until estate closed.

Contests: Usually done by petitioning for formal proof of will. Appeal: To the Superior Court, within 60 days of admission of will.

P.R. Fees: Reasonable compensation, but in practice up to 5% of estate value.

Attorneys Fees: Reasonable compensation, but in practice up to 5% of estate value.

State Tax: (1) Inheritance Tax; (2) Credit Estate Tax.

Tax Due: Twelve months after death.

Notes: Information is available from Registry of Probate office. Formal administration requires the P.R. to appear before the probate court to for a final accounting review.

NEW JERSEY: SURROGATE'S COURT

Statutes: New Jersey's Revised Statutes Annotated, Title 3B, Chapters 1-29; Rules governing the courts of the state of NJ (Part IV).

Administration: Unsupervised *(Informal);* (1) Admin. Unnecessary: (1) For estates under $10,000 where there is a surviving spouse; (2) For estates under $5,000 when there is no surviving spouse (requires filing an "affidavit of next of kin").

Holographic Wills: Not recognized.

Proving Will: Informal: By testimony of one witness, or verification of signatures. *Formal:* By evidence required by court. Self-proved wills are recognized. Wills generally submitted within 30 days after death.

P.R.: Nonresidents may be appointed.

P.R. Notice: To all interested parties by mail within 60 days of admission of will. A copy of the will must be sent to all interested parties with this notice.

Creditor Notice: By newspaper publication once each week for two consecutive weeks within 20 days of court order requiring notice to creditors.

Inventory: Not required unless petitioned for by interested party.

Appraisals: Usually done by P.R. (if inventory requested).

Spouse's Automatic Share: An allowance for living expenses during probate, upon application by the spouse.
Order of Priority of Claims & Debts: (1) Funeral expenses, (2) administrative expenses, (3) debts and taxes with preference under federal or New Jersey law, (4) last-illness expenses, (5) judgments against the deceased and (6) all other debts.
Community Property or Common Law State: Common Law.
Claims: Due within six months of court order requiring notice to creditors. Creditors may request initiation of probate 40 days after death.
Accountings: Not required.
Contests: Before acceptance of will, objections filed in surrogate's court office. After admission of will, contests due within three months (six months if contestant lives out of state).
P.R. Fees: 5 % of estate value (may be reduced by individual counties); 6% on income of estate.
Attorneys Fees: Reasonable fee, usually charged by the hour.
State Tax: (1) Inheritance Tax; (2) Credit Estate Tax.
Tax Due: Eight months after death.
Notes: New Jersey is a UPC state. The P.R. is directly responsible to the interested parties alone. Any interested party may petition the P.R. to file an inventory and/or final account with the court, otherwise filing of the iinventory and the final account is not required. By a ruling of the New Jersey Attorney General, it is said that Certified Public Accountants may not prepare state inheritance tax returns.

NEW MEXICO: PROBATE COURT (Informal), District Court (all other types of admin.)

Statutes: New Mexico Statutes Ch. 45.
Administration: (1) Unsupervised *(Informal);* (2) Supervised *(Formal);* (3) *Summary* (4) *Admin. Unnecessary:* For estates under $20, 000 when 30 days have elapsed since death and no P.R. has been appointed (transfer by affidavit).
Holographic Wills: Not recognized.
Proving Will: *Infomal:* properly witnessed wills are accepted without further evidence. *Formal:* By affidavit or testimony of one witness. Self-proved will are not recognized. Will must be submitted within 3 years of death.
P.R.: Non-residents may be appointed.
P.R. Notice: To all interested parties by personal service or by certified mail within 10 days after appointment of P.R.
Creditor Notice: By newspaper publication once each week for 2 consecutive weeks within a reasonable time after appointment of P.R.
Inventory: Due within 3 months after appointment of P.R.
Appraisals: Estimated by P.R.
Spouse's Automatic Share: half of all community property; homestead up to $100,000 in certain cases; personal property up to $3,500; allowance for living expenses, $10,000.
Order of Priority of Claims & Debts: (1) Administrative expenses, (2) last -illness expenses, (3) funeral expenses, (4) debts and taxes with preference under federal law, (5) debts and taxes due under other New Mexico laws, and (6) all other debts.
Community Property or Common Law State: Community Property.
Claims: Due within 2 months after first newspaper publication, or within 3 years after death if no notice was published. All claims not rejected by P.R. within 60 days of claim filing deadline are automatically accepted.
Accountings: Final account due no sooner than 6 months after appointment of P.R.
Contests: Filed in district court.
P.R. Fees: Reasonable compensation, but in practice: first $3,000—10%; above $3,000—5%. For cash, U.S. savings bonds, and life insurance proceeds: first $5,000—5 %, above $5,000—1%.
Attorneys Fees: Reasonable compensation, but in practice follows P.R. fee schedule or higher.
State Tax: Credit Estate Tax.
Tax Due: 9 months after death.
Notes: New Mexico is a UPC and community property state. One-half of the property acquired during marriage is owned by the surviving spouse.

NEW YORK: SURROGATE'S COURT (DECEDENT'S ESTATES DIVISION)

Statutes: New York Consolidated Laws Service, Annotated Statutes with Forms: Vol. 32, 32A, 32B, Surrogate's Court Procedure Act, Estates, Powers and Trusts.
Administration: (1) Supervised *(Formal);* (2) *Summary:* For estates under $10,000 (excluding motor vehicles).
Holographic Wills: Recognized only for members of armed services in wartime.
Proving Will: By testimony or affidavits of witnesses, or other evidence. Self-Proved wills are recognized in almost every county. Wills are generally submitted within 2 months after death.
P.R.: Nonresidents may be appointed.
P.R. Notice: To all interested parties by regular mail before letters of authorization *(letters testamentary)* are issued. Notice to tax commissioner due within 2 months after appointment of P.R.
Creditor Notice: Not required. Can be given by newspaper publication once each week for 3 consecutive weeks.
Inventory: Estimated inventory is required.
Appraisals: Real estate (if sold): By privately hired appraiser. Personal property: By P.R. or privately hired appraiser.
Spouse's Automatic Share: household personal items up to $6,000; farm machines up to $10,000.
Order of Priority of Claims & Debts: (1) Administrative expenses, (2) funeral expenses, (3) debts with preference under federal and New York State laws, (4) property taxes assessed against deceased prior to death, (5) judgments and decrees against deceased from prior to death and (6) all other debts.

Claims: Due within 7 months after appointment of P.R., but accepted until estate is closed.

Accountings: Usually waived by consent of all beneficiaries. May be required by court. Estate must remain open for 7 months after admission

Contests: Generally due within the time stated in the *P.R. Notice.*

P.R. Fees: First $100,000—5% next $200,000—4%; next $700,0000—3%; next $4,000,000—2 1/2%; above $5,000,000—2%; plus 5% of all rents collected. *NOTE:* Estates valued at less than $100,000 permit one full P.R. commission as listed above. Estates valued between $100,000 and $300,000 may be charged up to two full P.R. commissions if two full P.R.s (and/or guardians) probate an estate. Estates valued above $300,000 may be charged up to three full P.R. commissions—if three or more P.R.s (and/or guardians) probate the estate.

Attorneys Fees: Reasonable fee, but in practice up to 4-5% of estate value.

State Tax: (1) Estate Tax; (2) Credit Estate Tax.

Tax Due: 6 months after death.

NORTH CAROLINA: SUPERIOR COURT

Statutes: General Statutes of North Carolina, Ch. 28A, 29-31, 31A; 47.

Administration: (1) Supervised *(Formal);* (2) *Admin. Unnecessary:* For intestate estates consisting solely of personal property under $10,000 excluding debts (transfer by affidavit).

Holographic Wills: Recognized.

Proving Will: Informal: By testimony or affidavits of 2 witnesses (without notice). *Formal:* By petition of interested party, requires testimony of interested parties. Holographic wills are verified by 3 persons. Self-proved wills are recognized if made after 1976.

Admin. Notice: To all interested parties by regular mail, within a few days after admitting will by probate court.

P.R.: A nonresident is required to appoint a resident agent.

P.R. Notice: Combined with admin. notice.

Creditor Notice: Due within 20 days after appointment of P.R. by newspaper publication once each week for 4 consecutive weeks.

Inventory: Due within 3 months after appointment of P.R.

Appraisals: By P.R. or privately hired appraiser. Real estate can be appraised by tax assessment.

Spouse's Automatic Share: Allowance for family living expenses between $5,000 and one-half of the deceased's annual income prior to his death.

Order of Priority of Claims & Debts: (1) Debts which by law are secured by a lien on specific property (preference is not to exceed the value of that property, however), (2) up to $2,000 in funeral expenses, (3) debts and taxes with preference under federal law, (4) debts and taxes with preference under North Carolina law, (5) judgments rendered against deceased prior to death, (6) employees' wages and last-illness expenses from one year prior to date of deceased's death, and (7) all other debts.

Claims: Due within the time estate is open (minimum of 6 months).

Accountings: Due 12 months and 30 days after appointment of P.R., usually completed within 12 months.

Contests: Only of informal proof of will, within 3 years after admission of will.

P.R. Fees: Up to 5% of receipts and 5% of disbursements, excluding unsold real estate; 5% of cash received from sale of real estate (separate from realtor's commission). Petition for fees must be filed with court.

Attorneys Fees: Requires petition for fees, but no correlation of services to fees. In practice, only basic outline of services is listed.

State Tax: (1) Inheritance Tax; (2) Credit Estate Tax.

Tax Due: 9 months after death.

Notes: Unless sale of real estate is directed by will, it is restricted by court. Check with the estates division of superior court for specific limitations.

NORTH DAKOTA: COUNTY COURT

Statutes: North Dakota Century Code Annotated, Title 30.1.

Administration: (1) Unsupervised *(Informal);* (2) Supervised *(Formal):* By petition of interested party and court agreement; (2) Summary; (4) Admin.Unnecessary: For estates under $15,000 (excluding debts).

Holographic Wills: recognized.

Proving Will: Informal: Properly witnessed wills are accepted without further evidence; *Formal:* By affidavit or testimony of one witness. Self-proved wills are recognized. Wills must be submitted within three years of death.

P.R.: Non-residents may be appointed

P.R. Notice: To all interested parties by regular mail within 30 days after appointment of P.R.

Creditor Notice: By newspaper publication once each week for three successive weeks.

Inventory: Due within three months after appointment of P.R.

Appraisals: Privately hired appraisers may be employed.

Spouse's Automatic Share: Lifetime use of homestead; personal property up to $5,000; allowance for family living expenses during administration of estate, or if estate is insolvent, then up to only 1 year.

Order of Priority Of Claims: (1) Administrative expenses, (2) funeral expenses, (3) debts and taxes with preference under federal law, (4) expenses during last sickness, (5) debts and taxes with preference under state law, and (6) all other debts.

Claims: Due within three months after first newspaper publication.

Accountings: Informal: By sworn statement of P.R.; *Formal:* By a final accounting

Contests: Should be filed before or at formal will hearing. *Formal.* Appeals must be filed before order approving distribution, or 12 months after order admitting will, whichever is first. *Informal:* An appeal must be filed within six months of closing, or 12 months after admitting will, whichever is first.

P.R. Fees: Reasonable Compensation.
Attorneys Fees: Reasonable compensation.
State Tax: Credit Estate Tax.
Tax Due: 15 months after death.
Notes: North Dakota is a UPC state.

OHIO: COMMON PLEAS COURT (PROBATE DIVISION)

Statutes: Page's Ohio Revised Code Annotated, Title 21 (Ch. 2102-2131).
Administration: (1) Supervised *(Formal);* (2) Admin. Unnecessary: For estates under $25,000.
Holographic Wills: Not recognized.
Proving Will: *Informal:* Properly witnessed wills admitted without further evidence. *Formal:* By testimony or affidavits of witnesses; or by other satisfactory evidence. Self-proved wills are recognized.
P.R.: Nonresidents who are heirs may be appointed.
P.R. Notice: To all interested parties within one month after appointment of P.R. by regular mail.
Creditor Notice: By newspaper publication once each week for three consecutive weeks.
Inventory: Due within three months after appointment of P.R.
Appraisals: Personal property: By court-appointed or privately-hired appraiser. Real Estate (whether sold or not) must be appraised by court-appointed appraiser.
Spouse's Automatic Share: allowance for living expenses up to $5,000 deducted from spouse's inherited share; use of homestead for one year.
Order of Priority of Claims & Debts: (1) Administrative expenses, (2) $2,000 in funeral expenses, (3) allowance to surviving spouse and children, (4) debts with preference under federal law, (5) last-illness expenses, (6) an additional $1,000 for funeral expenses not covered by priority 2, (7) debts and taxes with preference under Ohio law, (8) debts for mutual labor performed for the deceased from one year prior to date of death, but no more than $300 per person and (9) all other debts.
Claims: Due within three months after appointment of P.R Without newspaper publication, claims are valid for 21 years (four years for real estate claims).
Accountings: Due within four months after probate of will by filing civil action in probate court.
Contests: Due within 4 months after probate of will by filing civil action in probate court.
P.R. Fees: First $100,000—4%; next $300,000—3%; above $400,000—2%. 1% for unsold real property and nonprobate property subject to state estate tax.
Attorneys Fees: Guidelines and practice: first $2,000—6%; next $13,000—4%; next $15,000—3%; balance 2%. Minimum fee— $150. For non-probate assets: 2% on first $20,000 and 1% on balance.
State Tax: (1) Estate Tax; (2) Credit Estate Tax.
Tax Due: Nine months after death.

OKLAHOMA: DISTRICT COURT

Statutes: Oklahoma Statutes Annotated, Titles 58 and 84.
Administration: (1) Supervised *(Formal);* (2) *Summary:* Under $60,000; (3) Admin. Unnecessary: If homestead to surviving spouse is the only real estate, transfer by nonjudicial proceeding.
Holographic Wills: Recognized.
Proving Wills: By testimony or affidavit of one witness. Self-proved wills are recognized. Will must be submitted within 30 days after notice of death. Hearing on will set 10-30 days after petition to probate is filed.
Admin. Notice: To all interested parties at least 10 days before will hearing by regular mail, and to others by one newspaper publication at least 10 days before hearing.
P.R.: A nonresident is required to appoint a resident agent to receive notice.
P.R. Notice: By newspaper publication once a week for two consecutive weeks.
Creditor Notice: By newspaper publication once each week for two consecutive weeks after appointment of P. R. If no county newspaper exists, post notice in courthouse and two other public places.
Inventory: Due within three months after appointment of P.R.
Appraisals: Usually done by P.R. If necessary, court appoints two or three.
Spouse's Automatic Share: Use of homestead; certain personal property; allowance for living expenses at court's discretion.
Order of Priority of Claims & Debts: (1) Funeral expenses, (2) last-illness expenses, (3) court allowances to the family, (4) taxes due to the U.S., Oklahoma, or at any locality, (5) debts with preference under federal or Oklahoma law, (6) judgments and other liens rendered against the deceased prior to death, and (7) all other debts.
Claims: Due within two months after first newspaper publication (or posting of notice).
Accountings: Due within two months after appointment of P.R.
Contests: Due within three months after admission of will.
P.R. Fees: First $1,000—5%; next $4,000—4%; above $5,000—2%. Up to double these rates for extraordinary services.
Attorneys Fees: No statutory provision.
State Tax: (1) Estate Tax; (2) Credit Estate Tax.
Tax Due: Nine months after death.

OREGON: CIRCUIT OR COUNTY COURT

Statutes: Oregon Revised Statutes Sections 112.015-117.000.
Administration: (1) Supervised *(Formal);* (2) *Summary;* (3) Admin. Unnecessary: For estates consisting of personal property up to $15,000 and real property up to $35,000 (transfer by affidavit).
Holographic Wills: Recognized.
Proving Wills: By testimony or affidavit or witnesses, without notice. By other satisfactory proof of signatures. Self-proved wills are recognized.
P.R.: Nonresident may be appointed.
P.R. Notice: To all interested parties by regular mail within 30 days of appointment of P.R.
Creditor Notice: By newspaper publication once each week for three consecutive weeks.
Inventory: Due within 60 days of appointment of P.R.
Appraisals: Estimated by P.R.
Spouse's Automatic Share: Use of family home for 1 year, allowance for living expenses of up to 2 years at the court's discretion.
Order of Priority of Claims & Debts: (1) Family allowances, (2) administrative expenses, (3) funeral expenses, (4) debts and taxes with preference under federal law, (5) last-illness expenses, (6) taxes with preference under Oregon law, (7) certain miscellaneous debts, and (8) all other debts.
Claims: Generally filed within four months after first newspaper publication. Must be filed within one year after final account is filed. P.R. must reject claims within 60 days of claims period or claims are deemed accepted.
Accountings: Due within 30 days after one year from appointment of P.R. and annually thereafter until estate closed.
Contests: Due within four months after publication of notice of probate of will.
P.R. Fees: First $1,000—7%; next $9,000—4%; next $40,000—3%; above $50,000—2%. Additional 1% for non-probate property subject to estate tax (excluding insurance).
Attorneys Fees: Reasonable compensation.
State Tax: (1) Inheritance Tax; (2) Credit Estate Tax.
Tax Due: Nine months after death.

PENNSYLVANIA: COMMON PLEAS COURT (ORPHANS COURT DIVISION)

Statutes: Purdon's Pennsylvania Consolidated Statutes Annotated (Title 20, Ch. 1-4).
Administration: (1) Supervised *(Formal);* (2) *Summary:* For estates under $10,000, by petition of any interested party.
Holographic Wills: Recognized.
Proving Wills: By testimony of two witnesses or competent persons. Self-Proved Wills are recognized. .Wills must be submitted within 20 years after death.
P.R.: Nonresidents may be appointed.
P.R. Notice: To all interested parties and to creditors by newspaper publication once each week for 3 consecutive weeks, upon appointment of P.R.
Inventory: Due within 3 months after appointment of P.R.
Appraisals: By Inheritance Tax Division appraiser.
Spouse's Automatic Share: Allowance of up to $2,000 in living expenses.
Order of Priority of Claims & Debts: (1) Administrative expenses, (2) family exemptions, (3) various medical expenses from six months prior to death and funeral expenses, (4) cost of tombstone, (5) rent owed by deceased from six months prior to death, and (6) all other debts.
Claims: Must be presented "promptly."
Accountings: First account due within 4 months after first newspaper publication. Final account due to close estate.
Contests: Due within 10 days after first account is filed. Appeal to Orphan's Court within one year after admission of will.
P.R. Fees: Usually 5% of gross estate (including unsold real estate).
Attorneys Fees: Same as P.R. fees.
State Tax: (1) Inheritance Tax; (2) Credit Estate Tax.
Tax Due: 9 months after death.
Notes: Pennsylvania is considered a UPC state. Use of attorneys is often urged by the court. Fees for attorney and P.R. are among the highest in country—as much as 10% of each estate.

PUERTO RICO: SUPERIOR COURT

Statutes: Laws of Puerto Rico Annotated, Code of Civil Procedure, Titles 31-32.
Administration: (1) Supervised *(Judicial or Formal);* (2) Admin. Unnecessary: If decedent expressly prohibits formal administration by will, and has appointed at least one person to partition the estate.
Holographic Wills: Recognized.
Proving Will: Open Wills (notarized, witnessed, and court filed) and *Closed Wills* (sealed, notarized, and witnessed): By testimony of notary and witnesses or persons acquainted with their signatures.
Holographic Wills: By testimony of surviving spouse and other interested parties.
P.R. Notice: To all interested parties by summons between 8 and 50 days before hearing on will.
Creditor Notice: By newspaper publication as directed by the Superior Court, usually once each week for two months.
Inventory: Required.
Appraisals: By P.R. unless Court-appointed appraiser requested.

Spouse's Automatic Share: half of the community property and one-quarter of the decedent spouse's separate property.
Claims: Due within six months after newspaper publication.
Accountings: Quarterly statements due until estate is closed.
Contests: Before or at hearing to prove will, or by civil action in Superior Court.
P.R. Fees: First $1,000—5%; next $9,000—2 1/2%; above $10,000—1%.
Attorneys Fees: No statutory provision.
State Tax: Estate Tax.
Tax Due: 270 days after death.

RHODE ISLAND: PROBATE COURT

Statutes: General Law of Rhode Island, Vol. 6, Title 33.
Administration: (1) Supervised *(Formal)*; (2) Admin. Unnecessary: For estates under $10,000 (after certain personal property) when 45 days have elapsed since death and no P.R. has been appointed.
Holographic Wills: Not recognized except for soldiers or marines in active service.
Proving Will: By one witness. Self-proved wills are recognized.
Admin. Notice: Usually waived by consent of all interested parties.
P.R.: Nonresident is required to appoint a resident agent.
P.R. Notice: To all interested parties by regular mail at least 10 days before date set for proof of will.
Creditor Notice: By newspaper publication once each week for three successive weeks. Probate court clerk arranges for this publication.
Inventory: Due within 30 days after appointment of P.R.
Appraisals: Usually done by P.R.
Spouse's Automatic Share: Certain personal property and allowance for 6 months worth of family living expenses.
Order of Priority of Claims & Debts: (1) Administrative expenses, (2) funeral expenses, (3) last-illness expenses, (4) debts to the U.S., (5) debts and taxes with preference under Rhode Island law, (6) wages due to employees of deceased from six months prior to date of death, but no more than $100 per person, and (7) all other debts.
Claims: Due within six months after first newspaper publication. P.R. must disallow any claims within 30 days after claims filing period.
Accountings: Due within two years after appointment of P.R., annually thereafter until estate is closed.
Contests: Filed with probate court. Appeal: Due within 20 days of admission of will, filed in superior court.
P.R. Fees: Just compensation, but in practice: 3-3 1/2% of estate value.
Attorneys Fees: Just compensation, but in practice: usually 4-5% of estate value.
State Tax: (1) Estate Tax; (2) Credit Estate Tax. Due:
Tax Due: Ten months after death.
Notes: Each city or town, except New Shoreham, has its own probate court. The Town Council acts as probate court in New Shoreham.

SOUTH CAROLINA: PROBATE COURT

Statutes: Code of Laws of South Carolina, Vol. 20B, Sections 14-23-10, 21-7-10.
Administration: (1) Supervised *(Formal)*; (2) *Summary:* For intestate estates under $10,000 (less liens and encumbrences), court administered.
Holographic Wills: Not recognized.
Proving Will: *Informal.* Hearing before probate judge (without notice). *Formal:* Upon petition within six months after will is admitted informally. No provision for self-proved will. Wills must be submitted within 30 days of knowledge of death.
P.R.: Nonresident may be appointed.
P.R. Notice: To all interested parties *and creditors* within 30 days after appointment of P.R., by newspaper publication once each week for three consecutive weeks.
Inventory: Due 30 days after appointment of P.R.
Appraisals: Must be filed 30 days after filing inventory. Three appraisers are appointed by the court.
Spouse's Automatic Share: Certain personal property and $5,000.
Order of Priority of Claims & Debts: (1) Administrative expenses and funeral expenses, (2) last-illness expenses, (3) debts and taxes with preference under federal law, (4) debts and taxes with preference under South Carolina law, and (5) all other debts.
Claims: Due within five months after first newspaper publication.
Accountings: Due five months after appointment of P.R., six months that, and annually thereafter until estate is closed.
Contests: Usually made within six months after will is admitted informally.
P.R. Fees: Up to 2 1/2% of receipts and 2 1/2% of disbursements. Additional fees for extraordinary services.
Attorneys Fees: No statutory provision.
State Tax: (1) Estate Tax; (2) Credit Estate Tax.
Tax Due: Nine months after death.

SOUTH DAKOTA: CIRCUIT COURT
Statutes: South Dakota Codified Laws, Vol. 9B, Titles 29 and 30.
Administration: (1) Unsupervised *(Independent or Informal);* (2) Supervised: *(Formal);* (3) *Summary:* For estates under $60,000 (with notice as required below); (4) Admin. Unnecessary: For estates under $5,000 (transfer by affidavit).
Holographc Wills: Recognized.
Proving Will: Informal.: Properly witnessed wills accepted without further evidence if copies of the will mailed to all interested parties with admin. notice. *Formal:* By testimony of one witness, or persons with knowledge of signing of will and testator. Self-proved wills are recognized.
Admin. Notice: To all interested parties by regular mail at least 15 days before hearing on probate petition.
P.R.: A nonresident is required to appoint a resident agent.
P.R. Notice: Combined with admin. notice.
Inventory: Due within 90 days after appointment of P.R.
Appraisals: By P.R., or by privately hired or court-appointed appraiser.
Spouse's Automatic Share: Lifetime use of homestead before creditors; personal property up to $1,500; allowance for family living expenses during administration of the estate, but for only 1 year if the estate is insolvent.
Order of Priority of Claims & Debts: (1) Administrative expenses, (2) funeral expenses, (3) last-illness expenses, (4) debts to servants and employees for service for 60 days prior to death, (5) debts with preference under federal law, and (6) all other debts.
Claims: Due within 2 months after newspaper publication.
Accountings: First account is due within 90 days after appointment of P.R., and annually thereafter until estate is closed.
Contests: Due within 2 months after will admitted.
P.R. Fees: First $1,000—5%; next $4,000—4%; above $5,000—2%.
Attorneys Fees: No statutory provision, but in practice: by the hour, or up to 3% of estate value.
State Tax: (1) Inheritance Tax; (2) Credit Estate Tax.
Tax Due: 12 months after death.
Notes: Independent administration differs from the *formal* process only in granting the P.R. more power to settle the estate. Otherwise the process is the same.

TENNESSEE: CHANCERY COURT, (Probate Court in Davidson and Shelby Counties)
Statutes: Tennessee Code Annotated Vol. 6, Titles 30-32.
Administration: (1) Supervised *(Formal);* (2) *Summary:* For estates under $10,000 if 45 days have elapsed since death.
Holographic Wills: Recognized.
Proving Will: Informal: By testimony of at least one witness (without notice).
Formal: By testimony of all available witnesses or other satisfactory evidence (with notice to all interested parties). Holographic wills proved by verification of handwriting by two persons. Self-proved wills are recognized.
P.R.: A nonresident is required to appoint a resident co-P.R.
P.R. Notice: Not always required. Check with your local Register of Wills.
Creditor Notice: By newspaper publication once each week for 2 consecutive weeks, within 30 days after appointment of P.R. Estates under $1,000 may post notice at court alone.
Inventory: Due before the court's next term, usually within 30 days after appointment of P.R.
Appraisals: By a privately hired appraiser.
Spouse's Automatic Share: Homestead: up to value of $5,000; allowance for living expenses for 1 year.
Order of Priority of Claims & Debts: (1) Administrative expenses, (2) federal and state taxes, (3) funeral expenses, and (4) all other debts.
Claims: Due within 6 months after first newspaper publication.
Accountings: Due within 15 months after appointment of P.R. and annually thereafter until estate is closed.
Contests: Due within 7 years after *informal* proof of will. No appeal from *formal* proof of will.
P.R. Fees: Reasonable compensation.
State Tax: (1) Inheritance Tax; (2) Credit Estate Tax.
Tax Due: 9 months after death.

TEXAS: COUNTY OR PROBATE COURT
Statutes: Vernon's Civil Statutes of the State of Texas Annotated, Vol. 17A, 17B, 17C (Probate Code).
Administration: (1) Unsupervised (Inde*pendent or Informal);* (2) Supervised *(Formal);* (3) Admin. Unnecessary: Generally for estates under $50,00 where 30 days have elapsed since death and no P.R. has been appointed.
Holographic Wills: Recognized.
Proving Will: By testimony or affidavit of at least one witness; or by proof of the handwriting of the testator and subscribing witnesses. Holographic wills proved by two persons. Self-proved wills are recognized. Will usually must be submitted within four months of death.
P.R.: A nonresident is required to appoint a resident agent.
P.R. Notice: To all interested parties by regular mail.
Creditor Notice: To holders of recorded claims by registered mail within four months after appointment of P.R. To all others by newspaper publication within one month after appointment of P.R.
Inventory: Due within 90 days after appointment of P.R.

Appraisals: Usually by 1 to 3 court-appointed appraisers. Sale of real estate requires appraiser.

Spouse's Automatic Share: Half of community property; at court's discretion, lifetime use of homestead and 1 acre in the city, or 200 acres outside, plus certain personal property; allowance for living expenses for 1 year, or $10,000 if there's no home in the estate.

Order of Priority of Claims & Debts: (1) funeral expenses and last-illness expenses, not to exceed $5,000, (2) administrative expenses, (3) tax liens and other secured liens, (4) various Texas state tax debts, and (5) all other debts.

Claims: Due within six months after appointment of P.R.

Accountings: Due 12 months after appointment of P.R and annually thereafter until estate is closed.

Contests: Due within two years after will is admitted.

P.R. Fees: Up to 5% of estate value; additional compensation by petition.

Attorneys Fees: By statutory provision.

State Tax: (1) Inheritance Tax; (2) Credit Estate Tax.

Tax Due: Nine months after death.

Notes: Texas is a UPC and community property state. One-half of the property acquired during marriage is owned by the surviving spouse.

UTAH: DISTRICT COURT

Statutes: Utah Code Annotated, Vol. 8A, Title 75.

Administration: (1) Unsupervised *(Informal);* (2) Supervised *(Formal):* by petition of interested parties and court agreement; (3) *Summary;* (4) Admin. Unnecessary: in certain cases for estates under $10,000, court administers estate.

Holographic Wills: Recognized.

Proving Will: Informal: Properly witnessed wills are accepted without further evidence. *Formal:* By affidavit or testimony of one witness. Self-proved wills are recognized. Wills must be submitted within three years of death.

Notice of Admin.: To all interested parties by regular mail, 10 days before hearing.

P.R.: Nonresident may be appointed.

P.R. Notice: Not required.

Creditor Notice: By newspaper publication once each week for three consecutive weeks.

Inventory: Due within three months after appointment of P.R.

Appraisals: Privately hired appraisers may be employed.

Spouse's Automatic Share: Homestead: up to $10,000; certain personal property; up to $5,000; up to 4 vehicles worth no more than $25,000; allowance for living expenses during administration of the estate, but for only up to 1 year when estate is insolvent.

Order of Priority of Claims & Debts: (1) Funeral expenses, (2) administrative expenses, (3) debts and taxes with preference under federal law, (4) last-illness expenses, (5) debts and taxes with preference under Utah law, and (6) all other debts.

Claims: Due within three months after first newspaper publication or within three years after death if no notice was published.

Accountings: Final accounting due to close estate.

Contests: Should be filed before or at formal will hearing. *Formal:* Appeals must be filed before order approving distribution, or 12 months after order admitting will, whichever is first. Informal: An appeal must be filed within six months of closing, or 12 months after order admitting will, whichever is first.

P.R. Fees: Reasonable compensation, but in practice: First $1,000—5%; next $4,000—4%; next $5,000—3%; next $40,000—2%; next $50,000—1 1/2%; above $100,000—1%.

Attorneys Fees: First $20,000—5%; next $40,000—4%; next $140,000-3%; next $550,000—2 1/2%; next $750,000-2%; balance—1%.

State Tax: (1) Estate Tax, (2) Credit Estate Tax.

Tax Due: Fifteen months after death.

Notes: Utah is a UPC state.

VERMONT: PROBATE COURT

Statutes: Vermont Statutes Annotated, Title 14; Rules of Probate Procedure.

Administration: (1) Supervised *(Formal);* (2) *Summary:* For estates consisting solely of personal property under $10,000 where the spouse or minor children are living; (3) *Admin. Unnecessary:* For estates under $300.

Holographic Wills: Not recognized.

Proving Will: By testimony of one witness, by proof of signatures of testator and witnesses, or by other competent evidence. Self-proved wills are not recognized. Will must be submitted within 30 days after death.

Admin. Notice: To all interested parties by regular mail, at least 10 days before hearing on will.

P.R.: A nonresident is required to appoint a resident agent.

P.R. Notice: Combined with admin. notice.

Creditor Notice: By newspaper publication once each week for 3 consecutive weeks.

Inventory: Due within 30 days after appointment of P. R., 60 day extension by petition.

Appraisals: By P.R. unless interested party requests appraisal (court appoints 2 appraisers).

Spouse's Automatic Share: Homestead: up to $30,000; allowance for family living expenses during administration of the estate, but for only up to 8 months when estate is insolvent.

Order of Priority of Claims & Debts: (1) Administrative expenses, (2) funeral exprenses up to $1,000 and last-illness expenses, (3) wages due to deceased's employees from three months before death up to $300 per person, and (4) all other claims.

Claims: Due within 4 months after first newspaper publication.

Accountings: Final settlement due within 12 months after appointment of P.R. May be extended 2 years (with yearly accounts) by court permission.
Contests: By appeal to the Supreme Court.
P.R. Fees: Hourly rate, must be approved by court.
Attorneys Fees: Hourly rate, must be approved by court.
State Tax: Credit Estate Tax.
Tax Due: 9 months after death.

VIRGINIA: CIRCUIT COURT
Statutes: Code of Virginia, Title 64.
Administration: (1) Supervised *(Formal)*; (2) *Admin. Unnecessary:* for estates less than $5,000 where 60 days have elapsed since death and no P.R. has been appointed, banks, employer of decedent, Virginia and U.S. governments may release up to $5,000 to beneficiaries.
Holographic Wills: Recognized.
Proving Will: Informal: By testimony of one witness (without notice). *Formal:* By request of interested party. Hearing requires appearance of all interested parties. Self-proved wills are recognized. Holographic wills are proved by two disinterested persons.
P.R.: A nonresident is required to appoint a resident co-P.R.
P.R. Notice: To all interested parties by regular mail.
Creditor Notice: By one newspaper publication (optional). Commissioner of Accounts posts notice on front door of courthouse at least 10 days before hearing to receive proof of debts.
Inventory: Due within 4 months after appointment of P.R.
Appraisals: By P.R. or privately hired appraiser (must be officially accepted by the clerk of court).
Spouse's Automatic Share: Homestead up to $5,000, deducted from the spouse's inherited share; personal property up to $3,500; allowance for living expenses during the administration of the estate, but for only up to 1 year when the estate is insolvent.
Order of Priority of Claims & Debts: (1) Administrative expenses, (2) family allowances, (3) funeral expenses up to $500, (4) debts and taxes with preference under federal law, (5) last-illness expenses up to $400 per hospital and $150 per person, (6) debts to the State of Virginia, (7) any debts the deceased had in any capacity as a trustee or fiduciary, and (8) all other debts.
Claims: Due by date of hearing on claims, set by the Commissioner of Accounts. Usually P.R. requests date for a hearing on claims.
Accountings: Due within 16 months after appointment of P.R.
Contests: Due within one year after admission (or rejection) of will, 2 years for nonresidents and interested parties who received notice only by newspaper publication.
P.R. Fees: In practice up to 5% of estate value.
Attorneys Fees: Reasonable compensation and expenses.
State Tax: Credit Estate Tax.
Tax Due: 9 months after death.
Notes: Virginia requires a Commissioner of Accounts to review the final accounting. A commissioner fee schedule and helpful probate information is available through the circuit court clerk's office.

VIRGIN ISLANDS: TERRITORIAL OR DISTRICT COURT
Statutes: Virgin Islands Code Annotated, Vol. 2, Probate and Fiduciary Rules Appendix, Vol. 3, Title 15.
Administration: (1) Supervised *(Formal)*; (2) *Summary:* Generally for estates under $300.
Holographic Wills: Recognized only if made by member of armed services, valid until one year after discharge.
Proving Will: By testimony, affidavits or statements of witnesses, or by other satisfactory evidence.
P.R.: A nonresident is required to appoint a resident agent.
P.R. Notice: To all interested parties by regular mail, and newspaper publication for 3 consecutive weeks.
Creditor Notice: By newspaper publication once each week for 4 consecutive weeks and by posting notice in post office and 2 other public places designated by court.
Inventory: Due within 30 days after appointment of P.R.
Appraisals: By 2 court-appointed appraisers.
Spouse's Automatic Share: Court determines, and sets aside property; homestead and living allowance as deemed necessary by the court.
Order of Priority of Claims & Debts: (1) Administrative expenses, (2) funeral expenses, (3) taxes, (4) last-illness costs.
Claims: Due within 6 months after first publication of notice to creditors.
Accountings: Due 3 months after appointment of P.R., and every 3 months thereafter until estate is closed.
Contests: Due before final distribution of estate.
P.R. Fees: No statutory provision.
Attorneys Fees: Reasonable compensation.
State Tax: Inheritance Tax.
Tax Due: Check with your local Internal Revenue Service Office.

WASHINGTON: SUPERIOR COURT (PROBATE DIVISION)
Statutes: Revised Code of Washington Annotated, Title 11.
Administration: (1) Unsupervised *(Informal):* For all estates except if creditor appointed as P.R.; (2) Supervised *(Formal)*; (3) *Summary:* For estates under $30,000 (excluding debts and one half community property interests), if 40 days have elapsed since death and no P.R. has been appointed.

Holographic Wills: Not recognized.
Proving Will: By affidavits of witnesses.
P.R.: A nonresident is required to appoint a resident agent.
P.R. Notice: To all interested parties by personal service within 20 days after appointment of P.R.
Creditor Notice: By newspaper publication once each week for 3 consecutive weeks
Inventory: Due within 4 months after first newspaper publication.
Appraisals: By P.R., usually, or privately-hired appraiser.
Spouse's Automatic Share: Half of community property; at court's discretion, home and other personal property up to $30,000 (after payment of debts and administration, funeral and last-illness expenses); allowance for reasonable living expenses during the administration of the estate.
Order of Priority of Claims & Debts: (1) Administrative expenses, (2) funeral expenses, (3) last-illness expenses, (4) wages due to deceased's employees from 60 days prior to death, (5) debts with preference under federal law, (6) taxes, or any debts to the State of Washington, (7) judgments against deceased from prior to death and which are liens against the deceased's real estate, and (8) all other debts.
Claims: Due within 4 months after: first newspaper publication.
Accountings: Due 12 months after appointment of P.R. and annually thereafter until estate is closed.
Contests: Due within 4 months after admission (or rejection) of will.
P.R. Fees: Reasonable compensation.
Attorneys Fees: No statutory provision.
State Tax: (1) Inheritance Tax; (2) Credit Estate Tax.
Tax Due: 9 months after death.
Notes: Washington is a UPC state. A probate manual is available from the state bar's "attorney information service." Washington is a community property state. One-half of the property acquired during marriage is owned by the surviving spouse. Assistance on taxes is available from the Dept. of Revenue Inheritance Tax Division. A simple affidavit may be used if no state tax is due.

WEST VIRGINIA: COUNTY COMMISSION
Statutes: West Virginia Code, Vol. 12, Ch. 41-44.
Administration: (1) Supervised *(Formal);* (2) *Summary:* For estates under $50,000 ($100,000 in Braxton, Kanawah, Marion, Putnam or Summers counties) or estates with only one beneficiary.
Holographic Wills: Recognized.
Proving Will: By testimony, affidavits or statements of witnesses, by proof of signatures of testator and witnesses, or by other evidence. Will must be submitted to Clerk of County Commission within 30 days of death.
Admin. Notice: To all interested parties by regular or certified mail for estates above $25,000, excluding all estates with only one beneficiary.
P.R.: Nonresidents may not be appointed.
P.R. Notice: Combined with admin. notice.
Creditor Notice: By newspaper publication once each week for 2 consecutive weeks.
Inventory: Due within 2 to 3 months after first newspaper publication.
Appraisals: By 3 to 5 appraisers appointed by county commission.
Spouse's Automatic Share: Homestead: use of family home until the children are 21 or dower share is taken; $1,000 in personal property.
Order of Priority of Claims & Debts: (1) Administrative expenses, (2) funeral expenses up to $600, (3) up to $100 per creditor for last-illness expenses, (4) debts to the U.S., (5) debts to the State of West Virginia, (6) taxes, (7) any debts incurred by deceased in serving as a trustee or in a similar function, and (8) all other debts.
Claims: Due 4 to 6 months after first newspaper publication.
Accountings: Due 8 months after appointment of P.R., and every 6 months thereafter until estate is closed. Completed by Fiduciary Commissioner or Supervisor.
Contests: By appeal to circuit court.
P.R. Fees: Reasonable compensation, but in practice up to 5% of estate value.
Attorneys Fees: Reasonable compensation, usually charged by the hour.
State Tax: (1) Inheritance Tax; (2) Credit Estate Tax.
Tax Due: 11 months after death. 3% discount if taxes are paid within 9 months after death.
Notes: West Virginia requires a "Fiduciary Commissioner" (a political appointee) to file inventory, accounting reports, and to review supervised probates. Summary procedures exclude fiduciary review, formal inventory, and accounting—except in Brackton, Kanawha, Marion, Putnam and Summers Counties. In these counties, a Fiduciary Supervisor (or Fiduciary Commissioner for contested estates) files the inventory, and accounting, and reviews summary probate. Distribution of estate assets is not permissible sooner than 4 months after appointment of the P.R. in all summary probates, and no sooner than one year thereof for supervised probates.

WISCONSIN: CIRCUIT COURT

Statutes: Wisconsin Statutes Annotated (1980), Ch. 851-879.

Administration: (1) Unsupervised *(Informal)*; (2) Supervised *(Formal)*; (3) *Summary:* For estates under $100,000 if spouse or minor children are living; or estates under $50,000 if solely owned property (transfer by affidavit).

Holographic Wills: Not recognized if written and signed in Wisconsin. Recognized if written and signed in a state that does recognize holographic wills.

Proving Will: *Informal.:* Properly witnessed wills are accepted without further evidence. *Formal:* By sworn statement and testimony of one witness, or by proof of competency of testator and all signatures. Self-proved wills are not recognized.

P.R.: A nonresident is required to appoint a resident agent.

P.R. Notice: Required for intestate estates. Usually waived by consent of all interested parties for all other estates.

Creditor Notice: By newspaper publication 3 times. If claims require hearing (which is rare), first publication within 15 days of court order fixing date for hearing claims. Hearing is set for about 3 months after order.

Inventory: *Informal:* Inventory must be shown to court, but not filed. *Formal:* Due within 6 months after appointment of P.R.

Appraisals: Real property: By court-appointed appraiser. Personal property: Estimated by P.R.

Spouse's Automatic Share: Half of all community property acquired during marriage as from Jan. 1, 1986; personal property up to $1,000 and, at the court's discretion, lifetime use or full ownership of family home up to $10,000; allowance for living expenses during the administration of the estate.

Order of Priority of Claims & Debts: (1) Administrative expenses, (2) funeral expenses, (3) family allowances, (4) last-illness expenses, (5) debts to federal, state, or local authorites, (6) wages to deceased's employees from three months prior to death up to $300 per employee, (7) up to $10,000 in property for the spouse which the court can order, and (8) all other claims.

Claims: Due before hearing on claims, which is set by court order (usually 3 months).

Contests: Due before or at the hearing on probate petition. Appeal: due within 60 days after admission of probate.

P.R. Fees: Reasonable compensation, additional fees for extraordinary services.

Attorneys Fees: Reasonable compensation.

State Tax: (1) Inheritance Tax; (2) Credit Estate Tax.

Tax Due: 12 months after death.

Notes: Attorneys are noted to almost always use formal administration, despite availability of informal procedures. Self-help probate guide is available from a Wisconsin state senator, Senator David Berger.

WYOMING: DISTRICT COURT

Statutes: Wyoming Statutes Annotated, Vol. 2, Title Two.

Administration: (1) Supervised *(Formal)*; (2) *Admin. Unnecessary:* For estates under $30,000, excluding debts, consisting solely of personal property where 30 days have elapsed since death and no P.R. has been elected.

Holographic Wills: Recognized.

Proving Will: By oral or written testimony of at least one witness; by two disinterested persons verifying testator and witnesses' signatures. Sef-proved wills are recognized.

P.R.: A nonresident is required to appoint a resident agent.

P.R. Notice: By certified mail to all interested parties.

Creditor Notice: By newspaper publication once each week for three consecutive weeks.

Inventory: Due within three months after first newspaper publication.

Appraisals: By three court appointed appraisers.

Spouse's Automatic Share: In certain cases, family home up to $30,000; allowance for reasonable family living expenses at the court's discretion.

Order of Priority of Claims & Debts: (1) Court Costs, (2) administrative expenses, (3) funeral expenses, (4) allowances for surviving spouse and children, (5) debts and taxes with preference under federal law, (6) last-illness expenses, (7) taxes with preference under Wyoming law, and (8) other miscellaneous creditors and all other debts.

Claims: Due within three months after first newspaper publication.

Accountings: Due 12 months after appointment of P.R. and annually thereafter until estate closed.

Contests: Due within three months after first publication of notice of admission of will.

P.R. Fees: First $1,000—10%; next $4,000—5%; next $15,000—3%; above $20,000—2%. Additional fees for extraordinary services by petition.

Attorneys Fees: Practice follows P.R. fee schedule.

State Tax: (1) Inheritance Tax; (2) Credit Estate Tax.

Tax Due: Ten months after death.

Appendix B
LAWS OF INTESTACY IN ALL 50 & OTHER STATES: DISTRIBUTION FORMULA WHEN THE DECEDENT LEAVES NO WILL

INTRODUCTION TO UNDERSTANDING THIS APPENDIX

Each state's intestacy laws specifies a particular formula by which the property of a person who dies <u>WITH-OUT</u> leaving a valid will (called dying "intestate") will be divided among his or her heirs. This appendix outlines such a formula for making intestate distribution in each state or jurisdiction in the nation when and where a person, a resident of the state, dies without a will. *Please note that the outline of laws given in the appendix is an overview primarily intended only to provide a simple but general idea of the distribution formula for each state.* For the most part, the essential information has been included in this appendix. If and when you should find it necessary to obtain a more specific or detailed treatment, you should not hesitate to check the state's statutes directly. [The applicable codes and laws for each state is listed under each state in Appendix A.]

For example, it may often be necessary to determine how your state decides what assets are included in the estate that is to be shared. (Most UPC states, for example, calculate the total estate as including the surviving spouse's share of property owned jointly by both spouses, but not the funeral or last-illness costs.) Or, you may not be sure as to what is includable as your "separate property" under your state's laws. And so on. Such will be a proper occasion to check the state probate code or to ask the probate clerk.

IN ANY CASE, SPECIFIC DETAILS OF LAWS AND COURT RULES MAY—AND DO—CHANGE FROM TIME TO TIME. SO, BEFORE PROCEEDINGS, IT MAY BE WISE TO CHECK YOUR STATE'S PROBATE CODE, ANY WAY, FOR THE MOST UP-TO-DATE FIGURES, PROVISIONS OR CHANGES, IF ANY.*

SOME FEW DEFINITIONS

A few definitions may be useful in following the information set forth in this appendix.

The term **"ISSUE"** refers to the decedent's children, or the children of any of the decedent's children who have died. In every state, property that passes to an issue is divided equally between the decedent's children; but if a child of the decedent has died, all children of the deceased child share the statutory portion of the estate that their parent would have received (this is called distribution **PER STIRPES**); any property which passes to brothers or sisters of the decedent, or to their issue, is divided according to the same principle.

A **LIFE ESTATE** interest grants a receiving heir the use of property for the remainder of the heir's life; **ENTIRE ESTATE** simply refers to the transfer of all the decedent's property to the surviving spouse. **SEPARATE PROPERTY** is all property acquired by either spouse prior to marriage, or by means of gift or inheritance.

Unless otherwise stated, all terms used in the appendix refer to blood relatives of the decedent. Many states, however, allow adopted children to inherit property as if they were natural children of the decedent. For specific information regarding adopted children, half-brothers and sisters, illegitimate children, and step-children, refer to the appropriate state code. Further reference to a state's intestacy statutes may also be required if all the categories of heirs applicable in your case contain no living members.

---

*The material applied in this Appendix is largely current as of 1993 probate laws and rules.

Here Now Are The Legal Distribution Formulas In No-Will Situations For Each State:

ALABAMA

If there is a spouse, but no living children or parent(s), the entire estate goes to spouse; $100,000 and 1/2 of balance go to spouse and 1/2 of balance to parent(s), if there are living parents but no living children; $50,000 and 1/2 of balance of estate go to spouse and 1/2 of balance to children, if the living children are all the decedent spouse's.

If there are children, but no spouse surviving, all children share estate equally or their children per stirpes; if there are parent(s), but no spouse or children surviving, the parent(s) share estate equally; if there are no spouse, children, or parent(s) surviving, entire estate goes to the brothers and sisters per stirpes, or if none, then to grandparents or their children per stirpes, and if none, then to deceased spouse's next of kin.

ALASKA

If there is a spouse, but no living children or parent(s) surviving, entire estate goes to spouse; $50,000 and 1/2 of balance go to spouse and 1/2 of balance to parent(s), if there are living spouse and parents but no living children, or if the living children are all the surviving spouse's; $50,000 and 1/2 of balance of estate go to spouse and 1/2 of balance go to the children or grandchildren per stirpes, if there is a spouse and living children; 1/2 of the estate go to spouse and 1/2 to children or grandchildren per stirpes, if there is a spouse and children who are all surviving spouse's.

If there are children but no spouse surviving, the entire estate go to the children equally or to their children per stirpes; if there are parent(s), but no spouse or children surviving, the parent(s) share the estate equally; if there are no spouse, children, or parent(s) surviving, entire estate goes to the brothers and sisters per stirpes; or if none, then 1/2 go to paternal grandparents and their children per stirpes, and 1/2 to maternal grandparents and their children per stirpes.

ARIZONA

State is a Community Property state. If there is a spouse, but no living children or parent(s), the entire estate goes to spouse; if there is a spouse and parents but no living children, the entire estate goes to the spouse; if there is a living spouse and children of the spouse, all of the decedent's 'separate property' and 1/2 of his/her "community property" go to the spouse and 1/2 of the decedent's "community property" go to the children; if there are a living spouse and living children who are all the surviving spouse's, 1/2 of the decedent's separate property go to the spouse and 1/2 of the decedent's separate property and all of his/her community property go to the children.

If there are children, but no spouse surviving, the entire estate go to the children equally or to their children per stirpes; if there are parent(s), but no spouse or children surviving, the parent(s) share the estate equally; if there are no surviving spouse, children, or parent(s), the entire estate goes to the brothers and sisters per stirpes, or if none, to the next of kin.

ARKANSAS

If there is a spouse, but no living children or parent(s), the entire estate goes to spouse if married over 3 years, or if married less than 3 years, 1/2 of the estate goes to spouse and 1/2 to brothers and sisters equally or their children per stirpes. If there are living spouse and children of the spouse, distribution is as follows: Real Estate: 1/3 life estate goes to the spouse and 2/3 to children equally or their children per stirpes; Personal Property: 1/3 goes to the spouse and 2/3 to children equally or their children per stirpes. If there are living spouse and living children who are all the surviving spouse's, the division is as follows: Real Estate: 1/3 life estate to the spouse and 2/3 goes to children equally or their children per stirpes; Personal Property: 1/3 goes to spouse and 2/3 to children equally or their children per stirpes.

If there are spouse and parent(s), but no living children, the entire estate goes to the spouse if married over 3 years, or if married less than 3 years, 1/2 goes to spouse and 1/2 to parent(s); if there are children, but no spouse surviving, all the children share the entire estate equally or their children per stirpes; if there are parent(s), but no living spouse or children, the entire estate goes to the parent(s) equally; if there are no spouse, children, or parent(s) surviving, the entire estate goes to the brothers and sisters per stirpes, or if none, then to grandparents and their children per stirpes.

CALIFORNIA

(State is a Community Property state). If there is a spouse, but no living children or parent(s), all of the decedent's entire community property goes to the spouse, 1/2 of the decedent's "separate property" goes to the spouse and the other 1/2 of the decedent's "separate property" goes to the brothers and sisters equally or to their children per stirpes. If there are a living spouse and children of the spouse, all of the decedent's "community property" go to the spouse; 1/2 of decedent's "separate property" go to the spouse, if there is only one child, and the other 1/2 goes to the child per stirpes; if more than one child, 1/3 of the decedent's "separate property" goes to the spouse and 2/3 to the children per stirpes.

If there are a spouse and parent(s) but no living children, all of the decedent's "community property" goes to the spouse; 1/2 of the decedent's "separate property" goes to the spouse and the other 1/2 of his/her "separate property" goes to the parent(s) equally; if there are children, but no living spouse, the entire estate goes to the children equally or to their children per stirpes; if there are parent(s), but no spouse or children surviving, the entire estate goes to the parent(s) equally; if there are no spouse, children, or parent(s) surviving, the entire estate goes to the brothers and sisters per stirpes, or if none, to the next of kin.

COLORADO

If there is a spouse, but no living children or parent(s), the entire estate goes to spouse; or if there is a spouse and parent(s) but no living children, the entire estate goes to the spouse; if there are children, but no spouse surviving, the entire estate goes to the children equally or to their children per stirpes; $25,000 and 1/2 balance of the estate goes to spouse, and 1/2 of the balance of the estate to the children and grandchildren per stirpes, if there are a living spouse and children, or if surviving children are not of surviving spouse, distribution is as follows: 1/2 of the balance of the estate to spouse and 1/2 to children.

If there are parent(s), but no spouse or children surviving, the parent(s) share the entire estate equally; if there are no spouse, children, or parent(s) surviving, the entire estate goes to the brothers and sisters per stirpes, or if none, then to grandparents and their children per stirpes, or if none, then to the nearest lineal ancestors and their children.

CONNECTICUT

If there is a living spouse, but no living children or parent(s), the entire estate goes to spouse; $100,000 and 3/4 of the balance of the estate goes to the spouse, and 1/4 of the balance of the estate to the parents or surviving parent, if there are surviving spouse and parents but no living children. If there are a surviving spouse and children, $100,000 and 1/2 of the balance of the estate goes to spouse and the other 1/2 of the balance of the estate go to the children or grandchildren per stirpes; if there are a surviving spouse but children who are all the surviving spouse's, 1/2 of the estate goes to spouse and 1/2 to children or grandchildren per stirpes;

If there are living children, but no spouse surviving, the entire estate goes to the children equally or to their children per stirpes; if there are parent(s), but no spouse or children surviving, the parent(s) share the entire estate equally; if there are no spouse, children, or parent(s) surviving, the entire estate goes to the brothers and sisters per stirpes, or if none, then it goes to next of kin.

DELAWARE

If there is a spouse, but no children or parent(s) surviving, the entire estate goes to the spouse; if there are a spouse and parents but no children surviving, distribution is a as follows: Real Estate—Life estate to spouse, and the rest of the estate to parents or surviving parent; and Personal Property: $50,000 and 1/2 of the balance of the estate to the spouse and the other 1/2 of the balance of estate to parents or surviving parent; if there are a surviving spouse and children, distribution is a follows: Real Estate— Life estate to spouse, and the rest to children or grandchildren per stirpes; Personal Property—$50,000 and 1/2 of the balance of the estate goes to spouse and the other 1/2 of the balance of estate to children or grandchildren, per stirpes.

If there are a living spouse and children who are only the surviving spouse's, distribution is as follows: Real Estate—Life estate to spouse, and the rest of the estate to the children or grandchildren per stirpes; Personal Property—1/2 to the spouse and 1/2 to children or grandchildren per stirpes.

If there are surviving children, but no spouse surviving, the entire estate goes to the children equally or to their children per stirpes; if there are living parent(s), but no spouse or children surviving, the parent(s) share the entire estate equally; if there are no spouse, children, or parent(s) surviving, the entire estate goes to the brothers and sisters or their children per stirpes, or if none, then to the next of kin.

DISTRICT OF COLUMBIA (WASHINGTON D.C.)

If there is a spouse, but no living children or parent(s), distribution is a as follows: Real Estate—1/3 life estate to the spouse, and the balance of the estate to the parent's children per stirpes, or if none, to the collaterals, or if none, to the grandparents, or if none, the entire real property goes to the spouse. And Personal Property: 1/2 to the spouse and 1/2 to the parent's children per stirpes, or if none, to the collaterals, or if none, to the grandparents, or if none, the entire personal property go to the spouse. If there is a surviving spouse and children, distribution is a follows: Real Estate— 1/3 life estate to spouse, and the balance to the children equally or their children per stirpes; Personal Property—1/3 to the spouse and 2/3 to the children equally, or their children per stirpes; or if the surviving children are only the surviving spouse's, distribution is as follows: Real Estate—1/3 life estate to spouse and balance to the children equally or their children per stirpes; Personal Property: 1/3 to spouse and 2/3 to children equally, or their children per stirpes.

If there are a living spouse and parent(s), but no surviving children, distribution is as follows: Real Estate—1/3 life estate to spouse and the balance to the parents; Personal property—1/2 to the spouse and 1/2 to the parent(s); if there are surviving children, but no spouse surviving, the entire estate goes to the children equally or their children per stirpes; if there are surviving parent(s), but no spouse or children surviving, the entire estate goes to the parent(s) equally; if there are no spouse, children, or parent(s) surviving, entire estate goes to the brothers and sisters or their children per stirpes, or if none, to their collaterals, or if none, to grandparents.

FLORIDA

If there is a surviving spouse but no children or parent(s) surviving, or a spouse and parents but no children surviving, the entire estate goes to the spouse; if there are children, but no spouse surviving, the children share the estate equally or their children per stirpes; if there are a spouse and children of the spouse surviving: $20,000 and 1/2 of the balance of the estate go to the spouse, and the other 1/2 of the balance of the estate go to the children and grandchildren per stirpes; and if there are a surviving spouse and children who are only the surviving spouse's, 1/2 of the estate goes to the spouse and 1/2 to children and grandchildren per stirpes.

If there are parent(s), but no spouse or children surviving, the entire estate goes to the parent(s) equally; if there are no living spouse, children, or parent(s) surviving, entire estate goes to the brothers and sisters or their children per stirpes, or if none, 1/2 goes to the maternal next of kin and 1/2 to paternal next of kin beginning with grandparents.

GEORGIA

If there is a surviving spouse but no surviving children or parent(s), or a spouse and parent(s), but no surviving children, the entire estate goes to the spouse; if there are a surviving spouse and children, distribution is as follows: estate is shared in equal shares by the children or grandchildren and spouse, but spouse must get at least 1/4 of estate; if there are a surviving spouse and children, but the children are only the surviving spouse's, children or grandchildren and spouse all take equal shares but spouse must net at least 1/4 of estate.

If there are children, but no spouse surviving, the entire estate goes to the children equally or to their children per stirpes; if there are parent(s), but no spouse or children surviving, the entire estate go to the parents, brothers and sisters equally, or to their children per stirpes; if there are no spouse, children, or parent(s) surviving, entire estate goes to the brothers and sisters or their children per stirpes; or if none, to paternal and maternal next of kin.

HAWAII

If there is a spouse, but no living children or parent(s), the entire estate goes to the spouse; if there are a surviving spouse and parent(s), but no children, then 1/2 of the estate goes to spouse and 1/2 to the parents; 1/2 of the estate goes to the spouse and 1/2 to the children equally or to the grandchildren, if there are living spouse and children who are either the decedent spouse's, or the surviving spouse's;

If there are Children, but no spouse surviving, all the children share estate equally or their children per stirpes; if there are parent(s), but no spouse or children surviving, the parent(s) share estate equally; if there are no spouse, children, or parent(s) surviving, entire estate goes to the brothers and sisters per stirpes, or if none, then to grandparents, or if none, to the uncles and aunts equally.

IDAHO

State is a Community Property state. If there is a surviving spouse but no living children or parent(s), the entire estate goes to the spouse, if there are a living spouse and children of the spouse, all of the decedent's "community property" goes to the spouse, $50,000 and 1/2 of the balance of the decedent's "separate property" goes to the spouse while the other 1/2 of the decedent's "separate property" goes to the children or grandchildren per stirpes; if there is a spouse and children but the children are not of the surviving spouse's, then all of the decedent's community property goes to the spouse, 1/2 of the decedent's "separate property" goes to the spouse, and the other 1/2 goes to the children or grandchildren per stirpes.

If there are a spouse and parent(s) but no living children, all of the decedent's "community property" goes to the spouse, $50,000 and 1/2 of the balance goes to the surviving parent(s); if there are children but no spouse surviving, the entire estate goes to the children equally or to their children per stirpes; if there are parent(s), but no spouse or children surviving, the entire estate goes to the surviving parent(s) equally; if there are no spouse, children, or parent(s) surviving, the entire estate goes to the brothers and sisters or their children.

ILLINOIS

If there is a surviving spouse and parents, but no living children or parent(s), or there is a spouse but no surviving children or parents, the entire estate goes to the spouse; if there is a spouse and children living, 1/2 of the estate goes to the spouse and the other 1/2 goes to the children equally, or to the grandchildren per stirpes; if there is a spouse and children but the children are not the decedent's, then the spouse gets 1/2 of the estate and the other 1/2 goes to the children equally or to the grandchildren per stirpes.

If there are children but no spouse surviving, the entire estate goes to the children equally or to their children per stirpes; if there are living parent(s), but no spouse or children surviving, the entire estate goes to the parents, brothers, sisters or children of brothers and sisters per stirpes, except that the others will take a double share if there is only one parent surviving; if there are no spouse, children, or parent(s) surviving, 1/2 of the estate goes to the maternal and paternal grandparents equally or to surviving grandparents, or if none, to their children per stirpes, or if none, the maternal great-grandparents and the paternal great-grandparents get 1/2 equally or the surviving great-grandparent; or if none is surviving, then it goes to their children per stirpes, or if none of the above is surviving, then the estate goes to the next of kin.

INDIANA

If there is a spouse but no living children or parent(s), the entire estate goes to the spouse; if there is a surviving spouse and parent(s), but no surviving children, then 3/4 of the estate goes to the spouse and 1/4 to the parent(s); if there are children but no spouse surviving, the children share the entire estate equally or their children per stirpes; if there is a spouse and children of spouse living, distribution is as follows: 1/2 of the estate goes to the spouse if there is one child, if there is more than one child, 1/3 to spouse and 2/3 to children; if there are a spouse and children surviving but the children are not the decedent's, distribution is as follows: Real Estate: life estate to spouse, the balance to the children; Personal Property: 1/2 to the spouse and 1/2 to the children, if there is only one child, and 1/3 to the spouse, and 2/3 to the children, if there is more than one child.

If there are parent(s) living, but no spouse or children surviving, 1/2 of the estate goes to the parents if both are surviving, and the other 1/2 to the brothers and sisters and their children per stirpes, and if only one parent is surviving, then 1/4 of the estate goes to the parent and 3/4 to the brothers and sisters and their children per stirpes; if there is no spouse, children, or parent(s) surviving, the entire estate goes to the brothers and sisters or their children per stirpes, or if none is surviving, then to grandparents, or if none, to the uncles and aunts per stirpes.

IOWA

If there are a surviving spouse and parent(s) but no surviving children, or a spouse surviving but no children or parent(s) surviving, or a spouse and children who are only the surviving spouse's, the entire estate goes to the spouse; if there is a spouse and children surviving but the children are not the surviving spouse's, distribution is as follows: $50,000 and 1/2 of the balance goes to the spouse and the other 1/2 of the balance goes to the children.

If there are children surviving but no spouse surviving, the children share estate equally or their children per stirpes; if there are parent(s) but no spouse or children surviving, the parent(s) share entire estate equally; if there are no spouse, children, or parent(s) surviving, entire estate goes to the brothers and sisters or their children per stirpes; or if none is surviving, then it goes to their ancestors and their children per stirpes, or if none is surviving, then to spouse or heirs of spouse.

KANSAS

If there is a surviving spouse and parents but no children or parent(s) surviving, or a spouse but no children or parent(s) surviving, the entire estate goes to the spouse; if there is a spouse and living children, 1/2 of the estate goes to the spouse and 1/2 to the children or the grandchildren per stirpes, whether or not the children are the decedent spouse's.

If there are children but no spouse surviving, the children share the entire estate equally or their children per stirpes; if there are parent(s) but no spouse or children surviving, the parent(s) share the entire estate equally; if there are no spouse, children, or parent(s) surviving, the entire estate goes to the decedent's brothers and sisters per stirpes.

KENTUCKY

If there is a surviving spouse but no children or parent(s) surviving, the entire estate goes to the spouse; if there are a surviving spouse and parent(s) but no surviving children, then 1/2 of the estate goes to the spouse and 1/2 to the surviving parents; if there is a surviving spouse and children of the spouse, distribution is as follows: Real Estate: life estate use of 1/3 of fee simple property acquired during marriage and 1/2 of other real estate owned by the deceased at death goes to spouse, and the balance goes to the children or grandchildren per stirpes; Personal Property: 1/2 goes to the spouse and 1/2 to the children equally or grandchildren per stirpes.

If there are children but no spouse surviving, the children share the entire estate equally or their children per stirpes; if there are parent(s) but no spouse or children surviving, the parent(s) share the entire estate equally; if there are no surviving spouse, children, or parent(s) surviving, the entire estate goes to the brothers and sisters or their children per stirpes, or if none is surviving, then 1/2 goes to the maternal next of kin and 1/2 to the paternal next of kin and their children per stirpes.

LOUISIANA

The State is a Community Property state. If there are a surviving spouse and parent(s) but no surviving children, distribution is as follows: all "community property" goes to the spouse, all "separate property" goes to the brothers and sisters or their children per stripes, or if none is surviving, to the parents, or if none is surviving, all goes to the spouse; if there is a surviving spouse and children, the spouse gets lifetime use of all community property which terminates when the spouse remarries, at which point the property goes to the descendants per stirpes. All separate property go to the children equally or to the grandchildren per stirpes;

If there are parent(s) but no surviving children or spouse, the children share the estate equally or their children per stirpes; if there is no surviving spouse, children, or parent(s), the entire estate goes to the parent(s) equally; if there is no spouse, children or parent(s) surviving, the entire estate goes to the brothers and sisters equally or their children per stirpes, or if none is surviving, to the next of kin.

MAINE

If there are a surviving spouse and parent(s) but no surviving children, distribution is as follows: $50,000 and 1/2 of the balance of the estate goes to the spouse, and the other 1/2 of the balance goes to the surviving parents; if there is a spouse and children, distribution is as follows: $50,000 and 1/2 of the balance of the estate to the spouse, and the other 1/2 of the balance of the estate to the children or grandchildren per stirpes; if there is a spouse and living children who are not the surviving spouse's children, distribution is as follows: 1/2 to spouse and 1/2 to children or grandchildren per stirpes; if there is a spouse but no surviving children or parent(s), distribution is as follows: $50,000 and 1/2 of the balance of the estate go to the spouse and the other 1/2 of the balance to the parent's children per capita, or if none is surviving, 1/4 of the balance to the paternal and 1/4 to the maternal grandparents or their children per capita.

If there are children but no spouse surviving, the children share the estate equally or their children per stirpes; if there are parent(s) but no spouse or children surviving, the parent(s) share the entire estate equally; if there are no surviving spouse, children, or parent(s), 1/2 of the estate goes to the paternal grandparents or their children per capita, and 1/2 to the maternal grandparents or their children per capita.

MARYLAND

If there is a surviving spouse but no children or parent(s) surviving, the entire estate goes to the spouse; if there are a surviving spouse and parent(s), but no surviving children, then 1/2 of the estate goes to spouse and 1/2 to the surviving parents; if there is a surviving spouse and children, distribution is as follows: 1/2 of the estate to spouse and 1/2 to the children equally or grandchildren per stirpes, if any of the children are minors, or $15,000 and 1/2 of the balance of the estate to the spouse and the other 1/2 to the children equally or grandchildren per stirpes, if none of the surviving children are minors.

If there are children but no spouse surviving, the children share the entire estate equally or their children per stirpes; if there are parent(s) but no spouse or children surviving, the surviving parent(s) share the entire estate equally; if there are no surviving spouse, children, or parent(s), the entire estate goes to the brothers and sisters equally or to their children per stirpes, or if none, to collateral next of kin.

MASSACHUSETTS

If there are a surviving spouse and parent(s), but no surviving children, distribution is as follows: $200,000 and 1/2 of the balance of the estate goes to the spouse and 1/2 of the balance goes to the parent(s) equally; if there is a surviving spouse and children who are either the decedent's or the spouse's, distribution is as follows: 1/2 to the spouse and 1/2 to the children equally or grandchildren per stirpes; if there is a spouse but no surviving children or parent(s), distribution is as follows: $200,000 and 1/2 of the balance to the spouse and 1/2 of the balance to the brothers and sisters equally or their children per stirpes, or if none is surviving, to next of kin, or if none is surviving, the entire estate to the spouse.

If there are children but no spouse surviving, the children share the entire estate equally, or their children per stirpes; if there are parent(s) but no spouse or children surviving, the surviving parent(s) share the entire estate equally; if there are no surviving spouse, children, or parent(s), the entire estate goes to the brothers and sisters equally or their children per stirpes, or if none is surviving, to the next of kin.

MICHIGAN

If there is a surviving spouse but no surviving children or parent(s), the entire estate goes to the spouse; if there is a surviving spouse and parent(s) but no surviving children, distribution is as follows: $60,000 and 1/2 of the balance of the estate goes to the spouse and the other 1/2 of the balance of the estate goes to the surviving parent(s) equally; if there is a surviving spouse and children, who are either the decedent's or the surviving spouse's, distribution is as follows: $60,000 and 1/2 of the balance of the estate goes to the spouse and the other 1/2 of the balance of the estate goes to the children per stirpes.

If there are children but no spouse surviving, the children share the entire estate equally or their children per stirpes; if there are parent(s) but no spouse or children surviving, the surviving parent(s) share the entire estate equally; if there are no surviving spouse, children, or parent(s), the entire estate goes to the brothers and sisters equally, or to their children per stirpes, or if none is surviving, 1/2 to the maternal grandparents or their children per stirpes and 1/2 to the paternal grandparents or their children per stirpes.

MINNESOTA

If there are a surviving spouse and parent(s), but no surviving children, or there is a spouse but no surviving children or parents, the entire estate goes to the spouse; if there are children but no surviving spouse, all the children share the estate equally or their children per stirpes; if there is a surviving spouse and children, distribution is as follows: $70,000 and 1/2 of the balance of the estate to the spouse and the other 1/2 of the balance of the estate to the children or grandchildren per stirpes (the $70,000 does not go to the spouse when the surviving children involved are not the surviving spouse's. Rather, the estate is merely divided 1/2 to the spouse and 1/2 to the children or grandchildren per stirpes in such a situation.)

If there are parent(s) but no spouse or children surviving, the surviving parent(s) share estate equally; if there are no surviving spouse, children, or parent(s), the entire estate goes to the brothers and sisters equally or their children per stirpes, or if none is surviving, to the next of kin.

MISSISSIPPI

If there are a surviving spouse and parent(s) but no surviving children, or there is a spouse but no surviving children or parent(s), the entire estate goes to the spouse; if there are children but no surviving spouse, the children share the entire estate equally or their children per stirpes; if there is a surviving spouse and children, who are either the couple's or the decedent's or the surviving spouse's only, distribution is as follows: Spouse and any surviving children each take equal shares.

If there are parent(s) but no spouse or children surviving, the entire estate goes to the parents, brothers and sisters equally, or to children of brothers and sisters per stirpes, or if there are no brothers or sisters or children of brothers or sisters surviving, the entire estate goes to the surviving parent(s) equally; if there are no surviving spouse, children, or parent(s), the entire estate goes to the brothers and sisters equally or to their children per stirpes, or if none is surviving, to the grandparents, uncles and aunts equally, or to their children per stirpes.

MISSOURI

If there is a surviving spouse, but no surviving children or parent(s), the entire estate goes to the spouse; if there are a surviving spouse and parent(s) but no surviving children, distribution is as follows: $20,000 and 1/2 of the balance of the estate goes to the spouse, and the other 1/2 of the balance goes to the surviving parent(s); if there is a surviving spouse and children, distribution is as follows: $20,000 and 1/2 of the balance of the estate to the spouse, and the other 1/2 of the balance of the estate to the children or grandchildren per stirpes. (The $20,000 does not go to the spouse when the children involved are not the surviving spouse's. Rather, the estate is merely divided 1/2 to the spouse and 1/2 to the children or grandchildren per stirpes in such a situation).

If there are children but no surviving spouse, the children share the entire estate equally or their children per stirpes; if there are parent(s) but no spouse or children surviving, the entire estate goes to the parents, brothers and sisters equally, or to their children per stirpes; if there are no surviving spouse, children, or parent(s), the entire estate goes to the brothers and sisters equally or to their children per stirpes, or if none is surviving, to the grandparents, uncles and aunts and their children per stirpes.

MONTANA

If there are a surviving spouse and parent(s), but no surviving children, or a spouse but no surviving children or parents, or a spouse and children all of whom are only the surviving spouse's, then the entire estate goes to the spouse; if there is a surviving spouse and children who are not the surviving spouse's, distribution is as follows: if only one child is surviving, 1/2 of the estate goes to the spouse and 1/2 to the child; if more than 1 child, 1/3 to the spouse and 2/3 to the children equally.

If there are children but no surviving spouse, the children share the estate equally or their children per stirpes; if there are parent(s) but no spouse or children surviving, the surviving parent(s) share the entire estate equally; if there are no surviving spouse, children, or parent(s), the entire estate goes to the brothers and sisters equally or their children per stirpes, or if none is surviving, 1/2 to paternal and 1/2 to maternal grandparents or their children per stirpes.

NEBRASKA

If there is a surviving spouse but no surviving children or parent(s), the entire estate goes to the spouse; if there are a spouse and parent(s) but no surviving children, distribution is as follows: $50,000 and 1/2 of the balance of the estate goes to the spouse and the other 1/2 of the balance of the estate goes to surviving parent(s); if there are children but no surviving spouse, the children share entire estate equally or their children per stirpes; if there is a surviving spouse and children, distribution is as follows: $50,000 and 1/2 of the balance of the estate goes to the spouse and the other 1/2 of the balance of the estate goes to the children. (The $50,000 does not go to the spouse when the children involved are not the surviving spouse's. Rather, the estate is merely divided—1/2 to spouse and 1/2 to the children, in such a case.)

If there are parent(s) but no spouse or children surviving, the entire estate goes to the surviving parents equally; if there are no surviving spouse, children, or parent(s), the entire estate goes to the brothers and sisters equally, or their children per stirpes, or if none is surviving, 1/2 to paternal and 1/2 to maternal grandparents or their children per stirpes.

NEVADA

(The State is a Community Property State). If there are a surviving spouse and parent(s) but no surviving children, distribution is as follows: all of the decedent's "community property" goes to the spouse, 1/2 of decedent's "separate property" goes to the spouse, and the other 1/2 goes to the surviving parent(s). If there is a surviving spouse and children who are either the couple's or only the decedent's, distribution is as follows: all of the decedent's "community property" goes to spouse, if there's only 1 child surviving, 1/2 of decedent's "separate property" goes to the spouse and 1/2 to child or grandchildren per stirpes, and if more than 1 child surviving, 1/3 of decedent's "separate property" goes to the spouse and 2/3 to the children or grandchildren per stirpes.

If there are children but no surviving spouse, the children share the entire estate equally or their children per stirpes; if there are parent(s) but no spouse or children surviving, the entire estate goes to the surviving parents equally; if there are no surviving spouse, children, or parent(s), the entire estate goes to the brothers and sisters equally, or to their children per stirpes, or if none is surviving, to the next of kin.

NEW HAMPSHIRE

If there is a surviving spouse but no surviving children or parent(s), the entire estate goes to the spouse; if there is a spouse and parent(s) but no surviving children, distribution is as follows: $50,000 and 1/2 of the balance of the estate goes to the spouse and the other 1/2 of the balance of the estate goes to the surviving parent(s); if there is a surviving spouse and children, distribution is as follows: $50,000 and 1/2 of the balance of the estate goes to the spouse and the other 1/2 of the balance of the estate goes to the children or grandchildren per stirpes (the $50,000 does not go to the spouse when the surviving children involved are not the surviving spouse's. Rather, the estate is merely divided—1/2 to the spouse and 1/2 to children or grandchildren per stirpes in such a case.)

If there are children but no surviving spouse, the children share the estate equally or their children per stirpes; if there are parent(s) but no spouse or children surviving, the entire estate goes to the parents equally; if there are no surviving spouse, children, or parent(s), the entire estate goes to the brothers and sisters equally, or to their children per stirpes, or if none is surviving, 1/2 to maternal and 1/2 to paternal grandparents or their children per stirpes.

NEW JERSEY

If there is a surviving spouse but no surviving children or parent(s), the entire estate goes to the spouse; if there is a spouse and parent(s) but no surviving children, distribution is as follows: $50,000 and 1/2 of the balance of the estate goes to the spouse and the other 1/2 of the balance of the estate goes to the surviving parent(s); if there is a surviving spouse and children, distribution is as follows: $50,000 and 1/2 of the balance of the estate goes to the spouse, and the other 1/2 of the balance of the estate goes to the children or grandchildren per stirpes (the $50,000 does not go to the spouse when the surviving children involved are not the surviving spouse's. Rather, the estate is merely divided—1/2 to spouse and 1/2 to children or grandchildren per stirpes in such a case.)

If there are children but no surviving spouse, the children share the estate equally or their children per stirpes; if there are parent(s) but no spouse or children surviving, the entire estate goes to the parent(s) equally; if there are no surviving spouse, children, or parent(s), the entire estate goes to the brothers and sisters equally, or to their children per stirpes, or if none is surviving, 1/2 to maternal and 1/2 to paternal grandparents or their children per stirpes.

NEW MEXICO

(A Community Property State). If there is a surviving spouse and parent(s) but no surviving children, or a spouse but no surviving children or parent(s), the entire estate goes to spouse; if there are children but no surviving spouse, the estate goes to the children equally or to their children per stirpes; if there is a surviving spouse and children who are either the couple's or only the decedent's, distribution is as follows: all of the decedent's "community property" goes to the spouse, 1/4 of the decedent's "separate property" goes to the spouse and 3/4 to the children or grandchildren per stirpes.

If there are parent(s) but no spouse or children surviving, the entire estate goes to the parents equally; if there are no surviving spouse, children, or parent(s), the entire estate goes to the brothers and sisters equally, or their children per stirpes, or if none is surviving, 1/2 to maternal and 1/2 to paternal grandparents or their children per stirpes.

NEW YORK

If there is a surviving spouse but no surviving children or parent(s), the entire estate goes to the spouse; if there is a spouse and parent(s) but no surviving children, distribution is as follows: $25,000 and 1/2 of the balance of the estate goes to the spouse and the other 1/2 of the balance of the estate goes to the surviving parent(s); if there is a surviving spouse and children who are either the couple's or only the decedent's, distribution is as follows: if only 1 child or grandchild, $4,000 and 1/2 of the balance of the estate goes to the spouse and 1/2 of the balance of the estate goes to the child or grandchild; if more than 1 child or grandchild, $4,000 and 1/3 of the balance of the estate goes to spouse and 2/3 of the balance of estate goes to the children or grandchildren per stirpes.

If there are children but no surviving spouse, the children share the estate equally or their children per stirpes; if there are parent(s), but no spouse or children surviving, the entire estate goes to the parents equally; if there are no surviving spouse, children, or parent(s) surviving, the entire estate goes to the brothers and sisters equally, or their children per stirpes, or if none is surviving, to grandparents equally or their children per capita, or if none, to the next of kin.

NORTH CAROLINA

If there is a surviving spouse but no surviving children or parent(s), the entire estate goes to the spouse; if there is a spouse and parent(s) but no surviving children, distribution is as follows: $25,000 (from any personal property, if any) plus 1/2 of the balance of the estate, goes to the spouse, and the other 1/2 of the balance of the estate goes to the surviving parent(s); if there is a surviving spouse and children who are either the couple's or only the decedent's, distribution is as follows: if only 1 surviving child is involved, $15,000 in personal property, if any, plus 1/2 of the balance of the estate, goes to the spouse, and the other 1/2 of the balance of the estate goes to the children or grandchildren per stirpes; if more than one child is involved, it's $15,000 (from any personal property) and 1/3 of the balance of the estate goes to the spouse, and 2/3 of the balance of the estate to the children and grandchildren per stirpes.

If there are children but no surviving spouse, the children share the entire estate equally or their children per stirpes; if there are parent(s) but no spouse or children surviving, the entire estate goes to the parent(s) equally; if there are no surviving spouse, children, or parent(s), the entire estate goes to the brothers and sisters equally, or their children per stirpes, or if none is surviving, 1/2 to maternal and 1/2 to paternal grandparents or their children per stirpes.

NORTH DAKOTA

If there is a surviving spouse but no surviving children or parent(s), the entire estate goes to the spouse; if there is a spouse and parent(s) but no surviving children, distribution is as follows: $50,000 and 1/2 of the balance of the estate goes to the spouse and the other 1/2 of the balance of the estate goes to the surviving parent(s); if there is a surviving spouse and children, distribution is as follows: $50,000 and 1/2 of the balance of the estate goes to the spouse and the other 1/2 of the balance of the estate goes to the children or grandchildren per stirpes (the $50,000 does not go to the spouse when the surviving children involved are not the surviving spouse's. Rather, the estate is merely divided 1/2 to spouse and 1/2 to children or grandchildren per stirpes in such a case.)

If there are children but no surviving spouse, the children share the entire estate equally or their children per stirpes; if there are parent(s) but no spouse or children surviving, the entire estate goes to the parent(s) equally; if there are no surviving spouse, children, or parent(s), the entire estate goes to the brothers and sisters equally or their children per stirpes, or if none is surviving, 1/2 to maternal and 1/2 to paternal next of kin.

PUERTO RICO

If there is a surviving spouse and living parent(s) or grandparent(s) but no living children, distribution is as follows: lifetime use of 1/3 of the estate goes to the spouse, and 2/3 of the estate to the parents or grandparents; if there is a living child or grandchild, the spouse gets lifetime use of the property which reverts to the decedent's issues upon the spouse's death; if there is a spouse but no living issue, parent, grandparent, great grandparent, sibling or their issue, the spouse gets 1/2 of the estate.

OHIO

If there is a surviving spouse and parent(s), but no surviving children, or a spouse but no surviving children or parent(s), the entire estate goes to the spouse; if there are children but no surviving spouse, the children share the entire estate equally or their children per stirpes; if there is a surviving spouse and children, distribution is as follows: if there is only one surviving child involved, $60,000 ($20,000 when the children are not the surviving spouse's) plus 1/2 of the balance of the estate, go to the spouse and the other 1/2 of the balance of the estate go to the children or grandchildren per stirpes , and if more than one surviving child is involved, $60,000 ($20,000 when the children are not the surviving spouse's) plus 1/3 of the balance of the estate, go to the spouse and 2/3 of the balance of the estate go to the children or grandchildren per stirpes.

If there are parent(s) but no spouse or children surviving, the entire estate goes to the surviving parent(s) equally; if there are no surviving spouse, children, or parent(s), the entire estate goes to the brothers and sisters equally, or their children per stirpes, or if none is surviving, 1/2 to maternal and 1/2 to paternal grandparents or their children per stirpes, or if none, to the next of kin.

OKLAHOMA

If there is a surviving spouse and parent(s) but no surviving children, distribution is as follows: all property acquired during the marriage by "joint industry" goes to the spouse, 1/3 of other property goes to the spouse, and 2/3 of that go to the surviving parent(s) per stirpes; if there is a surviving spouse and children, distribution is as follows: 1/2 goes to the spouse and the other 1/2 of the balance of the estate goes to the children or grandchildren per stirpes; if there is a surviving spouse and children who are not the surviving spouse's, distribution is as follows: 1/2 of the property acquired during the marriage by "joint industry" goes to the spouse, and the balance goes to the children and the spouse in equal shares; if there is a spouse but no surviving children or parent(s), distribution is as follows: all property acquired during the marriage by "joint industry" plus 1/3 of the balance go to the spouse, while 1/3 of the said balance go to the maternal and 1/3 to the paternal grandparents or their children per stirpes, or if none is surviving, to the next of kin.

If there are children but no surviving spouse, the children share the estate equally or their grandchildren per stirpes; if there are parent(s) but no spouse or children surviving, the entire estate goes to the parents equally; if there are no surviving spouse, children, or parent(s), the entire estate goes to the brothers and sisters equally, or their children per stirpes, or if none is surviving, 1/2 to maternal and 1/2 to paternal grandparents or their children per stirpes, or if none, to the next of kin.

OREGON

If there is a surviving spouse and parent(s) but no surviving children, or there is a spouse but no surviving children or parent(s), the entire estate goes to the spouse; if there are children but no surviving spouse, the children share the entire estate equally or their children per stirpes; if there is a surviving spouse and children who are either the couple's or only the decedent's children, distribution is as follows: 1/2 to the spouse and 1/2 to the children or grandchildren per stirpes.

If there are parent(s) but no spouse or children surviving, the entire estate goes to the surviving parent(s) equally; if there are no surviving spouse, children, or parent(s), the entire estate goes to the brothers and sisters equally, or their children per stirpes, or if none is surviving, to the next of kin.

PENNSYLVANIA

If there is a surviving spouse but no surviving children or parent(s), the entire estate goes to the spouse; if there is a spouse and parent(s) but no surviving children, distribution is as follows: $30,000 plus 1/2 of the balance of the estate go to the spouse, and 1/2 of the balance of the estate go to the surviving parent(s); if there are children but no surviving spouse, the children share the estate equally or their children per stirpes; if there is a surviving spouse and children, distribution is as follows: $30,000 plus 1/2 of the balance of the estate go to the spouse and the other 1/2 of the balance of the estate go to the children or grandchildren per stirpes (the $30,000 does not go to the spouse when the surviving children involved are not the surviving spouse's. Rather, the estate is merely divided 1/2 to spouse and 1/2 to children or grandchildren per stirpes, in such a case).

If there are parent(s) but no surviving spouse or children, the surviving parent(s) share the entire estate equally; if there are no surviving spouse, children, or parent(s), the entire estate goes to the brothers and sisters equally, or their children per stirpes, or if none is surviving, 1/2 to maternal and 1/2 to paternal grandparents, or if none, all to aunts and uncles or their children per stirpes.

RHODE ISLAND

If there is a surviving spouse and parent(s) but no surviving children, distribution is as follows: Real Estate—$75,000 in real estate (at court's discretion) and lifetime use of real estate (after some real estate claims) goes to the spouse, and the balance of the real estate goes to the surviving parent(s); Personal Property: $50,000 and 1/2 of the balance of the estate goes to spouse and 1/2 of balance of the estate to the surviving parent(s); if there are children, but no surviving spouse, the children share the entire estate equally or their children per stirpes. If there is a surviving spouse and children who are either the couple's or only the decedent's, distribution is as follows: Real Estate: Lifetime use of property by the spouse and the balance to the children equally or the grandchildren per stirpes; Personal Property: 1/2 to the spouse and 1/2 to the children or grandchildren per stirpes. If there is a spouse but no surviving children or parent(s), distribution is as follows: Real Estate—$75,000 in real estate (at court's discretion) and lifetime use of real estate (after some real estate claims) goes to the spouse, and the balance of real estate goes to the brothers and sisters equally, or if none is surviving, 1/2 to maternal and 1/2 to paternal grandparents, or if none, to aunts and uncles equally or their children per stirpes, or if none, to the next of kin.

If there are parent(s) but no spouse or children surviving, the entire estate goes to the surviving parents equally; if there are no surviving spouse, children, or parent(s), the entire estate goes to the brothers and sisters equally, or their children per stirpes, or if none is surviving, 1/2 to maternal and 1/2 to paternal grandparents or their children per stirpes, or if none is surviving, to the next of kin.

SOUTH CAROLINA

If there is a surviving spouse and parent(s) but no surviving children, distribution is as follows: 1/2 of the estate to spouse and 1/2 to the parents, brothers, and sisters or their children per stirpes; if there are children but no surviving spouse, the children share the entire estate equally or their children per stirpes. If there is a surviving spouse and children who are either the couple's or only the decedent's, distribution is as follows: if only one child surviving, 1/2 of the estate goes to the spouse and 1/2 to the child or grandchildren; if more than one surviving child is involved, 1/3 of the estate goes to the spouse and 2/3 to the children equally or their children per stirpes; if there is a spouse but no surviving children or parent(s), distribution is as follows: 1/2 to the spouse and 1/2 to the brothers and sisters per stirpes, or if none is surviving, to lineal ancestors, or if none is surviving, to the spouse.

If there are parent(s) but no spouse or children surviving, the entire estate goes to the surviving parent(s) equally; if there are no surviving spouse, children, or parent(s), the entire estate goes to the brothers and sisters equally or their children per stirpes, or if none is surviving, to lineal ancestors equally or to survivor, or if none is surviving, to aunts and uncles equally or their children per stirpes, or if none, to the next of kin.

SOUTH DAKOTA

If there is a surviving spouse and parent(s) but no surviving children, distribution is as follows: $100,000 and 1/2 of the balance goes to the spouse, and 1/2 of the balance to the surviving parent(s); if there are children but no surviving spouse, the children share the entire estate equally or their children per stirpes. If there is a surviving spouse and children who are either the couple's or the decedent's only, distribution is as follows: if only 1 child is involved, 1/2 of the estate goes to the spouse and 1/2 goes to the child or grandchild(ren); if more than one surviving child is involved, 1/3 of the estate goes to the spouse and 2/3 to the children or grandchildren per stirpes; if there is a spouse but no surviving children or parent(s), distribution is as follows: $100,000 and 1/2 of the balance goes to the spouse, and the other 1/2 of the balance goes to the brothers and sisters equally or their children per stirpes, or if none is surviving, to the spouse.

If there are surviving parent(s) but no spouse or children surviving, the entire estate goes to the parents equally; if there are no surviving spouse, children, or parent(s), the entire estate goes to the brothers and sisters equally, or their children per stirpes, or if none is surviving, to the next of kin.

TENNESSEE

If there is a surviving spouse and parent(s) but no surviving children, or there is a spouse but no surviving children or parent(s), the entire estate goes to the spouse; if there is a surviving spouse and children who are either the couple's or only the decedent's, distribution is as follows: spouse gets family homestead and one year's support allowance, plus at least 1/3 of the balance of the estate, and the remainder of the estate goes to the children equally or grandchildren per stirpes.

If there are surviving children but no surviving spouse, the children share the entire estate equally or their children per stirpes; if there are parent(s) but no spouse or children surviving, the entire estate goes to the surviving parent(s) equally; if there are no surviving spouse, children, or parent(s), the entire estate goes to the brothers and sisters equally, or their children per stirpes, or if none is surviving, 1/2 to maternal and 1/2 to paternal grandparents or surviving grandparents, or if none is surviving, then to the children of grandparents per stirpes.

TEXAS

(A Community Property State). If there is a surviving spouse and parent(s) but no surviving children, distribution is as follows: spouse gets all the "community property," plus all of the decedent's separate personal property and 1/2 of the decedent's "separate" real property, and the balance of the estate goes to the parents, if both are surviving, or if only one is surviving, the 1/4 of the balance to the parent and 1/4 to the brothers and sisters equally or their children per stirpes. If there is a surviving spouse and children who are either the couple's or only the decedent's, distribution is as follows: the spouse gets 1/2 of the community property, 1/3 life estate in the decedent's separate real property, and 1/3 of the decedent's separate personal property, while the balance of the estate goes to the children or grandchildren per stirpes; if there is a spouse but not surviving children or parent(s), distribution is as follows: spouse gets all the community property, plus all the decedent's separate personal property and 1/2 of the decedent's separate real property, while the balance of the estate goes to the brothers and sisters equally, or their children per stirpes, or if none is surviving, to grandparents or their descendents.

If there are surviving children but no surviving spouse, the children share the entire estate equally or their children per stirpes; if there are parent(s) but no spouse or children surviving, the entire estate goes to the both parent(s) equally, or if only one parent is surviving, 1/2 goes to the parent and 1/2 goes to the brothers and sisters equally or their children per stirpes; if there are no surviving spouse, children, or parent(s), the entire estate goes to the brothers and sisters equally or their children per stirpes, or if none is surviving, 1/2 to maternal and 1/2 to paternal grandparents or their children per stirpes.

UTAH

If there is a surviving spouse but no surviving children or parent(s), the entire estate goes to the spouse; if there is a surviving spouse and parent(s) but no surviving children, distribution is as follows: $100,000 and 1/2 of the balance of the estate goes to the spouse, and the other 1/2 of the balance of the estate goes to the surviving parent(s); if there is a surviving spouse and children, distribution is as follows: $50,000 and 1/2 of the balance of the estate goes to the spouse and the other 1/2 of the balance of the estate goes to the children or grandchildren per stirpes (the $50,000 does not go the spouse when the children are not the surviving spouse's. Rather, the estate is merely divided 1/2 to the spouse and 1/2 to children or grandchildren per stirpes, in such a case).

If there are surviving children but no surviving spouse, the children share the entire estate equally or their children per stirpes; if there are parent(s), but no spouse or children surviving, the entire estate goes to the surviving parent(s) equally; if there are no surviving spouse, children, or parent(s), the entire estate goes to the brothers and sisters equally, or their children per stirpes, or if none is surviving, then 1/2 to maternal and 1/2 to paternal grandparents or their descendants per stirpes, or if none is surviving, to the next of kin.

VERMONT

If there is a surviving spouse and parent(s) but no surviving children, distribution is as follows: $25,000 and 1/2 of the balance of the estate goes to the spouse and the other 1/2 of the balance of the estate go to the surviving parent(s); if there is a surviving spouse but no surviving children or parent(s), distribution is as follows: $25,000 and 1/2 of the balance goes to the spouse and the other 1/2 of the balance go to the brothers and sisters equally or to their children per stirpes, or if none is surviving, to the next of kin, or if none is surviving, to the spouse. If there is a surviving spouse and children, whether they are the couple's or only the decedent's, distribution is as follows: if only one child is surviving, 1/2 of the real estate and 1/3 of personal property goes to the spouse, and the balance of the estate goes to the child or grandchildren per stirpes; and if there are more than one surviving child, 1/3 of the real estate goes to the spouse while 1/3 goes to the children or grandchildren per stirpes, and 1/3 of the personal property goes to the spouse while 2/3 goes to the children or grandchildren per stirpes.

If there are children but no surviving spouse, the children share the entire estate equally or their children per stirpes; if there are parent(s) but no spouse or children surviving, the entire estate goes to the surviving parent(s) equally; if there are no surviving spouse, children, or parent(s), the entire estate goes to the brothers and sisters equally, or their children per stirpes, or if none is surviving, to the next of kin.

VIRGINIA

If there is a surviving spouse and parent(s) but no surviving children, or there is a surviving spouse but no surviving children or parent(s), the entire estate goes to the spouse; if there is a surviving spouse and children of the spouse, the entire estate goes to the spouse; however, if the children are not the surviving spouse's children, then distribution is as follows: 1/3 to spouse and 2/3 to the children or grandchildren per stirpes.

If there are surviving children but no surviving spouse, the children share the entire estate equally or their children per stirpes; if there are surviving parent(s) but no spouse or children surviving, the entire estate goes to the parents equally; if there are no surviving spouse, children, or parent(s), the entire estate goes to the brothers and sisters equally, or their children per stirpes, or if none is surviving, 1/2 to maternal grandparents or maternal next of kin (or if none, to paternal side) and 1/2 to paternal grandparents, or their children, or paternal next of kin (or if none, to maternal side).

WASHINGTON

(A Community Property State). If there is a surviving spouse but no surviving children or parent(s), the entire estate goes to the spouse; if there is a spouse and parent(s) but no surviving children, distribution is as follows: all decedent's "community property" and 3/4 of the decedent's "separate property" go to the spouse, and 1/4 of the decedent's separate property goes to the surviving parent(s) or their children. If there is a surviving spouse and children, whether they are the couple's or only the decedent's, distribution is as follows: the spouse gets all of the decedent's community property and 1/2 of the decedent's separate property, and the remaining 1/2 of decedent's separate property go the children and grandchildren per stirpes.

If there are children but no surviving spouse, the children share the estate equally or their children per stirpes; if there are parent(s) but no spouse or children surviving, the entire estate goes to the surviving parent(s) equally; if there are no surviving spouse, children, or parent(s), the entire estate goes to the brothers and sisters equally, or their children per stirpes, or if none is surviving, to grandparents or their children.

WEST VIRGINIA

If there is a surviving spouse and parent(s) but no surviving children, or there is a surviving spouse but no surviving children or parent(s), the entire estate goes to the spouse; if there is a surviving spouse and children, whether they are the couple's or the decedent's, distribution is as follows: the spouse gets 1/3 life estate in real estate and 1/3 of the personal property, and the balance of the estate go to the children or grandchildren per stirpes.

If there are surviving children but no surviving spouse, the children share the entire estate equally or their children per stirpes; if there are surviving parent(s) but no spouse or children surviving, the entire estate goes to the surviving parent(s) equally; if there are no surviving spouse, children, or parent(s), the entire estate goes to the brothers and sisters equally, or their children per stirpes, or if none is surviving, 1/2 goes to maternal grandparents or their children or maternal uncles and aunts or their children, or maternal next of kin (or if none is surviving, to paternal side) and 1/2 goes to the paternal grandparents, or their children, or paternal uncles and aunts or their children, or paternal next of kin (or if none is surviving, to maternal side).

WISCONSIN

If there is a surviving spouse and parent(s) but no surviving children, or there is a surviving spouse but no surviving children or parent(s), the entire estate goes to the spouse; if there is a surviving spouse and children, the entire estate goes to the spouse but if the child(ren) is not the surviving spouse's child, then distribution is as follows: 1/2 to the spouse and the other 1/2 of the estate goes to the children or grandchildren per stirpes. If there are surviving children but no surviving spouse, the entire estate goes to the children equally or their children per stirpes.

If there are no surviving spouse, children, or parent(s), the entire estate goes to the brothers and sisters equally, or their children per stirpes, or if none is surviving, to surviving grandparents, or if none is surviving, to the next of kin.

WYOMING

If there is a surviving spouse and parent(s) but no surviving children, or there is a surviving spouse, but no surviving children or parent(s), the entire estate goes to spouse; if there are a surviving spouse and children, whether they are the couple's or the decedent's, distribution is as follows: 1/2 to the spouse and the other 1/2 of the estate to the children or grandchildren per stirpes.

If there are surviving children but no surviving spouse, the children share the entire estate equally or their children per stirpes; if there are surviving parent(s) but no spouse or children surviving, the entire estate goes to the surviving parent(s), brothers, sisters equally, or children of brothers and sisters per stirpes; if there are no surviving spouse, children, or parent(s), the entire estate goes to the brothers and sisters equally, or their children per stirpes, or if none is surviving, to grandparents, uncles, or aunts or their children per stirpes.

Appendix C
SPOUSE'S RIGHT OF ELECTION IN ALL STATES

The following chart illustrates the *spouse's right of election,* indicating the shares which may be taken in each state against the provision in a Will. In these states, the surviving spouse has a 'right," which he/she may or may choose to exercise (it's totally up to him or her), to the specified share of the deceased spouse's estate, regardless of any provisions in the decedent spouse's will which may give the spouse less than the property share specified herein. *Fundamentally, it is a way of protecting husbands and wives from ever being totally disinherited.* In states which allow **"intestate shares"** as the applicable share under the right of election, the spouse inherits same share that he/she would have inherited in a situation of death without a will (Appendix B).

In virtually every state, a decision by a spouse to "elect against the will" generally means that the electing spouse forfeits any rights to his/her share as given in the will, if any, with the balance of the estate then divided up proportionately among the remaining beneficiaries. ***NOTE, HOWEVER, that to elect against a will, the electing spouse must often complete the necessary 'right of election' forms and file them with the probate court clerk's office before the deadline (given below) lapses.***

State	**Limitation or Share Under the Right of Election**	**Time Within Which Election Choice Must Be Filed**
Alabama	1/3 of the decedent spouse's "augmented" estate.	Within 6 months of death or of proving the will, whichever later.
Alaska	On third of augmented net estate	Within 9 months of death or 6 months after proving will, whichever is later.
Arizona*	No specific provision, but surviving spouse has right to one half of the couple's "community property."	
Arkansas	(1) 1/3 real estate owned by the deceased during marriage and 1/3 of the personal property owned at death if married to the deceased for more than 1 year and there are are living issue(s); (2) 1/2 of the estate before heirs or 1/3 before creditors, if there are no living issues (3) lifetime use of 1/2 of the real estate before heirs or 1/3 before creditors and 1/2 of personal property if real estate has been owned by the family for at least two generations.	Within 1 month after deadline for filing claims expires.
California*	none	

*Indicates a 'community property' state—i.e., a state where the property acquired by the husband and wife, or by either of them *during* (but usually *not* before) their marriage, is considered 'community property' owned by BOTH together. Generally, the surviving spouse always inherits one-half of such property. Property acquired by either party by gift, inheritance, by exchange for other separate property, is <u>not</u> generally counted as community property.

State	Limitation or Share Under the Right of Election	Time Within Which Election Choice Must Be Filed
Colorado	One-half of "augmented" estate of the decedent spouse	Within 6 months after first creditor notice for filing claims or 1 year after death, whichever is earlier.
Connecticut	Lifetime use of 1/3 of estate	Within 2 months of first administrator appointment
Delaware	1/3 of adjusted gross estate as defined for federal estate taxes.	Within 6 months after grant of Letters Testamentary or of Administration.
District of Columbia	Either intestate share up to a maximum of 1/2 of estate after debts, or lifetime use of 1/3 of real estate and 1/2 of other property after debts.	Within 6 months after grant of Letters Testamentary or of Administration.
Florida	30% of appraised fair market value of net assets (i.e., after debts have been subtracted). Estate property may not include jointly held savings and trust.	Within 4 months of first publication of notice to creditors.
Georgia	No provision	
Hawaii	One-third of augmented estate.	Within 9 months after death or 6 months of grant of Letters Testamentary/Administration, whichever is later.
Idaho*	One-half of quasi community property (property acquired during the marriage when the couple was not living in Idaho).	Within 6 months after publication of first notice to creditors.
Illinois	If there are surviving issues, one-third of entire estate after debts, if there are none, 1/2 of the entire estate	Within 7 months after admission of will to probate.
Indiana	One-half of entire estate. When, however, the surviving spouse is the second or subsequent spouse and did not have children by the deceased and the deceased left a child or descendent from previous marriage, then the spouse's share is limited to 1/3 net personal estate plus lifetime use of 1/3 of the real property.	Within 5 months and 10 days after time for filing claims or publication of creditor notice.
Iowa	1/3 of the real estate owned by the decedent during the marriage and 1/3 of personal property after debts.	Within 2 months after second notice of probate; 4 months after notice by executor.
Kansas	Intestate share (i.e., entire estate if no living	Within 6 months of proving will.

*Indicates a 'community property' state—i.e., a state where the property acquired by the husband and wife, or by either of them *during* (but usually *not* before) their marriage, is considered 'community property' owned by BOTH together. Generally, the surviving spouse always inherits one-half of such property. Property acquired by either party by gift, inheritance, by exchange for other separate property, is not generally counted as community property.

State	Limitation or Share Under the Right of Election	Time Within Which Election Choice Must Be Filed
	issue; otherwise one-half of estate).	
Kentucky	The state has elective rights, but for all practical purposes the provision is irrelevant in that it is virtually identical to dower or curtesy (automatic share) rights of a spouse.	Must elect within 6 months of proving will.
Louisiana	No provision, but state is a community property state.	N/A
Maine	One-third of the entire estate (including gifts and joint property).	Within 9 months of death or 6 months of proving will, whichever is later.
Maryland	One-half of the estate if there are no living issues; only one-third of estate if there are living issues.	Within 30 days after date of expiration of notice to creditors.
Massachussets	If the testator leaves no issues or relatives, spouse takes $25,000 plus 1/2 of the remainder of the estate; if testator leaves kindred (relatives) but no issues, it's $25,000 plus 1/2 of balance of personal property in trust, and 1/2 of balance of real estate for lifetime use; if there are issue(s), it's 1/3 of the estate. Alternatively, spouse may elect lifetime use of 1/3 of real property (dower).	Within 6 months after proving will.
Michigan	Either one-half of the estate (which includes 1/2 of certain legacies made by the decedent and joint property), or lifetime use of one-third of real estate owned during marriage.	Within 60 days after entry or order closing estate to claims (the deadline for claims or the taking of the inventory).
Minnesota	One-third of the estate (which includes certain legacies made by the decedent).	Within 6 months after proving will, or 9 months after death, whichever is later.
Mississippi	One-half of the estate (which includes joint property), if decedent left no issue; one-third of the estate (which includes joint property) if there are issues; and nothing, if the surviving spouse's property equals the intestate share.	Within 90 days of proving will
Missouri	One-third of estate if there are lineal descendants surviving testator, otherwise one-half of the estate.	6 months and 10 days after first creditor notice or proving of will
Montana	One-third of the "augmented" estate	Within 9 months of death, or 6 months after publication of first notice to creditors, whichever is later.
Nebraska	One-half of the "augmented" estate	Within 9 months of death or 6 months after issuance of Letters Testamentary, whichever is later.

State	Limitation or Share Under the Right of Election	Time Within Which Election Choice Must Be Filed
Nevada*	None	none
New Hampshire	One-third of the estate if there are living children; if there are no living children but only living parents or bothers and sisters, it is $20,000 and half of the rest of the estate; if there are no living children, parents or bothers and sisters, it is $10,000 plus $2,000 for each full year of marriage, plus half of the remainder of the estate.	Within 6 months of the appointment of the Executor.
New Jersey	One-third of the "augmented" estate, or lifetime use of one-half of real estate owned during the marriage between Jan 1, 1929 and May 28, 1980	Within 6 months of the appointment of the Executor.
New Mexico*	No provision	N/A
New York	The first $4,000 to $25,000 of the estate plus one-third of the "augmented" estate, if there is any living issues; one-half of the "augmented" estate if there are no living issues.	Within 6 months after issuance of Letters Testamentary or Letters of Administration-with-will-annexed.
North Carolina	Either lifetime use of the home or take one-third of the real estate owned during the marriage, whichever is greater. Election may be made only if the share under the will is less than what the surviving spouse would have received as intestate share.	Within 12 months after death, or 13 months after limit for filing claims if executor is appointed.
North Dakota	One third of "augmented" estate	Within 9 months of death or 6 months after proving will, whichever is later.
Ohio	One-half of the estate if there is one living issue; otherwise, it's one-third of the estate.	Within 1 months after service of citation to elect; or if no citation is issued or applicable, then within 7 months after appointment of executor or administrator.
Oklahoma	Half of all property acquired by "joint industry" during the marriage.	No fixed period, but on or before a final date for final distribution hearing.
Oregon	One-fourth of net estate (reduced by gifts and inherited share under the will up to 1/2 of the estate). Spouse may not elect if waived in writing.	Within 90 days after admission of will to probate or 30 days after filing inventory, whichever is later.

---

*Indicates a 'community property' state—i.e., a state where the property acquired by the husband and wife, or by either of them *during* (but usually *not* before) their marriage, is considered 'community property' owned by BOTH together. Generally, the surviving spouse always inherits one-half of such property. Property acquired by either party by gift, inheritance, by exchange for other separate property, is not generally counted as community property.

State	Limitation or Share Under the Right of Election	Time Within Which Election Choice Must Be Filed
Pennsylvania	One-third of estate (which estate includes all property given by decedent to the spouse and any gifts over $3,000 given by decedent to anyone other than the spouse within 1 year of death.)	Within 6 months after death or of proving will.
Puerto Rico	No provision.	N/A
Rhode Island	Lifetime use of all of the estate's real estate.	Within 6 months of proving will.
South Carolina	One-third of the estate.	Within 8 months of death or 6 months of probate, whichever is later.
South Dakota	$100,000 or 1/3 of all the decedent's property.	6 months of death or before court's order of distribution, whichever is earlier.
Tennessee	One-third of the decedent's net estate.	Within 9 months after death or 6 months after appointment of Executor.
Texas*	No provision	N/A
Utah	One-third in value of all personal and real property of decedent spouse.	Within 12 months of death or 6 months of the proving of Will, whichever is later.
Vermont	If there's only 1 living issue and the issue is the surviving spouse's, one-half of the real property owned at death, after debts; if otherwise, one-third of real property.	Within 8 months of proving will.
Virginia	One-third of the estate if there are any surviving issues or adopted children, if there are no surviving issues, it is one-half of the estate.	Within 1 year of proving will.
Washington*	No provision	N/A
West Virginia	One-third of the estate. Or, alternatively, lifetime use of 1/3 of the real estate dower.	Within 8 months of proving will; if will is contested, 2 months after final decision.
Wisconsin*	No provision. State is a modified community property state.	N/A
Wyoming	Half of the decedent's estate if there are no surviving children or they are all the surviving spouse's; one-fourth of the estate if one or more of decedent's living children are not the surviving spouse's.	Within 3 months of proving will or 30 days after notice, whichever is later.

---

*Indicates a 'community property' state—i.e., a state where the property acquired by the husband and wife, or by either of them *during* (but usually *not* before) their marriage, is considered 'community property' owned by BOTH together. Generally, the surviving spouse always inherits one-half of such property. Property acquired by either party by gift, inheritance, by exchange for other separate property, is <u>not</u> generally counted as community property.

Appendix D
FEDERAL ESTATE TAX DETERMINATION AND PROCEDURES

It has been explained in a preceding passage of the manual (Chapter 7-A on pp. 93-4) that there are a variety of federal as well as state tax returns (and payments) which may invariably become the responsibility of the executor (or administrator) to undertake—depending on the state involved and the size and nature of the estate or inheritance. Such taxes range from state death taxes of sorts (inheritance tax, estate tax or credit estate tax), to the federal estate taxes, and state and federal income taxes on the last-earned income of the decedent.

Here, in this Chapter, we shall concern ourselves mainly with the *ESTATE* and death-related tax part of probate taxation, leaving aside the *INCOME* tax dimensions as *they (the "income" tax aspects) are, in the author's view, relatively less important for the primary purposes of the average executor for reasons that shall soon be elaborated.*

A. Estate Tax Assessments In General

The basic principle relating to estate tax assessments is no different here: for a given estate to owe—or pay—an estate or inheritance tax to the government, a determination must first be made as to whether or not there is a tax liability, in the first place.

How do you make this determination in an estate situation? Basically you do so by filling out the necessary tax returns and filing them with the proper taxing authorities. With regard, particularly, to estate taxation, there are essentially two basic kinds of taxes to which an estate may be subject: a) **Federal Estate Tax**—which is a tax assessed by the federal government on the decedent's *entire* "taxable estate," and not just on the share received by particular beneficiaries; and b) **State Inheritance Tax** (also called by such names as state "estate," "transfer" or "succession" tax)—which is a kind of a right-to-transfer-property tax imposed by all state governments (except Nevada) upon that part (and only that part) of the decedent's estate transferred as inheritance to particular beneficiaries.

In this present Chapter (Appendix D) we deal with the *Federal Estate Tax* methods. And in the next Chapter (Appendix E), we treat the *state inheritance tax* dimensions.

B. Is Your Estate Big Enough To Be Even Federally Taxable In The First Place?

As an executor (or administrator) administering an estate, the filling out and filing of the relevant tax returns may well turn out to be something you may eventually have to do alright. **Coming first, though, is an important point for you to bear in mind:** *before you get yourself lost in some fancy details of the mechanics and arithmetic of estate tax return preparations and filings, you had better devote your energies to one aspect that is of more immediate and actual relevance to your job as an executor— namely, to the question of determining whether the estate you're handling is of such size and value as to require having a return filed, in the first place!*

Actually, this question may be the for more relevant one for an estate planner or estate executor, then you may ordinarily think. True, in theory when one dies his or her estate may possibly be subject to some sort of estate taxation. In practice, however, since the enactment of the **Economic Recovery Tax Act of 1981,** followed by the **Taxpayers Relief Act of 1997,** only very few estates pay or need to pay any federal estate taxes at all. Primarily through the device of increasing the size of estates that are exempt from the federal estate taxes, this law dramatically reduced the number of estates subject to estate taxes so that the result is that *only a tiny 1/3 of 1 percent of all estates in the United States, that is, those estates which fall within the society's uppermost wealth brackets, will actually have to pay any federal estate taxes, according to a Congressional staff report! Hence, it is not at all certain that the estate you are probating would indeed be subject to any federal estate tax, in the first place. Not even by a long shot!*

For example, for someone who dies in 1999, an estate tax may be chargeable <u>only</u> if the value of his/her "taxable estate" is in excess of $650,000. (see the table below). This amount – commonly called the "estate tax threshold" or "personal exempt amount" to donate the value of one's estate below which no federal estate taxation applies—will rise to $1 million by year 2006. But, WHAT IS EVEN MORE IMPORTANT IS THIS: the many exemptions to estate tax allowed under the law make it possible for people to transfer or leave behind estates that are far larger than that figure without owing tax.

The point to be made here is that, as an executor of an estate, the actual mechanics of physically preparing the necessary tax return forms for an estate should be the secondary concern or task. For one thing, that aspect of the estate tax task is a relatively simple and routine matter—certainly far less complex or involved than you might ordinarily be led to think. In deed, other than the US Estate Tax Return, IRS Form 706, which is by common consensus the most complex of all the estate tax returns, such forms as are involved in the average estate case are fairly easy and straightforward to complete! All you generally need do is follow carefully the explicit instructions given in the IRS "Instructions Booklet" which comes with the forms, and you shouldn't have much trouble completing the returns. Secondly, IRS tax accountants and tax return preparation experts frequently stand ready to figure out the tax liability (or tax credits) for you on request. Finally, you still have another option; you may just do what many executors/administrators and most practicing estate attorneys do, anyway: simply hand over the returns to a professional tax accountant to complete for you for a modest fee!!

Here, therefore, we'll concern ourselves not so much with the mechanics of physically filling out the estate tax returns, but with the broad principles and procedures governing estate taxation—the aspects whose understanding is, in the author's view, the more fundamental in the tasks required of an estate administrator.

C. Procedures By Which An Estate's Federal Estate Tax Is Determined

As stated above, as an estate executor the primary question—and probably the most relevant one—you should concern yourself with and find an answer to is: Is the estate you are administering of the size and value to have to file a federal estate tax return, in the first place, or to be subject to a tax liability?

The answer is simple. ***Whether an estate will be taxable will be dependent entirely on one major consideration:*** THE SIZE AND NATURE OF THE ESTATE ASSETS. Under the Internal Revenue Code of 1997, the federal estate tax return (from which a tax liability, if any, is determined) is not even required to be filed, <u>unless</u> the value of a decedent's "gross estate" approximately exceeds the following "estate tax threshold" amounts as of the date of death.

No filing required unless gross estate

For death in or gifts made in:	*Is more than:*
1999	$650,000
2000-2001	$675,000
2002-2003	$700,000
2004	$850,000
2005	$950,000
2006 and after	$1 million

NOTE: Note that these limits cease to apply if the beneficiary is the giver's spouse. That is, when the gift is between spouses, the tax-free amount that may be transferred is "unlimited," meaning that it would then be any amount whatsoever (see footnote on p.202 below). Furthermore, if you made any gifts of "taxable" nature to others (i.e., gifts made to others during your lifetime that are over and <u>above</u> the $10,000 per person permitted annually), such gifts—to the extent that they exceed the $10,000 per person that is allowed—will be used to reduce the amount of your gross estate that can pass tax-free at your death.

To put it simply, therefore, here's the "acid test": if the value of the decedent's "gross estate" is not likely to exceed the above amount in the given years, the estate would probably not be a "taxable estate" for federal estate tax purposes! (Another way of saying this, is that these amounts represent for the appropriate years, what you (the decedent) can transfer to anyone(s) you prefer, free of federal estate tax.) To put it another way, what this means for you, as an estate administrator or planner (or Will-maker), is this: if you can't see the size of the "gross estate" being worth in excess of the above-given "maximum exemption" limits (basically, $6),000 as from 19 onwards), then for all practical purposes you shouldn't worry about having any major federal estate tax problems or liability. *And, if you determine that the estate is in that situation, you should just as well skip the rest of this chapter and forget all the big, fancy talks about estate tax planning for your estates!*[2]

D. First, Determine (Or Estimate) The Size Of Your "Gross Estate"

As explained above, the size of the "gross estate" is a central figure in determining whether or not you may have to file a federal estate tax return, or possibly have a federal estate tax liability. Hence, the all-important question is: how do you determine this figure—THE <u>SIZE</u> OF THE GROSS ESTATE?

THE GROSS ESTATE

With respect to determining a person's (or decedent's) "gross estate" for tax purposes, technically speaking there is really one (and only one) important thing to bear in mind: namely, that as defined by the IRS, the "gross estate" comprises MORE THAN just the property owned outright by the decedent or only intended by him to pass through his Will, and that it does, rather, also, include different other kinds of property, including even those property which he may not have owned completely or outrightly.[3] Briefly summarized, a decedent's "gross estate" can be defined as *roughly the total of everything the decedent owned or shared an interest in, or that is due to his estate.*

---

[3]More specifically, as more fully defined by the IRS (See IRS Publications 559 and 448, for example), one's gross estate would include such items as the following:

   i) All property of any kind owned by the decedent (or testator) at the time of his death, regardless of where it is located, and that was transferred at death by Trust or Will or by local intestacy laws: real property, stocks, bonds, furniture, personal effects, jewelry, works of art, interest in a business, cash surrender value (or installment proceeds) of life insurance on another's life, notes, and other evidences of indebtedness to the decedent, etc.

   ii) Gifts made or property transferred for less than full and adequate consideration within 3 years of decedent's death. (Bona fide sales made for adequate consideration, or gifts (other than a life insurance policy) for which the decedent was not required to file a gift tax return, are <u>not</u> includable as part of the decedent gross estate. However, gift taxes paid on any gifts made during this 3-year period is includable.]

   iii) Under most circumstances, the proceeds of a life insurance policy, including accidental death policies, even if they are paid directly to the named beneficiary by the insurance company.

   iv) The value of any annuities (or other payments) payable to any other person surviving the decedent (to the extent of the contributions made to it by both the decedent and the employer, if payment to the beneficiary is under a "non qualified plan," and by the decedent only, if payment to the beneficiary is made under a."qualified plan.") [The value of any long term (over 36 months of) annuity payment to a beneficiary—other than an executor—under the Individual Retirement Arrangement (IRA), is generally excluded, however, part of a decedent's gross estate.]

   v) With respect to all pre-1977 joint interests, the total value of property owned (or held) by the decedent and others as joint tenants (or as tenants by the entirety) with the right of survivorship—except the part, if any, proven as paid for by the other surviving joint tenant or tenants.

   vi) With respect to all "qualified joint interests" (as well as pre-1977 joint interests for which an election is made to treat them as qualified joint interests), only one-half of the fair market value of the joint interests is includable in the gross estate of the spouse who died first, even if the surviving spouse furnished the total purchase money for the property. (The term "qualified joint interest" for an estate of a person dying after 1981 is defined as any interests in property held by the decedent and the decedent's spouse as: 1) tenants by the entirety, or 2) as joint tenants with the right of survivorship, but only if the spouses are the only joint tenants.)

   vii) Life insurance proceeds on decedent's life, if it is payable to his estate or to another person for the benefit of his estate; the proceeds of a policy payable to other beneficiaries but over which the decedent had some "incidents of ownership" (meaning things like the tight to change the beneficiary, or to cancel, assign or borrow against the policy);

   viii) Insurance proceeds on another's life (to the extent of the cash surrender value of the policy);

   ix) Any income earned but still uncollected by the decedent at the time of his death;

   x) Property over which the decedent had 'a general power of appointment' (meaning the right to na*me who the property should go to);

   xi) Distributions from pension and profit-sharing plans made in lump-sum to decedent's beneficiaries;

   xii) Dower or curtesy (or statutory estate in lieu thereof) of the surviving spouse.

For our limited purposes in this manual, however, it will suffice for you to simply define your (the decedent's) estimated "gross estate" as follows: ESTIMATED "NET WORTH"—that is, his/her assets minus liabilities. This should suffice for the purposes here, since, after all, you really don't need to know the precise value of the gross estate to be able to do the planning work intelligently; you merely need to have, for our purposes here, a rough but educated estimate so that you can assess the likelihood of the estate being liable for (federal) estate taxes, if at all.

A short-cut way of doing this is as follows. First, you apply a "fair market" price to each item of property you've listed in your inventory of the things the decedent owns—his assets.

Next, add up the value of all property the decedent owns or in any way controls. This should include the following: all property he/she owns individually, such as stocks, bonds, jewelry, artwork, furniture, business interests, debts owed to him and property owned solely or "in common" with other persons; then one-half of the value of all "community property" that may apply, if decedent was married and lived in one of the 9 community property states; and one-half of the property owned jointly with a spouse, regardless of who actually paid for it. For any property owned jointly with someone other than the decedent's spouse, add as his share of the property the value of his specific contribution to the purchase of that property.

Other assets you should include as the decedent's estate, if applicable, are: The full face value of every life insurance policy owned or in any way controlled by him; retirement benefits that will be transferred to his heirs in a lump sum or in monthly installments; all trusts in which he retains control of the principal or from which he retains the income or some other benefit; any property he has given away but from which he retains some benefit.

Once you have totalled the value of all his assets, *deduct* the value of any mortgages on the property and all debts (the total liabilities) that he owes others.

The dollar value you come up with at this point is the decedent's GROSS ESTATE.

E. Next, Determine If The Estate Is A "Taxable Estate" By Subtracting From It The "Allowable Deductions"

Alright. Let's say you have now calculated the value of the decedent's gross estate, meaning, actually, the value of his/her net worth. The next relevant question for you is this: *is the estate big enough to be classified as a "taxable estate"?*

How do you make this determination of an estate? It's simple: from your "gross estate" (i.e., your net worth) figure, you then subtract the total of all the "allowable deductions" (see below). And whatever balance you have left thereafter (if any), is the "taxable estate." *If no balance is left, then the estate at issue is a NON-TAXABLE ESTATE—one that would owe no federal estate tax whatsoever.*

What constitutes the "allowable deductions" of an estate?

THE ALLOWABLE DEDUCTIONS (FROM THE GROSS ESTATE)

In a word, "allowable deductions" are simply the kinds and amounts of deductions the law says are allowable under the tax code as legitimate to be made from the "gross estate" to arrive at one's "taxable estate." (This would seem logical since the taxable estate is defined as the "gross estate," minus the total "allowable deductions," remember?)

Briefly defined, the following are what constitute the 'allowable deductions' of an estate.

   i)   the total funeral expenses of the decedent;
   ii) the total amount of expenses made (or losses suffered) in administering the estate;
   iii) the total debts owed by, or claims made against, the estate;
   iv) losses in the estate arising from theft or casualties (storms, fires, and the like), incurred during the settlement of the estate—to the extent that is not compensated for by insurance or otherwise;

v) marital deduction allowance[4]—the value of any and all property left to decedent's surviving spouse through joint ownership, by Will, by being a beneficiary under life insurance upon decedent's death, by gift or in trust for which the principal of the trust passes to the survivor's own estate at her death, or for which the survivor has a "general" (i.e., sole) power to appoint whom the trust principal would go to, or any other property passing by other means, and which "qualifies" for the marital deduction; and

vi) charitable deduction allowance—the value of all property or gifts in the decedent's gross estate donated by the decedent either during his lifetime or by Will to tax-exempt charity.

Hence, illustrated graphically, a decedent's taxable estate is as follows:

ESTIMATING YOUR TAXABLE ESTATE

Gross Estate Value...		$_____
Less: Funeral expenses..................$_____		
Administrative expenses.........$_____		
Estate debts & Losses........... $_____		
Marital deduction amount.......$_____		
Charitable deduction amount...$_____	-$_____	
Add: Any taxable gifts made during lifetime[*] ....+$_____		
TAXABLE ESTATE.......................................=$_____		

F. Computing The "Net" Federal Tax Liability Of An Estate

Now, it has been explained above that the "taxable estate" (what is left after you deduct the total "allowable deductions" from the "gross estate"), is the amount upon which the estate tax liability is assessed. Using the tax table, called the *Unified Federal Estate And Gift Tax Rate Schedule* (see p. 206), you can easily determine what is known as the "tentative tax" on the taxable estate you have arrived at—the tax which an estate of a given size would likely be liable for.

In using this schedule to compute the tentative tax, however, there's one more factor of great importance to take into account. The law provides for a system of **"credits"** that can be applied, on a straight dollar-for-dollar basis, as offsets against the tentative tax amount—that is, credits that may be used to reduce the tax (the "tentative tax") assessed on one's estate, dollar-for-dollar. A "credit" is a direct reduction of the tax itself, as distinguished from a "deduction." In other words, what this means is that an estate may show a "tentative tax" liability but still not necessarily owe or have to pay any tax, nevertheless. So long as the amount of previously unused "credits" available to the estate (if any), is in excess of the "tentative tax" amount assessed to it, then that estate would have no "net" estate tax payable, and would in effect be a non-taxable estate.

There are five types of **"credits"** allowable against an estate's tentative tax (on the combined total of the taxable estate and the adjusted gifts) to determine the "net estate tax payable": Unified credit (representing credit for lifetime gifts); credit for state death taxes paid; credit for gift taxes paid; credit for tax on prior transfers; and credit for foreign death taxes.

---

[4] NOTE THIS: Marital deduction is a deduction allowable to only a surviving spouse from the decedent partner's gross estate, providing the property on which such allowance is made "qualifies." For estates of spouses who die after 1981, this allowance is unlimited—i.e., it could be any amount or proportion of the estate property, even to the extent of the whole estate, and which "qualifies."

Basically, in making the estate tax computation, the way the marital deduction allowance works out is that the total of any property that have gone or will go to the surviving spouse, say the wife, is deducted from the estate of the deceased spouse, and any property inherited by the surviving spouse as a marital deduction allowance goes untaxed, but is later taxable in her (the surviving spouse's) own estate when she dies. (See pp. 203-6 for more on actual estate tax computation procedures.)

To be eligible for this deduction, the property involved must "qualify"; that is: i) the property must actually be going to or have gone to the surviving spouse; ii) the spouse must survive the decedent and must be legally married at the time of death; iii) the property must have been denoted or bequeathed to her/him under conditions which make the property includable in his/her own taxable estate when he/she dies and iv) the property must have been left to a U.S. citizen spouse.

[*] See footnote on p. 204 for explanation of "taxable gift."

To illustrate the computation method, let's look at some examples just to see how the tax Schedule (see p. 206 below) is read.

G. Schematic Illustrations Of Federal Estate Tax Computation Method For 4 Different Estates

EXAMPLE 1: Assume the following facts: Mr. A, a married man, died in 1999. His gross estate was valued at $850,000. He made no lifetime taxable gifts. His surviving spouse was to receive all the assets of the estate.

The estate tax is computed as follows:

Gross Estate (use, essentially, the net worth)..$850,000

Minus: ("allowable deductions")	i) Funeral expenses............................$20,000	
	ii) Administration expenses.....................40,000	
	iii)Estate debts & losses........................100,000	
	iv)Charitable deductions.........................<u>40,000</u>	
		<u>-200,000</u>

Adjusted Gross Estate.. 650,000
Minus: Marital deduction (Mr. A left everything to spouse)..<u>-650,000</u>
Taxable Estate..-0-
Add: Adjusted taxable gifts* (assuming none)..-0-
Taxable Amount...<u>-0-</u>
NET ESTATE TAX PAYABLE BY MR. A's ESTATE...-0-

EXAMPLE 2: Assume the following facts: Mr. B estimates that the value of his gross estate (his net worth) in year 2001 is about $4.9 million. He anticipates the exemptions and allowable deductions and expenses (funeral and administrative expenses, charitable gifts, etc.) will amount to approximately $400,000, as listed in the illustration below, leaving him a Net Estate of about $4,5000,000. He plans to leave $3,250,000 to his wife, and $1,250,000 to his children.

Explanation: First, the property Mr. B leaves his wife ($3,250,000) is totally exempt from any federal estate tax because of the "unlimited marital deductions." Mr. B is thus left with a remaining net estate of $1,250,000 which is subject to federal estate tax. Looking at Column C of the Tax Rates Chart (p. 206), you find that the tax assessable on a $1,250,000 estate is $448,300. Then, looking at the Uniform Gift/Estate Tax Credit (p.206), to get the applicable "tax credit", Mr. B deducts from this $448,000, the applicable amount for "tax credit" allowed every individual for that year, $220,550. That leaves the balance of $227,750, which represents the estimated federal estate tax that Mr. B's estate will pay.

Gross Estate (use, basically, the net worth)..$4,900,000

Minus: ("allowable deductions")	i) Funeral expenses............................$60,000	
	ii) Administration expenses.....................90,000	
	iii)Estate debts & losses........................150,000	
	iv)Charitable deductions.........................<u>100,000</u>	
		<u>-400,000</u>

Adjusted Gross Estate..4,500,000
Minus: Marital deduction (Mr. A left everything to spouse)..<u>-3,250,000</u>
Taxable Estate..1,250,000

---

* A "taxable" gift is any gift which is <u>in excess</u> of the $10,000 per recipient per year permitted under the law, and the amount to include is the total of all amounts by which each persons gift per year exceeds $10,000, if any.

* See footnote on p. 205 for more on this concept.

Add: Adjusted taxable gifts[*] (assuming none)..-0-
Taxable Amount..1,250,000

Tax assessable on $1,250,000....................$448,300
Less "credits": Unified Credits[*].................-220,550

NET ESTATE TAX PAYABLE BY MR. B's ESTATE..$227,750

EXAMPLE 3: Let's just say that Mr. C (in year 2000-2001) has a net taxable estate (that is, what would be left of the estate after all the 'allowable deductions', such as the funeral and administrative expenses, charitable gift exemptions, marital deductions, etc., shall have been deducted), amounting to $1,300,000. But, the individual exemption of $675,000 for that year has not been deducted at this point. He's leaving $300,000 only to his wife.

His estate is computed as follows:

Gross Estate...$1,800,000

Minus:
       i) Funeral expenses.............................$50,000
       ii) Administration expenses.....................40,000
       iii)Estate debts & losses........................100,000
       iv)Charitable deductions..........................10,000

-200,000

Adjusted Gross Estate...1,600,000
Minus: Marital deduction (that is, all he leaves his wife)...-300,000
Taxable Estate...1,300,000
Add: Adjusted taxable gifts[*] (assuming none)..-0-
Taxable Amount..1,300,000

Tax assessable on $1,300,000 ($448,300 + 43% of excess over $1.25 million)....................$469,800

Less "credits": Unified Credits[*] ....-220,550
NET ESTATE TAX PAYABLE BY MR. B's ESTATE..$249,250

EXPLANATION OF METHOD OF CALCULATION:

1. Enter the numbers in Column A and B between
   which the value of your Net taxable Estate Falls

   Column A= $1,250,000
   Column B= $1,500,000

2. Subtract from the value of your net estate the amount in Column A

$1,300,000
-1,250,000
50,000

3. Multiply this remainder by the applicable percentage in Column D................................50,000

X.43
$21,500

4. Add together the resultant amount and the tax for $1,250,000 listed in Column C

21,500
+448,300
469,800

5. Subtract the applicable yr's federal estate tax credit (p. 206) from the last amount...........469,800

-220,550

This is your ESTATE TAX PAYABLE⟶ 249,250

EXAMPLE 4: (Illustrating how the "credits" are made use of): Assume the following: In 1979, while still alive, Mr. D gave his daughter a gift of property valued at $253,000, for which he had filed a gift tax return and paid a net gift tax of $32,800 (tentative tax, $70,800, minus unified credit of $38,000). He made no other prior gifts. Mr. D died in 1999 with a gross estate valued at $607,000. State death taxes of $25,000 were paid by the estate. The estate is valued as of the date of death. The value of the gift as of that date was $300,000.

The net estate tax on Mr. D's estate is computed as follows: [the value of the gift to the daughter at date of Mr. D's death—$300,000—is not included in the gross estate; but the value of the gift taxes paid ($25,000) would be. However, since the gift ($250,000) is a taxable gift, it is added to the taxable estate for purposes of determining the gross estate tax. No marital deduction is applicable.]

Gross Estate			$607,000
Minus:	i) Funeral expenses	$15,000	
	ii) Administration expenses	45,000	
	iii)Estate debts & losses	37,000	
	iv)Charitable deductions	10,000	
			-107,000
Taxable Estate			500,000
Add: Adjusted taxable gifts[5] ($253,000-$3,000)			+250,000
Taxable Amount			750,000
Tentative Tax (computed on Taxable Amount from the Unified Rate Schedule on p.206)			248,300
Minus "credits":	Gift taxes payable	$32,800	
	Unified credit	211,300 (limit for the 1999 year)	
	State death tax credit (based on adj. Taxable estate of $440,000)	10,000	
			- 221,300
NET ESTATE TAX PAYABLE BY MR. D's ESTATE			27,000

---

[5] "**Adjusted taxable gifts**" include only the value of the taxable gifts that were made by the testator (or decedent) after 1976 and that are not includable in the testator's gross estate. (The permissible amount for non-taxable gifts under the law operating since 1981 is $10,000 per recipient. Hence, any in excess of that amount is a "taxable gift")

*NOTE THIS: This is where the "tax credit" comes from. For every individual, the federal tax law exempts from federal estate tax property value worth up to $650,000 in 1999 and increasing to $1 million in 2006 and after, no matter who he or she leaves the property to—i.e., you are allowed to transfer that much property free of federal estate tax. But, with this one important qualification: this exemption is reduced by "taxable gifts," if any, that one may make during one's lifetime, to the extent that such gifts exceed $10,000 per person per year. Thus, let's say you give $40,000 to your son in a single year, then $30,000 ($40,000 - $10,000) will be subject to gift tax. However, the gift tax assessed is not paid in the year you make this gift; rather, the total amount of the excess taxable gift is deducted from your $650,000 or more estate/gift exemption, depending on the year of death. The $650,000 exemption works, however, by means of "tax credits" which, in effect, exempts the first $211,300 (for 1999) of tax due in an estate—the equivalent of the tax payable on $650,000.

There are five types of "credits" allowable against an estate's tentative tax before the "net" estate tax payable is finally arrived at. These are: 1) unified credit (representing credit for lifetime gifts); 2) credit for state death taxes paid; 3) credit for gift taxes paid; 4) credit for tax on prior transfers; 5) credit for foreign death taxes. A "credit" is a direct reduction of the tax itself, as distinguished from a "deduction."

In particular, the **"unified credit"**—which is so-called because it may be used to cover tax-free gifts made before death—is a credit of $211,300 that can be used to reduce the transfer tax (which is different from the income tax) on both taxable gifts and estates. And, if a decedent did not make any taxable gifts at all during his/her lifetime, the totality (100%) of the credit can be used to reduce the tax on his estate at his death. (A "non-taxable gift" is one that does not fall into any of these categories: e.g. gifts made by one spouse to another, annual gifts of $10,000 or less per recipient, or charitable contributions).

Take, for example, the case of a person who dies in 1999, meaning that his applicable "unified credit" for that year is $211,300. What this means, in effect, is that lifetime gifts of this decedent, and/or his estate, can escape tax entirely if they, together, total no more than $650,000—since $211,300 is exactly the "tentative" tax chargeable on an estate of that ($650,000) size. Thus, this decedent could have made a taxable gift of, say, $100,000 and left a $550,000 estate—without becoming subject to any federal transfer tax. That is, a combined gifts and estate worth up to $650,000 will not be subject to any federal estate tax for a decedent who dies in 1999.

H. Unified Federal Estate And Gift Tax Rates (Schedule)

The following table, *Unified Federal Estate and Gift Tax Rates,* gives the federal estate and gift tax rates for estates of people who have died after 1999. As discussed elsewhere in this manual (see, for example, pp. 199-201), these taxes will ONLY begin to apply if and when the decedent's taxable estate is worth $650,000 or more, depending on the year of death (see table on p. 200). Basically, to calculate the tax owed, here's the process: first determine the decedent's taxable estate—his net worth, minus the exempt amounts (funeral expenses, charitable gifts, any amount left to a surviving spouse) as elaborated on p. 201. Then, check on the Tax Rates chart below for the tax owed on the taxable estate. Finally, subtract from that amount the "tax credit" that is allowed for the amount that would be owed on the exempt amount applicable for the year of death (see table on p. 200).* For example, the exempt amount for a death in 1999 would be $650,000 and the tax credit would be $211,300; while the equivalent amounts for 2005 would be $950,000 and $326,300 respectively. (Of course, you'll recall from our previous discussion that if decedent has given gifts of more than $10,000 per year per person during his life, then this "credit" will have to be reduced by the total excess amount of excess gifts over the limit). Estate taxes apply only to those that are worth more than anywhere from $650,000 in 1999 to $1 million in 2006 and thereafter.

The Tentative Tax Bill

Column A *If taxable estate* *Is more than*	Column B *But not* *more than*	Column C *Tax owed on* *amounts in A* (tentative tax)	Column D *Rate of tax on excess* *over amounts in A*
$ 0	$10,000	$ 0	18%
10,000	20,000	1,800	20%
20,000	40,000	3,800	22%
40,000	60,000	8,200	24%
60,000	80,000	13,000	26%
80,000	100,000	18,200	28%
100,000	150,000	23,800	30%
150,000	250,000	38,800	32%
250,000	500,000	70,800	34%
500,000	750,000	155,800	37%
750,000	1,000,000	248,300	39%
1,000,000	1,250,000	345,800	41%
1,250,000	1,500,000	448,300	43%
1,500,000	2,000,000	555,800	45%
2,000,000	2,500,000	780,800	49%
2,500,000	3,000,000	1,025,800	53%
3,000,000	____	1,290,800	55%

---

* In strict terms, the specific requirements are that this form (Form 1041) is to be filed if : 1) the estate has a gross annual income in excess of $675,000 in 2000-2001; or 2) if it has a beneficiary who is a non-resident alien.

CHECKLIST OF ESTATE-RELATED TAX FORMS AND DUE DATES
For Executor, Administrator, or Personal Representative

Form No.	Title	Due Date
SS–4	Application for Employer Identification Number	As soon as possible for the identification number to be included in return, statement, or other document.
56	Notice Concerning Fiduciary Relationship	As soon as all of the necessary information is available.
706	United States Estate (and Generation-Skipping Transfer) Tax Return (Citizen or resident)	9 months after date of decedent's death.
706A	United States Additional Estate (and Generation-Skipping Transfer) Tax Return (Section 2032A)	6 months after cessation or disposition of special-use valuation property.
706CE	Certification of Payment of Foreign Death Tax	9 months after decedent's death. To be filed with Form 706.
706GS (D)	Generation-Skipping Transfer Tax Return for Distributions	See form instructions.
706GS (D-1)	Notification of Distribution from a Generation-Skipping Trust	See form instructions.
706GS (T)	Generation-Skipping Transfer Tax Return for Terminations	See form instructions
706NA	United States Estate (and Generation-Skipping Transfer) Tax Return, Estate of Nonresident not a citizen	9 months after date of decedent's death.
706 (Schedule S)	Increased Estate Tax on Excess Retirement Accumulations	9 months after date of decedent's death — generally filed with Form 706
712	Life Insurance Statement	Part I to be filed with estate tax return.
1040	U.S. Individual Income Tax Return	Generally, April 15th of the year after death.
1040NR	U.S. Nonresident Alien Income Tax Return	15th day of 6th month after end of tax year
1041	U.S. Fiduciary Income Tax Return	15th day of 4th month after end of estate's tax year
1041s	Trust Income Tax Return	
1041-ES	Estimated Income Tax for Fiduciaries	Generally, April 15, June 15, Sept. 15, and Jan. 15 for calendar-year filers.
1310	Statement of Person Claiming Refund Due a Deceased Taxpayer	To be filed with Form 1040 or Form 1040NR if refund is due. If the person claiming the refund is a surviving spouse filing a joint return with the decedent, this form is not required.
2758	Application for Extension of Time To File U.S. Partnership, Fiduciary, and Certain Other Returns	Sufficiently early to permit IRS to consider the application and reply before the due date of Form 1041.
4768	Application for Extension of Time to File U.S. Estate (and Generation-Skipping Transfer) Tax Return and/or Pay Estate (and Generation-Skipping Transfer) Tax	Sufficiently early to permit IRS to consider the application and reply before the estate tax due date.
4810	Request for Prompt Assessment Under Internal Revenue Code Section 6501(d)	As soon as possible after filing Form 1040 or Form 1041.

Note. An executor must report the termination of the estate, in writing, to the Internal Revenue Service. Form 56 may be used for this purpose.

Appendix E
State Death (Estate) Tax Procedures For All 50 States

The FEDERAL government (the IRS) isn't the only government that is interested in getting a piece of the decedent person's estate when he or she dies. Quite to the contrary, aside from the federal government, the STATE in which the decedent permanently resided (or owned substantial property) at his death may also impose a separate death tax of its own on the estate assets. Only one state has no death taxes at all, and that state is Nevada. State-imposed estate taxes go by a variety of names in different states—"estate," "inheritance," "succession," "transfer," or "credit estate" tax, and so forth.

A. The Three Basic Types Of State Death Taxes

By whatever specific name they are called in a specific state, however, there are three basic types of death-related taxes imposed by states on estates. They are:

- (state) estate tax
- inheritance tax
- credit estate tax

1. State Estate Tax

Imposed by just a few states, a *state* estate tax is a tax on the estate itself. Just as in the case of the *federal* estate tax, the <u>STATE</u> estate tax is a set percentage of the total value of the decedent's estate. The more valuable the estate, the higher the percentage, and vice versa. Another way of putting it, is that the (state) estate tax is imposed, not on the inheritor, but on the <u>*taxable estate*</u> itself.

For states which impose state estate tax, the taxable estate on which the tax is imposed is: all real estate in the given state no matter where the decedent lived, and all the personal property of the decedent who was domiciled in the state.

2. Inheritance Tax

A good way to define this type of tax, is to contrast it with the state "estate" type of tax. Whereas, on the one hand, the **estate** type of tax is based and imposed on the size of the estate, the ***inheritance*** tax, on the other hand, is based and imposed on the relationship of the heir (the person inheriting the given property) to the deceased person and the amount each heir inherits. (Note that states impose either an estate tax, or an inheritance tax, but never both.)

To put it another way, the inheritance tax is imposed on the <u>receiver</u> of inherited property (the <u>inheritor</u>) and not on the estate, and the amount payable is based on the value of the estate received, and on the relationship of the inheritor to the deceased person. As a rule, inheritance tax tables of states provide for property left to the decedent's spouse, children, and grandchildren, to be taxed at a lower rate than property left to brothers and sisters, while other categories of beneficiaries, such as cousins and friends, are taxed at a higher rate. The way this works, under state rules, is that state inheritance tax laws and schedules divide inheritors into different "classes" (categories) (see pp. 210-4). And each "class" is then assigned a different inheritance tax rate, as well as different personal exemption.

3. Credit Estate Tax

In many states, the states do, technically, impose death taxes to estates that are required to pay federal estate taxes, namely, those that are worth more than $600,000. However, the amount of this state death tax is exactly equal to the rebate ("credit") allowed by the IRS. That is, the amount of tax is the estate tax credit the IRS will allow the heirs to deduct from the federal estate tax the estate owes.) Thus, in effect, overall the net effect is that the only tax you pay is the federal tax.

Because this state tax has no real effect on one's estate, as it does not actually increase what one's estate owes, it is said that there is "effectively" no death tax in such states; state death taxes are, in such states, a simple matter of accounting. Overall, some 27 states and the District of Columbia fall under this category of states which, effectively, have no state death taxes.

B. State Estate Or Inheritance Tax Rates In All 50 States

As mentioned at the beginning of this Appendix (p. 208 above), the various categories of death-related taxes imposed by the states—as distinguished from that imposed by the federal government—fall under three basic types: *inheritance tax, estate tax,* and the *credit estate tax.* (The credit estate tax is defined as one which applies only to estates which are liable for the federal estate tax.)

Presented below, is a chart giving the following state information: **i)** the type of death-related or estate tax (whether "inheritance," "estate" or "credit estate" tax) that is applicable for the various states; **ii)** estate tax rates (the maximum and the minimum rates) which apply in each state, and **iii)** the value of property which is exempt from taxation in each state for each heir after all the claims, funeral costs, estate administration expenses, and other allowable deductions, have been taken into account.

> *NOTE:* It almost goes without saying that tax rates and levels of exemptions do often change from time to time without notice. Hence, readers should take it upon themselves to check the information given for their individual states with the local state department of taxation for the more up-to-the-minute details.

1. States That Effectively Do Not Have Death Taxes

The following states "effectively" have no state-imposed death taxes, in that they have a credit estate tax—that is, the state inheritance or estate tax imposed is equal to the federal credit for the state's death tax:

Alabama	Alaska
Arizona	Arkansas
California	Colorado
District of Columbia	Florida
Georgia	Hawaii
Idaho	Illinois
Maine	Minnesota
Missouri	Nevada (no inheritance tax of any kind)
New Mexico	North Dakota
Oregon	Puerto Rico
South Carolina	Utah
Vermont	Virginia
Washington	West Virginia
Wyoming	

2. States Which Have Inheritance Taxes

The following states have inheritance taxes:

Connecticut	Louisiana	New Jersey
Delaware	Maryland	North Carolina
Indiana	Michigan	Pennsylvania
Iowa	Montana	South Dakota
Kansas	Nebraska	Tennessee
Kentucky	New Hampshire	Wisconsin

The associated (inheritance) tax rates for each of these states is set forth in the following charts

Chart E-1

Connecticut

Class AA: Surviving spouse

Class A: Parent, grandparent, adoptive parent or natural or adopted descendant

Class B: Son or daughter-in-law of child (natural or adopted) who has not remarried. Stepchild, brother or sister (full or half or adopted), brother or sister's children (descendants, natural or adopted)

Class C: All other persons

Taxable Amount			Tax Rate
Class AA			No Tax
Class A	50,000 to	150,000	3%
	150,000 to	250,000	4%
	250,000 to	400,000	5%
	400,000 to	600,000	6%
	600,000 to	1,000,000	7%
	1,000,000	And Over	8%
Class B	6,000 to	25,000	4%
	25,000 to	150,000	5%
	150,000 to	250,000	6%
	250,000 to	400,000	7%
	400,000 to	600,000	8%
	600,000 to	1,000,000	9%
	1,000,000	And Over	10%
Class C	1,000 to	25,000	8%
	25,000 to	150,000	9%
	150,000 to	250,000	10%
	250,000 to	400,000	11%
	400,000 to	600,000	12%
	600,000 to	1,000,000	13%
	1,000,000	And Over	14%

Delaware

Class A: Spouse

Class B: Parent, grandparent, child (by birth or adoption), son- or daughter-in-law, lineal descendant, or stepchild

Class C: Brother, sister, their descendants; aunt, uncle, their descendants

Class D: All others

Taxable Amount			Tax Rate
Class A	70,000 to	100,000	2%
	100,000 to	200,000	3%
	200,000	And Over	4%
Class B	25,000 to	50,000	2%
	50,000 to	75,000	3%
	75,000 to	100,000	4%
	100,000 to	200,000	5%
	200,000	And Over	6%
Class C	5,000 to	25,000	5%
	25,000 to	50,000	6%
	50,000 to	100,000	7%
	100,000 to	150,000	8%
	150,000 to	200,000	9%
	200,000	And Over	10%
Class D	1,000 to	25,000	10%
	25,000 to	50,000	12%
	50,000 to	100,000	14%
	100,000	And Over	16%

Indiana

Class A: Spouse, parents, children, grandchildren

Class B: Sibling, nieces and nephews, son- or daughter-in-law

Class C: All others

Taxable Amount		Tax		
		Base Tax	Plus %	Of Amt Over
Class A 0 to	25,000	0 +	1%	0
25,000 to	50,000	250 +	2%	25,000
50,000 to	200,000	750 +	3%	50,000
200,000 to	300,000	5,250 +	4%	200,000
300,000 to	500,000	9,250 +	5%	300,000
500,000 to	700,000	19,250 +	6%	500,000
700,000 to	1,000,000	31,250 +	7%	700,000
1,000,000 to	1,500,000	52,250 +	8%	1,000,000
1,500,000	And Over	92,250 +	10%	1,500,000
Class B				
0 to	100,000	0 +	7%	0
100,000 to	500,000	7,000 +	10%	100,000
500,000 to	1,000,000	47,000 +	12%	500,000
1,000,000	And Over	107,000 +	15%	1,000,000
Class C				
0 to	100,000	0 +	10%	0
100,000 to	1,000,000	10,000 +	15%	100,000
1,000,000	And Over	145,000 +	20%	1,000,000

Exemptions:

1. Spouse: All tax

2. Child under 21 at death: $10,000

3. Child over 21 at death: $5,000

4. Parents: $5,000

5. Other Class A: $2,000

6. Class B: $500

7. Class C: $100

Iowa

Class 1: Spouse

Class 2: Parent, child, lineal descendant

Class 3: Sibling, son- or daughter-in-law, stepchild

Class 4: All others

Taxable Amount			Tax Rate
Class 1			No Tax
Class 2	0 to	5,000	1%
	5,000 to	12,000	2%
	12,000 to	25,000	3%
	25,000 to	50,000	4%
	50,000 to	75,000	5%
	75,000 to	100,000	6%
	100,000 to	150,000	7%
	150,000	And Over	8%
Class 3	0 to	12,500	5%
	12,500 to	25,000	6%
	25,000 to	75,000	7%
	75,000 to	100,000	8%
	100,000 to	150,000	9%
	150,000	And Over	10%
Class 4	0 to	50,000	10%
	50,000 to	100,000	12%
	100,000	And Over	15%

Exemptions:

1. Each son and daughter: $50,000

2. Father or mother: $15,000

3. Any other lineal descendant: $15,000

4. Charitable, educational, religious gifts: All tax

5. Any estate not exceeding $10,000

Kansas

Class A: Lineal ancestors and descendants; stepparents, stepchildren, adopted children, lineal descendants of adopted child or stepchild, spouse or surviving spouse of son or daughter, spouse or surviving spouse of an adopted child or stepchild

Class B: Siblings

Class C: All others

	Taxable Amount			Tax Rate
Class A	0	to	25,000	1%
	25,000	to	50,000	2%
	50,000	to	100,000	3%
	100,000	to	500,000	4%
	500,000	And Over		5%
Class B	0	to	25,000	3.0%
	25,000	to	50,000	5.0%
	50,000	to	100,000	7.5%
	100,000	to	500,000	10.0%
	500,000	And Over		12.5%
Class C	0	to	100,000	10%
	100,000	to	200,000	12%
	200,00	And Over		15%

Exemptions: (Taxable amount begins after taking applicable exemption)

1. Spouse: All tax

2. Class A: $30,000

3. Class B: $5,000

4. Qualified real estate: To $750,000, if left to family member and used for family farm or business

Kentucky

Class A: Parent, spouse, child, stepchild, adopted child, or grandchild

Class B: Sibling, nephew or niece, daughter- or son-in-law, aunt or uncle

Class C: All others

	Taxable Amount			Tax Rate
Class A	0	to	20,000	2%
	20,000	to	30,000	3%
	30,000	to	45,000	4%
	45,000	to	60,000	5%
	60,000	to	100,000	6%
	100,000	to	200,000	7%
	200,000	to	500,000	8%
	500,000	And Over		10%
Class B	0	to	10,000	4%
	10,000	to	20,000	5%
	20,000	to	30,000	6%
	30,000	to	45,000	8%
	45,000	to	60,000	10%
	60,000	to	100,000	12%
	100,000	to	200,000	14%
	200,000	And Over		16%
Class C	0	to	10,000	6%
	10,000	to	20,000	8%
	20,000	to	30,000	10%
	30,000	to	45,000	12%
	45,000	to	60,000	14%
	60,000	And Over		16%

Exemptions:

1. Spouse: All tax

2. Infant/child: $20,000

3. Mentally disabled child: $20,000

4. Parent: $5,000

5. Child or step-child: $5,000

6. Grandchild: $5,000

7. Class B: $1,000

8. Class C: $500

Louisiana

Class 1: Spouse, descendants, lineal ancestors

Class 2: Collateral relatives (siblings, their children)

Class 3: All others

	Taxable Amount			Tax Rate
Class 1	0	to	20,000	2%
	20,000	And Over		3%
Class 2	0	to	1,000	No Tax
	1,000	to	21,000	5%
	21,000	And Over		7%
Class 3	0	to	500	No Tax
	500	to	5,500	5%
	5,500	And Over		10%

Exemptions:

1. Spouse: All tax if death in 1992 or after

2. Class 1: $25,000 if death is in 1987 or after

Maryland

Class 1: Spouse, parent, children, grandparent, descendants, stepchild, stepparent

Class 2: All others

	Taxable Amount	Tax Rate
Class 1	All Amounts	1%
Class 2	All Amounts	10%

Exemptions:

1. Spouse: First $100,000 of personal property; all real property

2. Property administered under small estates law

Special tax rates:

Spouse of descendant: 1% for first $2,000 of jointly-owned savings; thereafter at 10%

Michigan

Class 1: Spouse, parent, grandparent, sibling, son- or daughter-in-law, children and adopted children

Class 2: All others

	Taxable Amount			Tax Rate
Class 1	0	to	50,000	2%
	50,000	to	250,000	4%
	250,000	to	500,000	7%
	500,000	to	750,000	8%
	750,000	And Over		10%
Class 2	0	to	50,000	12%
	50,000	to	500,000	14%
	500,000	And Over		17%

Exemptions:

1. Spouse: All tax

2. All other Class 1: $10,000

Wisconsin

Class A: Spouse, child or parent (Tax rate go from 2.5-12.5% of taxable estate)

Class B: Brother or sister (Tax rate is from 5-20% of taxable estate)

Class C: All others (Tax rate is from 7.5-20%)
Exemptions: All for spouse, $10,00 for:
1. Class A: $50,000 after July 1, 1985
2. Class B: $1,000
3. Class C: $500-$1,000

Montana

Class 1: Spouse, lineal descendant or child, and lineal ancestor

Class 2: Siblings, their offspring, son- or daughter-in-law

Class 3: Uncle, aunt, or first cousins

Class 4: All others

	Taxable Amount			Tax Rate
Class 1	0	to	25,000	2%
	25,000	to	50,000	4%
	50,000	to	100,000	6%
	100,000		And Over	8%
Class 2	0	to	25,000	4%
	25,000	to	50,000	8%
	50,000	to	100,000	12%
	100,000		And Over	16%
Class 3	0	to	25,000	6%
	25,000	to	50,000	12%
	50,000	to	100,000	18%
	100,000		And Over	24%
Class 4	0	to	25,000	8%
	25,000	to	50,000	16%
	50,000	to	100,000	24%
	100,000		And Over	32%

Exemptions:

1. Spouse or child or lineal descendant: All tax

2. Lineal ancestors: $7,000

3. Class 2: $1,000

4. Charitable, educational, religious gifts: All tax

New Hampshire

Class 1: Spouse, lineal ancestors, and descendants, their spouses and all adopted children in descendant's line of succession

Class 2: All others

Taxable Amount		Tax Rate
Class 1	Any Amount	No Tax
Class 2	Any Amount	15%

Exemptions:

1. Property left to care for cemetery lots

2. Contributions to charities

3. Members of household of deceased (must have lived with deceased from age 5-15): All taxes

4. Step-children, step-parents, descendants and their spouses: All taxes

Nebraska

Class 1: Spouse, parent, child, son- or daughter-in-law

Class 2: Uncle, aunt, niece, nephew or their descendants or spouses

Class 3: All others

	Taxable Amount			Tax Rate
Class 1	0	to	1,000	No Tax
	1,000		And Over	1%
Class 2	0	to	2,000	No Tax
	2,000	to	60,000	6%
	60,000		And Over	9%
Class 3	0	to	5,000	6%
	5,000	to	10,000	9%
	10,000	to	20,000	12%
	20,000	to	50,000	15%
	50,000		And Over	18%

Exemptions:

1. Spouse: All tax

2. Class 1: $10,000

3. Class 2: $2,000

4. Class 3: $500

New Jersey

Class A: Spouse, parent, grandparent, children, step-children, direct descendants

Class B: Sibling, daughter- or son-in-law

Class C: All others

	Taxable Amount			Tax Rate
Class A				No Tax
Class B	0	to	1,100,000	11%
	1,100,000	to	1,400,000	13%
	1,400,000	to	1,700,000	14%
	1,700,000		And Over	16%
Class C	0	to	700,000	15%
	700,000		And Over	16%

Exemptions:

1. Class B: First $25,000

2. Life insurance proceeds: All tax

3. Pension to surviving spouse: All tax

North Carolina

Class A: Spouse, lineal descendants, ancestor, stepchild, adopted child, or son- or daughter-in-law whose spouse is not entitled to any beneficiary interest in property of deceased

Class B: Sibling, their issue, aunt or uncle

Class C: All others

Taxable Amount			Tax Rate
Class A	0 to 10,000		1%
	10,000 to 25,000		2%
	25,000 to 50,000		3%
	50,000 to 100,000		4%
	100,000 to 200,000		5%
	200,000 to 500,000		6%
	500,000 to 1,000,000		7%
	1,000,000 to 1,500,000		8%
	1,500,000 to 2,000,000		9%
	2,000,000 to 2,500,000		10%
	2,500,000 to 3,000,000		11%
	3,000,000 And Over		12%
Class B	0 to 5,000		4%
	5,000 to 10,000		5%
	10,000 to 25,000		6%
	25,000 to 50,000		7%
	50,000 to 100,000		8%
	100,000 to 250,000		10%
	250,000 to 500,000		11%
	500,000 to 1,000,000		12%
	1,000,000 to 1,500,000		13%
	1,500,000 to 2,000,000		14%
	2,000,000 to 3,000,000		15%
	3,000,000 And Over		16%
Class C	0 to 10,000		8%
	10,000 to 25,000		9%
	25,000 to 50,000		10%
	50,000 to 100,000		11%
	100,000 to 250,000		12%
	250,000 to 500,000		13%
	500,000 to 1,000,000		14%
	1,000,000 to 1,500,000		15%
	1,500,000 to 2,500,000		16%
	2,500,000 And Over		17%

Exemptions:

All Class A beneficiaries and gross estate less than $250,000

Pennsylvania

Class A: Grandparents, parents, spouse, lineal descendants, widower or widow of child, spouse of child

Class B: All others

	Taxable Amount	Tax Rate
Class A	All Amounts	6%
Class B	All Amounts	15%

Exemptions:

1. Spouse: All property held jointly

2. Family: $2,000

3. Life insurance proceeds

4. Social security death payments

5. Employments benefits

6. Family exemption

South Dakota

Class 1: Issue, adopted child, child

Class 2: Ancestor or descendant

Class 3: Sibling or their issue or son- or daughter-in-law

Class 4: Aunt or uncle

Class 5: All others

Class 6: Sibling if in business with descendant for 10 or 15 years before death of descendant

Taxable Amount			Tax Rate
Class 1	0 to 30,000		No Tax
	30,000 to 50,000		3.75%
	50,000 to 100,000		6.00%
	100,000 And Over		7.50%
Class 2	0 to 3,000		No Tax
	3,000 to 15,000		3.00%
	15,000 to 50,000		7.50%
	50,000 to 100,000		12.00%
	100,000 And Over		15.00%
Class 3	0 to 500		No Tax
	500 to 15,000		4.00%
	15,000 to 50,000		10.00%
	50,000 to 100,000		16.00%
	100,000 And Over		20.00%
Class 4	0 to 200		No Tax
	200 to 15,000		5.00%
	15,000 to 50,000		12.50%
	50,000 to 100,000		20.00%
	100,000 And Over		25.00%
Class 5	0 to 100		No Tax
	100 to 15,000		6.00%
	15,000 to 50,000		15.00%
	50,000 to 100,000		24.00%
	100,000 And Over		30.00%
Class 6	0 to 15,000		3.00%
	15,000 to 50,000		7.50%
	50,000 to 100,000		12.00%
	100,000 And Over		15.00%

Exemptions:

1. Spouse: All tax

Tennessee

Class A: Spouse, child, lineal ancestor or descendant, sibling, stepchild, son- or daughter-in-law, adopted child

Class B: All other

Taxable Amount		Tax		
		Base Tax	Plus %	Of Amt Over
0 to 10,000		No Tax		
10,000 to 60,000		0	+ 6.5%	10,000
60,000 to 110,000		3,900	+ 9.5%	60,000
110,000 to 160,000		8,650	+ 12.0%	110,000
160,000 to 210,000		14,650	+ 13.5%	160,000
210,000 And Over		21,400	+ 16.0%	210,000

Exemptions: (Taxable amount begins after taking applicable exemption)

1. Class A: $600,000

2. Class B: $600,000

The applicable tax rates for states which have state ESTATE taxes (MA, MS, NY, OH, and OK) are set forth in the following charts.

Chart E-2

Massachusetts

Taxable Amount		Base Tax	Plus %	Of Amt Over
All Classes				
0 to	50,000	5% the taxable estate		
50,000 to	100,000	2,500 +	7%	50,000
100,000 to	200,000	6,000 +	9%	100,000
200,000 to	400,000	15,000 +	10%	200,000
400,000 to	600,000	35,000 +	11%	400,000
600,000 to	800,000	57,000 +	12%	600,000
800,000 to	1,000,000	81,000 +	13%	800,000
1,000,000 to	2,000,000	107,000 +	14%	1,000,000
2,000,000 to	4,000,000	247,000 +	15%	2,000,000
4,000,000		547,000 +	16%	4,000,000

Exemptions:

Estates under $200,000

Tax credits

Estates over $200,000, credit equal to Massachusetts estate tax liability or $1,500, whichever is less

New York

Taxable Amount		Base Tax	Plus %	Of Amt Over
0 to	50,000	0 +	2%	0
50,000 to	150,000	1,000 +	3%	50,000
150,000 to	300,000	4,000 +	4%	150,000
300,000 to	500,000	10,000 +	5%	300,000
500,000 to	700,000	20,000 +	6%	500,000
700,000 to	900,000	32,000 +	7%	700,000
900,000 to	1,100,000	46,000 +	8%	900,000
1,100,000 to	1,600,000	62,000 +	9%	1,100,000
1,600,000 to	2,100,000	107,000 +	10%	1,600,000
2,100,000 to	2,600,000	157,000 +	11%	2,100,000
2,600,000 to	3,100,000	212,000 +	12%	2,600,000
3,100,000 to	3,600,000	272,000 +	13%	3,100,000
3,600,000 to	4,100,000	337,000 +	14%	3,600,000
4,100,000 to	5,100,000	407,000 +	15%	4,100,000
5,100,000 to	6,100,000	557,000 +	16%	5,100,000
6,100,000 to	7,100,000	717,000 +	17%	6,100,000
7,100,000 to	8,100,000	887,000 +	18%	7,100,000
8,100,000 to	9,100,000	1,067,000 +	19%	8,100,000
9,100,000 to	10,100,000	1,257,000 +	20%	9,100,000
10,100,000	And Over	1,457,000 +	21%	10,100,000

Tax credits:

Tax	Credit
$0 to $2,750,	Full credit (No tax)
$2,750 to $5,000	Difference between tax and $5,500
$5,000 or more	$500

Mississippi

Taxable Amount		Base Tax	Plus %	Of Amt Over
0 to	60,000	0	1%	0
60,000 to	100,000	600 +	1.6%	60,000
100,000 to	200,000	1,240 +	2.4%	100,000
200,000 to	400,000	3,640 +	3.2%	200,000
400,000 to	600,000	10,040 +	4.0%	400,000
600,000 to	800,000	18,040 +	4.8%	600,000
800,000 to	1,000,000	27,640 +	5.6%	800,000
1,000,000 to	1,500,000	38,840 +	6.4%	1,000,000
1,500,000 to	2,000,000	70,840 +	7.2%	1,500,000
2,000,000 to	2,500,000	106,840 +	8.0%	2,000,000
2,500,000 to	3,000,000	146,840 +	8.8%	2,500,000
3,000,000 to	3,500,000	190,840 +	9.6%	3,000,000
3,500,000 to	4,000,000	238,840 +	10.4%	3,500,000
4,000,000 to	5,000,000	290,840 +	11.2%	4,000,000
5,000,000 to	6,000,000	402,840 +	12.0%	5,000,000
6,000,000 to	7,000,000	522,840 +	12.8%	6,000,000
7,000,000 to	8,000,000	650,840 +	13.6%	7,000,000
8,000,000 to	9,000,000	786,840 +	14.4%	8,000,000
9,000,000 to	10,000,000	930,840 +	15.2%	9,000,000
10,000,000	and Over	1,082,840 +	16.0%	10,000,000

Ohio

Taxable Amount		Base Tax	Plus %	Of Amt Over
0 to	40,000	0 +	2%	0
40,000 to	100,000	800 +	3%	40,000
100,000 to	200,000	2,600 +	4%	100,000
200,000 to	300,000	6,600 +	5%	200,000
300,000 to	500,000	11,600 +	6%	300,000
500,000	And Over	23,600 +	7%	500,000

Exemption:

Marital deduction for the lesser of the federal marital deduction or one-half of adjusted gross estates greater than $500,000

Tax Credit:

Lesser of $5,000 or amount of tax

Exemption:

$600,000, taxable amount begins after taking exemption

C. States' Death Tax Procedures In General

As stated earlier, every state (except Nevada) imposes one or more of the three types of death-related taxes listed above on the inherited property transferred to a person. And, as further stated in the preceding sections of this chapter, each state uses a different tax schedule of its own in computing the applicable local tax payable by an estate, and the allowances for personal deductions and exemption (see charts on pp. xxx above).

As an estate executor or administrator, though, what is of greater relevance for you in regard to *state estate taxation,* is probably this questions: ***what are the major state estate tax filing policies and procedures involved, and how do you handle these tasks?*** With respect to this question, probably nothing can be more helpful to you as an executor than this: directly contacting your local state tax authorities for assistance with information. You can generally count on getting a routine supply of the necessary tax forms, instruction booklets, procedural tax counseling, and other pertinent information and assistance for getting this task accomplished. Among other things, as an executor (or administrator) in any of the states which impose a death-related type* of tax, you should learn from your local probate tax authorities (the state's Department of Finance or Taxation) whether or not it is the estate executor that is responsible for calculating the inheritance tax payable under that state's rules, and whether or not he is the one responsible for arranging payment or directly making the payments of taxes payable, especially in situations when the decedent either leaves no will or did not specify therein whether such inheritance taxes should be paid out of his estate funds or directly by the persons inheriting the estate property.

In general, the procedures involved in the mechanical filing of the necessary state estate tax returns, computing the tax due, and paying the tax, when payable, is a fairly simple matter requiring no special expertise. (The same is still true even in the few states which require a state tax referee or a brief court hearing in determining the amount of tax chargeable.)

In a majority of the estates, only the state estate tax (but not the federal tax) would often be payable since the size of the average estate is often too small to warrant being federally taxable. On the other hand, state estate taxes—where and when they become applicable—generally amount to a fraction of the federal tax rate. Furthermore, when and where the state estate tax is payable by an estate, such taxes are almost always allowed the decedent, in part or in whole, as a "credit" against any federal tax paid.

NOTE: Note that a state's tax rates and exemption levels may change at any time, hence you should always check the most current tax information for your state with your state department of revenue, finance and taxation.

D. New York State's Estate Tax Procedures

New York State's estate tax procedures are fairly representative of the general practice in most states across the United States. Hence, they are broadly illustrative of the typical procedures of state estate taxation. As with many other states, basically New York State would use the federal return as the basis for determining its own applicable gross estate and deductions. [For example, in estates having a federal gross estate value that are big enough to require the filing of a federal estate tax return (as in Chart on p. 199), the state probate court and taxing authorities would simply accept a copy of the federal estate tax returns in lieu of requiring a separate itemized property schedule. Where the gross estate is below the federal size limitation for the given year of death, however, meaning that no federal return need to be filed, the petition made for New York State tax would then have to contain detailed schedules with full particulars of the estate assets or property.]

---

*NOTE: Whereas the question of who bears the responsibility for filing and making the payment can often be an "open" question with respect to the inheritance type of state taxes, the responsibility is clearly defined in states that use "estate" type of tax systems—the executor or administrator is the one who definitely must file and pay the estate tax in the latter, if due.

Briefly, the New York state procedures for making an estate tax liability determination and paying the tax due, if any, are as follows:

• Which estates must file a tax return? The estate of every individual who was a resident of New York State at the time of death, if the New York adjusted gross estate and New York adjusted taxable gifts are $108,333 or more in the aggregate. (New York's adjusted gross estate is basically the same as the total federal gross etate).

Or, if it is the estate of an individual who was not a resident of the state at the time of death, the estate must file the state estate tax return if the New York's adjusted gross estate and the New York adjusted taxable gifts are $108,333 or more, in the aggregate, and the estate includes real property or tangible personal property actually located in the state.

• Obtain the New York State Estate Tax Return package of forms. You can obtain them by calling toll-free (from <u>within</u> New York only) 1-800-462-8100, or from areas <u>outside</u> New York state, call (518) 438-1073. You can also write to: NYS Tax Department, Taxpayer Assistance Bureau, W.A. Harriman Campus, Albany, NY 12227. (Information of general nature on state estate taxation can be obtained by calling, from within New York only, 1-800-641-0004, and from outside the state, 518-485-8585 or 8586.

• Basically, the principal state Estate tax form you'll have to complete is ET-90, *New York State Estate Tax Return* (see sample on p. 217), which comes with 4 other forms having to do with various schedules. The forms also come complete with elaborate explanations of the forms required, and instructrions for completing them.

• To complete Form ET-90, when the federal gross estate is insufficient to require the filing of a federal estate tax return, the gross estate assets are to be entered on the appropriate Schedules A through I on Forms ET-90.1 through ET-90.4, and the deductions entered on Schedules J through N.

• If, on the other hand, a Federal Form 706 is required to be filed for the estate (meaning that the federal gross estate is big enough to require the filing of a federal estate tax return), then you'll need to complete Form ET-90 through page 4 and omit Schedules A through N on Forms ET-90.1 through ET-90.4, but attach a copy of the federal Form 706 and all schedules and supporting documents.

• Next, you complete the applicable lines of the recapitulation sections on Form ET-90, page 2, and the applicable Schedules 1 through 5 on pages 3 and 4.

Then, complete the Tax Computation section on page 1.

Next, file the completed state tax return (mostly filed within 9 months of the decedent's death) with the State Tax Department as follows: Simply mail it to this address:

NYS Estate Tax, Processing Center
P.O. Box 5556
New York, NY 10087-5556

• If there's an estate tax due on the estate, enclose a check or money order to cover that, made out to "Commissioner of Taxation and Finance," as the state law requires that 90% of the tax be paid within 6 months of death, with the balance payable within 9 months, to avoid the imposition of interest and/or penalty.

Upon filing the state estate tax return with the Tax Department, the estate must at the same time also file a copy of the New York estate tax return with the Surrogate's Court in the county wherein the probate proceedings are being undertaken. There's a filing fee charged for this by the court, calculated on the basis of the value of the New York gross estate of the estate as follows:

Value of the NY Gross Estate	Fee
Less than $10,000	$ 35
$10,000 but under $20,000	60
20,000 but under 50,000	170
50,000 but under 100,000	225
100,000 but under 250,000	335
250,000 but under 500,000	500
500,000 and over	1,000

New York State Department of Taxation and Finance

New York State Estate Tax Return

ET-90
(1/94)

For estates of decedents dying after May 25, 1990

For office use only

Decedent's last name	First	Middle initial	Social security number
Demanto,	Mary	A.	059 14 5034

Address of decedent at time of death *(number and street)*
72 Joseph St.,

Date of death 1 24 94   Check box if copy of death certificate is attached ✔

City, village or post office	State	ZIP code	County of residence
Staten Island,	NY	10302	Richmond

On the date of death, decedent was a: ☐ Resident of New York State   ■ Nonresident of New York State

Executor - If you are submitting Letters Testamentary or Letters of Administration with this form, indicate in this box the type of letters. Enter L if regular, LL if limited letters. If you are not submitting letters with this form, enter N.

Attorney's last name	First	Middle initial	Check box if POA is attached	Executor's last name	First	Middle initial
Pro Se				Demanto,	Charles	

In care of *(firm's name)*

If more than one executor, check box and see *Instructions* ☐

Address of attorney

Address of executor
2 Garden Street

City, village or post office	State	ZIP code	City, village or post office	State	ZIP code
			Newark,	NJ	07102

Social security number of attorney	Telephone number	Social security number of executor	Telephone number
	( )	035 40 9141	(201) 281-7494

☐ Walvers are requested Attach Form(s) ET-99 *(see instructions)*   Releases of lien are requested Attach Form(s) ET-117 *(see instructions)* *(enter number of counties)* 1 x $25.00 = 25 Total fee attached

If a proceeding for probate or administration has commenced in a Surrogate's Court in New York State, enter county **Richmond**

Was a copy of this return filed with the Surrogate's Court? ☐ Yes ✔ No

Federal estate tax return required ☐ Yes ✔ No   Federal gross estate   Federal taxable estate

<table>
<tr><td>1</td><td>New York adjusted gross estate (from page 2, line 34)</td><td>1</td><td>172,575</td></tr>
<tr><td>2</td><td>Total New York allowable deductions (from page 2, line 50)</td><td>2</td><td>10,484</td></tr>
<tr><td>3</td><td>New York adjusted taxable estate (subtract line 2 from line 1)</td><td>3</td><td>162,092</td></tr>
<tr><td>4</td><td>New York adjusted taxable gifts (from Worksheet I in the instructions)</td><td>4</td><td></td></tr>
<tr><td>5</td><td>Preliminary tentative tax base (add lines 3 and 4)</td><td>5</td><td>162,091</td></tr>
<tr><td>6</td><td>Preliminary tentative tax on the amount on line 5 (from Table A in the Instructions)</td><td>6</td><td>4,484</td></tr>
<tr><td>7</td><td>Unified credit (from Table B in the instructions)</td><td>7</td><td></td></tr>
<tr><td>8</td><td>Net preliminary tentative tax (subtract line 7 from line 6)</td><td>8</td><td>4,484</td></tr>
<tr><td>9</td><td>Tax attributable to New York adjusted taxable gifts (line 4 divided by line 5; multiplied by line 8; see instructions)</td><td>9</td><td>0</td></tr>
<tr><td>10</td><td>Tax not attributable to New York adjusted taxable gifts (subtract line 9 from line 8) 10 4,484</td><td></td><td></td></tr>
<tr><td>11</td><td>Multiply line 10 by the decimal on line 37</td><td>11</td><td>4,484</td></tr>
<tr><td>12</td><td>New York tentative tax (add lines 9 and 11)</td><td>12</td><td>4,484</td></tr>
<tr><td>13</td><td>Gift tax payable for gifts made after 1982 (from Worksheet II in the instructions)</td><td>13</td><td>---</td></tr>
<tr><td>14</td><td>New York estate tax before other credits (subtract line 13 from line 12)</td><td>14</td><td>4,484</td></tr>
<tr><td>15</td><td>Agricultural exemption credit (from Form ET-411) 15</td><td></td><td></td></tr>
<tr><td>16</td><td>Credit for New York estate tax on prior transfers (from Form ET-190) 16</td><td></td><td></td></tr>
<tr><td>17</td><td>Credit for New York gift tax paid on pre-1983 gifts (from Form ET-412) 17</td><td></td><td></td></tr>
<tr><td>18</td><td>Total other credits (add lines 15, 16 and 17)</td><td>18</td><td></td></tr>
<tr><td>19</td><td>New York net estate tax (subtract line 18 from line 14) or minimum tax (see instructions)</td><td>19</td><td>4,484</td></tr>
<tr><td>20</td><td>Prior tax payments (attach a schedule of date(s) and amount(s) of payment(s))</td><td>20</td><td></td></tr>
<tr><td>21</td><td>If line 20 is less than line 19, enter balance due (payable to Commissioner of Taxation and Finance)</td><td>21</td><td>4,484</td></tr>
<tr><td>22</td><td>If line 20 is greater than line 19, enter overpayment (to be refunded)</td><td>22</td><td></td></tr>
</table>

Tax Computation

Attach check or money order here.

Under penalties of perjury, I declare that I have examined this return, including accompanying schedules and statements, and to the best of my knowledge and belief, it is true, correct, and complete. Declaration of preparer other than the executor is based on all information of which preparer has any knowledge.

Signature of executor	Date	Signature of coexecutor	Date

Signature of preparer other than executor			Date

Address of preparer	City	State	ZIP code
2 Garden St.,	Newark	NJ	07102

See *Instructions* regarding your obligation to file a copy of this return with the Surrogates Court.

Page 2   ET-90 (1/94)

Recapitulation *(Attach federal Form 706 if applicable)*

Do you, the executor, elect alternate valuation in accordance with section 954(b) of the Tax Law? ☐ Yes   ☑ No

Gross assets *(see instructions)*		Value at Date of Death *or*	Alternate Value
23 Schedule A — Real Estate	23	118,000	
24 Schedule B — Stocks and Bonds	24	3,236	
25 Schedule C — Mortgages, Notes, Cash and Bank Deposits	25	51,339	
26 Schedule D — Insurance on the Decedent's Life	26		
27 Schedule E — Jointly Owned Property	27		
28 Schedule F — Other Miscellaneous Property	28		
29 Schedule G — Transfers During Decedent's Life	29		
30 Schedule H — Powers of Appointment	30		
31 Schedule I — Annuities	31		
32 Total *(add lines 23 through 31)*	32	172,575	
33 * Enter the net amount of additions (or subtractions) from line 69, page 3 . . .	33		
34 New York adjusted gross estate *(line 32 and add or subtract line 33; enter here and on line 1, page 1)*	34	172,575	

Computations

35 For resident decedent *(enter amount from line 70, page 3)*	35		
36a New York gross estate for resident decedent *(subtract line 35 from line 34)*	36a	172,575	
36b New York gross estate for nonresident decedent *(enter amount from line 71, page 4)* . .	36b		
37 Divide line 36a or 36b by line 34 *(carry the decimal to four places; cannot be more than 1.0)*	37	1	

Deductions *(see instructions)*

38 Schedule J — Funeral Expenses and Expenses Incurred in Administering Property Subject to Claims . . .	38	10,484	
39 Schedule K — Debts of Decedent, Including Mortgages and Liens	39		
40 Schedule L — Net Losses During Administration	40		
41 Add lines 38, 39 and 40	41	10,484	
42 * Federal estate tax on excess retirement accumulations *(section 4980A(d) of the IRC)*, if any . . .	42		
43 Subtract line 42 from line 41	43	10,484	
44 Enter the amount from Form ET-90.4, Schedule M, line 8 or from federal Form 706, page 3, Recapitulation Schedule, line 18	44		
45 * Enter amount, if any, from line 72, page 4	45		
46 New York bequests to surviving spouse *(line 44 and add or subtract line 45)* . . .	46		
47 Enter the amount from Form ET-90.4, Schedule N, line 9 or from federal Form 706, page 3, Recapitulation Schedule, line 19	47		
48 * Enter amount, if any, from line 73, page 4	48		
49 New York charitable deduction *(add lines 47 and 48)*	49		
50 Total New York allowable deductions *(add lines 43, 46 and 49; also enter on line 2, page 1)*	50	10,484	

* For use only when a federal estate tax return, Form 706, is attached.

51 Decedent's business or occupation *(if retired, check the box ☐ and state decedent's former business or occupation below)*

Business or occupation	Occupation code *(from Table C in instructions)*

52 Marital status of decedent at the time of death:

☐ Single	☐ Legally separated	☐ Divorced - date divorce decree became final

☑ Widow or widower	Name of deceased spouse	
	Social security number of deceased spouse	Date of death of deceased spouse

☐ Married	Name of surviving spouse	
	Social security number of surviving spouse	Amount distributed

If the surviving spouse is not a citizen of the United States and a marital deduction is elected for New York estate tax purposes, both the executor and the surviving spouse must signify by signing below:

Executor N/A	Date	Surviving spouse	Date

Estate of Mary A. Demanto	Social security number 059 14 5034	ET-90 (1/94) Page 3

Check the *Yes* or *No* box for each question

		Yes	No
53	Do you elect a marital deduction for qualified terminable interest property under section 955(c) (QTIP)?	☐	☑
54	Do you elect the special use valuation in accordance with section 954-a of the Tax Law?	☐	☑
55	Do you elect to pay the tax in installments as described in IRC section 6166 (NY 997)? If *Yes* attach Form ET-415 in duplicate	☐	☑
56	Did the decedent, at the time of death, own any interest in a partnership or unincorporated business; own stock in an inactive or closely held business; or have an interest in any commercial property or incorporated business?	☐	☑
57	Does the gross estate contain any IRC section 2044 property?	☐	☑
58	Was there any insurance on the decedent's life, or were there any annuities or lump sum distributions that are not included on the return as part of the gross estate?	☐	☑
59	Was the decedent a party to litigation within three years preceding death, or is there any pending or contemplated cause of action relative to decedent's death?	☐	☑
60	Were there in existence at the time of the decedent's death any trusts created by the decedent during his or her lifetime or any trusts not created by the decedent under which the decedent possessed any power, beneficial interest or trusteeship?	☐	☑
61	Are there any assets wholly or partially excluded from the gross estate other than jointly-held assets with the surviving spouse?	☐	☑
62	Did the decedent at the time of death own any artwork, stamp collections, coin collections or other collections?	☐	☑

Schedule 1 - Adjustments to Federal Gross Estate

		Additions	Subtractions
63	Property subject to a limited power of appointment created prior to September 1, 1930, includable in the New York estate under section 957 of the Tax Law	63	
64	Federal gift tax, if any, included on Schedule G of federal Form 706		64
65	New York State gift tax, if any, paid by decedent or decedent's estate for gifts made by decedent or spouse within three years of decedent's death	65	
66	Enter the full value of property included in the federal gross estate under the provisions of section 2044 of the Internal Revenue Code (QTIP)		66
67	Enter the full value of property includable in the New York gross estate under the provisions of section 954(a)(4) and (5) of the Tax Law	67	
68	Totals *(add lines 63, 65 and 67 in Additions column and add lines 64 and 66 in Subtractions column)*	68	
69	Net difference - plus or minus *(enter here and on line 33, page 2)*	69	

Schedule 2 - Real Property and Tangible Personal Property Having an Actual Situs *Outside* New York State

To determine the New York gross estate of a **resident** decedent:

List each property, indicating the item number and the schedule on which it is listed *(do not include bank accounts or other intangible assets located outside New York State)*.

70 Total value of property listed on this schedule *(enter here and on line 35, page 2)*	70

Schedule 3 - Real Property and Tangible Personal Property Having an Actual Situs *in* New York State

To determine the New York gross estate of a **nonresident** decedent:

List each property, indicating the item number and the schedule on which it is listed *(do not include bank accounts or other intangible assets located in New York State).*

71 Total value of property listed on this schedule *(enter here and on line 36b, page 2)* **71**

Schedule 4 - Adjustment to Federal Marital Deduction

If an addition to, or deduction from, the federal marital deduction is required:

List the property and indicate the federal schedule(s) on which it is listed. Also, indicate the amount of the adjustment *(see instructions).*

72 Total value of property listed on this schedule *(if negative amount, enter minus; enter here and on line 45, page 2)* . . **72**

Schedule 5 - Additions to Federal Deduction for Charitable, Public and Similar Gifts and Bequests

List property passing under a limited power of appointment created before September 1, 1930, that passes or has passed to a qualified charitable organization, if such property is included in the amount on line 63, page 3 *(Tax Law, section 957(c)).*

73 Total value of property listed on this schedule *(enter here and on line 48, page 2)* **73**

New York State Department of Taxation and Finance

ET-90.1
(8/91)

New York State Estate Tax Return / Schedules A - D

Estate of	Social security number
Mary A. Demanto	059	14	5034

Schedule A - Real Estate *(report jointly owned property on Schedule E; attach additional sheets if necessary)*

A Item Number	B Description	C Assessed Value	D Alternate Valuation Date	E Alternate Value	F Value at Date of Death
1	2-family frame house, 72 Joseph St., Staten Island, NY 10302				118,000
	Total from additional sheet(s) attached to this schedule				
1	**Total -** If alternate valuation was elected, enter the total of column E on Form ET-90, page 2, line 23; otherwise, enter the total of column F **1**				118,000

Schedule B - Stocks and Bonds *(report jointly owned property on Schedule E; attach additional sheets if necessary)*

A Item Number	B Description	C Unit Value	D Alternate Valuation Date	E Alternate Value	F Value at Date of Death
1	Liberty U.S. Govt-Money Mkt trust account.				2,206
	250 Shares, Kin-Ark Corporation Stock @ $4.12 per share				1,030
	Total from additional sheet(s) attached to this schedule				
2	**Total -** If alternate valuation was elected, enter the total of column E on Form ET-90, page 2, line 24; otherwise, enter the total of column F **2**				$3,236

ET-90.1 (8/91) (back) **Attach additional sheets if necessary**

Schedule C - Mortgages, Notes, Cash and Bank Deposits *(report jointly owned property on Schedule E)*

A Item Number	B Description	C Alternate Valuation Date	D Alternate Value	E Value at Date of Death
1	CD's with Richmond County Savings bank, SI, NY			27,098
2.	Savings Account balance (same bank)			20,00
3.	Check account balance (same bank)			4,241
	Total from additional sheet(s) attached to this schedule			
3	**Total** - If alternate valuation was elected, enter the total of column D on Form ET-90, page 2, line 25; otherwise, enter the total of column E 3			51,339

Schedule D - Insurance on the Decedent's Life

A Item Number	B Description	C Alternate Valuation Date	D Alternate Value	E Value at Date of Death
1				
	Total from additional sheet(s) attached to this schedule			
4	**Total** - If alternate valuation was elected, enter the total of column D on Form ET-90, page 2, line 26; otherwise, enter the total of column E 4			

New York State Department of Taxation and Finance

ET-90.2
(10/93)

New York State Estate Tax Return / Schedules E - G

Estate of	Social security number
Mary A. Demanto	059 14 5034

Schedule E - Jointly Owned Property *(attach additional sheets if necessary)*

Part I - Qualified joint interests *(interests held by the decedent and decedent's spouse as the only joint tenants)* **Note:** If the surviving spouse is not a citizen of the United States, the interest is not a qualified joint interest and must be reported in Part II below, even when the election provided in section 955(e)(2) of the Tax Law is made.

A Item Number	B Description	C Alternate Valuation Date	D Alternate Value	E Value at Date of Death
1				

Total from additional sheet(s) attached to this schedule *(Qualified joint interests)* ....

1 Total *(Qualified joint interests)*	1	
2 Amounts included in gross estate *(one half of line 1 total)*	2	

Part II - All other joint interests

A Item Number	B Description	C Name of Joint Tenant and Relationship to Decedent	D Alternate Valuation Date	E Alternate Value	F Value at Date of Death
1					

Total from additional sheet(s) attached to this schedule *(All other joint interests)* ....

3 Total *(All other joint interests)*	3	

Part III - Summary Add *Part I*, line 2 and *Part II*, line 3 (each column). If alternate valuation was elected, enter the total of the *Alternate Value* column on Form ET-90, page 2, line 27; otherwise, enter the total of the *Value at Date of Death* column........ | 4 |

ET-90.2 (10/93) (back)　　　　**Attach additional sheets if necessary**

Schedule F - Other Miscellaneous Property not Reportable Under Any Other Schedule

A Item Number	B Description	C Alternate Valuation Date	D Alternate Value	E Value at Date of Death
1				
Total from additional sheet(s) attached to this schedule				
5	**Total** - If alternate valuation was elected, enter the total of column D on Form ET-90, page 2, line 28; otherwise, enter the total of column E	5		

Schedule G - Transfers During Decedent's Life

A Item Number	B Description	C Alternate Valuation Date	D Alternate Value	E Value at Date of Death
1	New York gift tax paid *(under Article 26A)* by the decedent or decedent's estate for all gifts made by the decedent or decedent's spouse within three years before the decedent's death *(section 954(c) - see instructions)*			
2	Transfers made by decedent after December 31, 1982, *(under section 1009 of Article 26A)* In accordance with provisions of IRC sections 2035(a), 2036, 2037 or 2038			
Total from additional sheet(s) attached to this schedule				
6	**Total** - If alternate valuation was elected, enter the total of column D on Form ET-90, page 2, line 29; otherwise, enter the total of column E	6		

New York State Department of Taxation and Finance

New York State Estate Tax Return / Schedules H - L

ET-90.3
(8/91)

Estate of	Social security number
Mary A. Demanto	059 14 5034

Schedule H - Powers of Appointment *(attach additional sheets if necessary)*

A Item Number	B Description	C Alternate Valuation Date	D Alternate Value	E Value at Date of Death
1				
Total from additional sheet(s) attached to this schedule				
1	**Total** - If alternate valuation was elected, enter the total of column D on Form ET-90, page 2, line 30; otherwise, enter the total of Column E.	**1**		

Schedule I - Annuities *(attach additional sheets if necessary)*

A Item Number	B Description	C Alternate Valuation Date	D Alternate Value	E Value at Date of Death
1				
Total from additional sheet(s) attached to this schedule				
2	**Total** - If alternate valuation was elected, enter the total of column D on Form ET-90, page 2, line 31; otherwise, enter the total of column E	**2**		

Schedule J - Funeral Expenses and Expenses Incurred in Administering Property Subject to Claims *(attach additional sheets if necessary)*

A Item Number	B Description	C Amount Claimed as a Deduction
1	Funeral expenses - *Identify:* Agnes Funeral Home ($7,012); for engravement to Emerson Monument Inc. ($4,165); Luncheon with Jimmy Max ($512) Total funeral expense	$7,689
2	Administration expenses - *Identify:* Telephone, photocopying, transportation ($250) Surrogate Court fee for probate filing ($340) Total administration expense	590
3	Executor's commissions - *Identify:* Total executor's commissions	
4	Attorney fees - *Identify:* Total attorney fees	
5	Accountant fees - *Identify:* Total accountant fees	
6	Miscellaneous fees - *Identify:* Professional appraisal of home ($325); home insurance $525; Real Estate tax ($1,355) Total miscellaneous fees	2,205
	Total from additional sheet(s) attached to this schedule	
3	**Total amounts claimed as a deduction** *(enter here and on Form ET-90, page 2, line 38)*	**3** 10,484

226

ET-90.3 (8/91) (back)

Schedule K - Debts of Decedent, Including Mortgages and Liens *(attach additional sheets if necessary)*

A Item Number	B Debts of Decedent	C Amount Claimed as a Deduction
1	List creditor and nature of claim	
	Total from additional sheet(s) attached to this schedule	
4	Total amounts claimed as a deduction	4
1	List mortgages or liens *(describe)*	
	Total from additional sheet(s) attached to this schedule	
5	Total amounts claimed as a deduction	5
6	Total amount of debts claimed as a deduction *(add lines 4 and 5; enter here and on Form ET-90, page 2, line 39)*	6

Schedule L - Net Losses During Administration and Expenses Incurred in Administering Property Not Subject to Claims *(attach supplemental schedules; attach additional sheets if necessary)*

A Item Number	B Description	C Amount
1	List net losses during administration	
	Total from supplemental schedules or additional sheet(s) attached to this schedule	
7	Total net losses during administration	7
1	List expenses incurred in administering property not subject to claims	
	Total from supplemental schedules or additional sheet(s) attached to this schedule	
8	Total expenses incurred in administering property not subject to claims	8
9	**Total** *(add lines 7 and 8; enter here and on Form ET-90, page 2, line 40)*	9

New York State Department of Taxation and Finance

ET-90.4
(1/93)

New York State Estate Tax Return / Schedules M - N

Estate of	Social security number
Mary A. Demanto	059 14 5034

Schedule M - Bequests, etc., to Surviving Spouse *(attach continuation schedules or additional sheets if necessary)*

Terminable interest (QTIP) marital deduction - If you elect the marital deduction for qualified terminable interest property (QTIP) under section 955(c) of the Tax Law, check the box on Form ET-90, page 3, line 53, and enter on *Part II* below the trust property for which you are claiming the marital deduction.

Marital deduction for noncitizen spouse - If you elect the marital deduction for the surviving spouse who is not a citizen of the United States, sign in the area provided on Form ET-90, page 2, line 52, and enter the property in the appropriate part or parts below.

Did any property pass to the surviving spouse as a result of a qualified disclaimer? *(If Yes, attach a copy of the written disclaimer required by IRC section 2518(b).)* ☐ Yes ☐ No

Election out of QTIP treatment of annuities - Do you elect under section 955(c) of the New York Tax Law (as specified in section 2056(b)(7)(c)(ii) of the Internal Revenue code) to **not** treat as qualified terminable interest property any joint and survivor annuities that would otherwise be treated as qualified terminable interest property under section 2056(b)(7)? ☐ Yes ☐ No

If you do not elect out of QTIP treatment of the annuities or elect QTIP for some or all of the annuities, enter on *Part II* below the annuities for which you do claim QTIP.

Part I - Property interests which are not subject to a QTIP election

A Item Number	B Description of Property Interests Passing to Surviving Spouse	C Value
1		
Total from continuation schedule(s) or additional sheet(s) attached to this schedule		
1 Total value of property interests not subject to a QTIP election		1

Part II - Property interests which are subject to a QTIP election

A Item Number	B Description of Property Interests Passing to Surviving Spouse *(describe portion of trust for which allocation is made)*	C Value
1		
Total from continuation schedule(s) or additional sheet(s) attached to this schedule		
2 Total value of property interests subject to a QTIP election		2

Part III - Reconciliation

3	Total interests passing to surviving spouse *(add lines 1 and 2 above)*	3
4	New York State estate taxes payable out of property interests listed in Parts I and II above	4
5	Other states' death taxes and GST taxes, and federal section 4980A taxes payable out of property interests listed on Parts I and II above	5
6	Expenses payable out of property interests listed on Parts I and II above	6
7	Add lines 4, 5 and 6	7
8	Net value of property interests listed on Schedule M *(subtract line 7 from line 3; enter here and on Form ET-90, page 2, line 44)*	8

ET-90.4 (1/93) (back) **Attach additional sheets if necessary**

Schedule N - Charitable, Public and Similar Gifts and Bequests *(attach additional sheets if necessary)*

A Item Number	B Name and Address of Organization	C Paragraph of Will	D Amount
1			

Total from additional sheet(s) attached to this schedule ....

9   Total *(enter here and on Form ET-90, page 2, line 47)* .... | **9** |

You may use the space below to show us how you calculated the estate tax due.

Appendix F
GUARDIANSHIP APPOINTMENT
PROCEDURES IN PROBATE

Having a guardian appointed generally becomes necessary when, for example, the estate at issue has beneficiaries who are minors, or are under legal disability, or are adjudicated incompetent.

A guardian is a person or institution appointed by the court to look after the interests of an incompetent, or an infant (a minor). Such appointment is evidenced by **LETTERS OF GUARDIANSHIP** issued to the appointed person.

Under most state laws, not even the parent of an infant (unless he also acts as a legal guardian) has the legal authority to appear for or represent the infant's interests before the probate court; only his guardian, may do so on his behalf.

There are three basic types of guardians:

1) Guardian of the Infant's Person: The guardian's control and jurisdiction is limited to the infant's person only.

2) Guardian of the Infant's Property or Estate: The guardian's control and jurisdiction is limited to the infant's property only. (A "general guardian" is one with control OVER both the person and the property combined.)[1]

3) Guardian ad litem (also called a "special guardian"): A guardian appointed by the court to represent and protect the interests of an infant but only during the pendency of a particular suit or court proceeding. [A guardian ad litem will become necessary when and where, for example, there are infants or indeterminate beneficiaries who will not be receiving an immediate distributive share, but who have an ultimate interest in the estate; or where an infant or an incapacitated person or an adjudicated incompetent fails to be represented before the court by a regular guardian of his property or person. Or, when a possible conflict of interests exists, e.g., when the guardians of the property of the infant (who are usually the infant's parents or close relatives) must also share in the same estate.]

The appointment of a guardian may be either by will, or by deed. Under New York's procedures, if the appointment is by deed, the person so appointed, must record the deed in the office of the recording deeds in the county of the decedent's domicile within 3 months of his death, otherwise the appointee is presumed to have renounced his appointment. In any event, whether the appointment is by will or by deed, the person so appointed must likewise file a petition for a grant of "Letters of Guardianship" with the court *within* the same 3 months from the decedent's death, or else be presumed to have renounced the appointment.

---

[1]A Guardian in Socage is a guardian involved only where an infant has acquired real property.

PETITION FOR LETTERS OF GUARDIANSHIP

The petition for the appointment of a guardian of the person or property, or both, may be made by any person in behalf of the infant. (Infants over the age of 14 may make their own petitions to have someone appointed in New York.) Generally, but by no means always, the appointee is the infant's parent.

The procedure is simple. The guardian-to-be (or the infant himself, if over 14 years of age) obtains the official form from the court clerk's office—titled *"Petition for Appointment of a Guardian."* The petitioner then completes and notarizes the form, and further secures the consent of certain designated persons to the proposed guardianship by having such persons* sign and notarize the last page of the form, captioned *"Waiver of Process, Renunciation and Consent of Guardianship."* The completed form is then submitted to the clerk of court (the birth certificate of the infant is to be attached).

Now, if the consent of the necessary parties have been obtained, service of citation notice will not be necessary. If otherwise, the clerk will issue the petitioner copies of some "citations" (written notices) to be served on the designated persons.[2] Upon return of the proof of service of the citations to the clerk's office, if no legitimate person registers any valid objection with the clerk by the return date thereof, the court will grant the petition. The court will sign the order granting **LETTERS OF GUARDIANSHIP** to the appointee.

The guardian is required to file periodic annual accounts of his guardianship with the court (N.Y.'s official form *"Annual Account of Guardian,"* is used for this). The term of office of a guardianship ceases when the infant attains majority; or, if a female, when she marries. To accomplish this, the guardian would file the official form, *"Petition to Close Guardianship Account,"* with the court and obtain a final discharge therefrom.

NOTE: For the added convenience of the reading public, the Publisher's Legal Forms Division carries the New York guardianship petition papers for public distribution. See p. 239 for form ordering information.

---

[2]Persons whose consent are usually required are the following: A parent or both parents of the infant who reside in the state, *unless* he/she has abandoned the child, or is incompetent, or has been judicially deprived of the infant's custody, or is divorced from the parent having legal custody of infant; the caretaker or custodian of the infant; the infant himself, if he is over 14 yers of age; and the husband of a married female infant on behalf of whom the petition is being made, if such husband is 21 years of age or over.

Appendix G
GLOSSARY OF PROBATE, ESTATE & LEGAL TERMS

Abatement Clause	A clause in a Will by which the Will-maker ensures that in the event he had overestimated the value of his estate, or that it had substantially decreased in value at the time of his death or became smaller than he had anticipated when he made his will and the bequests therein, certain bequests would have preference or priority over others.
Acknowledgment	A declaration in front of a person who is qualified to administer oaths (such as a Notary Public) that a document bearing your signature was actually signed by you.
Act Of God	An accident which could not have been foreseen or prevented, e.g., those caused by earthquakes, storms, forest fires, and the like.
Ademption	The cancellation of a bequest by reason of some act of the will-maker, such as the subsequent sale of a bequeathed item by the will-maker.
Administration	The conservation, management and distribution of the property (estate) of a dead person.
Administrator	A male person (or a corporation) appointed by a court to manage and settle the estate of a person who died "intestate"—i.e., without leaving a will. The female counterpart is called Administratrix.
Administrator Cum Testamento Annexo	(With the will annexed, abbreviated c.t.a) A person or corporation appointed by a court to manage and settle the estate of a deceased (dead) person who left a will but failed to name an executor in the will; or a person so appointed when the person named in the will fails to qualify or is unable to act.
Affinity	Relationship by marriage. (This contrasts with "consanguinity," which is relationship by blood)
Ancestor	One who precedes another in the line of inheritance (father, mother, grand-parents, children, etc., are said to be in "direct" line of ancestry, and uncles, aunts, and cousins, in "collateral" line of ancestry)
Ante-nuptial (Contract)	A contract made by a man and a woman prior to their marriage, in which they detail their property-rights.
Appraisal	A valuation of property; the opinion of an expert as to the true value of real or personal property based on facts and experience.
Appreciation	Increase in value; opposite of depreciation.
Attest	To witness a document in writing, such as the witnessing of the signing of a will.
Attestation Clause	That clause in a will which contains the statement of the persons witnessing the signing of the will; the clause that immediately follows the signature of the will-maker.
Augmented Estate	The balance left of an estate after the deduction of funeral expenses, homestead and family allowances, exemptions, and claims. In general, the deceased spouse's aug-mented includes both the property that passes under the will and any other property that passes by other means of transfer, e.g., joint tenancy, trust, etc.
Authenticated Copy	A copy of a document certified by a court official to be a true and correct copy of the original.

Beneficiary	One who is the recipient of benefits, such as: 1) the profits or rents of an estate or transaction; or 2) the proceeds of an insurance policy; or 3) the income or profits from a trust fund.
Bequest	A gift of personal property by will (same as Legacy, but contrasts with devise, which is a gift of real property).
Bond	A written pledge or obligation, usually issued by a bonding company for a fee, by which the bonding company is to pay a sum of money in case of failure to fulfill an obligation, or of conflicting damages or mishandling of funds
Charitable Bequest	A gift of personal property by will to a charity.
Codicil	An addition or amendment of a will.
Collateral	Incidental; something that is additional to, or an off-shot to a matter. E.g., the term "collateral heir," means a person who falls outside the "direct line" of inheritance, such as a nephew, uncle or aunt.
Community Property	The property owned in common or together by husband and wife during their marriage, based on the legal doctrine in certain states that property acquired by either or both parties during marriage belongs to the "marital community."
Competent	(Testator or witness). A person who, at the time of his making and signing of his will, had a reasonably sound mental capacity to do so. When used in connection with a witness, the term is generally used to refer to the fitness of the witness to a will to testify credibly in court concerning his role as a witness to the signatory.
Conservator	A guardian, protector or preserver.
Corpus	Latin word meaning the "body" or principal of an estate, as contrasted with its income or interest.
Curtesy	The right of a surviving widower, under an old commmon law practice, to have an interest in the real property the wife leaves, irrespective of the provisions of her will to the contrary, and irrespective of any debts she might owe, etc.
Death Taxes	Same as estate and inheritance taxes.
Decedent	The dead person.
Demise	1) Death, decease; 2) To pass by Will or inheritance.
Depreciate	To decrease in value; the opposite of appreciate.
Descendant	One who descends (proceeds) from the body of another, e.g., a child, grandchild, etc.
Descent	The passing on of an estate to another person by inheritance.
Devise	A gift of real property by will. The giver is called the devisor, and the person to whom it is given, the devisee.
Direct Heir	A person in "direct" line of descent, such as a child or parent.
Distribution	Generally, the distribution or apportionment of property or money by an Executor or the court to the heirs or beneficiaries of an estate. More commonly, the term is used to describe a situation where the court distributes the property of a person who dies without leaving a will to those entitled to receive them under the applicable state law. (A "distributee" is one who gets or is entitled to a share in the distribution).
Domicile	One's permanent or legal home, as opposed simply to his temporary place of abode. This differs from a person's "residence" which is used to describe where the person may be living for the time being.
Dower	The right of a surviving widow under an old common law practice, to have an interest in the real property the husband leaves, irrespective of the provisions of his will to the contrary, or any debts he might owe, etc.
Election	The choice of an alternative, such as the right of a widow (or widower) to take the share of her deceased husband's estate to which she is entitled under the law, if she dissents from the provision made in her husband's will.

Encumbrance	A right in real property which, while it diminishes the net value of the property, does not prevent its transfer from one person to another, e.g., liens, outstanding debts or taxes on a house.
Entail	To restrict an inheritance to a certain succession of heirs—e.g., to limit passage of the title to male heirs only.
Entirety	The phrase "ownership or tenancy by the entirety," is used to describe a situation where two or more persons (but more commonly a husband and wife) jointly own a real property, so that the property cannot be divided up between them. Hence, if one of the parties should die, the whole property goes to the remaining survivor(s).
Escheat	The reversion of property to the state if no heirs or beneficiaries can be found.
Estate	The sum total of the property, both real and personal, owned by a decedent at the time of his death.
Execution	The completion of the making of a document (such as a deed, contract or Will) by officially signing it.
Executor	A male person (or a corporation) named in a Will to see that the terms of the Will are carried out. If a female, she is called an Executrix.
Exemplified Copy	A copy of a record or document certified by a proper official as required by law.
Fiduciary	A general term used to describe a relationship that requires a high trust and confidence. Persons like guardians, trustees, executors and administrators of estates, fall under such a category.
Gift Causa Mortis	A gift of personal property made by a person in contemplation or expectation of death, which is actually delivered by the gift-maker but effective only if the gift-maker dies.
Gift inter Vivos	A gift of personal property made by a living person to another, which becomes effective only if actually delivered by the gift-maker.
Gift tax	A tax imposed upon the value of a gift.
Guardian	A person who is legally assigned the responsibility of taking care of and managing the property of another person who is incapable of managing his own affairs (e.g., a minor or an incompetent)
Guardian ad Litem	A person assigned by a court to represent a minor or an incompetent while a court action or probate proceedings are pending.
Heir	A person who inherits by virtue of descent or relationship from a deceased person.
Heir at Law	One who automatically succeeds to a deceased person's estate by operation of law.
Holographic Will	A will written, dated and signed entirely by the will-maker in his own handwriting.
Income	The returns from a property or asset, as opposed to the principal or capital itself (the "corpus"). Rents, interest and dividends are examples of income.
Incompetent	A person who lacks the ability or fitness to understand and manage his own affairs or to discharge the required function.
Infant	A person who is not of the required legal age. (Same as minor)
In Extremis	Something done in extreme circumstance, e.g., the one's last illness.
Inheiritance Taxes	A tax assessed on the person who receives a proprty by inheritance. This tax is based on the recipient's right to receive such a gift, and differs from an "estate" tax, which is assessed on the decedent's estate itself.
Inter Vivos	A trust or gift between living persons; something done during one's lifetime.
Intestacy	The state or condition of dying without having made a valid will. One who dies without having left a valid will is said to have died "intestate."
Issues	One's offspring, children or descendents.

Joint Tenancy	The phrase "joint tenancy or joint ownership" is used to describe a situation where two or more persons (usually non-marital partners) own or hold property in joint names, so that if any of them should die, the entire property goes to the remaining survivors. (Nearly the same as "tenancy by the entirety," especially when non-marital partners are involved)
Kin (or Kindred)	Persons related by blood, or with a common ancestry. (Next-of-kin is a person who is next closest relation to a decedent by blood).
Lapse	A gift which fails, usually by reason of the death of the intended recipient, during the donor's or testator's lifetime.
Legacy	A gift of personal property by will. (Same as bequest). One who receives or is entitled to receive a personal property under a will is known as a legatee.
Letters Testamentary	A document issued by a court to an executor, by which the said executor is authorized to settle a particular estate.
Life Estate	An estate meant for the use or enjoyment of the designated beneficiary only for the life of the person.
Linear Descendent	A person in "direct" line of descent, such as a child or grandchild.
Lien	A claim on the property of another resulting from some charge or debt.
Mutual Wills	Two separate wills in which each testator (usually a husband and wife) make similar or reciprocal provisions concerning the beneficiaries and executor or executrix.
Natural Guardian	The mother, father or grandparent of a minor.
Non Compos Mentis	Latin for "not of sound mind." Term is used to indicate a state of insanity or intoxication when one has no knowledge of the full meaning or consequences of his act.
Noncupative Will	An oral statement by a person on his death bed or under similar circumstance, as to what should be done with his property, which then becomes the basis of his last will if he should die.
Pecuniary Legacy	A gift of money by will.
Per Capita	Latin, meaning "by the head." When used in wills, it is taken to mean that the property or gift involved should be distributed in equal or share-by-share parts to each of the beneficiaries named.
Personal Representative	The person named in the Will or appointed by the court to administer an estate in whatever capacity; the general term for "administrator" or executor. Same as fiduciary.
Per Stirpes	This is the opposite of "Per Capita." When a will-maker makes a gift to a group of beneficiaries 'per stirpes,' it means that if any of the named beneficiaries should die before he could receive the gift, then his children would get, as a class or family, that portion to which their parent would have been entitled if alive.
Perjury	False testimony made under oath.
Personal Property	Any other property other than real property. (Same as personalty)
Posthumus Child	A child born after the father's death.
Power of Appointment	A right given to a person to dispose of property which he does not own.
Primary Beneficiary	A beneficiary entitled to receive the property or other benefits immediately.
Principal	The capital of an estate or trust; or the original fund of money or deposit on which interest is paid.
Probate of Will	The formal presentation of the will to a proper court for the purpose of establishing that the will presented is actually the maker's last will.
Pro Se	A person, usually a non-lawyer, who is acting for himself or representing himself in a court case.
Public Administrator	A government official who acts as the administrator of a deceased person's estate when there is no one else named or available or qualified to assume the duty.

Real Property	Land and everything growing or erected on it.
Residuary Estate	The property that is left over in a testator's estate after all the liabilities, bequests and devises are paid out.
Reversion	The return of real property to the original owner or his heirs, after the expiration of a stated period. E.g., when a testator gives a house to his wife for her lifetime only, the house 'reverts' (goes back) to the testator's estate upon the death of the wife.
Revocation of Will	The cancelling or renouncing of an existing will by a subsequent act of the testator, such as making a new will or destroying the old one.
Settlement	The final distribution of an estate by an executor or administrator.
Statutory Share	That portion of a person's property or estate which is allowed to his spouse by the law of the state.
Signature	A signed name or mark on a document to identify the person who made the document.
Specific Legacy	A gift made by will of a specifically designated article of personal property.
Spendthrift Clause	A provision made in a Will or trust instrument which limits the right of the beneficiary to dispose of his interests and the right of his creditors to reach it.
Subscribe	To write your name yourself, by putting your signature to a written statement or document, such as a will.
Subscribing Witness	One who signed his name on a will as a witness to its execution by the will-maker.
Succession	The state of someone becoming entitled to the property of a deceased person, whether by law or by the provision of a will.
Summary (Probate) Administration	This refers to one of the three basic administration categories in probate (the other two are "supervised" and "unsupervised" administrations). *Summary administration* is the procedure used for "small estates"—estates with assets that do not exceed the minimum dollar limits set by the given state.
Supervised Probate Administration	Refers to one of the three basic administration types in probate. Also called "formal" or "regular" administration, this refers to when the rules require direct and close court supervision of the probate process, involving prior court consent and approval for most major steps. This type of administration—which is the type more fully detailed for the state of New York in this manual—is still the most widely used in the nation, used in about 35 states. (See the Chapters on New York probate procedures if a closer look at this administration "type" is sought.)
Tenancy by the Entirety	See "Entirety."
Tenancy in Common	The holding of property by two or more persons on such terms that each has an <u>undivided</u> interest in the property, and on the death of one of them, his undivided interest automatically passes to his heirs or devisee(s) and <u>not</u> to the other survivors.
Testamentary Capacity	(Testamentary power). The competency or mental capacity sufficient to make a will.
Testamentary Guardian	A guardian named in the will of a decedent.
Testamentary Trust	A **trust** established by the provisions of a will.
Testate	The opposite of intestate; the state of having made or left a valid will at one's death.
Testator	A person (male) who dies leaving a valid will. (Called a testatrix, if a female)
Trust	An obligation upon a person (the "trustee") which arises out of the terms of a special grant, to hold or apply property according to those terms, for the benefit of others (the "beneficiaries").
Uniform Probate Code	Some 12 states (AL, AZ, CO, FL, HA ID, MN, NE, NM, ND and UT) have adopted the so-called Uniform Probate Code (UPC) enacted since the 1970's.

Unsupervised Probate Administration	This refers to one of the three basic administration types in probate. "Unsupervised" administration (also called "informal," "independent," or "abbreviated" administration), is when little court supervision is used with very few formal reporting requirements. In the 13 unsupervised administration states which have adopted the Uniform Probate Code, for example (see Appendix A), the personal representative is responsible only to the heirs once the letters of administration are issued, and may settle and close the estate thereafter without further contact with the probate court. If, however, any interested parties were to petition the court requesting, say, court supervision of the distribution of assets, or that the personal representative file a final accounting with the court, then the court may in its discretion, require a more formal, supervised administration.
Verification	Written confirmation of the truth of a document made out and sworn to by a person.
Void	An act or statement which has no legal force, effect or legitimacy from the beginning. (When something is "voidable," it means it has a legal force or legitimacy until and unless someone takes an action that makes it void, or a court declares it so.)
Ward	A person who is under the protection of a guardian.
Widow's allowance	The allowance given to a widow for her immediate needs after the death of her husband.
Will	A legal written instrument (or declaration) by which a person declares his wishes as to the distribution of his property after his death.

Appendix H
SOME RELEVANT BIBLIOGRAPHY

A list of readings is included below. They are recommended as possible aids to persons who may, for whatever the objective, want to explore the subject of estate planning, probate and estate settlement.

ALL-STATES WILL & ESTATE PLANNING GUIDE: BASIC PRINCIPLES AND A SUMMARY OF STATE AND TERRITORIAL WILL AND INTESTACY STATUTES. The Editors, Chicago: American Bar Association Section of General Practice, 1990. *An excellent overview treatment of the subject.*

THE ESSENTIAL GUIDE TO A LIVING WILL, by B.D. Cohen, published by Prentice Hall Press, N.Y. 1991. Book by a Pulitzer-Prize winning reporter, is a competent primer on the subject it addresses.

EVERYTHING YOU'VE ALWAYS WANTED TO KNOW ABOUT THE LAW BUT COULDN'T AFFORD TO ASK, by Edward E. Colby. Published by Major Books, 21335 Roscoe Blvd., Canoga Park, California 91304, and by Drake Publishers, 801 Second Ave., New York, N.Y.

FEDERAL ESTATE AND GIFT TAXES, Revised Sept. 1984-US Internal Revenue Service publication (Publication #448). Revised periodically and available from the IRS Form Distribution Center of your state. Good for reference information on federal estate tax provisions that apply to the estate of individuals dying in 1981 or thereafter.

HANDBOOK OF PROBATE LAW—PRACTICE & PROCEDURE, by Robert O. Angle. Published by Good Life Press, 658 S. Bonnie Brae St., Los Angeles, California 90057. The price is a little on the upper side, $31.50, but it is a comprehensive work with some important helpful insights for the non-technician.

HOW TO AVOID LAWYERS: A LEGAL GUIDE TO LAYMEN, by Edward Siegel. Published by Fawcett World Library, New York, N.Y.

THE LIVING WILL HANDBOOK, by Alan D. Lieberson, published by Hastings House Book Publishers, Mamaroneck, NY (1991). An excellent and comprehensive guide on the Living Will written by an author who is both a physician and a lawyer.

THE NEW YORK TIMES GUIDE TO MAKING THE NEW TAX LAW WORK FOR YOU, by Karen N. Arenson. Published by Times Books, 3 Park Avenue, N.Y., N.Y. 10016. Explains, in non-technical language, the major aspects of post-1981 tax law, estate and gift tax planning: from tax-saving techniques, to items that are of relevance to a Will-maker from the standpoint of estate taxation.

Other Sources: "Passing On as Much as You Can," in The N.Y. Times, May 30, 1982; "New Unlimited Marital Deduction Changes Estate and Gift Planning," in The N.Y. Times, August 7, 1981, pp. Al & D4; "Estates and Gifts: Planning Simplified," in The New York Times, Sept. 4, 1981, pp. DI & 4.

HOW TO SETTLE AN ESTATE, A manual of Executors & Trustees, by Charles K. Plotnick and Stephan R. Leimberg, Consumer Reports Books, Yonkers, NY (1991).

HOW TO ADMINISTER AN ESTATE, A Step-By-Step Guide For Families and Friends, by Stephan G. Christanson, Carol Publishing Group, New York: 1993.

PROBATE; SETTLING AN ESTATE: A Step-By-Step Guide by Kay Ostberg in Association with HALT, Random House, New York: 1990.

THE LIVING TRUST, by Henry W. Abts III, Contemporary Books, Chicago: 1989, esp. Chapters 1, II, 13 & 15, which discuss aspects of probate and/or estate settling process.

HOW TO SETTLE AN ESTATE OR PREPARE A WILL, by Toni P. Lester. Putnam Publishing Group, New York, 1988.

HOW TO AVOID PROBATE!, by Norman F. Dacey, New York: Harper Publisher, 1992. (Deals, essentially, with do-it-yourself living trust methods by which to "avoid" having an estate subjected to the probate process, in the first place).

ESTATE, GIFT, TRUST, AND FIDUCIARY TAX RETURNS: PLANNING AND PREPARATION, by George M. Schain, Shephard's/McGraw-Hill, Colorado Springs, Colorado: 1991.

HOW TO LIVE—AND DIE—WITH NEW YORK PROBATE, Gulf Publishing Co., Texas.

THE TROUBLE WITH LAWYERS, by Murray Bloom (Pocket Books, NY: 1970).

Appendix I
ORDERING YOUR BLANK FORMS FOR FILING FOR PROBATE & SETTLING AN ESTATE

For our readers' added convenience, the **Do-It-Yourself Legal Publishers,** the nation's original and leading self-help law publisher, makes available to its readership a package of standard forms specific to each state for use in filing for probate. Please indicate on the Order Form below the particular state or states for which the forms apply. Note that not all states' forms are available; forms for a handful of states, few in number, are presently not being supplied by The Legal Publishers.

- -

(Customers: For your convenience, just make a zerox copy of this page and send it along with your order. All prices quoted here are subject to change without notice.)

TO: **Do-It-Yourself Legal Publishers,** Legal Forms Division
   60 Park Place #1013,
Newark, NJ 07102

Order Form

Please send me the publisher's "all-in-one" STANDARD PROBATE PACKAGE for the states checked below: [Prices: $24.90 per set]

Check off which ones please [✔]

States	With Will	No Will	States	With Will	No Will	States	With Will	No Will
1. Alabama			18. Louisiana			35. Ohio		
2. Alaska			19. Maine			36. Oklahoma		
3. Arizona			20. Maryland			37. Oregon		
4. Arkansas			21. Massachusets			38. Pennsylvania		
5. California			22. Michigan			39. Rhode Island		
6. Colorado			23. Minnesota			40. S. Carolina		
7. Connecticut			24. Mississippi			41. S. Dakota		
8. Delaware			25. Missouri			42. Tennessee		
9. Florida			26. Montana			43. Texas		
10. Georgia			27. Nebraska			44. Utah		
11. Hawaii			28. Nevada			45. Vermont		
12. Idaho			29. New Hampshire			46. Virginia		
13. Illinois			30. New Jersey			47. Washington		
14. Indiana			31. New Mexico			48. W. Virginia		
15. Iowa			32. New York			49. Wisconsin		
16. Kansas			33. N. Carolina			50. Wyoming		
17. Kentucky			34. N. Dakota					

Total number of sets_____ X $24.90 = $_____

Plus Shipping & Handling @ $4 per set $_____

Sales Tax (NJ residents please

enclose 6% of price).................................$_____

GRAND TOTAL......................................$_____

Answer the following questions:

Did the dead person leave a will? Yes____ No____
If there's a will involved, does the will have a trust (testamentary trust) provision? Yes____ No____
I bought your book, or read, or learned about it from this source (bookstore, library, medium)_____
                                                   (Name and address, please)

Enclosed is the sum of $_____ to cover the order, which includes $4 per set for shipping and local sales tax,* as applicable.
Send this order to me:
    Mr/Mrs/Ms/Dr_____Address:_____
    City & State:_____Zip_____ Tel. # (   )_____
*New Jersey residents enclose 6% sales tax.

IMPORTANT: Please do NOT rip out the page. Consider others! Just make a photocopy and send.
And have your please completed our 'Readers Opinion Sheet' on p. 241?

Appendix J

PUBLICATIONS FROM DO-IT-YOURSELF LEGAL PUBLISHERS/SELFHELPER LAW PRESS

The following is a list of books obtainable from the Do-it-Yourself Legal Publishers/Selfhelper Law Press of America.

(Customers: For your convenience, just make a photocopy of this page and send it along with your order. All prices quoted here are subject to change without notice.

Please DO NOT tear out this page. Consider others!

1. How To Draw Up Your Own Friendly Separation/Property Settlement Agreement With Your Spouse
2. Tenant Smart: How To Win Your Tenants' Legal Rights Without A Lawyer (New York Edition)
3. How To Probate & Settle An Estate Yourself Without The Lawyers' Fees ($35)
4. How To Adopt A Child Without A Lawyer
5. How To Form Your Own Profit/Non-Profit Corporation Without A Lawyer
6. How To Plan Your 'Total' Estate With A Will & Living Will, Without a Lawyer
7. How To Declare Your Personal Bankruptcy Without A Lawyer ($29)
8. How To Buy Or Sell Your Own Home Without A Lawyer or Broker ($29)
9. How To File For Chapter 11 Business Bankruptcy Without A Lawyer ($29)
10. How To Legally Beat The Traffic Ticket Without A Lawyer (forthcoming)
11. How To Settle Your Own Auto Accident Claims Without A Lawyer ($29)
12. How To Obtain Your U.S. Immigration Visa Without A Lawyer ($25)
13. How To Do Your Own Divorce Without A Lawyer [10 Regional State-Specific Volumes] ($35)
14. How To Legally Change Your Name Without A Lawyer
15. How To Properly Plan Your 'Total' Estate With A Living Trust, Without The Lawyers' Fees ($35)
16. Legally Protect Yourself In A Gay/Lesbian Or Non-Marital Relationship With A Cohabitation Agreement
17. Before You Say 'I do' In Marriage Or Co-Habitation, Here's How To First Protect Yourself Legally
18. The National Home Mortgage Escrow Audit Kit (forthcoming) ($15.95)

Prices: Each book, except for those specifically priced otherwise, costs $25, plus $4.00 per book for postage and handling. New Jersey residents please add 6% sales tax. ALL PRICES ARE SUBJECT TO CHANGE WITHOUT NOTICE.

- -

(CUSTOMERS: Please make and send a xerox copy of this page with your orders)

Order Form

TO: *Do-It-Yourself Legal Publishers* (Books Division)
    60 Park Place #1013,
    Newark, NJ 07102

Please send me the following:

1._____copies of_____
1._____copies of_____
1._____copies of_____
1._____copies of_____

Enclosed is the sum of $_____to cover the order. *Mail my order to:*

Mr/Mrs/Ms/Dr._____
Address (include Zip Code please):_____
_____Zip_____

Phone No. and area code: (_____)_____Job: (_____)_____

*New Jersey residents enclose 6% sales tax.

IMPORTANT: Please do NOT rip out the page. Consider others! Just make a photocopy and send. And have you please completed our 'Readers Opinion Sheet' on p. 241?

Index